Axe of Iron—The Settlers

by

J. A. Hunsinger

Published by
Vinland Publishing, LLC
16192 Coastal Hwy.
Lewes, DE 19958-3608

ISBN: 978-0-9801601-0-9

Library of Congress Control Number: 2007942927

Printed in the United States of America

Dedication

I dedicate this novel to them, the four thousand Norse Greenlanders who disappeared from the Greenland settlements so long ago.

Acknowledgment for a job well-done must go to my editors, Jan Weeks, Week's Literary, CO, and Dave Jordon, RJ Communications, NY. Their expertise and tireless attention to detail prompted me to polish the manuscript to its final iteration. My appreciation and gratitude must also go to artist Glenda Scheuerman, CO. Her expertise and talent translated my vision of the cover jacket scene into reality.

And most of all I owe a debt of gratitude to my wife, Phyllis; she never allowed me to falter. Without her love and advocacy I would not have arrived here.

J. A. Hunsinger
2007

Author's Note

A lthough I have attempted to give the reader a sense of reality in the telling of this story by associating the travels of my characters with many of the actual discovery sites of Norse artifacts on this continent and archaeological evidence supporting the Norse lifestyle I depict, the events and characters portrayed, with the exception of men I mention who are of historical significance, are fictitious products of my imagination.

Some of the names of my characters may be difficult and unfamiliar, for they were in common usage among Northmen and native peoples more than a thousand years ago. The most notable will be the protagonist, Gudbjartur Einarsson. He is an Icelander and his name, phonetically, Goo-d-bjar-toor, is of Icelandic origin. His nickname is Gudbj, pronounced Goo-j. His surname, Einarsson, means literally that he is Einar's son. A female offspring of Einar would be Einarsdattur, i.e., Helga Einarsdattur. This naming system remains in use among many modern day descendants of the Northmen.

The Historical Perspective and the Glossary of Terms, while unusual in many novels, are included for the reader with an interest in the history of the period and to provide a grasp of terms that may be unfamiliar.

J. A. Hunsinger
2007

Historical Perspective

A	*xe of Iron—The Settlers* is a tale of the Northmen, or Vikings, who journeyed across the North Atlantic Ocean from Iceland during the latter half of the tenth century to explore and settle portions of Greenland and North America. I have followed history insofar as is known; however, the extent of the Northmen's exploration of North America, a land they referred to as Vinland, is unknown.

It happened so long ago scholars cannot agree on what the word Vinland means. Nor do they agree on where it is, but more on that later.

The Northmen did not leave their home country because of wanderlust, although a quest for land probably played a part. It may also have been a result of the still common practice of deeding settled farmland to the firstborn son, leaving younger sons no option but to settle elsewhere.

In order to understand these Northmen and the indigenous peoples they contacted in their quest for a new homeland, I offer the following to give perspective to the reader of a time, more than one thousand years ago; in this land we now call North America.

We know that Northmen not only reached North America between 997 and 1003,[1] they regularly sailed back and forth from Greenland to North America, Iceland, Norway, and perhaps other northern European destinations for about five hundred years.[2]

The term Norse, or Norsk, is used to describe all peoples of Scandinavian origin, e.g. Swedish, Danish (including Greenland and the Faeroe Islands), Norwegian, Icelandic, and the Orkney and Shetland islanders. Norse is also a reference to their common language—for in those days they all spoke the same language—and to differentiate them from other Germanic peoples.[3]

For the purpose of this story, reference will be made to both Northmen and Norsemen in a general and interchangeable sense. They were no longer Vikings, and I will not refer to them as such. When they sailed across the Atlantic, they became something else entirely.

The Medieval Warm Period, between the ninth and fourteenth centuries, made these voyages possible. Benevolent weather allowed them first to settle Greenland and later to reach and explore unknown portions of North America. The weather was considerably warmer during this period than it is today in North America and Greenland.[4]

The Northmen, under Eirik Thorvaldsson (Eirik the Red) colonized Greenland. Their sheep, goats, cattle, and horses grazed the lush green pastures while they traded in walrus hides and ivory with their European homeland. However, the fragile environment soon became overgrazed and could not support their domestic animals in viable numbers, forcing a gradual shift from an agrarian to a hunter-gatherer society, as the contents of their middens indicate.[5] Wild game was plentiful during the early years, but after a time, the hunting moved farther and farther afield as yak and caribou herds were depleted. Finally no game remained except a few ring seals.[6]

It is particularly important for the reader to be aware that *not a single document originating in Greenland exists.* The Norse Greenlanders may have been illiterate for the most part. Everything about their personal history is conjecture because none of it comes to us from the source, they themselves. The runic alphabet they employed did not lend itself to lengthy dissertation.

Everything about the five-hundred-year history of the two main Greenland settlements comes to us from sources with no vested interest in telling the true story of these hardy people. In all cases, the information was compiled as long as two hundred years after the fact by saga writers who had never been to Greenland.[7]

The man responsible for centuries of misconceptions, Adam of Bremen, a German cleric of the eleventh century, wrote a four-volume treatise on the Vikings. Volume IV deals specifically with Greenland and Vinland. It is his reference to "the profusion of grapes and self-sown wheat" found in Vinland that has perpetuated the myth of grapes and grain to the present day.[8] In fact, grapes have never grown north of the forty-fifth parallel—Nova Scotia and Maine—at any time in history, and the wet weather of the Canadian Maritimes will not support the growth of wheat.[9]

The Norse Greenlanders were not wine drinkers so grapes would have been of little importance to them. Their preferred alcoholic beverages were beer, when barley and hops were available, and mead, made from honey and water.[10]

The Norse word *vin*, the root of Vinland, is incorrectly associated with grapes. It means pasture or meadow in Old Norse, hence literally Pastureland. Norway and Sweden have many place names where the word *vin* is used as either a root syllable or as a suffix, e.g., Vinje, Vinnan, Granvin, etc. Invariably the meaning is associated with pasture or meadow, not wine, as was the case with Vinland when Leif Eiriksson named it more than one thousand years ago.[11]

The Greenland saga, the real one, began sometime between 982 and 984. In reality it bore little resemblance to the *Groenlendinga Saga* written long afterwards. Eirik the Red, exiled from Iceland because of continuing trouble, and his eldest son, Leif, explored the western coastline of Greenland sometime between 982 and 984.

They remained for at least one winter—presumably hauling their ship from the water before freeze up and constructing winter quarters—before continuing their exploration during the following spring and summer. They finally chose two suitable fjords on the southwestern coast, some four hundred miles apart. These sites were to become the Eastern and Western Settlements.

They set sail for Iceland during the summer of 985, planning to gather settlers, ships, livestock, and equipment. Eirik called the new land Greenland, making no reference to the vast ice sheet covering most of the island, to induce people to come back with them.

The strategy worked, and in the spring of 986, a fleet of twenty five ships sailed for Greenland. Fourteen of the ships made it to Eiriksfjord, the southernmost of the two settlement sites selected. Of the remaining eleven ships, a few made it back to Iceland; the fate of the others is unknown.[12]

Later that same summer, Bjarni Herjulfsson of Iceland, while sailing to the newly established settlement in Greenland to visit his father who recently arrived with the rest of the settlers, was storm-driven far off course and sighted unknown land to the west.[13] His sightings were probably Labrador and Baffin Island; however, he did not land, continuing instead to Greenland, a decision decried by his crew and the Greenland settlers.[14]

The Norse knew about North America for at least fourteen years before exploration began, or that is what the sagas tell us. The sagas also tell us that Leif Eiriksson purchased Herjulfsson's ship and, with a crew of thirty five men, set sail for North America sometime between 997 and 1002. Many do not believe that avid explorers such as the Northmen were content to wait fourteen years before someone checked into Herjulfsson's discovery.[15]

With life spans averaging forty odd years, fourteen years would make the difference between a young man and an old man. And exploration was definitely for the young. I doubt they waited.

I believe these people mounted other expeditions almost immediately after Herjulfsson told them what lay to the west. They were famous for being impulsive, and they were inveterate explorers. Curiosity alone would guarantee they did not linger fourteen years before setting off into the unknown.

The sagas tell us Leif Eiriksson landed on both Baffin Island and Labrador before finding what he sought, a land of bountiful timber and pasture for livestock near the northeastern tip of Newfoundland Island. Nobody knows what Leif called Newfoundland Island. Nor is it known whether he called the new land Vinland.[16]

Leif Eiriksson wrote nothing down; we do not know what he called the settlement he constructed on Newfoundland. The sagas refer to the site as *Leifsbudir*, or Leif's Booths.[17]

The Norwegian Helge Ingstad, and his wife, Dr. Anne Stine Ingstad, an archaeologist discovered and excavated Leifsbudir between 1961 and 1968.

This momentous but oft–ignored discovery proves that Northmen were the first Europeans on the North American continent. They regularly sailed from Greenland to North America, Iceland, and Norway for more than four hundred years before Columbus was born.[18]

Between 997 and 1002, Leif and his men completed construction of the houses and support buildings of Leifsbudir, at the head of the small bay where he landed. The buildings were not temporary huts, but permanent all-weather structures.

According to the Norse sagas, Leifsbudir was one of at least three permanent settlements built and utilized by Greenlanders and Icelanders. The other settlements referred to in the sagas, *Hop* (meaning tide pools), and *Straumfjord* (meaning stream fjord), have never been located.[19]

Greenlanders used three place names, attributable to Leif Eiriksson, to describe areas where they landed: *Helluland* (Flat Stone Land) believed to be Baffin Island; *Markland* (Wood Land) most likely heavily wooded Labrador; and *Vinland* meaning and exact location unknown—a general area, not a specific place.[20]

Given the Northmen's propensity for exploration, as well as the need to constantly find new hunting grounds, it is safe to assume they also explored much of the northeastern coast of North America and made forays into the interior. Like the natives they encountered, they hunted and traded. Their simple lifestyle left no sign of their passage.

Norse artifacts have been found on the south shore of Ungava Bay in Hudson Strait, the western and eastern shores of Hudson Bay itself, Baffin Island, Labrador, Newfoundland Island, and many other sites in the Canadian North. A Norse penny recently turned up in Maine, and a rune stone was unearthed in Minnesota during the latter portion of the nineteenth century.[21]

Norse artifacts have been found as far inland as the state of Oklahoma. With the exception of the Norse penny found in Maine, archaeologists continue to disagree about the authenticity of all other Norse artifacts discovered in the United States.[22]

The Norse Greenlanders, primarily livestock farmers and hunters, were also warriors by nature and necessity and fully capable of defending themselves against all comers. The indigenous people they encountered as they explored were numerically superior. Weaponry was similar enough that the outcome of protracted armed conflict tended not to favor the Northmen.

Not surprisingly, the natives were friendly and anxious to trade in the beginning. After all, they had no reason to dislike their Norse visitors; they had never seen one before.

Had the Northmen been more amicable toward the people they initially contacted, a very different early history for North America might have resulted. Instead, the sagas tell us they cheated in trade, killed the natives indiscriminately, and eventually had them so incensed that a state of war existed, making all attempts at settlement impossible. At least that is the presently accepted theory among academics.[23]

By today's standards, the Northmen were a cruel and savage nationality. The Dark Ages, in which they existed and became a force with which to be reckoned, was a period of eight hundred years of almost continuous warfare. The Northmen were some of the most accomplished warriors of that violent time.

The native tribes they came in contact with seemed to tolerate their presence better when the Northmen came only to trade. Any attempt at permanent settlement — Hop, Straumfjord, and Leifsbudir — always led to violent confrontation.[24]

This situation only existed initially. We know nothing about the remainder of the four hundred years of association between the Northmen and the people we now collectively refer to as Indians. *And there most certainly was an association.*

Greenlanders referred to the indigenous people of North America as *Skraelings*, generally thought to be an epithet, but the meaning is not known. We do not know whether Skraeling is a reference to the Tornit (pronounced Dornit) they contacted initially, the Inuit (Eskimo) who followed the Tornit later in the twelfth and thirteenth centuries, or includes all the indigenous people they contacted.[25]

Some believe that the Northmen interbred with the Inuit of Baffin Island and other groups of people in the far north, as tall, fair-skinned Inuit were reported by the next influx of explorers in the fifteenth and sixteenth centuries. This is not a fanciful contention at all when consideration is given to the fact that women were always in short supply. The lack of sufficient females caused many fights and blood feuds among the Northmen.[26]

Farther south the Northmen contacted ancestors of several other Indian tribes. At some point approximately one thousand years ago the ancestors of Indian tribes we now identify as belonging to the Algonquian and Iroquoian language groups, e.g., Ojibwa, Cree, Huron, Mohawk, Iroquois, etc, began to emerge. Various tribal bands of these people occupied all the land from Hudson Bay, south to Lake Superior, and east to the Canadian Maritimes, the area in which this story takes place. They fought over the hunting grounds and ancestral lands annually, alternately claiming or losing lands as ongoing warfare involved subsequent generations.[27]

We do not know what they called themselves one thousand years ago. It is believed by some that they referred to themselves simply as the People. Most still have a name in their language that translates to the People. I have endeavored to use their names for themselves, if we know it, or a diminutive of that name, throughout this novel.

The two known Norse Greenland colonies prospered into the late fifteenth century. The population eventually swelled to as many as four thousand people at any given time, spread among farms in the areas around these settlements.

At some point late in the fourteenth or early in the fifteenth century, all settlement attempts and trading voyages to Greenland from Iceland and other points to the east were abandoned. Sometime in the middle of the fourteenth century (Western Settlement), and just after the turn of the fifteenth century (Eastern Settlement), the Greenland populations disappeared without a trace.[28]

Perhaps most of the inhabitants of the Greenland settlements had already moved west having migrated to successful settlements already established by other Northmen with the native populations of North America over the ensuing years.[29]

In any case, I maintain they eventually gave up the sea. Like thousands of their compatriots in Europe, they settled ashore. All impetus and desire for undertaking the perilous voyages became a thing of the distant past.

Around 1450, winters became colder in the far north, a lot colder. The ice in the harbors and fjords began remaining well into summer, and then it just remained. Greenland became uninhabitable for the Northmen. The Medieval Warm Period ended. A mini-ice age gripped the Arctic and northern portions of North America for the next four hundred years, into the last half of the nineteenth century.[30]

During the late fourteenth or early fifteenth century, a Catholic Prelate voyaged to Greenland, ostensibly to check on his flock. Although a few domestic animals grazed the hillsides, he found no people, living or dead. No ships, supplies, or tools remained. The people and their possessions had simply vanished into the mists of time.

The Icelandic bishop Gisli Oddsson, quoting church records, stated in the sixteenth or seventeenth century (the exact date is unknown) that the Norse Greenlanders joined the natives of America in 1342, giving up Christianity in the process. The record notes a firm date for the migration, not sometime in the fourteenth century.[31]

We know three things for certain if one considers the disappearance of these people objectively: they did not sail to Iceland or Europe; they did not remain on Greenland until they died of hunger or exposure; they did not simply disappear. No, they had been migrating slowly to North America for five hundred years. Assimilation with the indigenous peoples became, over time, the Norse Greenlanders' only option for survival. It is the only logical answer to the one-thousand-year-old mystery.[32]

Since their assimilation, almost everything the Northmen left behind on this continent has turned to dust, become locked under the permafrost, or disappeared under many feet of debris in the forests and along the seashores of North America.

I have attempted to tell a tale of what might have happened, what could have happened, and considering the options available, what probably did happen to the Norse Greenlanders.

More than 30-generations have elapsed since they came to this continent. Now their very existence, everything they accomplished, has faded from the collective memory of all the peoples they contacted and lived among.

I prefer to believe the four thousand live on however, their genetic makeup diluted by the intervening centuries of time. They are still here, smiling back at us from the faces of the Inuit Greenlanders, Cree, Ojibwa, and Iroquois with whom they joined so long ago.[33]

J. A. Hunsinger
Colorado, USA

ENDNOTES

[1] William W. Fitzhugh, *Vikings The North Atlantic Saga* (Smithsonian Institution Press, Washington, DC, 2000) 11.

[2] Helge & Anne Stine Ingstad, *The Viking Discovery of America* (Checkmark Books, New York, NY, 2001) iv.

[3] Fitzhugh, 27.

[4] Fitzhugh, 330.

[5] Fitzhugh, 328–329.

[6] Paul Buckland, *The North Atlantic Saga* (Smithsonian Institution Press, Washington, DC, 2000), 148–149.

[7] Birgitta Linderoth Wallace, *Archeologists Interpretation of the Vinland Sagas* (Smithsonian Institution Press, Washington, DC, 2000) 225.

[8] Gisli Sigurdsson, *An Introduction to the Vinland Sagas* (Smithsonian Institution Press, Washington, DC, 2000) 218.

[9] Gisli Sigurdsson, *The Quest For Vinland* (Smithsonian Institution Press, Washington, DC, 2000) 234.

[10] Sigrid & Irmelin Martens Kaland, *Farming and Daily Life* (Smithsonian Institution Press, Washington, DC, 2000) 42.

[11] Wallace, 226.

[12] Gwyn Jones, *The Norse Atlantic Saga* (Oxford University Press, Oxford, NY, 1986) 73–79.

[13] Jones, 115.

[14] Jones, 116.

[15] Jones, 117.

[16] Jones, 117–118.

[17] Jones, 118–119.

[18] Ingstad, 141.

[19] Ingstad, 86–87.

[20] Wallace, 226–227.

[21] Patricia D. Sutherland, *The Norse and Native North Americans* (Smithsonian Institute Press, Washington, DC, 2000) 246–247.

[22] Fitzhugh & Wallace, *Stumbles and Pitfalls in the Search for Viking America*, (Smithsonian Institute Press, Washington, DC, 2000) 383–384.

[23] Jones, 226–227.

[24] Jones, 227–228.

[25] Robert McGhee, Contact *Between Native North Americans and the Medieval Norse*, (American Antiquity 49, no. 1, 1984) 22.

[26] Jones, 277–279.

[27] E. S. Rogers, *Indians of Canada*, (National Museum of Canada, Toronto, Canada, 1965) Bulletin 65.

[28] Jones, 95, 111.

[29] Jones, 95.

[30] Thomas H. McGovern, *The Demise of Norse Greenland* (Smithsonian Institute Press, Washington, DC, 2000) 327.

[31] Ingstad, 177–178.

[32] Ingstad, 179–180.

[33] History Channel, *The Vikings Fury From The North* (A&E Television Networks, New York, NY, 2000) VCR Tape.

Contents

Chapter One

Southwestern Greenland, spring, 1008

The sun appeared as a dull orange orb through the haze and sea mist as it began to rise above the horizon. The grey half-light of the northern night yielded to the brightness of the day. A chill offshore breeze, stirred to life by sinking cold air that flowed like a river from the vast inland icecap, began to stir the calm surface water of the fjord.

The last remnants of rotting pack ice dotted the water's surface. Icebergs could be seen shining in the distance as they drifted by the fjord entrance on the current that carried them north along the rocky coast.

A crowd of silent people stood among the rocks and grasses of the hillside. Below them, on the stony beach, a group of six men listened to a red-haired man who stood before them.

"The offshore wind comes off the icecap, and the tide begins to run from Eiriksfjord. It is time to make sail." He looked at each of the men before his eyes came to rest on one of them.

"I am in your debt, Eirik," the man said. "I could not have mounted this expedition without your help. I wish you were going with us."

Eirik turned his head to look at the four ships drawn up on the beach. "I have sailed from many shores in my time," he mused. "There have been many adventures. Too many some would say. No, this is your time, yours and your men's. I pass the sword of adventure and conquest, the spirit of our people, to you and to all those with you. Go now, Halfdan. Set sail for Lysufjord. Destiny awaits you."

Eirik shook hands with each of the men in turn. He saved Halfdan for last. The two men held each other's eyes for a heartbeat, their hands locked on forearms in a vice-like grip. A silent farewell passed between them. Halfdan turned away and followed his men toward the ships.

A groundswell of sound rose from the many throats, from ship and shore alike, as shouted farewells became raucous and tearful.

The mood became pensive as though a shroud settled over the watchers ashore when the long sweeps backed the ships from the beach and pointed their bows toward the mouth of the fjord. Sails rose to the mastheads and filled with the off-shore wind. The ships sailed from the fjord into the open sea and out along the coast to the northwest, to the rendezvous at Lysufjord, Greenland.

* * *

Six wooden ships laid sharply over in the brisk northwest wind as they sailed close-hauled on the port tack. Their destination was Leifsbudir, Vinland. Riotous ranks of steep swells surged by, dotted with islands of spume scattered indiscriminately on the surface. Spindrift off the wave tops pelted their hulls as the ships plunged into each deep trough and boisterously rose to the crest of the next swell.

Under the command of Halfdan Ingolfsson, the flotilla had sailed into the western ocean from the northernmost Greenland settlement of the Northmen, at Lysufjord. Halfdan took advantage of the north-flowing Greenland current to sail north along the coast to the narrowest part of the strait between Greenland and Helluland before he turned to the west. Dawn found the ships near the halfway point in the strait as the rising sun chased the twilight of the polar night to the west.

The ships were loaded to capacity with 163 Greenlanders and 152 Icelanders. The complement included men, women, children, and livestock. Each ship carried a share of the supplies and equipment deemed necessary for the establishment of a permanent settlement.

Every person had been carefully chosen to ensure all the trade skills of the Norse people were represented. All were young, as such things are reckoned, and without handicap. Halfdan accepted families among the settlers but refused their kin. Feuds among opposed kinfolk were common in Norse society; a duel with one became a duel with all. He wanted to avoid the possibility of any such trouble, even if it meant fewer settlers.

* * *

Halfdan and his second-in-command, Gudbjartur Einarsson, stand together on the bow platform of the lead ship. Their work-roughened hands gripped the ship's rail and forestay as they swayed in time with her roll off the crest of each swell. The bow platform is the only place aboard where people knew not to disturb them. Secluded and apart as much as possible from the normal activity aboard the crowded ship, the two men reflected on the past season and the decision to begin a quest for a new land to settle.

The decision to migrate had been made when new arrivals from Iceland, Vestfold, Gotland, and Svealand, the homelands for most of them, had made it apparent that Greenland could not long support the burgeoning population.

"We have listened to all the councils, Gudbj. We know the mistakes made by others who attempted to establish permanent settlements in Vinland. We must not repeat those mistakes." Halfdan pounded the rail for emphasis.

"If we learned nothing else, we know we are greatly outnumbered by the Skraelings." Gudbjartur's eyes swept the sea ahead. Serried swells covered the surface to the limit of his vision.

"Every person must understand. We are too quick to fight. This time we come in peace. We will fight to protect ourselves, but only to protect ourselves."

"They have all been told. It will be as you say."

"Our planned destination still does not feel right to me. We need to think on it. Perhaps a different area of Vinland would be better than Leifsbudir."

Both men lapsed into silence as they reflected on the importance of this voyage and what lay before them. Everything they possessed hung in the balance.

Gudbjartur glanced at his chieftain and realized he was in a world of his own. He knew in his heart he had done all he could to relieve the worry and lift some of the weight of command from Halfdan's shoulders. The final decisions were always Halfdan's. After careful consideration he made them without hesitation. But the strain told on his face. Gudbjartur watched the spume of the sea float by for a moment. The ship's bow sliced through the swells like a sword blade. He left Halfdan leaning on the ship's rail. *I doubt he will even be aware of my absence,* he thought. He turned and made his way aft to get something to eat.

* * *

Halfdan leaned on his forearms across the ship's top rail, hands clasped in front, oblivious to the icy wind that stung his face and caused his eyes to water. He gazed, lost in thought, on the surface of the sea.

People remembered the eyes when speaking of him. They were like the sky on a clear winter day, a pale blue color that fairly bored into you—intense with a touch of sadness, but also tempered hard as the best steel blade. His eyes, out of long habit, occasionally rose from the surface of the sea and swept the horizon.

His age would have been difficult to determine. Like all his kith, his face was tanned and deeply lined, sculpted by the timeless element of his world: the incessant chill wind of the northern sea. The scar of a sword cut turned a strip of his beard white and marred his face as it ran diagonally from his cheekbone through the corner of his lip and down across his chin. This small imperfection served to give him character. He was a handsome man, and his face mirrored a youthful exuberance. This characteristic had lulled more than one adversary into underestimating the man that dwelt within.

He emanated the power and force of his will, that which made him what he was, a chieftain.

In the prime of life, he stood about six feet with a powerful build. His shoulder-length, dark brown hair was braided on each side of his face to keep it out of his eyes. A full beard blew freely in the wind.

He wore a dark woolen pullover tunic that reached his thighs, trousers of the same material thrust into soft-tanned, high-topped leather boots. A seal fur leather vest protected him from the raw wind.

A knife and ornately carved scabbard hung from the right side of the broad leather belt that encircled his waist. Large, ornate, silver ring pins—the only indication of his rank—held each of the top ends of his laced vest together over his shoulders.

He thought about the councils he had called the previous summer at both the Eastern Settlement at Brattahlid in Eiriksfjord and the Western Settlement at Lysufjord. He and Gudbjartur made the three-day roundtrip sail several times before they found enough people for an expedition to Vinland. They spent most of the summer talking to the widely scattered farmers and gathering the people, ships, livestock, and equipment required for a voyage of settlement the next spring.

Four ships from Eiriksfjord, including three of last summer's arrivals from Iceland, had rendezvoused with the two ships from Lysufjord. The flotilla set sail with a fair wind on the ebb tide.

* * *

Gudbjartur walked up to the group of people clustered aft of the mast, greeted them with a nod, and winked at his wife. He picked a piece of dried cod from a food bag and stuffed it in his mouth. His eyes followed the movements of his wife as he chewed the tough fare.

A tall, young woman, Ingerd's intelligent, widely set blue-green eyes animated her comely face. A single, thick braid and bright blue wool scarf captured her long golden hair. Her angular chin and jaw indicated a firmness of character. The large hands and frame of a worker and the rounded hips and

ample breasts of a woman of childbearing age did not detract
from what some referred to as an almost regal bearing.

Ingerd was attired essentially the same as all Norse women,
although each woman adorned herself in accordance with personal tastes. Available clothing choices were limited by utilitar-
ian necessity. She wore a simple, full-length, long sleeved,
pullover shift of pale red wool. She wore no undergarments, nor
was such available. A full-length apron covered her front and
back. The apron provided additional warmth and served to protect her dress from work related damage. The apron consisted of
identical front and back panels fastened with over-the-shoulder
looped straps joined together by two large pinned broaches, one
above each breast. The dome shaped broaches were ornately
incised silver, a wedding present from Gudbjartur.

A beautifully worked bronze ringlet necklace hung about
her neck. Beyond its decorative value, it also provided a handy
place for the bronze ring that held the keys to the family's
chests. Scissors, tweezers, and needle case—the tools of all
Norse women of her station—hung from a silver chain connected between her broaches. In addition to this chain of
tools, Ingerd had belted about her waist, on the outside of her
apron, a pouch containing flax and wool thread, spare ring
pins, comb, hair brush, and a knife scabbard. Her feet were
encased in the ankle-length, soft tanned leather shoes common to both men and women. Her position as the wife of
Gudbjartur ensured others deferred to her.

"What were you two talking about?" Ingerd asked. Her
eyes studied her husband's face.

"This voyage. I will tell you about it later, Ingerd, when we
have a few minutes alone."

"All right, I will hold you to that." She smiled at the man
she loved above all else.

Gudbjartur bent down to look forward under the bottom
edge of the tightly braced sail. He noted that Halfdan remained
in the same position.

He turned his attention back to the food. He stooped to
pick up a medium-size wooden trencher from a pile near the
mast step. From the open food bags he selected four chunks
of dried fish and the same of dried meat.

The usual fare at sea was dried fish or dried meat, boiled eggs when available, and water. There was no set time for meals; people ate as they felt the need.

"Do you want a couple boiled eggs to go with that meal, Gudbj?" Thora asked. A solidly built woman with reddish-blond hair, she was one of several cooks who prepared the communal meals when the company was ashore.

"Aye, Thora. Make it four." He watched her ladle the eggs from the cask of whale oil that preserved them. She plopped the eggs, still in their shells, onto his trencher with a generous amount of the rich oil.

He made eye contact with her and smiled. "Dribble a little oil over the fish and meat. We need to keep up our strength."

She snorted at his humor and did as he bade. In spite of the lively action of the ship's deck in the quartering head seas, she did not spill a drop of oil. Whistles of appreciation came from those who witnessed her adeptness.

Gudbjartur grinned at the smug expression on Thora's face. He lifted his chin to Ingerd. She stepped over to him and planted a kiss on his hairy cheek.

They held the rail and stepped forward out of earshot. "Halfdan and I are discussing our destination. We may not go to Leifsbudir. Keep this to yourself until we make up our minds." Gudbjartur spoke to her in a low voice.

"No matter, you will decide what is best." An impish sparkle shined from her eyes. "You had best watch Thora, Gudbj. She wants a man and she would be happy to have you."

Gudbjartur stopped and turned around to appraise Thora. At that moment she happened to have her head thrown back to laugh at something said by a member of the group gathered near the mast. Her long reddish-blond hair blew in the wind. He got an eyeful as her ample breasts strained against the confines of her apron, each nipple plain to see. Of medium height, her hair framed an average looking face dominated by unusual pale brown eyes with green flecks— cat eyes some called them. Her nicely rounded hips and wide shoulders bespoke the strong, solid build of a worker. Thora was known as a woman who appreciated a good joke, especially at another's expense. Quick to laugh, the sharp tongue of a born wit and quick to anger—these pretty well described her.

"She looks very good from here. Perhaps I can have two of you. That way, if one is uncooperative, I will have a spare, to fill in, so to speak." He grinned at his wife.

"You!" She walked away in a huff.

"Me? You started it." He continued toward the bow and shook his head over his wife's reaction. *It is impossible to predict how she will take something. And she brought up Thora, not me.* He chuckled to himself at the thought. His free hand gripped the rail while he tried to balance the full trencher against the antics of the ship. Gudbjartur sat the trencher on the raised bow platform. "Here, Halfdan, you have thought long enough. I have brought food and water."

Halfdan selected a piece of meat from the trencher. "I did not realize I was hungry."

"Nor I. Food has a way of making us know that we are hungry."

They sopped their selection in the puddle of whale oil, gripped bite-sized chunks firmly in their teeth, and cut off the excess with their knives. This process was not without a certain element of danger, as evidenced by the scarred noses and lips of more than a few of those aboard.

By comparison, the fish was easy to consume. It, too, had been salted, smoked, and air-dried to the consistency of leather; however, when soaked in the puddle of whale oil for a short time, it gave up much of its toughness.

Ingerd watched the two men from her seat atop a pile of gear bags. She mended her son's pullover, her actions almost automatic as she plied the needle and thread. She glanced back and forth between the men and her mending. "Look at them, Thora. Except for clothes and hair color, they look like twins."

"Yes, they do. Halfdan and Gudbj have become legends. That status is usually reserved for those who are dead."

"I feel almost humble to be married to him, Thora. He is the most respected and feared man among us, and yet he can be as gentle as any man."

"Well, do not tell him that. It might give him a big head."

"No, he has not changed at all since Halfdan chose him to be his second-in-command. If anything, it has matured him. The responsibility of his position makes him more aware of our everyday problems. He feels especially protective of Halfdan. You will notice he is always close by."

"Him and that axe, Ingerd. He gives me the shivers sometimes. At the same time I am glad he is on my side. He is quite a man. Tell me if you tire of him."

Ingerd turned her head and fixed Thora with a direct look. "No, I will never tire of him. He is mine."

Thora slapped Ingerd on the shoulder in friendly fashion. "I think everyone knows that. Come on. I do not want to miss any gossip."

Ingerd waved a hand in dismissal. "You go ahead. I will be along shortly." Her eyes sought Gudbjartur again.

Thora shrugged and walked back to rejoin the women grouped around the mast. She resumed her place among them as though she had never left. Some made new apparel, others repaired old, and they gossiped, always gossiped.

Ingerd watched her man. She never tired of admiring that which made him what he was. He had the square jaw and facial structure people associated with a good, honest man. His countenance reflected a firm resolve. People often said he had fish eyes, a very pale blue, almost grey color depending on how he felt that day and the color of his clothing. His eyes were widely spaced with crows-feet etched in the corners. He squinted in the sun and wind, and of course, he smiled a good bit because he found humor in many of the adverse aspects of life. It was known among all the people that when he was provoked those same eyes and pleasant facial expressions could instantly change to a hardness few could look upon.

All the men were clothed essentially the same out of necessity and long practice. Most personalized their attire in various small ways. Gudbjartur preferred not to wear the pants worn by most men. Except for the coldest months of winter, he wore a mid-thigh length pullover tunic of bright blue, red, or green that left his legs bare. His footgear consisted of either knee-high boots or the common ankle-high leather shoes. If the day proved to be especially cold and windy he might throw on a wool cloak or seal fur vest, fastened with common but ornately fashioned iron ring pins.

He always wore a beautifully worked broad leather belt, incised intricately with favored mystical animals, to which he attached a pouch, belt knife, and the ever-present battleaxe. The long-handled axe was heavy, but he was never without it. After many accidental nicks and cuts from the sharp edge of the axe, he had developed a leather safety scabbard that fit over just the edge and attached to the carrying loop at his belt. He had found turning the axe edge to the rear in the scabbard made it easier and safer to carry, especially when he sat down. When he swung the axe handle forward as he took a seat, the edge was down instead of up.

None of the men shaved. Unlike many others he kept his beard neatly trimmed. But then, he was unlike any of the others in almost all respects, except Halfdan himself.

Finished with the appraisal of her husband, Ingerd smiled to herself. She shook her head at some cherished memory and turned away to rejoin her friends.

Gudbjartur looked aft at the full-bellied sail and spoke around a mouthful of meat. "We could not ask for better conditions. As heavily loaded as the ships are, we have made a fast passage. We are a little more than halfway across the strait and should soon feel the southerly current off Helluland's coast."

"You always know when to change the subject. I appreciate it." Halfdan peeled the shell from an egg, cut it in half lengthwise, dipped one of the halves into the whale oil, and popped it into his mouth.

"We may as well change the subject. It is done. We are on our way. I, for one, am excited about what lies ahead. Whatever it is, we can handle it."

"I agree with you, but there is always that nagging doubt in the back of my mind with something as big and important as what we have undertaken. But you are right, and I, too, am excited about this voyage, more than any I have ever before been on."

A hail from the masthead interrupted their conversation as the lookout voiced the age-old cry at the sighting of land.

"Land! Land off the steerboard bow!" The lookout pointed out over the right front side of the ship. Both men got to their feet and looked westward. Low on the horizon it was just possible to see a smear of clouds from the deck. The clouds hugged the mountain tops of Helluland.

Sometime later, the ship had drawn close enough for everyone aboard to see Helluland. After the turn south to parallel the coast, people crowded along the ship's weather rail to gaze at a shoreline that none had ever before seen. There was little to see, but the sighting of the treeless Helluland told the ship's company that the dangerous crossing of the open sea had been successful. The flotilla was on course, and people felt the influence of the southerly current.

Ingerd and Thora stood together at the rail. "It looks stark and cold from here. I am glad we are not going to land there." Ingerd shielded her eyes from the sunlight reflected off the water. "I doubt it is as nice as Greenland."

"I heard some of the men talking last night and they said Leif Eiriksson told Halfdan that Helluland is covered with great slabs of stone. There are no trees or brush and very little grass," Thora offered. "That is why he called it Helluland, land of flat stone."

The stark mountains, dimly visible through the sea mist, appeared black and featureless at this distance. With nothing to hold their attention, the ranks of people at the rail gradually thinned.

Halfdan and Gudbjartur finished their meal and rested with their backs against the planks of the ship's side. Their legs were draped over sealskin gear bags. Crew and passengers stowed personal belongings in these bags. They also doubled as sleeping bags. Their owners stowed them all over the ship wherever a suitable spot presented itself.

Neither man had said anything for awhile. Gudbjartur sharpened the shiny, razor-sharp edge of his battleaxe.

"You are going to wear that axe out with that whetstone."

Gudbjartur looked up at his friend from under bushy eyebrows and gave the same answer he always gave. "I like to keep it sharp. I take care of it, and it takes care of me." His hand never missed a stroke with the whetstone, although his eyes were on Halfdan.

Halfdan grinned at him. Gudbjartur and the long-handled battleaxe were the stuff of legend among the Greenlanders. He watched him whet the edge for a moment longer, and then told him what was on his mind. "I have decided we are not going to Leifsbudir, Straumfjord, or Hop."

"The other captains do not know this." Gudbjartur was surprised. He set the axe and whetstone aside.

"Not yet. I wanted to talk to you about it first."

"I seldom disagree with any of your decisions, unless I think you are wrong." Gudbjartur's eyes searched his chieftain's face.

Leaning toward his lieutenant, Halfdan kept his voice low. "I know. But this time I want your opinion after you have heard my reasons for the decision. What we do from here on is of paramount importance to our people."

Gudbjartur nodded. He watched Halfdan as the man gathered his thoughts.

"There is not much to it because we do not have enough information to talk about. Nonetheless, interrupt me if I say something you do not understand or do not agree with. I need your help to decide the best course of action. We will work it out with the others later, even if a *thing* is called for before the final decision is reached."

"All right, Halfdan."

Halfdan continued. "I told you we had to do it differently than any of the other settlement attempts. That is what has worried me. I did not know how to do it differently. Others have failed because of one thing. The Skraelings became hostile. Thorfinn Karlsefni and his group lived at both Hop and Straumfjord for three years before it became too dangerous to stay. Our challenge will be to somehow find a way to get along with the Skraelings without our men's pride being hurt. There must be a way. I have personally spoken at length with Karlsefni and the other leaders who came back to Greenland.

I believe they all failed for the same reasons. They cheated the Skraelings in trade and killed many of them without reason."

"Then all we need do is make certain this does not happen when we contact them." Gudbjartur placed the whetstone back in his pouch and then rubbed his axe blade with an oily bit of leather.

"It is not quite that simple. We cannot go back to any of the same places. The Skraelings are already wise to our ways. They will attack as soon as they know we have returned to their land. We probably all look the same to them. They will not give us an opportunity to tell them we are not the ones who wronged them."

Gudbjartur picked up a length of rope someone had cast aside and aimlessly tied a series of knots as he waited for Halfdan to continue.

Halfdan watched the ropework for a moment. "Karlsefni sailed as close as possible to the Markland coast. He told me there are numerous bays and narrow fjords along the coast all the way south to Leifsbudir. My suggestion is we find a fjord far enough north of Leifsbudir that we will contact a different group of Skraelings. Maybe we will have a chance to make friends with them." He glanced pointedly at his lieutenant. "What do you think about all this?"

Gudbjartur stood up and stretched. He nearly lost his balance as the ship took a lively plunge off a wave crest. He threw the length of rope overboard and turned to Halfdan, who had also gotten to his feet. "I think we should sail into the first bay or fjord we sight along the Markland coast and call a council. This decision involves all of us. You are our chieftain, and the final decision is yours. But this is too big a decision to make without the others. I agree with what you have said, and I stand with you. But the other captains must be told as soon as possible of the change in plans."

"We will do that. Have Gauk come down from the masthead and tell him what we seek along the Markland coast." He good-naturedly slapped his lieutenant on the shoulder.

Gudbjartur walked aft. He waved Gauk, the lookout, to the deck. His action was blocked by the sail. The curious eyes did not see the signal.

Halfdan remained where he was, once again thankful to have Gudbjartur at his side. He shared every thought with the man. Overtime, a bond had formed between them that neither could have explained.

Halfdan watched as Gudbjartur balanced himself against the ship's rail, forward of the mast and out of sight of most of those aboard. Gauk leaned against the ship's rail beside him. Gudbjartur gestured with his hands as he talked. They conversed for a moment and then Gauk made his way aft. He managed to retain his balance with a hand on the rail before he ducked under the foot of the sail and disappeared from sight.

"I told him he could stay on deck until we sight Markland," Gudbjartur told Halfdan.

"I doubt he will; he likes it up there. After he eats I would not be surprised to see him back on his perch."

"I do not see how he stands it. Every motion of the ship is amplified many times at the masthead," Gudbjartur said. "He talks to himself up there. He tells me there are spirits on top of the yard." He gestured up to the crossbeam that supported the ship's taut sail. "He says they are part of the ship's soul and they protect us from the gods who would do us harm."

Both men looked up to the top of the mast. Neither spoke; an awe of that which should forever remain unseen and that which is best left unknown rendered them silent.

* * *

The six ships of the flotilla were double-ended cargo vessels called knarrs. All were practically new and varied in length from seventy to eighty-five feet. Each had open cargo holds forward and aft of the single mast and deep wide hulls of overlapping oak planks. The ships had no permanent shelters of any kind, save for the sides.

Knarrs were a marvel of proven design capable in almost all sea conditions. They seemed a part of the sea itself. Of shallow draft for their length—the largest drew between three and four feet of water fully loaded—they could be beached if conditions permitted, and often were when cargo was to be loaded or unloaded.

Their captains had either purchased them outright from a builder or hired a crew to construct them in Vestfoldland, where good oak was still available.

Each ship carried two ship's boats, miniatures of the ship down to the small square sail. Constructed of thin pine planks, they were strong enough to endure rough handling yet light enough to be rolled upright on the deck and lowered over the side with a long boom pole and block rigged to the mast. Halfdan's ship carried two such boats inverted and secured in chocks on the deck to either side of the mast. Both were twenty-five feet in length. Propelled by six oars or a sail, they were typical of all the ships' boats.

A single, large, loose-footed square sail powered Halfdan's ship, Steed of the Sea, the longest at eighty-five feet. The sail was bellied out hard as iron in the stiff northwest wind of this day. The ship coursed through the sea, the white foam of her passage creaming from the graceful, raked bow.

The sail, woven by the women over the long winter, was made from panels of heavy wool wadmal cloth. The finished sail panels were whip-stitched tightly together with leather thongs. The edges were then bound with seal or walrus-skin thong whippings and heavily oiled with seal or whale oil. The sails were refurbished as necessary; they lasted many seasons unless sundered by a violent storm. Each ship carried an extra sail to preclude just such an eventuality.

Steed of the Sea carried a sail that consisted of ten panels, three feet wide by fifty feet tall. Reef points—two foot lengths of leather rope equally spaced from top to bottom and side to side over the forward surface of the sail—provided a means to divide the sail into four equal parts from top to bottom. In stormy weather, the crew could lower the sail yard to any one of four points on the mast and tie the sail's foot securely across its width with the reefing point ropes. This action shortened the sail's exposed surface and protected the mast—which could also be lowered—from being carried away by the wind.

The captains decorated their ships according to personal likes or idiosyncrasies. Each ship sported an ornate, intricately carved, removable figurehead affixed to the top of the bow and stern timbers. Typically they were the stylized head of a god or man or some mythical animal or serpent head.

The six ships of the flotilla sported sail panels of alternating colors, most decorated with the figurehead in profile. Steed of the Sea sported a black horse head. The long mane seemed to stream in the wind, and the head was centered in the red and blue sail.

These decorating efforts changed what would have been a rather somber and forbidding flotilla of vessels, intended to strike fear into an enemy's heart, into a gaily colored and outfitted fleet whose purpose was to convey openness and friendliness to strangers.

"Look at them, Gorm!" Halfdan exclaimed to his helmsman. "They are magnificent. I never tire of watching them slice through the swells."

Gorm looked over his shoulder at the five ships that followed astern. "Nor I. The colorful sails were a good idea, Halfdan. They can be seen for a great distance."

"That is the idea. I want the Skraelings to see us so they will know they have nothing to fear."

Gudbjartur joined the two men on the stern platform. "Is something amiss?" He looked astern at the other ships of the flotilla.

"No, nothing at all. We are discussing how the ships stand out with their new sails." Halfdan gestured aloft.

"Aye, they do," Gudbjartur agreed. "That is what we wanted."

The ships of the flotilla sailed on a broad reach, almost straight away from the wind's direction. The ship with the longest waterline had a slight speed advantage. The first two ships astern of Steed of the Sea decided to test that theory. They created an air of excitement and competition for a short time as they vied for second place.

Faint shouts carried over the water as the crews and passengers of each ship realized they were being challenged. The skill of captain and crew would decide the outcome. To that end, passengers shifted forward or aft to change the trim, the angle at which the bow entered the water, and the helmsmen and sheet handlers worked closely together to wring out the last bit of speed possible.

"Look at them!" Gudbjartur whooped. "That is what I like to see. Now we will have their full measure."

Passengers and crew vied for vantage points along the rail and on the stern platform with Halfdan and Gudbjartur to watch the excitement as the racers jockeyed for position.

The loud blast of the masthead lookout's warning horn froze the ship's company in place. All eyes were drawn to the masthead and then in the direction of Gauk's outstretched arm as his shouts of warning directed attention into the distance forward of the ship.

Chapter Two

"Halfdan, Gorm, a big wave comes at us!" Gauk shouted from the masthead.

Halfdan hurried forward through the onlookers to the bow platform to get an unobstructed view forward.

Gudbjartur grabbed a backstay and jumped onto the ship's rail. "All hands! Everyone down below the rails! Grab the sheer strake and hold tight!" Gudbjartur swept his arms to the side and down. The urgency and commanding tone of his voice brought unquestioned obedience as the emergency cry of "All hands!" swept throughout the ship.

The rogue wave was not yet in sight of the deck, but passengers and crew members scrambled to each side of the ship and gripped the narrow inboard plank affixed to the upright ribs that ran the full length just below the sweep holes. This plank normally functioned as a place to secure rigging or shore lines.

Mothers and fathers grabbed any children close to hand, regardless of whose children they happened to be, and huddled with them below the rail. Within a few heartbeats everyone was secured to the sheer strake and they awaited their fate in tense silence.

"Gorm, let her fall off downwind a little! Take the wave at more of an angle!" Halfdan shouted through cupped hands after he saw the giant wave.

Waves were almost equidistant in deep water. They usually gave everyone aboard sufficient time to become accustomed to the sea's state. A rogue wave—a confluence of several waves—although rare, could build to monstrous heights. It would have been disastrous had this particular wave caught them unaware and on the beam rather than the bow. The ship would be rolled onto her beam ends, almost certainly sinking with all aboard.

The long, sleek Steed of the Sea rose out of the trough of the preceding wave and charged at the crest of the giant. Up, up, up until a third of her length hung in the air before she slipped over the crest and swooped down into the trough on the other side. Shrieks of pure exhilaration filled the air.

The rest of the flotilla followed suit without mishap or pause. Each ship took all the sea had to offer. The ships of the Northmen were in their element; failure was usually caused by the crew, not the ship.

Gudbjartur joined Halfdan on the bow platform. They locked eyes. Halfdan shook his head once and hammered his fists on the oaken rail of his ship. "No wave will ever claim her," he shouted. "She is truly the Steed of the Sea!"

The wind ripped most of his words away, but his exuberance caused those within earshot to shout and laugh with him.

Gudbjartur organized a bucket brigade to deal with the water that had come aboard from the wave crest. They scooped water from the lowest part of the long keel, passed the buckets along the line, and tossed the water overboard. This simple act of maintenance served to calm people.

More than a few contemplated what could have happened had the monster been met in the dark of night, or at too great an angle. Several of them knew the flush of fear and were not possessed of the bravado of their shipmates when confronted with the terrors of the sea.

Many were affected in an entirely different way. They slowly expelled a collective breath of thanks to the gods, or laughed self-consciously; the merciless sea had missed them once again.

Halfdan and Gudbjartur made their way down each side of the ship, in order to reassure those who still cowered at the rail in white-knuckled fear that the danger had passed. Although everyone aboard, with the exception of some of the children, had been to sea many times, some never developed the acceptance of the dangers like the born sailor.

* * *

Gorm's eyes constantly swept the sea ahead from his place at the steering oar. He watched Halfdan and Gudbjartur as they conversed in a relaxed manner with those in need of a comforting word or a pat on the shoulder.

"The wave had begun to curl and break as we went over the top." Gorm glanced at his chieftain as Halfdan stepped up beside him and grabbed the backstay for support.

"I know. You should have been with Gudbj and me. It was exciting when almost half the ship hung over the crest before we crashed into the trough." Halfdan chuckled as he recalled. His eyes swept the ranks of swells ahead.

"It was exciting enough from here. It took my breath away to watch the ship climb the wave."

"No! Not you!" Halfdan's eyes widened and he peered at Gorm in mock surprise. "Did the wave scare you?"

"I was not afraid. But I talked to Steed of the Sea, and she listened to me."

"So did I, Gorm. So did I. She has been tested by the god Njord. She is a good ship."

"She is that."

The two men lapsed into silence. Their eyes swept the ranks of swells ahead.

"Do you need help at the steerboard?" Halfdan asked his helmsman as Gorm made adjustments to keep the ship on course.

"No. Not yet. I will call for help when the time comes."

Halfdan bobbed his head in assent and glanced at the horizon once more before he stepped from the stern platform.

"The wind has picked up and veered a little more north. Do you want to take a reef in the sail?" Gorm called.

"Let her fly for now. Call me if you think it necessary later," Halfdan called back over his shoulder as he made his way forward.

I will, Gorm thought. He took a quick bearing with a hand-held bearing compass and made a slight course change. *I doubt it will be necessary, unless the wind veers more to the north.* He saw Gudbjartur glance aloft at the fluttering sail, wave to him, and direct men to make the necessary adjustment to the sail sheets in response to the course change.

As the helmsman, Gorm stood above all but the masthead lookout on one of two areas of raised deck, the other being in the bow. He steered the ship along her course with a single large oar, called a steerboard, fixed to the outside of the hull on the right side near the stern. The blade of the steerboard extended into the water well below the bottom of the keel. The bottom edge was ironbound to protect the wood from damage as the ship beached. This assembly was secured in place by a heavy iron pivot that allowed the large blade to turn from side to side to steer the desired course, and to pivot up as the ship beached. The steerboard was essential not only to steer a course, but it also acted as a lever underwater to prevent the ship from skidding sideways as her course took her close to the eye of the wind. A wide leather strap, secured in slots cut in the top rail, kept the oar blade in the down position until the helmsman removed it to pivot the oar up out of the way.

Gorm's work-roughened hands gripped the heavy, removable, wooden tiller bar as he guided the ship on course. When the great ship had been built, he had carved the oaken tiller bar into an ornate serpent's head and body that extended to where it was pinned in place atop the steerboard itself. The tiller gave him leverage over the massive steerboard; it allowed him to easily control the ship's course in all but the worst sea conditions.

He whistled tunelessly to himself, the notes blown away on the wind. His eyes darted over the sea ahead and aloft at the trim of the sail and rigging. The heart of the ship pulsed through the soles of his feet, vibrated up through the steering oar and the palms of his hands, an inaudible hum that told him all was well in his world.

* * *

Gudbjartur sat down with a group of men aft of the mast. He cut a worn eye-splice from a coiled line at his feet and began to splice in a new eye. No one spoke for a moment. He occasionally glanced up from his splicing to watch two men as they repaired the worn foot of the spare sail.

"It is fortunate we changed sails. This one is wearing thin." Helge glanced at Gudbjartur. He threaded a new length of hard-twisted wool yarn into the needle's eye, and resumed the tedious task. His long steel needle whipstitched a new sheet rope into the worn doubled-over bottom edge of the heavy sail. A steel-reinforced leather palm protected his right hand as he pushed the needle through the heavy fabric.

"I see the wear. The sail served us well." Gudbjartur looked aloft at the trim of the new sail. "Our sails have a hard life. When this old sail is repaired and oiled it will serve for many seasons as a spare before it rips in two." He picked up the blade end of a sweep and examined a crack that extended through the center. "How many are split like this?" Gudbjartur looked at the two men repairing a similar crack in another sweep.

"Only two so far. We will take all of them down and check each one." Gisli pointed up at the vertical T-shaped supports where the sweeps and sail booming spars were stored when not in use. Secured on the supports, the twenty-four long sweeps were higher off the deck than the tallest man. This clearance allowed the crew and passengers unobstructed passage back and forth.

Gudbjartur watched Gisli and his helper, the thrall Ewyn, bore evenly spaced holes with a gimlet along both sides of the crack in the sweep blade. Ewyn then crisscrossed a wet rawhide thong between the gimlet holes and tied the ends together.

"There. As the rawhide dries it should pull that crack back together and this sweep will be good as new," Ewyn said as he inspected his work.

"We have just started. By the time you lace the rest of the split blades back together you will be good enough at it that Gudbj will let you repair them by yourself." Gisli winked at Gudbjartur. The men chuckled good-naturedly as the young man ruefully contemplated the large number of sweeps racked overhead that remained to be inspected and repaired.

The light, strong sweeps were carved from pine in different lengths to accommodate the curve and upsweep of the hull at bow and stern. The different lengths ensured each sweep entered the water at the same time to provide maximum thrust. When the sweeps were deployed, the crew passed them across the beam of the ship to their opposite number on the other side. These crew members guided the sweep blade through the slot in the waist high rowing hole and out to its full length. The crew plied the sweeps while they stood on the walkways down both sides of the ship, from just forward of the mast toward the stern. A round cover pivoted down and covered each rowing hole to keep water from coming aboard in rough seas when the sweeps were not in use.

* * *

At sea, passengers and idle crew sat or reclined in any suitable place that presented itself, a favorite being the mast step aft of the mast. Seated thusly, with one's back against the quivering mast, the very soul of the ship could be felt as she shouldered her way through the seas.

Today, however, not a single person lolled on deck. The southerly course took the flotilla closer to the Helluland shoreline and everyone was glad for a break in the monotony. The course took full advantage of the speed of the current that flowed south past Helluland and Markland. The ship's speed seemed to have doubled.

Passengers and unoccupied crew members lined the inshore rail as the ship rolled in the ranks of swells that charged at the coastline. For a time, each person was lost in their own thoughts as they gazed at the vast empty land through the sea mist.

"Whales, off the port bow!" Gauk shouted from the masthead. A large pod of small Minke whales and white-sided dolphins darted in and out of the flotilla. The playful animals soon had the onlookers in high spirits as they swam in close company.

"It is interesting how they always seem to know when we are not hunting them," Helge said from his place at the rail.

"Yes. I will wager they would disappear if one of us picked up a weapon. Look how they watch us." Ingerd laughed and pointed at one of the whales as the animal turned on its side next to the ship and looked up at the people along the rail.

"I doubt you would get any takers on that wager, Ingerd," Helge answered.

The remainder of his words were lost as a cacophony announced the arrival of clouds of crying seabirds. They dipped and dived at schools of frightened baitfish stirred up by the passage of the ships and whales. The squabbling seabirds added their own air of excitement to the ceaseless sounds of wind and sea.

The whales and seabirds soon lost interest and went their separate ways. The people huddled together in their sleeping bags, exhausted by the wind and the antics of the ship. Another day came to an end as the twilight of the northern night descended on the flotilla.

* * *

Halfdan and Gudbjartur found themselves on the bow platform after a sleepless night. Everyone aboard was restless because of the uneasy motion of the ship after the course change to the south. It had steadily worsened. Sometime before dawn the ship passed into an area of swells off the port quarter and now a corkscrew motion was added to the pitch and roll. This made for a most unpleasant ride.

Gudbjartur glanced at Halfdan in time to see him swallow several times.

"Are you sick, too?"

Halfdan shook his head. "Are you sick?"

"Not quite. But if I look aft at all those people hanging over the rail or take my eyes off the horizon for very long, I will be."

"I am in the same shape. The sea's surface is very confused here. There are back eddies off that cape to steerboard. Maybe the sea will calm down somewhat after we clear it. The sailing directions spoke of those two islands over there, so I believe that is the southernmost cape of Helluland."

"That is it, all right. We are about to enter the strait between Helluland and Markland. I hope you are right about calmer conditions when we are further offshore. I will give Gorm the course change to south by southeast to clear the north cape of Markland and then I want to check the ship and our people."

"Thank you, Gudbj. I am glad you remind me of my duty."

"This is my duty. You are to take care of the important things." Gudbjartur turned and made his way aft. He went from one handhold to the other as the ship continued her antics.

Halfdan watched the big man as he went from person to person, a word here, a pat on the shoulder there. Seasickness was a terrible thing and spared no one. Under the right conditions of storm-tossed turbulence, the most seasoned sailor could be struck down by its capriciousness.

The ship's corkscrew motion began to subside as the cape fell astern. Most of those aboard began a slow recovery. Halfdan knew that Gudbjartur would go down one side of the ship and return up the other side. He was aware of the slight course change toward the southeast and he glanced aft—but only for a moment, lest he too hang over the rail—in time to see Gudbjartur duck under the tightly braced sail, a sickly green cast to his face.

"You do not look too good. Try a swallow of water; it helped me."

Gudbjartur took a long drink from the water bag, tied the wooden plug securely back in place, and hung it back on a pinrail. "Everyone is sick except Ingerd and Thora. The rougher the sea, the better they like it." He shook his head as he thought of the two women. "I could not linger back there. There is vomit sloshing in the bilge. Most of the animals are sick too."

"All right!" Halfdan swallowed several times in an effort to maintain his dignity. "Do not talk about it anymore."

A weak smile was Gudbjartur's only acknowledgment.

Neither man spoke for a time as they struggled with nausea. They focused their attention on the distant horizon and the queasiness began to subside.

"We should sight Markland around dawn tomorrow, if I remember the sailing directions," Halfdan said. "Tomorrow morning, if sea conditions permit, let us plan to heave to. I will tell the other captains of the destination change and that we will find a bay or fjord we can sail into for a council."

"I agree. Why not also tell them we will tow a boat so it can quickly scout out a likely anchorage while the ships heave to offshore?"

Halfdan smiled appreciatively. "Now, why did not I think of that?"

Gudbjartur glanced at him through narrowed eyes as he considered the statement. But the wrinkles at the corners of his eyes gave him away. "You cannot think of everything. That is why you have me and the council."

"True, very true. Now, let us go over Leif's sailing directions once again to be certain we have not forgotten something. I want to cover them all the way to Leifsbudir, even though we are not actually going there."

The two men stood side by side, facing outboard. Their forearms rested comfortably atop the ship's rail; their bodies unconsciously swayed in time to the motion of the ship as they discussed the route to Vinland.

"Leif Eiriksson's sailing directions, verified by all who followed him, spoke of a westerly course on the approach to Helluland from Greenland, until a strong southerly current began setting the ship to the south," Halfdan said. "At that time, turn south until the southernmost cape of Helluland passes astern. Positive identification of the south cape of Helluland is two islands, one large and one small. There are several smaller islands toward the actual cape. These smaller islands are due south of the entrance to a large bay. The next landfall after Helluland, one day's sail farther south, will be Markland off the steerboard bow. When the northernmost cape of Markland is abeam, alter course a few points more to the southeast, to parallel the coast. Sail well off the wooded shoreline to avoid numerous submerged reefs and skerries. In the southern part of Markland, after a total of four to five days at sea, long, white sand beaches, Furdustrandir, are visible far out to sea. Half a day is required to sail past them. After Furdustrandir falls astern, the southeasterly course is maintained for another two days until abeam the southern tip of Markland. Across a narrow strait is the northernmost cape of a large island. Near the northeastern tip, inshore of five small islands, is the entrance to a small bay. Leifsbudir is on the south shore of that bay." Halfdan glanced at Gudbjartur. "Any questions?"

"No. No questions. I can find it if need be." He shoved himself erect from the rail.

"Good, I had no doubt you could." Halfdan glanced aloft at the brass wind gauge atop the masthead. "If this wind holds we should sight the northernmost cape of Markland on schedule."

"I do not like the look of the southern sky. It is much too dark for this time of day." Gudbjartur pointed at the ominous banks of dingy gray and blue-black clouds. "I have seen Thor hurling his lightning bolts."

"I, too, have seen the lightning. Whatever it is we will be in it before another day is done."

* * *

The night of the fourth day passed without incident. The lightning was a constant reminder of things to come. Thus far, conditions from Lysufjord had been ideal: strong steady wind, no fog, good visibility. At dawn, just about when they expected to sight the northern cape of Markland, the rising sun appeared as a dim, reddish-orange crescent. Banks of low lying clouds partially obscured the sun's face as it tried to chase the twilight of the northern night to the west. The entire southeastern sky was black in the center and tinted a dim red color around the edges, a sinister portent of the day to follow.

* * *

Gudbjartur sought Halfdan, reclined in fitful slumber amidships. He grabbed him by a foot and shook him rudely awake. Instantly alert, Halfdan lurched to his feet. The wind howled and steep seas covered with wind-blown spume met his glance as his eyes swept the sea. Both men fought to maintain their balance. The shrouds amidships saved them from a headlong fall into the animal pens below.

"We would have had many opportunities to find a safe fjord or bay somewhere along the Markland coast to convene a council." Gudbjartur pointed at the angry sea. "I think the gods have other plans for us."

Halfdan, a grim expression on his face, grabbed Gudbjartur by the arm and shouted into his ear to be heard. "Take another reef in the sail!"

Gudbjartur staggered away without comment. One hand grasped the ship's rail, and the other gestured at crew and passengers as all hands sprang to. The work was all accomplished with hand signals. It was impossible to communicate otherwise in the wind. With great difficulty crew members lowered the sail as it thrashed about like a mad thing in its death throes. Gauk, the lookout, came down the mast atop the sail yard and lent a hand. Reef points were quickly tied across the sail. Men at the halyards hoisted the reefed sail aloft. Others sheeted home the yard and foot of the sail as it filled with a boom, the drawing surface reduced by half.

The ship responded. The motion eased somewhat as the strain on her rigging and mast was diminished by the reefed sail. At the same time every available person secured livestock and loose cargo. Passengers and crew then wrapped themselves in sleeping bags as insulation against the icy wind, lashed themselves and their children to the shear strake, and hunkered down below the ship's side to seek the only shelter available.

Gudbjartur, after one last check of the preparations, waved to Halfdan and lashed himself between Ingerd and his son, Ivar. For the time being, his job was finished.

A wall of dark, ominous clouds swallowed the sun. Lightning flashed and thunder crashed continuously. The incandescent lightning backlit the wall of clouds as the ships and the storm rushed toward their inevitable collision.

Gorm, back at the tiller after a sleepless rest period, and his helper, Thorgill, a big, heavily built redhead and one of the strongest men among them, lashed themselves to the steering oar post. Even shouted speech became impossible as wind velocity increased to a sound reminiscent of a demented, shrieking woman.

Halfdan, as was customary at such times, lashed himself to the mast to direct the effort to survive the tempest. He remained erect as long as humanly possible; his eyes vainly sought other ships of the flotilla. Finally he sank to the deck, no longer able to keep his feet under him.

The wind shifted direction and increased velocity suddenly as the storm slammed down on them, nearly dismasting the flotilla. Gorm and Thorgill fought to control the ship's abrupt surge downwind as it conformed to the mindless will of the tempest. The two men reacted from long experience; guidance from their officers was unnecessary. Conditions worsened to the point that they secured the tiller handle to fore and aft lashings at the rail to trim the steering oar amidships. The ship could now blow downwind with the storm.

Halfdan and Gudbjartur forsook the safety of their lashings to rally the crew in a last-ditch effort on the ship's behalf. Crewmen fought to take additional reefs in the sail before it shredded. Finally forced to give up the uneven battle with the wind, the men fought the sail down and secured it and the yard to the mast base.

Wind-driven rain stung exposed skin like bees protecting their hive. Even the toughest crewmembers were forced to hunker below the weather rail and cover their heads. Water coming over the ship's windward side and sheets of wind-driven rain made constant bailing necessary. The shared misery of the task was endured without comment by every available person. Fresh people scuttled back and forth on the deck like crabs, to replace those in the bucket brigade exhausted by the effort. The end person in the bucket line, cowering below the rail, simply threw the water up in the air and the wind whisked it away.

* * *

Unknown to those aboard Steed of the Sea, two ships lost the uneven battle with the elements as sheets, shrouds, and stays parted. Lines snapped like whips in the withering blast.

Masts crashed down in a welter of cordage and tackle. The captains lashed to the mast and those nearby were lucky to avoid being crushed as the masts toppled. No longer under control, the two dismasted ships swung broadside to the wind, to lay a-hull, sideways, in swell and trough alike, as they plunged downwind like a balk of wood, their crews helpless in the teeth of the maelstrom.

* * *

Gray day turned to black night, then back to another gray day made more horrifying by the mountainous seas glimpsed through the opaqueness of the waterlogged atmosphere. Through the next night the ships were driven inexorably northwest before the gale, as if they were being led by an unknown and unrealized force. The wind took the ships well to seaward of all land. Had the storm slammed into the fleet at any position other than the strait between landmarks, the southeast wind would have blown them onto the rocky coast of either Helluland or Markland to a certain death.

During the third surreal night, the storm finally released the widely scattered ships from its grip and conditions gradually improved. Exhausted by the ordeal, people moved about in a state of torpor, unable to grasp the reality of their survival. The crews, more conditioned to storms at sea than the passengers, had never stopped tending to the needs of the ship. Their survival depended on it.

The weak sun, too, seemed exhausted by the ordeal. It peeked from the overcast and strove to brighten the otherwise somber dawn. But ragged storm clouds, not to be denied, hid its face from view until well into the afternoon.

Two ships found themselves within sight of one another. The rest of the flotilla was nowhere to be seen. Within hours, two more ships appeared on the eastern horizon and after their arrival, all four heaved to for a conference.

Halfdan cupped his hands and shouted to his captains. "Did anyone see what happened to Athils' and Gudrod's ships?"

"Both were having a rough time of it the last time I saw them; they were dismasted but still afloat," Bjorn Kjetilsson replied.

"We were too busy to even notice them." Brodir, a dark, hairy, giant of a man summed up the situation for all.

Although everyone heard the exchange, nothing more was said about the missing ships. They were feared lost. It was bad luck to speak of them.

The crews and passengers of the four ships that survived had more urgent needs.

A light mist from the ragged clouds, and occasional glimpses of blue-gray sky, accompanied by a steady, cold, wind out of the northwest heralded a gradual change in the weather. Passengers and crew began to emerge from the lethargy that had gripped them during the long storm. Dried rations and fresh water were passed out and this simple fare, even more than the change in the weather, lifted everyone's spirits for the first time in days.

"I have the crew busy with storm damage repairs," Gudbjartur reported to Halfdan. "We were lucky. Damage to the ship is minor. Some of the food stores packed in barrels and firkins are fouled by seawater. Most will be salvaged, but we lost too much to finish this voyage without replenishment. Dried meat and dried fish are edible, packed as they are in bags, but almost everything else got wet and will need to be spread out to dry. The fresh water supply stored in waterproof bags is unspoiled by saltwater. Everything in opened bags or barrels is spoiled and has been thrown overboard. We all soiled ourselves over the past four days, out of necessity. Clothing has been washed out and the ship is scrubbed clean. It already smells better."

Halfdan looked over his command, a sour expression on his face. "We do smell better, but we look pretty bad right now." His glance swept all four ships as they sailed in close company. Wet clothing and bedding flapped in the wind and festooned the rigging and every available line and surface. He thought it imparted an unkempt air to the flotilla. He looked at Gudbjartur as the man swayed in time with the ship. His face was gaunt and deeply lined from strain. "You do not look any better than the ships."

"Nor do you," Gudbjartur retorted. "Everyone is soaked to the skin and in need of a change. They need to get their

thoughts on something new. We must land and get the people ashore."

"I agree. Alter course within hailing distance of one of the
other ships and tell them we are landing."

Without comment, Gudbjartur worked his way aft to give
the necessary orders to the helmsman and alert the crew and
passengers.

The storm had blown the flotilla far off course. They found
themselves north of a rocky, treeless coast, lost in a strange
new land. The ships coasted slowly, close inshore. All eyes
strained to locate an ice-free bay that offered some protection
from the incessant wind.

"Bay off the port bow!" the lookout shouted.

"I do not see it yet. Gorm, turn to port and close the distance to the shore," Halfdan shouted as he grabbed the forestay
and jumped up on the bow rail. "There, Gorm!" Halfdan
pointed ahead and jumped down from the rail. He walked aft.
"Alter course a little to port and the ship will be lined up with
the entrance," he ordered as he stepped up beside Gorm.

"I see it, Halfdan. It does not look like much of a bay."

"No, it is small but maybe that rocky point will block some
of this wind," Halfdan said, gesturing.

The rocky shoreline inside the small bay made it too dangerous to beach the ships safely, so they rafted up, bow to the
shore in the shallows under the lee of the small headland.
Lines were secured at bow and stern and all four ships snuggled up alongside one another. The crews rigged two anchors
offshore and carried two ashore to secure among the rocks.
With the addition of spring lines from the sterns of the out-
ermost ships to the beach, the rafted ships were secured, as
one, in all directions.

As soon as this was done, Halfdan again jumped onto the
rail of his ship. He held onto the shrouds amidships and
addressed the occupants of all four ships. "When you have
things spread out to dry, have some of the hot soup the women
have heated." He gestured at the smoke rising from charcoal
braziers aboard each ship. "Rig awnings to keep out the mist
and everyone get some rest. We will do what needs to be done
after we have all gotten some sleep."

People complied without comment, most still languid from exhaustion. Women and children lined up for soup while most of the men rigged awnings aboard each ship.

"I need two volunteers, one aboard each end ship, as anchor watch; the rest of you go to sleep as soon as you can," Halfdan called.

"I will stay awake," Gudbjartur told him. "I am too keyed up."

"Are you sure? Someone else can do it." Halfdan looked at his lieutenant.

"I am sure. I could not sleep now. Later perhaps."

"All right." Halfdan looked toward the other end ship.

"And I, too, will stay awake, Halfdan," Sweyn called from the end ship.

"Good. I will see the rest of you later today." Halfdan waved as he jumped from his perch.

* * *

People awakened from fitful slumber in the mid-afternoon. Everybody knew what must be done and work parties formed to unload all the supplies and most of the animals. Horses, cattle, sheep, and goats were offloaded to graze on the lichen and scrub. Smaller animals, and the compact Norse cattle were picked up, dropped over the side, and left to swim or flounder the short distance to shore. The short, stocky horses jumped without being coaxed, as they were well accustomed to being loaded and unloaded. Pigs, being too hard to catch, remained penned aboard with the chickens that spent their days scratching in the manure from the larger animals. All of the cats and most of the dogs stayed aboard for their own reasons. This left only the larger animals to reload when the time came.

Gudbjartur gathered the captains of the other three ships and a council convened on Halfdan's ship. Crew and passengers gave their leaders some degree of privacy on the crowded ship as they went about their work. The men lounged in a group in the stern. Some sat while others stretched out full length among the piles of supplies scattered about to dry in the wind and occasional heat rays from the sun as it peeked from the ragged overcast.

"Repairs are being made. Asa and her helpers attend to the injured, and people are recovering." Halfdan paced back and forth as he spoke, his eyes on the deck as he gathered his thoughts. "The livestock are grazing, and all our small boats are busy hunting and fishing. I think we should remain here for a few days of rest before we continue. I also think we should explore this unknown land.

"I disagree." Bjorn Kjetilsson, a tall, broad-shouldered, blond-haired man, given easily to disagreement, stood to make his argument. "We know what awaits us at Leifsbudir and south of there, but this land is unknown. I think we should sail back to a place we know."

Fatigue forgotten, a lively discussion ensued as the captains Bjorn, Sweyn, and Brodir voiced their opinions.

Halfdan listened patiently as the topic was cast about. He knew he would win them over in the end. Each man had his say and was entitled to voice an opinion. That was the way it had always been. He glanced at his men, lingering for a somewhat longer time in thoughtful contemplation of Bjorn before he spoke to him directly. "You are right, Bjorn, we do know what to expect at Leifsbudir. But it is at least ten days sail from here and we are in no shape to continue without rest and fresh food. Some of the food stores have been fouled by seawater. What remains will not last four days, much less ten."

Bjorn began to rise to the occasion until interrupted by the raised hand of Halfdan.

"Let me finish, my friend. You will have plenty of opportunity to present your arguments, as always." The others chuckled at the levity. "We have no option but to restock the food we lost. What we have that can be washed off with fresh water, re-dried and re-stored, will be saved. Fortunately none of the grain in sealskin bags got wet, but some of the barley meal stored in lock boxes was fouled. We must obtain fresh meat and fish to conserve the dried stores we have left for winter and emergencies. We came to find land to settle; land that will provide meat, fish, and pasture. We must secure the trade goods and raw materials to make what we need to live. We also came to explore unknown country, to find something no Northmen have seen before. We are explorers and traders, as our people have always been. I, for one, would like to know what lies around yon headland." He gestured to the west. "We may be on an island, and we can sail around it to return to our original course. Or it may be part of an unexplored new continent. I do not know. But I want to know before we leave here, so we can tell others who will follow. Leif called this new land Vinland, for the bountiful pastureland he found. It would be a shame to have been storm driven here by the gods and then leave before we have explored this area of Vinland."

He paused for a moment. He looked at the faces of his captains to gauge their state of mind. "I had already decided not to go to any of our settlements in Vinland before the storm hit us, and Gudbj agreed with my reasons for the change."

Grumbling arose from the group at this admission and Bjorn got to his feet again, to better position himself for another argument.

Gudbjartur entered the conversation. "Wait, let him finish! I, too, was skeptical. After you hear him out you will agree with him."

The group shuffled around and assumed positions along the rail. They acquiesced to Halfdan and Gudbjartur, for the moment, without further comment.

"I will begin my explanation with a question. What has caused every expedition to fail since Bjarni Herjulfsson first sighted this land twenty-two years ago?"

No one spoke. He took their silence as his cue to fill in the blanks in their knowledge of Greenland's early history. "Skraelings are the cause of every one, as far as we know. I have talked to everyone who was personally involved, or knew someone who was personally involved. In each case, hostilities with the Skraelings caused the expedition to fail. One expedition of two ships came to explore this land the summer after Bjarni sighted it. Neither was ever seen again, so we do not know what happened to them. They may still be here somewhere, living among the Skraelings. In addition, other expeditions came over in the early years to cut timber and hunt reindeer and moose on Markland. They saw Skraelings every time they came. But they had no contact with them. The most recent settlement attempt was Thorfinn Karlsefni, the Icelander. Some of you may know him?" Halfdan glanced from man to man; Sweyn and Brodir nodded. "His experience here lasted three seasons and he spent time at all three of our settlements. Again, hostile Skraelings made it too dangerous to stay. I talked with him about it." His glance swept over his audience. The men listened with more than a little interest, so he plunged on.

"Karlsefni admitted that relations with the Skraelings were very good when he first arrived. They deteriorated because some of his men cheated them in trade and several Skraelings were killed without cause. The key to our attempt at settlement here, and the only chance of success we will have, is to settle where the Skraelings do not live. When first contact is finally made, as it will be eventually, they will be treated fairly. Any attempt to cheat them will be dealt with instantly and in full view of them. If that sounds like a threat to any of you, it is. Let us get your response out of the way now."

"I have no problem with that, Halfdan. We all want this to work as much as you do," Bjorn answered.

"I think all of us have the same motive for this voyage. Whatever we have to do to make the settlement successful, I say we do it," Brodir rumbled in his deep voice.

Sweyn nodded his agreement and Halfdan continued. "Before the storm brought us to this place, I thought we could look for a suitable bay or fjord along the coast of Markland, well north of Leifsbudir. When we arrived off the Markland coast, we intended to launch a boat to explore any likely spots, while the ships heaved to a safe distance offshore. We were going to tell you of the change in plans when we could safely do so, but the storm changed all that. Now we are here; wherever here is." His men chuckled in response. "I propose we round this headland after we have restocked and rested and sail to the west for a few days. If we have not found what we seek in a reasonable time, we will turn around and sail for the east coast of Markland. In the meantime, we will have replenished our larders and obtained more fodder for the livestock. Now, what say you?

Who among you does not want to know what awaits us around that headland?"

"I would rather be somewhere on the east coast of Markland. It is closer to Greenland," Bjorn said.

"All right. But think about that before you give your final vote."

"I will think about it."

"Gudbj, what do you think?" Halfdan looked questioningly at his lieutenant.

The others watched as Gudbjartur regarded Halfdan. Always deliberate and one to speak his mind, Gudbjartur had disagreed with Halfdan in the past if he felt it necessary. As the second-in-command his opinion carried almost as much weight as their chieftain. That was the way of it. These men were expected to have an opinion and when Halfdan asked he expected them to voice it.

"I have already agreed with your plans. I always want to know what lies around the next headland. We may find all we seek, just as you have said. I do not know. However, we will not find it if we do not look. The sea god, Njord, sent the wind that blew us here and he had a reason for doing so. It is up to us to find that reason. So, I say sail west along this coast and explore. It is our destiny."

A general discussion ensued, which Halfdan had hoped to avoid. However, it became impossible to intervene before all had their say.

"What is 'a few days,' Halfdan? How long will we explore before we turn around?" Brodir asked.

"The moon is full now. What say we explore this coast for two more full moons, until the end of the Sun Time moon? That gives us plenty of time to replenish supplies and explore." Halfdan looked from man to man.

Brodir was the first to speak. "We have much to accomplish before winter sets in. But it does not matter where we winter as long as we stop somewhere in time to build longhouses, stock food stores, and harvest fodder for the livestock. I am concerned we might run out of time." He gestured with both arms for emphasis. He hawked loudly and leaned over the rail to spit. "I know you have already thought of all this. I say stick with the original plan. Find a suitable place on the east coast of Markland, closer to Greenland and Iceland. So, I stand with Bjorn." He pushed his long, curly black hair back with his hands as he leaned against the rail again.

"I agree." Sweyn the Icelander lolled comfortably with his hands clasped behind his head. In contrast to the unkempt Brodir, the large, somewhat thickset man kept his reddish-blond beard neatly trimmed and his blond hair gathered into a single braid down his back. Known to be a taciturn man not given to lengthy discussion, he surprised the others with his longest speech thus far. "We expected to spend the winter at Leifsbudir, where everything is ready except for stores of food. I, too, am convinced that Leifsbudir is not safe, especially since we have women and children with us. Now we are faced with exploration of a new land. We must build houses and collect food—all before winter. I do not think we can do it in time." He lurched to his feet. "We have the women and children to think about. All the heavy work of building houses will fall to us and we already have enough to do without more work for ourselves."

"Most of the women and some of the older boys can out-work you, Sweyn." Brodir laughed and punched him in the arm in a conciliatory fashion.

Everyone, including Halfdan, laughed at Sweyn's expense.

"Aye, Sweyn. What about Frida? You could not outwork her. By Loki, I doubt you could even catch her." Bjorn laughed and poked a finger in Sweyn's ample belly.

The men laughed uproariously, everyone save Sweyn, and joked around like small boys for a time before they returned to the discussion.

"We are all charged with the care and safety of the people. As your chieftain, I have the final say, but I always want each of you to have your say. I believe we have more than enough time to sail along this coast wherever it leads us. And enough time to choose a suitable place to winter and lay in all the supplies we need before freeze up." Halfdan glanced at his men. "If we cannot find a suitable area we will still have ample time to sail for Markland." Silent for a time, he continued to pace while he mustered his thoughts. "This full moon is the first of the spring. As our people have always reckoned the seasons, this is Sowing Time. Some of the smaller bays are still filled with pack ice and many icebergs are about. We have seven more moons before another winter approaches: Lambing Time, Sun Time, Midsummer, Haymaking Time, Harvest Time, Slaughtering Time, and Autumn Time. We have ample time to explore this new land. If I did not believe this to be true I would be the first to turn around and sail for Markland. Now, who agrees with me? I have given you the reasons for my decision. Do you have further concerns?"

None had further objection. One by one the men voiced their agreement with the plan. But Bjorn still remained unconvinced.

"What about trees? Markland is covered with trees, while this place has only driftwood, like Greenland. We need trees big enough to make lumber for our immediate needs and to trade to Greenland. I agree with much of what you say, but I see no useful trees at all, and we must have them to make it worthwhile to build a new settlement." Bjorn glanced from man to man in search of agreement. He found none.

Halfdan continued in the most conciliatory tone he could muster, certain he could both placate Bjorn and gain his support. "Bjorn, I have said we would turn around after two more moons, the end of Sun Time, if we have not found what we seek. That includes ample forests. Certainly this is one of our most important needs, as you pointed out. Now, what else are we to discuss before we have agreement?"

Before Bjorn could answer, an excited shout interrupted further discussion.

"Two boats come! They tow heavy loads!"

Two boats rounded the point from the west. Both were heeled sharply over in the wind. Their sails drew taut as they sailed as close to the eye of the wind as possible to make good a course toward the rafted ships. Forward progress was slowed by the small black whales each boat towed backward by a rope around their flukes. The ungainly burdens caused the boats to slew to and fro, and the helmsmen were hard put to maintain a straight course.

Halfdan watched Gudbjartur as he swung over the bow, dropped into the shallow water, and strode purposefully away. He gathered men to butcher the catch.

Brodir and Sweyn joined the crowd at the rail. This left Bjorn and Halfdan together.

"One day, Halfdan, the others will agree with me and you will lose because I will be the one who is right." Bjorn looked at Halfdan, a slight smile on his face.

"One day, Bjorn, when you are right, I will let you win." Halfdan grinned and slapped the man on the back. "For now though, let us go see what we eat tonight."

Shaking his head in resignation, Bjorn grinned good-naturedly and followed his chieftain. The men pushed their way through their jubilant shipmates to the ship's rail to view the catch.

To make himself heard over the din, Halfdan cupped his hands and shouted to the lead boat. "Did you have any trouble with those little pilot whales?"

"No!" shouted Tostig, the boat captain. "There are many of them and they are not wary of us. We killed these two with arrows. Snorri and his crew followed their whale clear across the bay before he died. We hit ours better and he died right away."

The second boat arrived with a single whale in tow. Snorri, the boat captain, gripped the forestay and stood athwart the bow to shout so all could hear. "Our other two ships are in sight to the northeast!"

A great roar of exultation arose as word passed from ship to ship. Women wept openly and hugged each other happily as everyone realized friends and family had come through the storm. Some of the men expressed emotion out of keeping with their normal taciturn personalities as the enormity of the good news became apparent to all.

"How far out at sea are they?" Halfdan asked.

"They were hull down, just their sails visible, to the northeast, when we entered this bay," Snorri answered.

"Do you think they saw you?" Halfdan asked.

"I doubt it. They could not have seen us through the sea mist against the dark shoreline from that far away."

Halfdan gazed silently at the entrance to the bay.

"We also found a big fjord, Halfdan. A river flows into it. It is better protected than this one and has a narrow entrance to block the wind. It is just west of yon point." Snorri indicated the headland they were sheltered behind as he looked up the ship's side at Halfdan. "There is a beach we can land on by the river. It is covered with pebbles and looks big enough for all six ships."

"Good! This anchorage makes it very difficult to replenish our stores. We must get the ships closer to shore," Halfdan said. "With the wind from the northwest and the tide beginning to ebb, it will be some time before the other ships can get here."

"Do you want us to go out to meet them?" Snorri asked.

"No! We will need you to lead us when we move to this new fjord of yours. As soon as Gudbj and his crew get the whales butchered, we will move the ships." He looked toward the activity around the two whale carcasses. Gudbjartur's crew of butchers had just taken the towline from Snorri's boat and fed it through a block aboard Sweyn's ship. His men heaved on the line and warped the third whale alongside the others as Halfdan watched.

The three whales, eighteen to twenty-five feet in length, were roped along the waterline of Sweyn's ship. A swarm of men rapidly reduced them to their usable parts. Deck crews peeled blubber with skin attached from the carcasses in long strips. They hauled lustily on lines routed through rigging blocks to which large iron hooks were attached. Men in small boats alongside wielded the short-handled flensing knives and cut the strips loose as the deck crew hauled them over the ship's side. All the rich dark meat, usable internal organs, flukes, and fins followed. Nothing remained save the offal. The stomach and large gut were saved. The remainder either floated away on the current or sank to the bottom, food for crabs and the clouds of squabbling seabirds. The cloying smell of fresh blood was everywhere but the people welcomed it as a measure of the success of the hunt. Almost everyone near at hand stuffed chunks of bloody blubber and skin into their mouths, chewed contentedly, and leered at others not fortunate enough, or close enough, to partake.

Halfdan called to Gudbjartur. "As soon as you are finished, Gudbj, we will move to a new fjord Snorri and his men have found."

Gudbjartur waved his understanding. He and his men continued to get the meat and blubber aboard ship as quickly as possible. They would render the blubber to oil, and dry and smoke the meat that was not consumed fresh after they moved the ships.

Halfdan turned his attention back to the whale boats. "Snorri, we hear your whale gave you some trouble."

"Yes, Rolf shot it too close to the tail. It bled badly but if we had not gotten a lance into it we would still be out there." Snorri cast a mock glare at his companion.

"I thought he was longer." Rolf, one of several thralls with the settlers, muttered in a subdued tone, his eyes downcast. "I aimed below his fin, but the water is rough out there and he rolled under faster than I thought he would."

Everyone laughed good-naturedly at his discomfort and the matter was dropped as preparations began to move the ships.

* * *

The livestock handlers ran into trouble when the time came to reload their charges. The animals resisted all attempts by the young herders to swim them to the sides of the rafted ships because of the strong smell of blood from the butchered whales.

Had safe beach conditions—sand or small smooth stones—been available, the ships would have been brought into the shoreline sideways, laid over with ropes and pulleys attached to stem, stern and suitable anchor points ashore, and the animals unloaded and reloaded over the low side. Since this method was not possible with the ships anchored bow to the beach, other means became necessary.

No amount of yelling and coaxing would get any of them to pass through the bloody offal between the shore and the ships. Bystanders offered helpful advice, shunned for the most part by the harried herders. Hoots of derision and laughter announced the arrival of several men as they surged into the milling animals.

"Look out boys, let a man show you how to get this done!" Thorgill bodily picked up a struggling animal and walked into the shallow water to pass it aboard the nearest ship. With the assistance of others of his ilk he soon sorted out and caught up the sheep and goats as they bucked and plunged hither and yon in their attempts at freedom. Hemmed in by water on one side and a semi-circle of bystanders on the other side, they were effectively contained for the loading process.

Larger animals, secured with rope halters and an additional rope around their rumps to help them along, were unceremoniously dragged through the water to each of the ships. Crewmen on board, utilizing a boom, sling, and block arrangement rigged from the mast, hoisted them up the side and swung them inboard, where they were lowered into the pens. Situated before and after the single mast and extending almost across the beam of the ship, livestock pens built into the deepest area of the hull amidships allowed passengers and work crews to pass from side to side as well as fore and aft over the penned livestock. The decking below each livestock pen, actually the thin hull planks of the ship, had the extra protection of raw hides nailed securely in place, hair side up, to preclude damage from the sharp hooves of the penned animals. Over these hides, dried hay, seaweed, or moss dunnage was thickly scattered to provide additional protection for the hull and more secure footing for the livestock. It also acted to trap accumulated manure and urine. The fouled dunnage was cast overboard or treated with sacked wood ash and reused.

Gudbjartur came to converse with Halfdan about the move to Snorrisfjord. Halfdan, content to let others solve the problems at hand without his input, stood with Gudbjartur at the forefront of the crowd enjoying the humor of the moment. As the last animal rose over the side of one of the ships, he and Gudbjartur turned away.

"After we have moved to Snorrisfjord, see that gangplanks are rigged to the ships' sides or careen them, if it is safe to do so, to make loading and unloading the animals easier. We will be there until provisions are replenished, so make it easier for people to get on and off the ships and move between them." Halfdan gave his orders as they walked through the crowd of busy people.

Gudbjartur nodded without comment and returned to the whale butchering.

"Tostig!" Halfdan bellowed above the din of activity. The idle boat captain looked in the direction of the hail. "Sail out and catch the other boats before they get here. After you have told them of our plans, intercept Gudrod's and Athils' ships and lead them to Snorrisfjord. We will meet all of you there."

Tostig waved his assent, and his crew set their small sail. The wind filled the sail with a boom and the boat heeled over and surged by the sterns of the anchored ships.

"Where are you going, Tostig?" a man shouted as he worked on the rigging of one of the ships.

"We are going to lead the boats and ships to another fjord that Snorri has found to the west," Tostig shouted as his boat swept past.

Chapter Three

Preparations to move the ships to Snorrisfjord began when Gudbjartur's crew pulled the last slab of whale meat over the bloody side of Sweyn's ship.

"We are ready over here!" Sweyn shouted over the noise.

Halfdan waved in acknowledgment. He stood on the stern platform with his helmsman while crewmen retrieved the anchors and cast off the lines between ships. Other crewmen pushed the ships apart with sweeps and stood by for the order to deploy them. The captains held a clenched fist overhead to indicate their readiness to put to sea.

Halfdan shouted the expected order: "Out sweeps, give way astern together!"

The sweeps rattled out and the crew began an even stroke to the cadence of the stroke drum. The ship backed away from the beach, guided along the offshore stern anchor line by Gorm at the helm.

Two crew members hauled in the slack until the ship passed over the anchor on the bottom, then cleated the line so the ship's momentum could break the anchor loose.

"Anchor is aweigh!" The hail indicated the heavy, iron-bound hook was free of the bottom and could be hauled aboard and stowed.

Halfdan looked aft at his ship's position. "Hold the stroke!" The stroke drummer stopped the cadence and the rowers held the sweeps out of the water. "Stow the sweeps!"

Halfdan waited for the sweeps to come inboard and the rowers to stow them. "Make sail!"

Four men walked the halyard aft and the sail rose up the mast with Gauk astride the yard. The sail boomed in confusion in the variable wind but provided enough thrust for the ship to get underway, both her boats in tow astern.

Steed of the Sea, the first in line astern of Snorri, rapidly overhauled the small boat in spite of his lead.

"Take two reefs in the sail! We are overhauling Snorri!" Halfdan shouted to the sail handlers.

The four men on the halyard lowered the sail halfway down the mast; others tied the foot of the sail with the reef lines and the halyard crew hoisted the yard and sail up the mast. The sail filled when they sheeted it home, its surface area reduced by a quarter.

Halfdan glanced astern at Brodir's ship in time to see him reef as well. He turned his attention forward and watched Snorri's boat a moment. Satisfied they were no longer overtaking the small boat, he looked aloft at the set of the sail, glanced at Gorm, winked, and walked forward.

Gorm watched Halfdan's receding back, a smug smile on his face. *Thanks to my ability at the steerboard, the sail was drawing tightly when Halfdan looked aloft.* He glanced aloft at the set of the sail. Satisfied with its trim he turned his attention to Snorri's boat in the distance.

Gudbjartur and his crew stayed aboard Sweyn's ship and continued to process the mountain of meat and blubber as the ship sailed to Snorrisfjord. Clouds of crying seabirds followed in the ship's wake, vying for the scraps thrown overboard.

One of the butchers swung a long piece of gut over his head to taunt the birds. Their cries quickly became deafening as individuals tried to grab the bait.

"Here, I will get rid of them! Watch this!" He threw the gut high in the air away from the ship. All the wheeling birds tried to grab it at the same time, but it proved too large to swallow and too heavy to fly with. The gull that won out over his fellows refused to let go and plunged into the water along- side the ship. With piercing cries, the rest of the flock dove into the water beside him and squabbled over the tidbit as the ship sailed away.

Halfdan closed his eyes briefly as the ship sailed from the bay. He threw his head back and took a deep draft of the heavy salt air. Scattered clouds scudded under a brilliant blue sky. His eyes swept the shoreline of the rocky headland and the open sea beyond.

"Head north, Gorm!" Halfdan shouted. He pointed with an outstretched arm toward the open sea.

The ship took the heavy swells full on the bow as Gorm turned her to a northerly heading to gain sea room from the bay's western headland, where it jutted into the strait. Wind- blown spray and spume drenched Halfdan and those near him in the bows as the ship pounded into the head sea.

"By Thor, it is rough out here!" Halfdan grinned and wiped the spray from his face.

"Here, I brought you a dry vest." Thora lurched onto the bow platform. She grabbed the ship's rail for support.

"Thanks." Halfdan made eye contact with her as he shrugged out of his wet vest and handed it to her.

She nodded and turned to the other men with him.

"We have more dry clothing if the rest of you want to change." There were no takers, so she made her way aft, hand- over-hand along the rail to maintain her balance.

Two men watched her every move until she dropped from sight behind the foot of the sail.

"Did you see her nipples sticking out? By the gods I could use some of that," Helge said to the other man.

"Go right ahead. You can have my share of her. I have had enough of her sharp tongue," Vilhjalm said.

"It might be worth an occasional tongue-lashing." Helge grinned at his companion.

"Not to me. Moreover, it will be a continuous tongue- lashing, not an occasional one. She will also make you clean up before you can have any. It is not worth the trouble."

"I do not blame her for that, my friend. You smell a little gamy to me."

The two men laughed together and returned to their duties as Halfdan ordered a course change. The ship shouldered her way around to a westerly course, coming up close-hauled on the steerboard tack.

"Come on, Vilhjalm." Helge grabbed the man's upper arm. "Halfdan will want the sail boomed out, so let us be about it."

As the ship steadied on the steerboard tack, the two men helped boom the steerboard foot of the sail outboard and then sheeted the port foot tightly inboard. Spars, or boom poles, of various lengths for different angles secured one bottom corner of the loose-footed sail and a socket cut in the mast step held the other end. The crew sheeted in the loose corner and trimmed the sail to the wind. The new angle at the sail foot allowed the ship to sail close to the eye of the wind on either upwind tack.

The sea mist cleared and the headland fell astern. "Two sails, broad on the steerboard beam!" Gauk hailed from the masthead.

Halfdan's eyes swept the distant horizon. He saw no sign of them from the deck. "Where away?"

"There!" Gauk pointed into the distance beyond the ship's steerboard side.

Halfdan leaped up on the rail, both hands held tight to the forestay, while his eyes swept the misty distance. He strained to pierce the mist and finally caught a flash of sail as one of the ships crested a swell. "I have them in sight!" He jumped down from his perch.

Both were still a long distance away and making slow progress to the west, close-hauled as they were in the stiff west-northwest wind. *Tostig's small boat must be having a rough time in these boisterous seas*, Halfdan mused.

Halfdan looked for Snorri's boat. He caught sight of the small square of sail some distance ahead and inshore of his position. Conditions would be somewhat better than offshore due to the dampening effect of the back eddies from the surf. The boat was almost invisible in the mist created by the surf.

It appeared briefly when it crested a swell and quickly disappeared as it swooped into the next trough.

Halfdan stood on the foredeck. He tilted his head back and savored the last swallow of cold broth from the drinking horn. He looked aft to study the trim of the sail as it vibrated like a live thing in the wind. The ship alternately soared and plunged under him. "Pull the port sheet in tighter, the sail luffs! Let her fall off a little, Gorm, and get help at the tiller!" He watched the helmsman struggle to hold the ship's head as close to the wind as possible. The sea's condition required the concerted efforts of two men at the tiller bar to hold the course close to the eye of the wind. The slight course change stopped the flutter of the sail, and it hardened with a full grip on the wind.

The ships of Athils and Gudrod, shrouded in the sea mist, were on their own as Snorri changed course for the narrow entrance to his fjord.

Halfdan tossed the empty drinking horn in the direction of a group of women clustered aft of the mast and looked aloft to the masthead. He cupped his hands and shouted at the lookout, who was perched atop the yard with his legs wrapped around the vibrating mast. "Hold on, Gauk! We are going to run into the fjord!"

Gauk gave Halfdan his wide, gap-toothed grin and waved that he understood. He seemed unaffected by the lively antics of the plunging ship. Heeled over as she was, the top of the mast hung over the water beyond the side of the ship. Had Gauk fallen from his lofty perch into the sea he would have drowned. Like the rest of them, he could not swim. No matter, the icy water would suck the life from his body in a short time anyway. To preclude a fatal fall, lookouts fashioned a safety line or harness that allowed them the free use of their hands. Gauk had fashioned his harness from a piece of old sail. It fit him loosely like a vest and included a stout, walrus-hide rope to loop round the mast. Oftentimes he could be seen relaxed against his harness, arms crossed comfortably over the safety lines as his eyes swept the sea.

Halfdan smiled and shook his head at the man's nonchalant acceptance of danger. He cupped his hands to shout the course change to the helmsmen. "Port full! Follow Snorri into the fjord entrance." He grabbed at the forestay to maintain his own balance and dignity as the ship plunged into a swell.

The helmsmen brought Steed of the Sea around to port. The course change made steering easier as the hull came up level and the ship surged downwind.

"Thanks for the help, Thorgill," Gorm said to the big man. Thorgill nodded and walked forward to help reset the sail to the new course.

Passengers and crew forward of the mast, warned of the turn to port, ducked as the sail's foot slashed out on the opposite side of the mast and filled with wind. The crew stowed the booming spar and sheeted the sail foot and top yard home to trim both to the downwind course.

Free to run now, the four ships, still in line astern, quickly passed Snorri and his crew. Foam creamed from their plunging bows as they surged toward the fjord entrance.

"Watch the rocks on the east side of the entrance! The deepest channel is on the west side next to the highest cliff!" Snorri shouted at Halfdan, as the great ship surged by the small boat.

Halfdan waved in acknowledgment. He grinned from ear to ear; several of those aboard shouted and whooped at the sheer exhilaration of the ride as the ship surfed rapidly toward the entrance of the fjord. Sheer cliffs marked both sides of the narrow entrance, but there was ample room to maneuver.

Although the wind and sea were boisterous on the outside, conditions past the entrance were exactly the opposite. The sail flapped and banged in the variable wind, and the ship slowed as if grasped by the hand of a giant. The wind continued to decrease to a light breeze and the ship moved slowly into the fjord.

"Sheet home the sail, she luffs!" Halfdan called. Crewmen retrimmed the sheet lines to take advantage of what wind remained. Once the ship was through the entrance, the fjord opened into a wide bay. It continued south far enough that features of the shoreline were indistinct in the distance.

Everyone aboard lined both rails as they gazed at the beautiful fjord that unfolded before them.

"This will be a good place for us to restock and rest the people." Helge stepped onto the bow platform beside Halfdan. "Snorri found the only pebble beach in this fjord. The rest of the shoreline appears to be jagged rocks."

"Yes. This is a land of rolling hills, with large, lichen-covered rocks and low brush as far as the eye can see. There appears to be little forage grass among the lichen but the livestock will make do. The narrow fjord entrance will protect us from the north wind and that is a good thing." Halfdan gestured inland. "Did you see the reindeer herd before that ridge blocked it from view?"

"No. I missed them. The sail needed attention around then. After the camp is set up we can go on a hunt." The two men glanced at each other, the beginnings of smiles on their faces.

"I will look forward to that, Helge."

"Consider it done, then."

They lapsed into silence as a flurry of activity off the steerboard bow got their attention.

Sunning seals dove into the water or lunged in their comical gait across a well-worn, rocky ledge some distance from the fjord entrance as the intruders disturbed their slumber.

"Look at them. There must be a hundred seals." Gorm shouted and gestured in their direction.

The dogs began barking and running about before many of the people lining the port rail saw the seals. Their excited barking soon had everyone aboard laughing at their antics and coaxing them on.

Halfdan caught sight of the beach Snorri had described, along the west shore of the fjord and beside a river. He turned to his crew. "Loose the sheets and halyards!"

Crew members loosed the halyards and sheets, and the sail slid down the mast, helped along by the weight of the top yard and the lookout still perched on top. They swung the yard around to trim it fore and aft and lowered it onto its T-support aft of the mast. An ornately carved prop fit into a hole in the mast step and secured the other end. The furled sail, gathered around the yard and secured with the reefing point lines, was shipshape and out of the way. During this frantic bustle, the ship gradually lost way.

Halfdan waited until his men had the sail secured and out of the way before giving the order, "Out sweeps!" Idle passengers congregated amidships while crewmen deployed the twelve sweeps.

"Steer for the beach to the left of the river mouth, Gorm." Halfdan guided the ships progress with hand signals as they made the straight-in approach to the beach. The bottom gradually shelved to the shoreline and a beach covered with small smooth stones provided the safe bottom conditions necessary to beach the ships.

"Hold the stroke! Toss your sweeps!" Halfdan called. The oarsmen stopped rowing, withdrew the sweeps, and held them in an upright position, waiting for orders to stow them.

The ship's momentum carried her forward slowly as the way went off. She rose up the slope of the bottom and ground to a halt on the beach. Just before the keel contacted the bottom, the helmsman pulled the leather strap loose from its slot and the steerboard pivoted out of the way.

"Stow the sweeps and secure the ship." Halfdan called. He leaped from the upswept bow onto dry ground, followed by others of the crew as they secured the ship beam-to the beach. Conditions near the river's mouth proved ideal for their purposes and Halfdan waved the other three ships in.

All three nosed into the beach beside Halfdan's ship, far enough apart so they could be swung beam-to the beach to unload.

* * *

Gudbjartur arrived from Sweyn's ship in time to organize a large group of men to rig gangplanks from each ship's side to the beach, making movements back and forth safer and easier. Cross cleats on each gangplank ensured secure footing and the planks, all part of the ships loose decking and walkways, came in different lengths to accommodate all the anticipated uses.

With the ships secured at bow and stern, every unemployed person, including older children, pitched in to unload the ships' deck cargo. There were many round trips before the decks were clear of supplies and equipment.

"Thorgill!" Gudbjartur motioned the man on board ship down to the beach with a wave of his arm. "While the cargo is being offloaded, walk inland a short distance and check the forage situation, then report back to me."

"Asgrim comes, Gudbj." Thorgill pointed inland to a figure winding his way through the jumble of rocks and low brush. "He looks for bog iron and he will know."

Gudbjartur nodded, and walked to meet Asgrim. "Did you find any iron?" Gudbjartur asked as he glanced in the bucket the man carried.

"A few lumps. About half a bucket, I guess." The smithy examined the contents of his bucket. "Haakon and Sigmund are still looking. Maybe they will have more luck. There are so many rocks here it is hard to get the sod loose to look for bog iron lumps among the roots."

"That is what I want to talk to you about. How is the forage out there?"

"Sparse. The goats and sheep will like the thick brush but there is not much grass for the horses and cattle. Thick lichen covers the rocks and they can eat that after the grass is gone."

"Are you and Haakon going to build a forge here?"

"Aye, a small, combination forge and smelter," the smithy answered. "Or maybe just a forge. It depends on whether Haakon and Sigmund find more iron than I did."

Both men faced toward the beached ships while they talked. Thorgill, one of many people unloading the ship, walked down the gangplank at that moment, burdened with food bags on each shoulder. Gudbjartur nodded to Asgrim and intercepted Thorgill. As the man dropped his load on a pile of food bags on the beach, he gave his orders. "After the decks are clear, you supervise careening the ship to unload the livestock. Get the horses off first, then the cattle and the rest of the livestock. Asgrim told me the grass is sparse. There is enough other forage for the time we will be here. I will be with Halfdan to pick the perimeter guards."

"All right, Gudbj. Do you want the ships moored and secured bow-to the beach when we get them unloaded?" Thorgill asked.

"Yes. I will return before you get to that. If I am delayed you know what to do."

Thorgill nodded his assent and walked back up the gangplank. Gudbjartur glanced over the beach area, his mind occupied with the myriad details of the encampment: unloading the ships, seeing to the livestock, and the assignment of guards for security. He went to look for Halfdan.

As equipment and supplies were unloaded, Gudbjartur handpicked men to guard the encampment. He and Halfdan spoke to them before they took up their positions.

"You all know we have much work to do before we sail from this place." Halfdan said. "Your vigilance is the only means we have to ensure the safety of everyone and allow them to perform their tasks without having to constantly look over their shoulders. We have all seen the great white polar bears in the distance. There are plenty of seals for them to hunt, so they are not hungry. I do not need to tell you how dangerous they are. Stay vigilant."

"I want the guard to change three times from sunup to sunup." Gudbjartur looked at each of the eighteen men in turn. "There will be six of you on guard at a time and you are responsible for your own relief. Work that part out among yourselves, just so you get the job done. You all know what must be done and how to do it."

"If you are not asleep or on guard I know you will help whoever needs help." Halfdan added.

"Take a dog with you," Gudbjartur said, as the first six men began to gather food, water, and weapons. He remained until the men moved inland to a point just beyond effective arrow range and formed a semicircular security perimeter from the shoreline around the encampment.

Each guard led a tethered dog and carried either bow and arrows or heavy spears.

* * *

Thorgill had little patience on the best of days. Trouble with the livestock on Steed of the Sea had almost unhinged him. Pigs were always difficult to handle, for they were the most intelligent of domestic animals. Consequently, they were almost impossible to herd and better left to their own devices. Of course, that would not get them unloaded. Today they decided to do what they wanted, and all ran in different directions through the livestock pens on the ship. They steadfastly refused to disembark, as Thorgill wanted them to. This in spite of, or perhaps because of, his shouted threats.

"Ewyn! Do not just stand there! Get over here and help!" Thorgill shouted at a young thrall who stood near a small herd of mixed livestock that milled about on the beach.

"I have been helping Finbar hold the livestock together until they are all unloaded," the slightly built, mild-mannered thrall explained as he walked up to Thorgill. "I was not just standing there. I was watching the animals. You told me to."

Thorgill grabbed a handful of the thrall's tunic and jerked him to his tiptoes. "Are you arguing with me?" His face was a hands-breadth away and Ewyn blinked in discomfort and fright as a gust of the big man's fetid breath washed over him.

"No! Please, Thorgill! I mean no disrespect. I am trying to tell you what I was doing."

Thorgill watched him through narrowed eyes as he grappled with his anger and the thrall's obvious sincerity. "All right. Do not ever argue with me," he warned through gritted teeth.

The thrall shook his head in speechless fright. He took an off balance step backward when Thorgill released his tunic.

"Finbar!" Thorgill roared at the other thrall.

Finbar jumped in surprise and ran the short distance up the gangplank to stand beside Ewyn.

"Both of you unload these god-cursed pigs. Never mind the other animals. They are not going anywhere. When you finish, put the chickens in their coops, and carry them ashore. Stack the coops with the rest of the deck cargo."

The two thralls nodded. Neither trusted his voice in the face of the threat posed by Thorgill's anger. They climbed down into the animal pens to round up the pigs before something else set off the unpredictable man. Finbar waited a few moments before he spoke. He wanted to give Thorgill time to move on. He climbed on the top rail of one of the pens and peeked over the ship's rail. "He is talking to Gudbj." Finbar climbed down from his perch and looked at his troubled companion. "Relax, Ewyn, he is gone for the time being."

"I thought he would hit me. He frightens me, Finbar. One day his temper will overflow and he will beat one of us to death."

"No, he will not kill us. Beat us, maybe. We belong to Halfdan. That alone protects us from everyone. Thorgill lost his temper, and the matter is finished. Forget about it. Now, open all the pen gates and we will herd the pigs into the pen closest to the gangplanks. After they settle down from being yelled at, we can carry them off one at time as we always do."

With the exception of the single-minded pigs, the livestock were tame and easily handled. The compact animals were suited for transport aboard ship. Each ship carried five each of sheep, goats, pigs, cats, and dogs, and four each of the small cows and horses. These numbers did not include small flocks of chickens. Duplication aboard each ship insured survival of a species in the event of a sinking.

Later that day, the two thralls and three of the older boys drove a mixed herd away from the encampment to graze. Under the watchful eyes of the herders and the perimeter guards, the livestock mingled with their kind from all four ships.

Dogs, trained from birth to both herd and protect the helpless livestock from dangerous wild animals, ranged back and forth as the animals scattered onto the pastureland. They were work dogs, not pets. They packed light loads, guarded the livestock, and provided meat during periods of meager food supplies.

The aloof pigs scattered about the countryside on their own, rooting in the mast under the low-lying brush and miniature pine trees or eating offal and scraps as they wandered in pig fashion about the encampment. One of the sows wallowed out a nest in the middle of a dense copse of brush and birthed a litter of piglets. The herders saw her ears above the top of the brush, alert for danger, as she watched them pass. They knew she would bring out her piglets in her own good time.

The herders allowed the animals to scatter somewhat as they moved along in their eternal search for fodder.

"Boys, you are with us to help. Stop throwing rocks and help Ewyn and me watch out for predators like you are supposed to," Finbar said.

"This is boring work. We do not have anything to do," a tall, blond-haired, blue-eyed boy complained. "You do not need us, and you can not tell us what to do, Finbar. You are a thrall and I will not listen to you."

"I am certain Gudbj will have something to say about that. Now all of you fill those sacks with lichen, as we are doing, but keep one eye on the livestock. Watch the dogs. They will sense danger before we see it."

"You would not tell my father," the boy said petulantly.

"No. I will not, Ivar, unless I have to because you will not do the work your father sent you here to do. However, I will tell you what to do, because I am a man and you are a boy. Now, do as you are told!"

Thick lichen covered most of the ground surface and projecting rocks, and the grazing animals munched contentedly on this abundance. The herders gathered the same lichen and stuffed it into skin bags as their charges grazed. When dried, the lichen provided a supply of absorbent material to twist into lamp wicks, stanch blood flow from wounds, or to wipe oneself after a trip to the toilet pit. Women also used it during the time of their monthly curse.

* * *

Gudbjartur directed the hectic activity as equipment accumulated on the beach. After completing the unloading, crew members floated the ships down the beach out of the way and moored them side-by-side from bow and stern, as before.

Everyone pitched into the myriad chores associated with setting up the encampment, and a sense of order began to emerge from the piles of equipment and supplies.

Gudbjartur selected the only naturally drained, level site that was large enough to accommodate all twenty-eight tents, and men began clearing the area of brush and rocks not needed for the fire pit. Located a short walk from the shore-line, the area commanded a good view in all directions and the slight rise in elevation ensured the wind would help keep the clouds of insects at bay.

Gorm, the first in a long line of people who carried equip-ment from the beach to the campsite, arrived with an arm-load of the flat, intricately carved, external tent-bracing boards.

"Start laying them out here, Gorm," Gudbjartur said, indi-cating the area of the encampment. "Put the frames together facing south and group them in three rows."

"All right. Which ones are yours and Halfdan's?" Gorm asked as others arrived with their loads of tent frames and assorted equipment.

"I will assign a tent to everyone after they are pitched. For now it does not matter who will be in them, for they are all the same."

Over the previous winter, large groups of women had joined the lightweight, tightly woven, wadmal panels together. The new tent design accommodated several people and all their possessions. Halfdan had specially ordered them for this expedition.

Mixed crews of men and women began assembly of the seven-piece tent frames. Three stout horizontal braces secured the two identical V-shaped frames front to back. Hardwood tenon pins secured each joint. The easily erected result was a strong, rigid, external tent framework that formed a wide, inverted V.

"Bring a tent over here." Gorm beckoned to two men who lugged one of the tents, as he and two others finished assem-bly of a framework. They unrolled the tent beneath the free-standing framework, spread it out, and tied the peaked top at several points to the ridgepole. They tied the sidewalls to the corresponding support members in like fashion. The erected tent consisted of chest-high externally braced sidewalls, and an externally braced peaked roof. The removable, enclosed back wall and closable entry flaps made for a snug shelter in almost any weather conditions.

Ulfar and Vilhjalm, two of the men who worked with Gorm, staked the bottom tent apron to the ground and then sat down and began to dig the trench around the outside of the apron that would channel water away from the tent interior. "Who have you been close to with red hair?" Vilhjalm plucked a long red hair from the shoulder of his friend's tunic. "Here is another. And another," he chuckled.

Ulfar pushed his hand away. "None of your business. We decided to meet in secret, and I will not tell you who she is."

Vilhjalm laughed aloud at his friend. "Secret! There are no secrets here. Come on, who is it?" He leaned toward the other man to keep his voice low. "You can tell me, I would never tell your secret."

Ulfar refused to rise to the bait. His silence alone guaranteed a continuation of the questions.

Vilhjalm glanced at Gorm, who eavesdropped on the conversation while he finished securing the ties to the tent frame. "Who do you think it is?"

"There are only so many women with that color hair," Gorm answered, as he examined the long strand closely. "It should be easy for you to guess the right one."

Vilhjalm took the strand of hair from Gorm's outstretched hand; he leered at his friend and sniffed at the evidence. "That smell seems familiar. Let me see. It is not Thora or Gudny, wrong shade."

"You had best forget it. Both of you." Ulfar warned the two grinning men.

"How about Frida?" Vilhjalm smelled success the moment he uttered her name. "It is all over your face. Frida it is, Ulfar!" He peered closely in triumph at his friend, who struggled to keep a smile off his face. "You had best watch yourself with her, she is fiery. You will have lots of competition with that one."

"There will be no competition. She is my woman." Ulfar glared from one to the other.

"Does Gizur agree with that? The last time I saw her with a man in the daylight," Gorm chuckled, "it was him."

"Gizur!" Ulfar spat the name passionately. "He will try at his own peril."

"All right, Ulfar. Settle down. We jest with you. You know that. Now, let us get back to work before somebody says something that cannot be taken back," Vilhjalm said in a level tone of voice.

"That sounds like very good advice," Gorm agreed, as he picked up a brazier for charcoal and carried it into the tent. The small iron braziers, vented through adjustable leather flaps in the peaked roof, took the morning chill off the interior and made the tents useful temporary winter shelters.

Vilhjalm and Ulfar finished the drainage ditch in silence, both irritated over the outcome of Vilhjalm's jest. They piled the dirt and gravel they laboriously dug from the packed soil onto the tent apron. This provided a ditch to drain water away and sealed the interior from the elements. After the last shovelful of dirt went on the apron, Vilhjalm stretched out full-length on the ground to rest. Ulfar lurched to his feet, stretched tired back muscles, and gazed out over the fjord in time to see a school of large fish feeding offshore. Seabirds marked the school's feeding frenzy. They followed overhead and dived into the water after the frightened baitfish.

"Come on, Vilhjalm. Get up. Help me with the benches so we can go fishing." Ulfar kicked his friend's foot.

"All right, all right." Vilhjalm got to his feet. "So, you are no longer angry at us?"

"I was not angry. Nevertheless, mind your own business. Next time I may not take your jest, as you call it, so well."

Vilhjalm grumbled to himself, got to his feet, and helped put together the raised benches that the tent's occupants sat and slept on. Assembled from easily joined components, the frames had the same type of mortise, tenon, and pin joint as the tent frame. Placed end to end along each side of the tent's interior wall, they provided the occupants with a comfortable knee-high bench that got them up off the damp stone and earthen floor.

After the benches were assembled, little remained to accomplish as far as the tent interior space was concerned. Everyone kept personal possessions in large, tightly rolled, rectangular leather bags, laced down the center for half their length. These bags doubled as snug sleeping bags. When unlaced they provided unrestricted full-length access.

Privacy was virtually unknown in temporary encampments and natural bodily functions and open copulation were accepted facts of daily life. Refuse pits for human waste and trash were dug a short walk from the living areas. At any given time, someone was either using these pits, or heading toward them, a wad of dried moss in hand.

Halfdan sought out Gudbjartur, finding him talking to a group of men. He watched the big man unobtrusively from a distance. Neither Gudbjartur nor those grouped around him knew their chieftain watched them. Whatever the subject was, Gudbjartur had the men's full attention as he gestured with his hands.

Halfdan had an unobstructed view of his lieutenant from the side and he unconsciously assessed him as he watched him in conversation with his men. What he saw was a man who was almost his twin, although neither man consciously knew it. He was heavily muscled and taller by a head than most of the men grouped before him. His hair was a very light brown color, worn shorter than most, about halfway down his neck.

A vain man, Gudbjartur parted his hair neatly down the center, gathered a hank of it at the front on both sides, and braided it to keep it out of his eyes. A leather thong secured the bottom end of each braid and the added weight ensured the braids hung straight rather than curled.

Shaking himself from the reverie that had caused him to become fixated on Gudbjartur, Halfdan approached the group. Gudbjartur had just finished issuing his orders to the men as Halfdan walked up to them.

He greeted the men with a nod, and drew Gudbjartur aside. "Gudbj, when we decided to have these big tents made there was concern about problems caused by jealousy or one thing or another. This will be the first time they have been used and I leave the whole matter in your hands."

"I thought you might do that, so I already have everything organized. Each of the twenty-eight tents will accommodate twelve people, and I have already assigned everyone to their tent. Family groups are together and each tent has a person I have placed in charge. He is to keep order, and if it gets out of hand he is to tell me."

Halfdan had a slight smile around his mouth and the corners of his eyes. "I do not know why I thought I had to tell you to take care of it, you always do. Most of the time I am just thinking out loud when I tell you something, but then you know that too, I suppose."

Gudbjartur looked at Halfdan, his thumbs hooked in his leather belt and a twinkle in his eyes. "Yes, I do know that. I am your lieutenant. Your second-in-command. When I see something that needs doing, I gather the men to do it. I will continue in this manner until you tell me to stop, or to change my methods."

"I doubt I will ever have occasion to change anything you do. We are too much alike. Many times I have been about to bring something to your attention, only to find you were already thinking the same thing. I value that, Gudbj. It is hard to come by."

Uncomfortable at the direction of the conversation, Gudbjartur changed the subject and pointed to the tent in the middle of the encampment. "That is your tent. There are four other people in there with you, and I have used it to store extra gear. That leaves one extra tent, and I decided it would not be pitched unless we need it for Asa and Thorkatla to tend wounded."

"And your tent?"

Gudbjartur pointed to the far end of the encampment. "The end one there. Ingerd, Ivar, and I will have nine others for company."

"All right, Gudbj. It looks like you have it under control." Halfdan glanced toward his tent. "I think I will go sit in my high seat. I see someone has already put it together."

Halfdan slapped Gudbjartur on the shoulder. He chuckled softly and turned toward his tent. "Call me if you need me."

"I will do that." Gudbjartur called as Halfdan walked away.

Between the tents and the shoreline, Gudbjartur and a work crew gathered to dig the long communal fire pit and line it with stones. Gudbjartur gave instructions as he scratched the outline in the dirt with a stick. "We will not stay in this place, so do not make a special effort to make the fire pit perfect. Thora wants a raised shelf, with an upright slab of rock to serve as a reflector at one end. She also wants a large round hole lined with stones at the other end."

"She wants a lot," one of the men complained.

The others laughed at his comment. They knew he meant it in jest.

Gudbjartur looked at the man, a smile played over his features. "Thora is a cook, Helge. I think we should give her whatever she wants."

"Yes, Helge! She might not feed us if we make her angry," offered another one of the workers.

"You are right. Do not say anything to her. It is hard enough to get along with her. What else does she want, Gudbj?" The ghost of a smile played around Helge's mouth and eyes.

Gudbjartur finished the outline in the dirt. "She wants an iron tripod with its assortment of pot hooks set up over the round part of the fire pit so she can hang her round pot over the fire."

"Is that all?" Helge asked. The others chuckled at his sarcasm.

"That is it, as far as I know," Gudbjartur said. "Now, let us be about it or we will have nothing to eat at the end of the day."

The thin soil contained so many rocks it was unnecessary to haul additional rock to line the pit. Gudbjartur watched the preparations for a time, and then turned his attention to the west to gauge the weather they could expect. "By the looks of those clouds to the west we may be in for more drizzle. Bring a spare sail or two up here and rig them over the fire pit for an awning."

Sails were heavy and it took several men to drag and carry two from the beach to the fire pit. By the time that was done, others had erected a framework of sweeps and walrus hide ropes to provide support. The result was an open-sided awning that covered a large area around the fire pit and provided good protection for the fire and the cooks from the occasional drizzle.

While the men built the fire pit, several boys and girls hauled in driftwood. When the pit was finished, a large pile of wood had accumulated and a couple men took to the damp wood with axes to expose the dry centers. They laid the fire and ignited dry tinder from their pouches with flint and steel.

The cooks arrived from the beach carrying large, riveted, sheet-iron cooking pots that they suspended from tripod hooks over the newly kindled fire. The pots contained a mixture of rich, dark whale meat, just the right amount of seawater for taste, diluted with fresh water from the river, and dried seal meat. The cooks decided the seawater-fouled ground barley was too valuable to discard, and although too salty for bread, it worked as a thickener for the stew. After a time the stew began bubbling, and hungry passersby salivated at the rich smells that wafted throughout the encampment as it cooked.

Two thralls placed soapstone pots directly in the coals of the fire pit to boil seawater for the salt it contained. As the water boiled away they scraped out the accumulated salt, refilled the pots with seawater, and the process began anew. The two women tended the salt pots and gathered edible sea-weed that the previous low tide had left on the beach in scat-tered piles. They filled two baskets for immediate use, and spread the rest out to dry above the high-water line on the stony beach. When dry enough they would rake it into piles and burn it to ash. This ash contained a very high concentra-tion of salt. It also provided another source of salt to cure dried meat and fish and to flavor other foods.

Thralls performed all the heavy work without supervision or complaint. They knew the penalty if they shirked their duties. A swift public whipping resulted from any refusal to work, or instant death for a violation of hard-earned trust. Thralls were captives, slaves, some from childhood, who lived with their owners and were an integral part of Norse social structure. Well treated for the most part, they had a well-defined place and never deviated from that which they knew to be their lot. Death could be instant and at the whim of their owner. No freeman or chief would intercede for them. They were private property, chattels.

* * *

Several kettles of whale blubber boiled over individual fires on the beach to render the valuable oil. The thick, rich oil, skimmed of the connective tissue—the crunchy fried meat and curled pieces of skin were a delicacy—had many uses. It was a valuable food source, preservative, and lamp fuel.

Hundreds of seabird eggs, collected during the annual nesting frenzy, would be stored in barrels and covered with hot oil. Both fresh and boiled eggs, stored in this way, lasted throughout the summer months and into winter; and people ate the oil right along with the eggs it preserved.

Excess oil was stored in barrels for later use. After cooling and solidifying—effectively sealing them—the oil barrels were stored aboard ship, gradually replacing some of the ballast stones in the lowest part of the hull along the keel.

Most of the chores associated with setting up the encampment were complete or being attended to. Those finished with their particular task scattered in all directions, their long confinement aboard ship forgotten or set aside. The twilight of the far northern night provided plenty of time to explore the new country and get some much-needed exercise.

Vast herds of grunting reindeer grazed in the distance. They were a species never before seen by either the Greenlanders or the Icelanders. As people scattered through the countryside, the reindeer trotted away a short distance while they watched these strangers. When no threat materialized from the people, the animals returned to their endless quest for lichen, their principle food.

Gudbjartur watched the reindeer herds and the wolf packs that shadowed them, and he assigned groups of hunters to scatter into the hinterland after fresh meat. "Helge, Ulfar, and Vilhjalm, each of you gather men to hunt with you. Shoot as many of those deer as possible before they get spooked. I will get a couple horse-drawn carts put together and will join you with crews to butcher the kills while the rest of us hunt.

"I spoke to Halfdan earlier, and he wants to hunt with us," Helge said.

"I am certain he will, Helge. Find him as you pick your men. Meet back here as soon as you have your gear together," Gudbjartur said.

The men scattered through the encampment. In less time than it took Helge to alert Halfdan, the hunters returned with spears, bows, and quivers filled with arrows.

Halfdan and Helge were equipped in similar fashion to the other hunters. The two men arrived at the assembly point at the same time as Gudbjartur.

Halfdan shaded his eyes from the glare of the sun with his free hand. "We better get out there before something spooks the deer."

"I agree. You two go ahead. I will wait for the carts. Thorgill is assembling some of them. They will be kept busy." Gudbjartur shaded his eyes and looked over the countryside.

"Come with us, Gudbj," Halfdan said. "Thorgill will know where you are when he arrives with the carts and butchers. If you wait, there will be nothing left to shoot."

Gudbjartur glanced toward the landing beach and saw no sign of the carts or Thorgill. "I will get my bow and arrows and be right back," he said enthusiastically.

The excitement of the hunt had a firm grip on the men as the three contingents fanned out through the hinterland. The plan varied little from hunt to hunt. The reindeer would run into one or the other group as they fled from their pursuers. The slaughter would continue until the men exhausted their arrow supply or ran out of targets.

Each ship carried the component parts of one horse drawn cart and Thorgill decided they needed all of them for the expected windfall of reindeer meat. By the time the hunters made their first kills, Thorgill had the carts and butchers filing out into the hinterland to begin butchering the carcasses and transporting the cartloads of meat back to the encampment.

Halfdan and Gudbjartur deemed the first organized hunt in Vinland a huge success. By early afternoon, all the hunters had expended their arrows; the hunt stopped to allow the butchers time to clear the field of carcasses.

* * *

On the nearby rocky cliffs, women and children used long-handled nets to scoop seabird eggs from the cliff edge. Others found eggs aplenty lying on the rocky ground. Within a couple hours, people returned to camp laden with eggs.

Ingerd walked toward a group of women who were cutting the last of the whale meat into strips to dry for later use. Because of the heavy load she carried in her apron, which she held by each bottom corner to create a sling bag, she waddled toward them like a duck. She was a comical sight and her friends made the most of it with ribald comments and laughter. Ingerd laughed with them good-naturedly. "Look at what we have found." She opened her apron to show them as they clustered around her. "We have enough for everyone and there are hundreds more."

The arrival of more egg gatherers markedly increased the pile of eggs Ingerd had started on the lichen-covered ground under the fire pit awning.

"We can add some of them to the stew." Helga squatted and picked through the pile of eggs. "Some are certain to be rotten."

"No matter, the dogs will eat them. When we boil them the rotten ones will float to the top," Ingerd said.

"Yes, they usually do. But I have been fooled many times because not all rotten eggs float," Olga said. "I will get my big kettle and we can boil some and pack the best in oil for the rest of the journey."

"That is a good idea, Olga." Thora finished cutting the last of the meat into strips and stood to stretch her tired back muscles. "We can boil most of the eggs in sea water, to pack in barrels for later, and beat the rest to add to our stew."

Olga and another woman returned from the shoreline with a large iron kettle half full of seawater and suspended between them on a staff. They walked down either side of the fire pit and hung it on one of several iron tripod hooks suspended above the bed of coals. Three similar kettles that contained stew bubbled over the same coals.

A boisterous egg fight developed between several children. "Stop!" Rannveig shouted. Several mothers looked up from their work, but did not bother to rise. "That is a waste of good food." The smell of rotten eggs drifted among the women where several eggs had broken on the rocky ground.

"Children!" Thora strode toward them. "Come here all of you!" They gathered around her, and she took the two oldest, a boy and a girl, by the arm. "Listen to me. You are the oldest, and you must watch that the little ones do not pick up old eggs. They are probably rotten. Old eggs are dirty and dull looking because the bird has left them for some reason. Just gather shiny warm eggs, and then we will not have this smell around our work. Play a little longer, until we get all the eggs boiled and packed away. Now, off with you."

Helga shouted after them as they ran to find more eggs. "Leave some in each nest for next year's birds." Everyone laughed to see the children enjoy their newfound freedom.

"They have been confined aboard ship too long. It is hard for children to be inactive. They need something to do with all that energy," Ingerd said as the women watched the children at play.

They all agreed and Grunhild voiced the unspoken concern of all mothers. "Yes, but their clothes will be a terrible mess. It will not be as much fun for them when we clean them up as it was for them to get dirty."

The women forgot the drudgery of work for a few minutes as they laughed among themselves at the antics of the children as they ran from nest to nest. The screams and shrill voices of the children had every bird in the rookery stirred up, and they squawked and wheeled overhead in agitation.

* * *

A lookout's horn called everyone's attention as he pointed at the fjord entrance. Three of the five boats still out entered the fjord. All towed heavy loads toward the people gathered on the beach.

"Whale hunting must be good out there," Gudbjartur said to Halfdan as they walked down to the beach. "Those whales are of a different species. The other three had long, slender jaws."

"They are minke whales. I saw them in Iceland one time years ago. They look fatter than the other whales," Halfdan said.

Another boat entered the fjord. It, too, towed a heavy load.

"It is Snorri. That leaves just one boat still out," Gudbjartur observed as he and Halfdan took hold of a towline to help draw one of the whales onto the beach.

Two of the first boats to arrive sailed out to assist the newcomer. The weight of his catch slowed the boat when the sail began to luff in the fjord's variable winds.

When the boats drew near, excitement ran through the crowd as those close enough to see the shape in the crystal-clear water identified what the boat had captured.

"It is a bull walrus!" Helge shouted from his place at the water's edge, when he caught sight of the long tusks.

"There are many more on the rocks to the west. We killed this one easily. I do not think they have been hunted before." Snorri and his boat crew collapsed on the beach to rest.

Although the animal weighed more than ten men, it soon joined the whales on the beach, drawn half out of the water by several men on the towline. Walruses furnished meat, blubber, and ivory; the hide provided the best rope for ship-board uses.

Gudbjartur gave his knife a couple swipes on his whetstone as he walked up beside one of the whale carcasses. He made the cuts behind the animal's head and forward of the tail that allowed the flensers with their short-handled knives to cut the blubber loose in long strips.

"You were right, Halfdan. They are fatter than the other whales. Look at how thick the blubber is." Gudbjartur pushed his fingers inside the cut he had made and pulled the blubber up for examination.

Halfdan stood beside the whale next to Gudbjartur's, sharpening his knife. "Yes, the blubber is twice as thick. I imagine the small fish they eat are more plentiful now that the water is warmer."

Helge and Ring plied the flensing knives on Gudbjartur's whale. They made each cut from head to tail in one long slice. Others impaled the bottom end of the strip on a hook and heaved on the attached rope until the thick strip peeled from the carcass and onto the stones of the beach.

"Come on you men. Pull!" Halfdan shouted, as the crowd got into the spirit of the process, making it an event instead of bloody drudgery. The four men on the hook-rope hauled mightily on one of the blubber strips. It suddenly tore loose, and all four landed in a heap accompanied by appreciative laughter at their expense. Every available person pitched in to butcher the catch. The sheer bounty had all of them in a jovial mood. Chunks of whale and walrus blubber joined that already piled on the rocky beach around the rendering pots.

Thora smiled and shook her head as she and her companions regarded the accumulated mountain of meat. She stood with bloody hands on hips and gestured toward the beach scene with her knife. Blood from the dismembered carcasses stained the water red. "We almost got finished. Our hunters are too good at their work." Her tone of voice reflected the appreciation felt for the bounty they must have to survive and the exhaustion they all felt from their labors.

"Yes, they are, and for that I am happy. Well, happy to have so much, but tired at the same time." Grunhild tossed another strip onto the pile. She straightened from her work and rubbed the muscles of her lower back without thought. Her bloody hands soiled her smock in the process.

"You are making a mess out of your smock, Grunhild," Ingerd admonished.

"You should talk. Look at what a mess you are," Grunhild fired back. The others laughed as they looked at the mess they had made of themselves. Grunhild's attention shifted to the two thrall women who salted meat strips as they added them to a long, deep, wooden trough with carrying handles. They picked up the full trough and trudged away to hang the meat on driftwood racks to dry in the steady wind. Grunhild watched them struggle across the uneven ground with their burden. "There will be a lot more meat, you two. You do not need to try to carry all of it at once."

"We know, but we do not need to make as many trips this way," Halla, the dark-haired thrall woman, tossed back over her shoulder.

Grunhild shrugged at the comment and returned to her work. "Well, I, for one am happy they do that work."

"Me too." Rannveig straightened up to watch the two thralls struggle with their load. "I am happy to have them do the heavy work. They will pack the dried meat and fish in bags and carry it aboard ship. They will carry all of it at least twice. That is why we have slaves, to work. Otherwise, the men would have us do it. We all know they would be too busy to do this kind of work."

"They are always too busy, or gone when we really need them," Grunhild offered. The others laughed in appreciation at the truth of her statement. They worked without comment for a time. Rapidly the immense pile of bloody meat became strips ready to dry.

Thora noticed the glances her companions made in the direction of a large group of men who worked at various tasks nearby. "I saw you follow Asgrim up the beach until you both disappeared among the rocks, Rannveig. What did you do? You were gone a long time."

"You know what we did, Thora. We coupled, as you and he did aboard ship before we got in that awful storm. Why, are you jealous?"

"No, I am not jealous. I just wondered when it would be my turn again. He seems to be popular."

Peals of laughter followed her answer as the group of women, without a knife stroke lost, talked about their favorite topic, sex. They stole sidelong glances in the direction of the newly constructed forge and smelter, where the two smithies, Asgrim and Haakon, worked at their craft. The conversation reduced to ribald comments and laughter loud enough to attract the attention of the smithies.

A smile passed between Asgrim and Haakon as they worked over their anvils on lumps of white-hot iron they drew out into forged iron bars. Their conversation about the women attracted the attention of their four helpers, who worked to erect a lean-to over the temporary smithy. The six men gathered around the warmth of the forge and talked about the women, while the women talked about them just a few steps away.

Haakon leaned over and whispered to Asgrim, a knowing grin on his face. "I wonder what they talk about."

"I would not know, but it is not about that pile of meat. It may be about meat, but not that meat." He slapped the other man on the back, and all laughed uproariously.

"Haakon is good too," Grunhild said. "He may be better than Asgrim."

"I think so too." Gudny, a thin, dark woman, joined the conversation.

"What, you too? I thought I was the only one he liked." Thora's statement brought snorts and laughter from her companions.

"I do not know about that. I have not tried either yet." Gudrun, a broad-shouldered redhead, paused for emphasis. "But that tall, blond, young man who pumps the bellows is my favorite in that group."

"Sigmund? Why, he is just a boy," Helga, his mother, said in mock concern.

"Not any more, Helga. His body is not the only part of him that is big," Gudrun added.

"Really, how big?" Gudny asked.

Gudrun stuck her knife in the pile of meat and spread her hands in a demonstration of length.

"No!" the women shouted in disbelief.

"Oh, yes it is. And thick too," she said emphatically.

The women dissolved in laughter, huddled closer together, and continued their conversation.

Halla and Genevra returned for another load of meat to find the meat cutters still overcome with laughter.

The two thralls looked at each other and smiled at the infectious laughter. Halla began to refill the trough with meat strips. Genevra stopped what she was doing and stood with her hands on her hips. "What is so funny?"

"Oh, we were laughing about the size of things." Gudrun was unable to continue as the women dissolved in another bout of laughter.

A perplexed look passed between the two thrall women before they happened to notice the smithies also laughed among themselves. It suddenly dawned on both Halla and Genevra what the topic of conversation had been.

"Size, yes! You talk about Sigmund, I will wager." Halla elbowed her companion in the ribs.

"You cannot keep such a nice thing a secret. Halla and I already know about him," Genevra added.

"It seems my son has become famous," Helga said appreciatively. "I wonder why I have not heard of this before."

"You are only his mother, Helga. They all grow up, and I can assure you Sigmund has grown up." Gudrun's attentive audience laughed uproariously.

"We are sorry to have missed most of this conversation. It would have been a welcome diversion. Maybe we can be here next time." Halla smiled as she looked at the group of women.

"The topic is certain to come up again," Thora said, as her companions convulsed again with appreciative laughter.

The two thralls laughed good-naturedly also, because sex was one of the favored gossip topics, and gossip, regardless of the topic, served to relieve the tedium of the daily work.

"I hate to change the subject." Halla waited for the others to stop laughing. "We are running out of bags to pack the dried fish and meat in. It dries fast in this wind."

"Pack it tight as you can. More bags will be made as soon as the reindeer hides have dried enough to be tanned," Thora said.

Halla was exasperated that Thora would think they would do otherwise. "Nobody could pack it tighter, Thora. We know how to do our job."

"I did not mean that at all, Halla. Do not be so defensive." Thora regarded the thrall from under a lowered brow, the laughter gone from her voice. "Store it in the tents until they get new bags made."

Ingerd joined them in time to hear Thora's comment. "I just came from the tents and we have several bags already stitched together. We knew you would need more bags. Gudbj told us not to dry and tan them but just sew the hides green and let the bags dry before they are used. As quickly as they are finished, we hang them under the fire pit awning. With the heat and smoke from the fire pit and this wind some of them may be dry enough tomorrow."

"Good. We have three more bags. They will last until tomorrow, unless we work all night." Halla looked from face to face, the crinkles of a smile around her dark eyes.

Everyone looked up from their work at her statement, as she knew they would. The thought that they might work all night affected freewoman and thrall, and none wanted that to happen. They felt they had done enough for one day.

"Surely Halfdan will call a halt soon," Ingerd said hopefully.

"Let us hope so, Ingerd." Grunhild stood up again and stretched her tired back. "Maybe you could have Gudbj ask Halfdan to let everyone stop? The food will be cooked soon and we will stop then, but we could work after we eat unless..."

Her voice trailed off as Ingerd interrupted her. "I would never ask Gudbj to do that. He would not ask Halfdan such a thing. If I asked him that, he would probably make everyone work all night. I do not interfere in his work and he does not interfere in mine, unless I do something wrong." Her eyes swept the group of women.

Ingerd wheeled and strode away. They watched her for a time before returning to their tasks.

Chapter Four

Frida sat curled on the lookout's lap, her arms around his neck. They had groped each other until they had almost reached the point of no return. The focus changed suddenly when the lookout's partially glazed eyes chanced to shift in the direction of the fjord entrance. A small boat, followed by two ships, entered the waters of the fjord.

"Get off me! Stand up, Frida! Quickly, my horn! Where in the name of the gods is my horn?" Gizur spat out as he scrambled about like a crab.

"Here!" Frida held the horn out to him. "You sat on it."

Gizur grabbed the horn from her and lurched to his feet, the horn at his lips. Frida jumped up and ran like a deer from the lookout post. The stentorian blast of the lookout's horn interrupted the encampment's work.

"Tostig comes, and the ships follow him!" Frida shouted. Her long, red hair flew in the breeze, and her large, scantily covered, unfettered breasts swung to and fro as she ran down the slope from the lookout post.

Halfdan and Gudbjartur turned at the sound of the horn and saw Frida run down the hill. "With all this work to do, what is she doing at the lookout post?" Halfdan asked.

Gudbjartur raised an eyebrow in surprise. "Everyone knows what she was doing up there with the lookout."

"What?"

"She is a troublemaker. She is with Gizur to make another jealous. I am surprised he even saw the ships enter the fjord. Frida demands a man's full attention." Gudbjartur looked at Halfdan with a smile; his vain attempt at humor failed to register.

"Who is the other man?" Halfdan turned to face his lieutenant, his manner gruff.

"It is not important. If it was not him it would be some other poor bastard."

"I will decide what is important." Halfdan spoke through gritted teeth, his irritation apparent.

"Easy, Halfdan." Gudbjartur extended his hands palms out to placate his chieftain.

An inarticulate growl came from Halfdan; he spoke a single word through gritted teeth. "Gudbj?"

With no choice in the matter, Gudbjartur answered. "It is Ulfar, but it could be any man. She likes to make trouble."

"Why have you not told me she caused trouble?"

"I did not tell you because you have more important problems to deal with. Who is coupling with who is not important. If her dalliance causes trouble, you will know. We cannot control everything these people do. Only important things will I tell you, the rest I will take care of. Is this not what you want of me?"

Halfdan regarded the man in silence for a time and then turned his attention back to the lookout post. Frida had disappeared into the crowd that gathered on the beach to meet the ships. "You are correct, Gudbj. I am too important to bother with such trivial matters." He chuckled, and threw his arm tightly around the shoulders of his friend. "You take care of it for me."

Before Gudbjartur could answer, a shout came from somebody in the crowd, something about a race.

Halfdan glanced thoughtfully at his lieutenant. He ignored the shouts of the crowd. "We will talk more about this later, perhaps. For now, continue as you have been."

Gudbjartur nodded and both men joined the people on the beach to watch the race.

* * *

Shouts of encouragement carried faintly to the ships from the shoreline. Both ships fanned out as they entered the broader part of the fjord and headed toward the landing beach. The race became one of equals as sails vanished from the masts in the light air and double-manned sweeps came into play. The sweeps slashed into the water. They left twin rows of eddies on the surface and wove a beautiful tapestry across the calm surface of the fjord as the ships sped neck and neck toward the landing beach.

The two captains, Athils and Gudrod, hurled taunts back and forth as they urged their crews onward.

"Maximum speed!" Athils shouted from the bow and swept his arm forward. "Gudrod reaches on us!"

The stroke drum beat a tattoo for maximum possible speed. Sweat beaded on the rowers' faces in spite of the chill air, as they strained to their utmost.

Athils turned to the excited passengers gathered amidships. "Everybody aft! Shift your weight aft to make the bow rise!" The weight shift brought immediate results as the ship closed the gap on the leader.

Gudrod tried to follow suit, but before the weight shift produced results, his ship suddenly stopped in a welter of spray. The crash of equipment tearing loose and the snap of splintering sweeps carried all the way to the shore as all forward momentum ceased. Everything loose within the hull wound up in a pile forward: people, equipment, and animals.

The heavy mast twisted and crashed forward, as backstays and shrouds parted one after another with loud snaps.

"Look out! The mast!"

"What happened?"

"The ship is aground! What did we hit?"

Cries of pain and consternation came from every quarter as individuals extricated themselves from under other people and the wreckage of the rigging that entrapped them.

"Help us, we are trapped!"

"Where is Gudrod?"

"I am here!" Gudrod fought his way upright from under the mast and the tangle of fallen rigging near the point of the bow. Blood flowed from a cut on his forehead into his eyes, and he swiped at it as two men pulled and cut the rigging away to free him from its embrace.

"I fell forward from the impact at the same time the mast came down. I ducked aside, and it smashed down on the bow rail—otherwise I would be dead," he said to the men with him as they hurried toward the cries for help. He pointed to the area of the mast step where the shrouds and most of the rigging formed a tangle. The tangle of lines had ensnared several people as surely as a moth in a spiderweb. "I am fine. Get those people out of there." He pulled and hacked desperately at the tangle.

Being close to the shipwreck, Tostig and his boat crew altered course to lay their boat alongside the stricken vessel. The three-man crew vaulted from their boat over the side of the ship in time to witness the discovery of the hapless victims under the mass of wreckage at the foot of the mast. They joined others who pulled and cut the tangle of rigging and broken sweeps away from the heavy mast. Several people managed to crawl to freedom. All sustained minor cuts and scrapes. Tostig made mention of what they all dreaded. "We saw several people fall toward the bow when the ship stopped, Gudrod. They landed in a heap forward of the mast. There are more people still trapped under here. Some were probably knocked into the livestock pens."

"Hold it!" Ring held up his hand. "I see something!" He fell to his knees and stuck his head in a hole he worried in the web of rigging, yard, and furled sail.

"What do you see?" Gudrod demanded.

He backed slowly out and pulled himself erect. He looked at Gudrod. "There are four people under there. Three are under the mast and yard, and one fell into the pens. Before they could get out of the way they were smashed to a bloody pulp. They are all dead, Gudrod."

Gudrod glanced around the suddenly still group of would-be rescuers with a sick look on his face. "By all the gods," he swore. "Are you sure?"

"I am sure. I doubt they knew what hit them." Ring spoke in a low voice, his eyes downcast.

A cry came from another crewmen as he inspected the ship's hull for damage. "Gudrod, we are taking on water fast. The ship is holed in two places amidships."

"Leave these people where they are, we cannot help them." Gudrod ordered. "Come, we must attend to the ship."

* * *

Onshore, the cries of surprise from occupants caught completely off guard and the tormented groan and screech of the hull as it halted, although muffled somewhat by the water and distance from the beach, grated on the nerves of every person within earshot. Someone quicker to respond than others shouted, "Gudrod's ship is aground!" Cries of distress and disbelief came from the crowd on the beach.

Athils, captain of the other ship, continued without pause toward the beach. Before he could assist those aboard the grounded ship, all his passengers and much of his cargo must be put ashore to make room for Gudrod's passengers and cargo.

Everyone on shore shouted at once as the bow of Athils' ship ground on the beach. The instant the ship came to rest passengers climbed over the bow and dropped into the shallow water or onto the pebbled beach, urged on by Athils and his crew.

Halfdan stood at the front of the crowd. He raised his arms and shouted above the tumult, "Quiet everyone! Athils, is Gudrod's hull holed?"

"I do not know. The noise when he grounded sounded bad. There may be a lot of underwater damage. I will bring his passengers and all the cargo we can carry back here, to lighten the ship, and then try to tow him off with the high tide if his hull is not holed. If it is holed they will try to make temporary repairs and then we will tow him off." He turned to look toward the stricken vessel.

Halfdan jumped up, grabbed the rail of Athils' ship at the bow, and swung into the ship for a quick conference. "If this works, Athils, and the ship does not sink in the process, tow her straight into the beach. Do not stop."

"Gudrod may want to bring her in with his own crew, Halfdan," Athils answered doubtfully.

"No! We do not know how bad the damage is. The patches will not hold very long and we will need to get her beached as soon as possible. Leave the livestock aboard. There is no time to transfer them. If the ship sinks on the way to shore the animals will make it to shore on their own. Tell him I told you this."

The two men locked eyes for a heartbeat. Athils nodded. Halfdan turned and dropped over the ship's side into the knee-deep water and waded ashore.

His passengers and cargo unloaded, Athils ordered the oarsmen to back them away from the beach. Several men on the beach pushed at the bow while others threw coils of heavy towrope aboard as the ship backed away.

* * *

"Listen!" Gudrod shouted to his crew and passengers as Athils' ship approached. "All the men remain aboard my ship. Women and children go with Athils. Pick up something, anything, when you board his ship. We will unload all the cargo we can in the time we have. The tide is near the end of the flood and we must beach the ship before she floats off whatever holds her. She is badly holed and will sink if we float off before the patches are in place. Speed is essential, so make haste when Athils' ship comes alongside."

Gudrod joined his crew members as they worked to clear the area of the keel where the underwater damage had occurred.

"The water that comes in has slowed down, Gudrod. The ship is held so tightly that no more can leak in." A man who knelt on the keel looked up at Gudrod as he dropped to his knees beside him and bent over to peer at the damage.

"I see that." Gudrod stretched out full length, stuck an arm into the water, through the holed planks, and felt around the outside of the hull until his hand contacted a mussel-encrusted point of rock.

"We might want to come back and harvest these mussels. The rock that knocked this hole in my ship is covered with them. Big ones, too." He glanced at his men as he got to his feet. He rubbed the circulation back into his chilled arm. "Let us take a look at the planks on the port side. We do not have much time."

It became apparent after inspection of the damage that the only thing that had kept the ship afloat was the vice-like grip of two points of rock. Spread like the fingers of a giant's hand, they appeared to be about three feet below the surface. The ship had driven at full speed between the two spires, to the widest area of the hull, amidships, and there she wedged.

"Half of you men come with me to help get our cargo and people off. The rest of you get started on temporary repairs and leather patches. We will come back to help as soon as we finish topside." Gudrod and several crew members climbed out of the hold.

Gudrod directed Athils alongside with hand signals. "We checked for rock alongside, Athils, and did not find any. Throw us some lines and my men will pull your ship in slowly just in case we missed something," he shouted as Athils turned his ship into the light breeze and slowly made his approach.

The moment the ships were secured side-to-side, passengers literally jumped between them. Most of the cargo and personal belongings followed closely behind.

"Halfdan told me to continue to tow you into the beach rather than stop to let you row in yourself. He also said leave the animals, there is no time for them. We must get you off before the flood tide floats you or sinks you," Athils shouted.

"I agree. I will keep only a couple men with me after the patches are in place. Put as many as possible on the sweeps. We will only have one chance to do this right, so let us be about it."

Athils waved in assent and the combined crews began the hectic salvage operation while others finished with the transfer of cargo. Athils then positioned his ship at the bow of the stricken vessel and his men secured the heavy towropes for the attempt.

Meanwhile, aboard Gudrod's ship, crewmen wedged fractured and sprung hull planks back in place. Then they nailed heavily greased leather patches in position on the inside of the hull, and sealed the edges with more grease. The patches would have been more effective on the outside of the hull, but the task was impossible in the near-freezing water. Others continued to bail the accumulated water outboard.

Gudrod shouted to Athils, the excitement plain in his voice, "We are finished! Take a strain on the towline!"

Athils motioned to the stroke drummer, from his position on the stern platform, and the man began the measured beat to take a slow strain on the towline. "Easy. Easy. Now!" Athils shouted. "Pull for all you are worth!"

With four strong backs at each sweep, instead of the normal one or two, success was certain provided the ship could be budged from the obstruction.

Sweeps rose and fell to the boom of the stroke drum, and slowly, painfully, with much creaking and groaning from the damaged hull, the ship cleared the rocks that held her captive. The sudden surge forward as the hull slid free caused several men at the sweeps to lose their balance and the cadence of the stroke, but they quickly recovered.

A great roar of exultation burst forth from both ship's crews as Gudrod's ship floated clear.

"Full speed to the beach!" Athils shouted excitedly as he swept his arm forward. "Put your back into it, men!" The beat of the stroke drum increased at a measured pace to the maximum possible beat. The arm and back muscles of the men at the sweeps bulged and flexed as they threw themselves into the effort.

Cries drifted across the water from the anxious witnesses ashore as they realized the ship was afloat and free.

Athils' ship sped toward the beach. He stood beside the man on the stroke drum and gauged the distance to the shoreline. He raised his fist. "Slow." The ships' speed began to decease and he motioned to the helmsman for a slight turn to port at the last moment to make room for Gudrod to beach his ship. "Hold the stroke." Athils paused for a heartbeat. "Back your sweeps!" he cried. The sweeps thrashed in reverse, and the ship crunched ashore on the pebble beach.

The moment the towline went slack, as Athils backed his sweeps, a crewman cast the towline loose so Gudrod's ship could continue into the beach by her own momentum.

When Athils turned to port, Gudrod turned to steerboard to clear Athils' stern. The ship's hull rose up the bottom as it shelved. A man standing high in the bow heaved a light messenger line ashore, attached to the towline coiled in the bow. "Here, catch this messenger and haul in the towline!" he shouted.

A group of men ashore caught the messenger line and hauled it in hand over hand until they had hold of the heavy towline. They ran with it straight away and hauled lustily to drag the ship as far forward as humanly possible as Gudrod drove his bow up on the inclined beach.

Secured tightly to the beach with a single line at the bow and two stern lines, the ship's keel rested firmly on the bottom for almost half its length.

The need to make haste gave the activity ashore an air of frenzy. With the hull damaged on both sides of the keel, the ship had to rest in an upright position while repairs were made.

Slack tide, the period between the flood and ebb tides, lasted only a short time before the rapid surge of the ebb began and the water poured from the fjord. To ensure the ship remained in the desired upright position, timbers had to be in place before the support of the water was lost as the tide ebbed. All the necessary equipment and shoring timbers lay piled in readiness on the beach.

The ship's contingent of livestock, their nervous voices adding to the bedlam, were left aboard. They would be unloaded after the critical work of shoring up the ship was completed.

Halfdan and Gudbjartur worked side by side with other men in the freezing water. Balks of timber, carried aboard each ship for just such a task, were wedged into place along the outside of the hull to support the ship in an upright position.

The extreme difference between high and low tide, twenty to thirty feet, would leave the damaged ship high and dry, supported along both sides in an upright position during the low and slack tide and before the onset of the next flood tide. During this period, an army of carpenters would complete the repairs to the hull.

* * *

One unpleasant task remained. Halfdan and Gudbjartur surveyed the bustle of the encampment. Those close by knew what was to come but chose to stay busy to keep their minds off the loss of life aboard Gudrod's ship.

Butchers cut up the last of the meat and fish before more accumulated; helpers salted the long strips and fillets before they laid them out to dry. Carpenters trimmed new planks and fit them in place on the hull of Gudrod's ship; others bored holes along the edges of the thin planks and riveted them together. Children ran around underfoot or engaged in light chores. Groups of women gossiped as they spun, sewed, and cooked. Livestock grazed under the watchful eyes of their guards. An argument heard here, the guffaw of a man's laughter there, the tinkle of a woman's giggle at some antic or other, and the buzz of conversation hung over the encampment as a hardy, happy people went about the business of life.

The two leaders watched these activities for a time. Halfdan turned his head and locked eyes with his lieutenant. He nodded once, as if to say, it is time.

Gudbjartur took a deep breath, raised his horn to his lips, and blew a long drawn out blast that echoed over the countryside.

Halfdan watched the facial expressions of his people as they gathered. Although most appeared neutral they all knew why he summoned them. He gestured for them to gather in closely. After the shuffling stopped and he was certain he had their attention, he spoke in a loud, clear voice. "You all know why you have been called. In yon ship," he gestured toward Gudrod's ship, "are the bodies of three men and a woman killed by the mast when Gudrod's ship ran aground."

A mutter swept through the crowd as people close to Gudrod parted and he came into everyone's view.

"It is not his fault," Halfdan said. "Tostig took us out to where Gudrod ran aground and we could not find the rocks. Gudrod told me that seaweed and mussels cover them and they are only visible at the lowest tide. We took soundings and the water has no bottom there. It is very deep. Gudrod's ship struck two long points of rock below the surface that we looked for and could not find, so he and his crew had no chance to see them. It could have happened to anyone. Even the lookout did not see any danger before they struck. He was one of those killed. Now, let us do what we must: bury them and get back to work. Forget what happened as quickly as possible. It is over. It is done."

People went about the business of burial as an unpleasant fact of life. Violent death was a specter that loomed over the lives of all of them and they were well accustomed to its grim visits. Consequently, people had little time to mourn or bury the dead unless the death required a special ceremony.

Thrall women washed the bodies of all signs of their violent deaths and dressed each in the finery they had possessed in life. The tools, weapons, and utensils they had used in life, and would need in the afterlife, were included with the corpses. They rested in a common grave, together, as they had lived and died.

Without further ceremony several men filled in the grave with the cold, rocky earth. Large stones were piled over the top to keep animals from digging up the corpses.

The massed onlookers stood for a time in silence, each with their own thoughts, before the crowd began to thin as individuals and small groups returned to their work.

* * *

Hunters returned from another successful reindeer hunt in the hinterland. Game continued to be plentiful a short distance from the encampment. Crews of butchers again made use of the horses and two-wheeled carts to transport the meat and hides to the riverbank, where others readied the meat for consumption or drying and selected the best hides for tanning. All unusable offal remained in the field, food for ravens and other eaters of the dead.

On the beach near the river's mouth, the green, undressed hides accumulated in piles. They awaited the tanners, who would stake them to the ground hair-side down and scrape off bits of fat and flesh. Some of the hides were left to dry while others were weighted with rocks in the river. The hair slipped off easily after a prolonged soak. The best of these hairless hides and all the bear hides—left hairy for bedding—were set aside to be tanned. The poorest quality hides became storage bags, or, cut into continuous rawhide strips, the twisted, multi-strand rope so essential to everyday work.

The smell of the fresh hides worsened with the passage of time. Soaking the hair loose in water, curing the heavy green hides into leather with the thick liquid of the tanbark, and the final tanning of the leather in the sunshine to a rich brown color took several days. Before the tanners completed their task, the smell wafted for a great distance around the encampment.

Over time, the smell permeated the clothing and skin of the tanners to the point that the smell they exuded was indistinguishable from their product.

Gudbjartur, who seemed to be everywhere at once, stopped by on his rounds and talked to the large group of men who worked on the fresh hides. "We need more rope, so save all the seal hides. If more is needed after all the hunters are in, pick the best of the reindeer bull hides for rope."

"We do not have many seals, Gudbj. That pile is all of them." Thorvard pointed toward a pile of seal hides.

"Unless some are brought in soon we will use bull hide." A short wiry man, tough as the leather he loved, whose beard and hair nearly covered his entire face (Gudbjartur had often wondered how he could see), Thorvard was the best rope maker among them. He took his trade seriously and required little or no suggestion or supervision. "I have selected all the best bull hides." He pointed to several large hides piled in the river shallows. "The hair will slip in a few days and then we will cut them into strips and twist the strips into rope."

"Good, Thorvard. Be sure to cut plenty of wide strips for anchor and towrope. We seem to be short of them."

"I will, Gudbj, I always do." The man shook his head and chuckled. "But you ask me anyway."

"Aye, I guess I do," Gudbjartur reflected. "I always will, and you expect me to. You all expect me to." He swept his arm to include Thorvard's whole crew. He matched the smiles of the tanners. "Now, I have others to check on. To make certain they, too, are doing what I already know they are doing."

It is good to do whatever it takes to keep order, whatever makes people happy and gets the work done, he thought as he walked away to find Halfdan.

The tremendous bounty of this new land became apparent to all when the tally of whales, bear, reindeer, fish, and seals was known. The work progressed rapidly, almost keeping pace with crews who brought in the carcasses. Strips of drying meat festooned every rock and bush in and around the encampment. It became necessary to rig much of the spare rope to accommodate the overflow.

Ingerd and Thora organized a group of children, provided them with sticks, and left them to make a game of keeping seagulls from the drying meat and fish. The shouts and swinging sticks of the children ensured limited success for the bold scavengers during the short period of full daylight.

Fishing had also been particularly good as attested to by the arrival of a ship's boat that rode so low in the water from its load of fish that it was in danger of swamping.

The two-man crew rowed in to the beach under the eyes of, and subjected to the derogatory comments of, those nearby.

"It looks like you almost caught too many fish," one observed from shore as the loaded boat gently touched the beach. Several hands dragged the boat up onto the beach as far as possible.

"Every cast of the jig brought a fish," Helge said. "The bottom of this fjord is covered with big cod."

Gudbjartur walked up in time to catch the last of the conversation. "Your fish are very welcome. We need fresh fish to eat now and many more to dry for winter."

"That will not be a problem. Next time Ring and I will take one of the larger boats and a net. We can also set fish traps," Helge said.

"Good," Gudbjartur said as he helped unload the catch. "Take all the boats not in use, and fish while the school is close by. Catch all you can."

Several of the men who had unloaded the catch, now piled high on the beach, volunteered to fish, and soon crews were assembled to man all available boats. The rest of the men gutted, boned, and split the fish into two fillets joined at the tail. These splits were later salted and hung to dry. The dry, leather like fillets were a winter staple.

"Has anyone seen Halfdan?" Gudbjartur asked.

The men laughed at the question.

Gudbjartur stopped unloading fish and looked from man to man. "What is so funny? Have I missed something?"

"Oh, you have missed something, all right." Ring reached down and hooked a big fish from the boat with one of the short-handled gaffs they all used to handle the slimy cod. "If you hurry you might still be in time to see what we find so funny."

Everybody laughed again and Gudbjartur turned to look around the encampment. For the first time he noticed a crowd had gathered. To judge from the way they acted, they watched something humorous.

"Halfdan's hair and beard are being trimmed. He is in the middle of yon crowd." Ring gestured toward the crowd.

In response to a quizzical look from Gudbjartur, Ring explained further. "He and Frida had an argument about something. It did not last long, and then they went over to Halfdan's tent. Halfdan is teaching her some manners. The crowd started to gather right away. They are still there because the crowd is bigger. You can see Frida's red hair but I do not see Halfdan."

"They are both still there all right," another said with a chuckle. "I just came from there."

Gudbjartur walked toward the crowd without another word; the men he had been talking to followed closely. This would be too good to miss. He pushed his way through the crowd and stopped in midstride. Halfdan sat smugly on an overturned barrel in front of his tent having his hair cut by a fuming Frida. He arrived in time to hear Halfdan speak to her.

"Trim the beard to blend into the length of my hair, Frida. Cut my hair evenly across the bottom, just above my pull-over." He ducked slightly to avoid a particularly aggressive slash she made in the direction of his hair. "Watch the ears with those scissors." Halfdan caught sight of Gudbjartur as he stepped to the front of the crowd and folded his arms, a slight smile on his face. "Gudbj, I am happy you are here. Frida had nothing to do so I asked her to cut my hair, and she happily obliged. You need a haircut, too. I am certain Frida would be happy to cut yours as well."

Frida was not happy. Her clenched teeth and the look she flung at Gudbjartur conveyed the intensity of her feelings.

The expectant crowd looked from Frida, to Gudbjartur, and back to Halfdan, intent on catching every aspect of the unfolding drama.

"Mine is all right, Halfdan, but thank you for the offer. Ingerd cuts mine when it gets too long." Gudbjartur smiled broadly.

"No, I insist. I can not have my lieutenant looking shabby when Frida is all set up to cut hair."

Noting the intensity of the look in Halfdan's eyes, Gudbjartur reversed himself. "All right, I guess I do need a haircut."

Frida almost exploded with fury. But she managed to regain control, biting off the retort before she lost what little composure remained in this test of wills.

Halfdan goaded her even more. "You do not mind, do you, Frida? Do you have time to cut Gudbj's hair?"

She answered through gritted teeth, her fury plain to see. "No, I do not mind, and yes, I have time. As you say, I have nothing else to do anyway."

"Excellent Frida, I am happy you agree with me," he said dryly.

Gudbjartur looked from Halfdan to Frida and realized this was much more than it seemed. Frida's aloof personality had gained her few friends and everyone rejoiced to see her humbled in this manner. Halfdan had her where he wanted her and she did not like it at all. However, she had no choice in the matter. He bent Frida to his will, humbled her publicly, and showed her who was in charge. Gudbjartur turned to the crowd at his back and spoke loud enough for everyone to hear. "All right everyone, I think that is enough." He knew the show was over, and that was what Halfdan wanted him to do. "I am sure you all have much to do."

The crowd grumbled a little but returned to their various tasks. They continued to observe the hair cutting drama from a distance. As such things happen, word passed quickly and soon every member of the community knew the story and most of the embellished variations. It became a favored part of camp gossip.

* * *

Another boat came onto the beach. The two-man crew had caught a large number of crabs in six collapsible traps that they had baited with offal and scattered in a line behind the moored ships.

Two of the cooks saw the full traps and walked down to the beach from the fire pit to watch the crew unload their boat.

"That is terrific! Carry them to the fire pit for us. We will get some seawater on to boil," Helga said.

Further down the beach two thrall women gathered edible seaweed on the tidal flats. When they had a full load, they picked up the heaping baskets and trudged toward the fire pit with the dietary staple. Today, most of the harvest would be used fresh. The remainder was chopped, dried, or burned to ash and stored for later use as a seasoning in stews and soups.

Thora tended several kettles of stew simmering over the coals of the fire pit. She gave each kettle a stir to prevent the gravy from sticking as she passed down the line. She looked up as the two thrall women came bearing baskets of seaweed. "Oh good, you found some. Drop some in each kettle and I will stir it in."

"It will add body to the stew." Halla shook a pile of seaweed onto a round, ironbound, oak chopping block and deftly chopped the rubbery seaweed into bite-sized pieces with a meat cleaver. She scooped the chopped greens back into a bucket and walked down the line of kettles to drop a portion into each. "It is easy to find. Unlike Greenland, we seem to be the only people here who use it for anything."

"If you have time later, harvest and dry all you can. We might not be so lucky at the next place we stop," Thora said.

"The problem we always have is that there is never enough time." Halla answered.

"If we do find a little free time, someone always has something else for us to do." Genevra, her companion, pouted.

"Oh, come now, Genevra. Things are not as bad as all that. All of us get free time when the work is done, even you," Thora chided.

Genevra nodded silently. She did not wish to cause a disagreement over something she could not change. As a thrall, she knew her place. And both she and Halla worked longer and harder as a consequence.

The two crab fishermen arrived burdened with their traps. Their arrival and the incessant clicking sound made by the crabs as they scurried around in the traps interrupted the silence that had descended over the cooks after Thora's remark to Genevra.

"Where do you want these?" the first man asked.

"Bring them down to this end. When the water boils you can empty your traps right into the kettles," Thora called.

The men stacked their crab traps off to the side of the fire pit and took the opportunity to catch up on the latest camp gossip with the cooks.

"How long did it take to catch all of these big crabs, Vilhjalm?" Halla asked.

"Not long." He glanced at his companion and nodded, as if to say, you answer her.

Ulfar always filled in where his friend left off with his short answers. "We set the traps out after the ships were moored, and before we went inland to hunt. The crabs came to the bait right away because of the blood and guts from the butchering. The traps were, no doubt, full within half a day. They are not only bigger than the crabs around Greenland, there are many more of them."

Vilhjalm nodded appreciatively at Ulfar and beamed at the women. "See, I told you it did not take long." Everyone laughed.

"This has been a most successful day. What would you two rather do, hunt or fish?" Halla asked Ulfar.

"Hunt. Fishing is just hard work most of the time." He glanced at his companion.

Vilhjalm agreed. "It does not really matter to me. The hunt today was fun while it lasted."

"Yes!" Ulfar responded enthusiastically. "When we began, there were so many deer we could not decide which one to shoot. The herd ran from one bunch of hunters to the next; we shot as fast as we could put arrow to bow, until our arrows were gone. I have never seen anything like it. So many animals."

"Go ahead and dump the crabs into those kettles." Thora pointed with a long-handled wooden spoon in the general direction of several kettles from which steam rose into the chill air.

"The water is just about ready to boil. It is already hot enough to kill the crabs before they can climb out."

From the riverbank, where the meat was being cut up, thralls and butcher's helpers hauled large stacks of bloody leg bones, piled high on two-man wooden trenchers, to the fire pit, where they placed them directly on the coals to bake.

"Stop here, Halla. I think we have enough on the coals for now. We can begin a pile of marrow bones and ribs and add more to the coals when there is room for them," Genevra said.

Halla stooped to retrieve a long-handled hook to turn the marrow joints in the coals. "We better tend to the roasting. Let the men carry the rest."

Genevra glanced toward Thora, who was busy at the other end of the fire pit. "That is fine with me. If Thora wants us to do something else, she is certain to tell us."

"Now that is a fact." Halla narrowed her eyes in the heat as she stooped to hook a rib rack from the coals. She straightened to look at her friend. "Do not make Thora mad. She is a good friend to us but she has a bad temper. She has always treated us well and we do not want that to change."

"Do not worry, Halla. I know what I am and what I can and cannot do."

As the leg bones and joints roasted through, the two women hooked them out of the fire pit and piled them with the others on the stone hearth. Racks of ribs turned a uniform brown color as the spitting, outer fat layer melted over them.

"Take a break from the cook fire, you two." Thora walked up to the two thralls. She took a fork from the sweaty hand of Halla and pointed to the other end of the fire pit. "Cut those cooked rib racks into smaller portions and pile them with the marrow bones on the hearth. Put the roasts on trenchers and cut them into smaller pieces. We are about ready to feed everyone."

* * *

A breeze freshened off the fjord and brought with it a light drizzle. The smell of roasted meat drifted throughout the encampment. The rich smells called the people from their work better than the loudest gong.

The buzz of conversation and occasional laughter from the press of people under the cook's awning brought a smile to Gudbjartur's face as he and Halfdan joined the queue. "Nothing like hot food and the warmth of a cook fire to drive the chill and fatigue away," he said.

Halfdan glanced at his friend and noted the water that dripped from his hair and beard. "You look a little the worse for wear."

"I am. And so are you. Food will fix everything."

Halfdan and Gudbjartur moved under a corner of the big awning so they could eat protected from the drizzle.

Everyone forgot their fatigue as they recounted the day's activities in many separate conversations. In an orgy of hunger, they wolfed down copious amounts of roasted meat smeared with the last of the butter, tender meaty ribs dipped in hot bone marrow, and boiled eggs. People milled about or sat with a wooden plate, bowl, or trencher balanced across their knees, intent only on the food and conversation between mouthfuls.

The three kettles of stew had cooked down to a rich broth filled with cooked seaweed and chunks of tender meat. Several scoops of barley and beaten eggs, added earlier, had thickened and added body to the broth. People consumed many bowls before the three kettles emptied.

Steam rose into the cold air from a large pile of cooked crabs on the hearth. There was more than enough for everyone who liked crabs, and the pile was eventually reduced to nothing as crabs were taken and dismembered. The tremendous variety of food was soon reduced to piles of bones and empty crab shells.

On behalf of everyone, Halfdan voiced appreciation for the food the women had prepared. "We are all exhausted from traveling; repairs of the storm damage and hunting have kept everyone busy. There is so much meat and fish that much work remains to do."

Good-natured groans came from the crowd. Halfdan laughed and continued, "This day is almost over. We are full of food and I think we can leave what remains of the work for tomorrow. Let us celebrate our safe arrival in this place and the bounty of fish and game provided by the gods."

There was loud agreement and several barrels of mead appeared, as if by magic.

"Before the celebration gets too far along, each captain will post additional guards. I want them doubled. We do not want bears to cause problems with all this meat in camp." Halfdan shouted over the din while they could still hear him.

Pairs of guards rekindled their fires as before. The security perimeter radiated from the water's edge in a semicircle around the encampment as the shadows lengthened. The flames flickered in the breeze and provided the guards with some illumination as the twilight of the northern night gathered. It lent a surreal air to the boisterous celebration as the light shimmered and danced off the milling crowd. With many lubricated by great quantities of strong mead and thick barley beer, the volume of sound that rose into the chill air reverberated through the countryside and out over the still, dark waters of the fjord.

Inevitably, those prone to drunkenness soon were thoroughly drunk. With seven men to every woman, trouble simmered just below the surface. Custom dictated women were free to choose regardless of attachment, unless their current mate disagreed, of course. Trouble came to the fore when the strong drink loosened tongues and eliminated all pretense at civility. A fight developed between two men who laid claim to the same woman.

Frida's wide, green eyes invited sexual advance from those she chose. She had goaded the two men who vied for her attention into a frenzy of jealous rage. Drunk with mead, Gizur fondled Frida's breasts and crotch openly. He pulled her into his lap and kissed her neck and ears in an unbridled display of lust. She returned his advances in full view of everyone. She rubbed his swollen manhood through the confines of his tunic with one hand while she gripped the back of his neck with the other. Their tongues wetly entwined as their bodies writhed in the full grip of passion. They seemed oblivious to the glances cast their way.

Ulfar chanced to glance in their direction in time to see Gizur's dalliance with the woman he regarded as personal property. He roared like a wounded bear and hit Gizur in the back of the head. The blow knocked Gizur and Frida into an untidy heap. Gizur lurched to his feet and whipped out a knife. Ulfar kicked him in the crotch and down he went once again.

Gizur lay curled up on the ground cradling his injured manhood. Ulfar aimed several hard kicks at his head. Gizur scrambled aside and made a vicious swipe with his knife. A long, deep cut appeared in Ulfar's lower leg.

The crowd surrounded the combatants. Several men forcibly separated them.

Ulfar roared, "I claim the right of the einvigi on this scum. He has coupled with Frida for the last time."

"Frida causes trouble, she likes it, and everybody couples with her anyway," a big redheaded man said. "She is not worth dying for."

"I will not be the one who dies, Thorgill. If you do not want to be next, shut your mouth about Frida," Ulfar shouted.

"Do not let your mouth run away with you. You do not want to fight me," Thorgill rumbled ominously.

"Enough!" Halfdan shouted. He shouldered his way through the circle of men.

The instant he saw the combatants, his previous conversation with Gudbjartur came to mind. He knew what the problem was: Frida. He had humbled her before everyone, but it had done no good. It was going to take more than two haircuts to tame Frida.

"What is the trouble here?" Halfdan looked between the antagonists.

"I claim the right of the einvigi. Gizur has coupled with my woman for the last time." Ulfar pointed his knife at Gizur, who remained on the ground cradling his manhood.

"Your woman? She is my woman!" Gizur made to rise from the ground. He groaned and sank back down.

"It looks like you have already won," Halfdan retorted.

"I am not beaten yet." Gizur rose slowly from the ground. "He kicked my eggs, but I am ready for whatever he wants to do now."

"It looks like both of you have been marked in this fight." Halfdan gestured at the blood that ran down Ulfar's leg. "Apologize and let it go."

"No!" Ulfar shouted. "As the one wronged here, I claim the right of the einvigi. I will teach him and every other man to leave Frida alone."

Halfdan looked at the two enraged men. He nodded in exasperation. "Bring two or three hides and a leather strap. These men can send each other to Valhalla."

"Here!" a man shouted as he and another dragged a freshly skinned bear hide into the open circle of onlookers. "They can use this."

Two more hides were dragged up to join the first, and all were staked to the ground hair side up. Both men moved onto this traditional arena of the duel. They stripped off their tunics and shoes and cast them aside. Both were naked, ready for single combat.

"You are both freemen, so you can do this thing, this einvigi. This duel will be fought until one of you is bleeding. That man can quit if he wishes and honor will be served if the other man agrees. You are already bleeding, Ulfar. You must choose to fight or quit. What say you?" Halfdan voice was devoid of emotion.

"No!" Ulfar raged. "I will see his guts on the ground before I quit!"

Halfdan looked from one to the other for some sign of hesitation. There was none. "The einvigi is a fight to the death for one or both of you. I ask you again to consider your honor served by the blood already drawn. What say you?"

Both men glared at each other and shook their heads.

Halfdan looked directly at Gizur. "As the challenged, it is your right to choose the weapons."

"Knives." Gizur spoke in a low tone of voice between gritted teeth.

Halfdan faced the two men. "Arm yourselves, and make ready. You both know the rules. You must hold the strap in your teeth. If you lose your hold on it, the fight stops until you have hold of it again. If you fight off the hides, you must stop until you are back on them. I will tell you to continue. If you do not stop, Thorgill or I will club you down." Halfdan indicated the man with a lift of his chin. Thorgill stood at the edge of the hides, a big grin on his face as he slapped a heavy club in his hand. "There is no quarter from this point on; none will be asked or given by either of you. If either of you dishonor the duel by trying to run, or strike your opponent when the fight has stopped for any of the reasons I have said, that man will be killed by Gudbjartur." He nodded toward Gudbjartur, who held his battle-axe easily in both hands, his face expressionless.

Neither combatant looked away. They locked their eyes on each other.

The crowd of men and women shuffled this way and that as individuals vied for position. Their faces mirrored the sick fascination that obsessed people who were to witness violent death. Nobody uttered a sound.

Halfdan stepped out of the way and spit out one word: "Fight!"

The two men warily circled one another; their wet skin glistened in the light drizzle and dancing firelight. The leather strap, the length of a man's extended arms, was held clamped in their teeth to restrict movement.

Sound from the crowd began as an undercurrent, the source indefinable. It almost sounded like the growl of a beast that built in volume until every mouth was involved.

Gizur drew first blood with a flick of his blade, swifter than the dart of an adder's tongue. The red-rimmed mouth of the deep cut grinned across Ulfar's chest. Ulfar grunted in pain. He grappled. Both men strained to throw the other off balance.

Ulfar suddenly dropped down and backward. He threw Gizur over his head. Ulfar followed through, turned completely over, and slammed astraddle Gizur's midsection. A long, drawn-out sigh rose from the throng. Shouts of encouragement filled the air as the weight of Ulfar's upper body and bulging shoulder muscles forced his knife down toward Gizur's naked chest. Blood from Ulfar's chest wound soaked both combatants. Each strained to hold the other at bay as the point of Ulfar's knife blade closed the gap. Gizur's grip on Ulfar's wrist slipped on the bloody skin. Just before the knifepoint would have entered his chest, Gizur growled and twisted convulsively under his opponent in a last-ditch effort. His paroxysm deflected the knife blade through the bunched muscles of his side, through the bear hide, and into the ground. Gizur bellowed in pain and rage. The strap fell from his mouth.

"Hold!" Halfdan shouted. Thorgill clubbed Ulfar off Gizur. Ulfar lay stunned by the blow.

The shouts from the crowd made conversation impossible. Both men were covered in blood. Gizur, his breath coming in ragged gasps, rested on his back while all waited for Ulfar to regain his wits.

Both men rose slowly from the hide. Ulfar shook his head to steady himself. They placed the leather strap back in their teeth.

Halfdan looked from one to the other. Their wet, lank hair hung unnoticed in front of their eyes. Neither paid it any attention. Each man fastened his eyes on the other; their mouths, wide-open around teeth clenched on the leather strap, gulped air like a beached fish. In spite of their bloody, crippling wounds, their expressions were wild; it would be a battle to the death. Halfdan shouted, "Fight!"

Both men, covered in blood and restricted by the length of the strap they clenched doggedly in their teeth, shuffled slowly in a circle on the hides.

Gizur, his right side weakened by the wound, shifted his knife into his left hand. He pressed his right arm against his side to stanch the flow of blood.

Ulfar sensed an advantage. He suddenly dropped his knife arm down from mid-chest and lunged forward. He swept the blade's cutting edge up at Gizur's unprotected belly.

Gizur pivoted desperately sideways. He deflected Ulfar's thrust with his right arm. His left hand flicked out, and his knife sliced the base of Ulfar's neck. The vicious swipe cut through to the collarbone at the juncture of neck and shoulder. Ulfar lost his grip on the strap. He sank slowly to his knees.

"Hold!" Halfdan leaped between the two men.

In a fit of murderous rage, oblivious to his wounds, Ulfar leaped up and knocked Halfdan aside. Halfdan fell away, off balance. Ulfar leaped on Gizur and drove him to the ground. He straddled Gizur's chest and pinned both arms with his knees. He grinned in triumph. Spittle ran from the rictus of his mouth. Ulfar raised his bloody knife above his head to drive it into Gizur's unprotected chest.

"No!" Halfdan struggled to grip the wet, slippery, bulging arms and bloody wrists of a man gone mad.

Ulfar laughed hysterically. The insanity of bloodlust glazed his eyes and suffused his face. He was intent only on the naked chest of his adversary. His fogged brain may have registered surprise at the moment Gudbjartur's battleaxe cleaved his skull in half. None of the men sprayed with his blood would ever know what he thought as the darkness of death enveloped him and he collapsed atop his adversary.

Gudbjartur placed his foot on Ulfar's body and wrenched his axe loose from the shattered skull. Rigid and tense, he held the heavy axe in both hands as blood dripped from the blade. Slowly he relaxed. He shifted the weapon to his right hand and lowered it to his side without conscious thought. As he viewed the untidy heap of that which had been a man, he became conscious of the silence and the stares of the crowd. His emotionless gaze slowly swung from man to man. His eyes stopped on Halfdan. "He dishonored you, the einvigi, and himself."

Halfdan regarded his friend in awe, wordless at the ferocity of his attack. They stared at each other for uncounted heartbeats. Both men averted their eyes. With the brief eye contact broken the tension drained away like water. The silence of the crowd accentuated the unreality of the scene as men and women surged forward and jostled for a better vantage point.

Only one woman stood at the front near Ulfar's body. Frida surveyed the gore with a look of excitement on her beautiful face. She chanced to look up from her examination of what remained of her erstwhile lover directly into Halfdan's eyes. The icy hand of fear gripped her heart as she looked into his steady blue eyes. She felt the heat of his passion caress her soul. She dropped her eyes from his, turned, and shoved her way through the crowd to distance herself from that malevolent stare.

A gasp of pain from under Ulfar's corpse called everyone's attention to Gizur. "Get him off me," he said weakly.

Thorgill reached down, grabbed an arm of the corpse, and flipped it off Gizur. "You look like something out of the Underworld! We forgot all about you." The big man chuckled in an attempt to ease the tension.

Several others laughed weakly, mindful of the palpable tension. Tempers flared anew as those to the rear of the surging crowd tried to shove their way ahead so they too could be a witness to the action. One of these, the fisherman Vilhjalm, shoved men out of the way and burst to the front beside the body of Ulfar, his best friend.

He glanced wildly from Ulfar to Gudbjartur. He summoned up the courage to speak. "You did not need to kill him!" he shouted.

Gudbjartur dropped into a crouch and pivoted to face the threat. His arm and shoulder muscles corded as he gripped the bloody axe at the ready. He fixed Vilhjalm with baleful eyes.

Gudbjartur's silence unnerved the hapless man. He made to bluster nonetheless, until Halfdan took control of the tense situation.

"Easy Gudbj. There is no need for any more." Halfdan gripped the iron-hard arm of his friend in an attempt to relax him. He looked at Vilhjalm. "You almost made a serious mistake. It is not wise to rush up on a man who has just violently killed another. No matter the reason."

Vilhjalm blustered loudly enough for all to hear. "He should not have killed him! I could have stopped Ulfar!"

"You could not stop him! You were not close enough. Gudbj stopped him from dishonoring himself and the einvigi the only way he could. He acted on my order." Halfdan's words carried passion to the silent onlookers.

Vilhjalm made to bluster again, but he quelled in the face of Halfdan's wrath.

"Enough! The duel is over and you will accept it. You must honor the einvigi. We all must or we are nothing! Without honor we are no better than animals!"

Vilhjalm averted his eyes. He muttered something unintelligible as he turned away.

Halfdan grabbed his arm and spun him around. He bathed the man in the force of his overpowering persona. "What did you say?" He spoke between gritted teeth. His hands crushed Vilhjalm's upper arms in a vice-like grip. "Do not mumble. Speak your mind, please!"

"I have nothing to say, Halfdan. Ulfar was my friend. I said what I felt about this fight. I will say no more, except he was a good man."

Halfdan relaxed his grip on the man and regained a semblance of control. "Yes, he was a good man. They are both good men. Ulfar dishonored us. He died for it. That is as it is, as it has always been with our people, and as it must be. He violated our law, our custom that makes us the people we are. He has paid the price for his mistake. Now, is there any man among you who wishes to take exception to the words I have spoken? Anyone?" His voice was flat. His eyes swept the crowd of men around the carnage.

No man came forward. Few looked directly at him. He continued in the same flat tone of voice. "Let this be the end to it then. Get Gizur to his tent and have his wounds bound up, Gudbj." He glanced at his lieutenant. He hoped the order would help calm the man.

The tension slowly ebbed from Gudbjartur. He shifted his feet from their rigidly held position and lowered the bloody axe. His eyes locked on Halfdan's for a moment. He nodded once and turned away. He pointed at Thorgill and Vilhjalm and motioned at Gizur with a lift of his chin. "Carry him to his tent. Somebody get Asa to tend to him." Gudbjartur wheeled away. He strode purposefully to the water's edge where he knelt on one knee and washed the congealed blood from the axe and himself.

Halfdan watched his friend as he walked away. As he turned back to the crowd, he saw that Thorgill and everyone else in the forefront stood suspended in the very same motionless stance as they gazed after Gudbjartur.

Halfdan caught Thorgill's eye in time to see him raise an eyebrow and shake his head once in wonder. Halfdan frowned and lifted his chin toward Gizur lying on the ground. Thorgill and Vilhjalm stooped, picked him up, and moved off toward the tents without a word. Two other men similarly removed the corpse of Ulfar.

The crowd began to disperse. None wanted to attract Halfdan's attention. He stood alone. His gaze rested on the only man he called friend. That man knelt at the waters edge and dried the blade of his axe with the bottom edge of his tunic.

Halfdan raised his eyebrows and sighed. He felt humbled, and more than a little awed. A flush of pride warmed his chest as he turned away.

Chapter Five

Fog crept inland from the fjord. It formed first in ragged pockets over the small ponds and puddles in the tundra before it cloaked the land in a damp, gray blanket.

A great white bear meandered through the tundra toward the fjord. His white coat was stained a dingy gray color streaked with rust and brown from the wetness of the tundra. He was a large solitary male. With forelegs bigger around than a man's waist, his every movement bespoke the awesome power of his rippling musculature.

He tested the faint onshore breeze with his sensitive nose. His head turned from side-to-side as he tried to filter the elusive scent of blood and smoke from the thickening fog. He came to a sudden halt, one foot suspended, his body gone rigid as the distinct odor of fresh blood filled his distended nostrils.

The fog drifted over him. He became all but invisible. He changed direction somewhat and picked up speed. Senses were on full alert. He homed on the blood spoor. It had been several days since he had feasted on the seal kill. Hunger alone drove him forward.

A dim glow was ahead, but the strong smell of wood smoke mixed with the hated smell of human caused him to veer to the side. He broke into a run. The frenzied bark of a dog close by further confused him. He swept by the startled guards and stumbled as a wave of intense pain came from the great bellows of his lungs. Wraith-like, the fog cloaked him. He wheeled on the barking animal at his heels. One swipe of a massive forepaw dashed the dog to gruel.

Thoroughly confused now by the pain in his chest and the cloying smell of blood, and disoriented by the noise and wood smoke that seemed to be all around him, he plowed in a frenzy of destruction into the packed humanity that materialized in his path.

He roared his challenge at the puny humans who scattered before his onslaught. His great forearms, tipped with rapier claws, ripped through all who stood in his path.

The unmistakable roars of an enraged bear, mixed with shouts of terror and confusion, came from the inshore portion of the large crowd of people still scattered around the scene of the einvigi.

Men grabbed spears, bows, arrows, and axes and ran toward the melee from every quarter. They quickly surrounded the animal. Their shouts added to his confusion and prevented further attacks on unarmed people. Every dog in the encampment circled and feinted. Their excited barks added to the noise and confusion. Two of their number came within range of his slashing forepaws and died for the effort.

The bear wheeled back and forth to confront each new threat. His confusion confined him within the circle of his tormentors. Each time he wheeled away toward a shout or feint another arrow slammed into his body from the opposite side. Several pierced his vitals.

In a fit of murderous rage at his tormentors, the brute heaved himself erect. He towered over the men who surrounded him and roared out his challenge.

Gudbjartur saw an opportunity when the bear stood up. He swept forward with a heavy spear poised at the ready. Every fiber of his being focused on the target, off center on the left side of the beast's chest, and he heaved the missile with all his strength. He followed through the cast into a crouch. His hand swept the axe from its belt loop. Coiled like a spring, he crouched in anticipation of the bear's next move.

The impact of the spear drove the bear back a step as the sharp blade sundered his vitals. The point narrowly missed the backbone as it slashed through tensed muscle to come out between his shoulder blades.

The ring of men drew back. They knew that Gudbjartur had dealt the bear a deathblow. Their shouts dwindled to murmurs as they warily watched their adversary.

The spear transfixed the bear, and his blood ran freely from many wounds. The great beast's roars stopped abruptly. A single lamb-like bleat came from his mouth. Abruptly he dropped to all fours. He stood still for a couple heartbeats, his face and lips slack. Slowly the great head began to swing back and forth. He continued to voice the soft, confused bleats of the cub he had been so long ago.

All the while, his heart pumped his lifeblood from the wounds. He bit at the spear shaft that protruded from his chest. His eyes squinted from the pain as his jaws worried the shaft. The beast swung weakly toward Gudbjartur. For a moment their eyes met. Then the bear collapsed in death without a sound.

His killers stood in silent tribute around the animal. Halfdan stood near the forefront of the men, his bow in hand, an arrow still nocked on the string. "By Thor, he is the biggest bear I have ever seen," he said.

"He is that," Gudbjartur agreed. He stood near the bear's head as the other men crowded around the corpse. First one, and then another slapped him on the back in congratulation for the deathblow.

"It took all of us. He was dying. I just finished him." Gudbjartur's glance swept the group of men and returned to the body of the bear.

"Perhaps." Halfdan looked across the bear's body at his lieutenant. "But your spear hurt him so badly he gave up the fight and bled to death."

Cries of pain and anguish drew the men's attention to the chaotic situation brought about by the bear's attack. Most of the injured had miraculously escaped fatal wounds, save for three untidy heaps. Two of these were dead and the third would soon join them.

Three men knelt beside the one who lived.

"It is Ottar. How can he still be alive? His head is crushed." Gorm looked at his companions as they knelt beside the man's body.

"Listen, he tries to say something." Bjorn leaned closer to hear over the din of the crowd. Ottar struggled to form words.

Gudbjartur held his arms above his head to get the attention of the crowd. "Quiet! Ottar tries to speak."

"Neck Cleaver." Ottar whispered faintly into Bjorn's ear.

"His sword! Neck Cleaver! He wants his sword. Quickly!" Bjorn pointed to the sword on the ground some feet away. One of the men slapped the haft of the bloody sword into Bjorn's outstretched hand. Bjorn placed it in Ottar's hand. He closed the stiffening fingers around the haft. Ottar's eyes flicked open for moment. He focused on Bjorn's face. Suddenly he stiffened out full length. A shudder shook the torn body. He sighed. A death rattle of air escaped his mouth and his eyes closed for the last time. Those close by bore witness as the spirit passed from his body.

Those who had been merely shaken up were helped under the awning to the warmth and comfort of the fire pit. Teams of men carried the seriously injured inside the tents.

Asa, the most gifted healer among them and a sorceress, seemed to be everywhere at once. "Thorkatla, bring my bag," she called to the crowd at large. The message passed from person to person until it reached her young daughter.

Thorkatla ran to fetch her mother's bag of potions and supplies from the tent where Asa had treated Gizur before the bear's attack. The young girl possessed many of her mother's gifts for healing and sorcery.

Mother and daughter quickly collected green leaves from certain of the low shrubs close at hand. They chewed the leaves to a paste as they worked over the injured. They spread a poultice of the paste over the wounds and bound them with leather or wool dressings. They cleaned and dressed minor cuts and scrapes with a salve concocted of equal parts goose grease, beeswax, and pine pitch. Their salve exhibited miraculous curative powers.

Asa organized the efforts of her many helpers, Ingerd, Thora, and Olga among them. She cared for the more seriously injured personally. Splints secured broken limbs; she stitched ripped flesh together and applied medicinal potions from her bag.

Claw marks and bite wounds were especially worrisome because of the danger of putrefaction. Asa had found the most effective remedy for serious wounds to be a red-hot iron. After she thoroughly washed the wounds with lye soap, she sealed all the deep gashes and puncture wounds in this manner.

"The irons are ready, Asa," Ingerd said, her voice low so as not to alarm the injured.

"Bring me one." Asa did not look up from stitching the ragged edges of a long rip in a woman's upper leg. When she had the hot iron, she nodded to her helpers and they took hold of the woman's legs and arms.

The woman's eyes flew open as she felt the heat of the iron near her flesh. She struggled against those who held her.

"What are you doing? No, Asa!"

"I must!" Asa grabbed the woman's face and turned it toward her. Thora forced a leather strap between her teeth. "Take it! Bite down! Or you will bite your tongue in half." Asa plunged the iron into the woman's flesh.

The woman screamed; the inhuman sound became muffled as she bit into the leather strap. The red-hot tip of the iron sizzled as it stanched the flow of blood and melted the edges of the wound together. The woman's screams echoed through the encampment. More than one gritted their teeth and silently thanked their favorite god it had not been them.

Halfdan sent Gudbjartur to gather the perimeter guards so they could explain why they failed to secure the encampment during the einvigi.

An obviously angry Halfdan paced in front of the guards as he berated them for what he regarded as dereliction of duty. "How could a white bear get into the camp so easily? By Hel, what were you all doing? You were to guard the encampment."

Gudbjartur watched his men become sullen at Halfdan's accusatory tone as they explained what happened.

"If not for the fog he could not have gotten by us," Gisli said. "When we saw him his head was up as he followed the blood spoor. He disappeared into the fog before we could do anything except blow a warning horn."

"Our dog started to bark just before the bear ran by our fire. We hit him with two arrows that made him stumble, but he did not slow down. We turned the dog loose; he died in the chase. We shouted and blew our horns, but most of you could not hear us because of the noise coming from the einvigi," Ormiga explained. "The boy who was killed must have heard the horns and turned just in time to receive the bear's charge. If the bear had not stopped to tear the boy to pieces we could not have gotten near enough to keep him from killing a great many more."

"We did our duty," another guard said. "It was as Gisli and Ormiga told you. The smell of meat and blood is everywhere. The fog came in and the bear was already running on the blood spoor when we saw him. By then it was too late."

"Blame the duel and the fog, Halfdan, not us," Ormiga said.

Halfdan glanced at each guard in turn before his eyes stopped on Ormiga, the last to speak. "We learned a lesson tonight. We know the great white bears are dangerous. Guards must be farther out from camp and closer together, as long as we are here in this place. We have enough meat now. It will be butchered and smoked as quickly as possible. Until then we must be more cautious. Gudbj, I am making you personally responsible for the safety of the encampment." Halfdan turned to his lieutenant. He felt the task would help get his friend's mind back to the present and off the einvigi. "Get as many men as you need. I want the camp guarded day and night. You all know what must to be done, now go and do it. I have other concerns here." He turned away and left the matter in the capable hands of Gudbjartur.

Halfdan approached the scene of the duel. He paused in thought. He happened to glance back toward the body of the bear and saw Gudbjartur detail two men to butcher the carcass.

He shook his head again in appreciation at the resiliency of his lieutenant and his attention to duty. He turned away, thankful the grisly work with the axe had not robbed Gudbjartur of his value to both himself and the expedition.

Halfdan seemed to be everywhere among his followers—a kind word here, a harsh word there, a hand extended where needed. His eyes darted around the assembly until they fell on Frida, the object of his quest. He strode toward her, grabbed her arm on the way by, and dragged her away from the others. "Come with me. I want to talk to you."

"Let go of my arm! You are hurting me," Frida said.

He ignored her plaintive cry and continued to drag her away from the camp proper.

She looked back at the people who witnessed her departure and extended her free hand in supplication. They ignored her. "You are hurting me," she repeated. She tried to pull free.

Halfdan stopped abruptly and grabbed both her upper arms. He pulled her face close to his. "Shut your mouth, Frida, or I will rip your arm off and beat you to death with it."

She slumped, cowed by his vehemence and helpless in his powerful grasp.

He held her helpless as a fly in a spider's web. His hot breath fanned her face as he struggled to form words through the red haze of his rage. "We are alone here. You have no crowd to perform for. I am not interested in anything you have to say. Listen carefully. You are responsible for two good men cutting each other to pieces in a duel. One is badly hurt. It will take him a long time to heal, if he ever heals. The other is dead. Three other people are also dead. Many are injured because the crowd made so much noise during the duel we did not hear the shouts and warning horns of the guards. I blame you for all of that."

Frida started to speak, but she snapped her mouth shut again as Halfdan's hands clamped down like a vise on her arms.

"Shut your mouth! Last warning!" Halfdan spoke through gritted teeth. "You can have every man in the expedition if you want. I do not care what you do. Unless you cause trouble. Then

I will care. You have fooled nobody. Gudbj had you figured out from the start. Now you have come to my attention. I will watch you. You are a troublemaker. But you will not cause any more trouble. Hear what I say, woman. No more!"

She stood extended on tiptoe, held in a grip that rendered her immobile. Her large, firm breasts, the nipples engorged with blood in her excitement, brushed his chest. A flicker of feeling briefly masked the anger in his eyes. He held her a little further away, inches from his face.

"You are a strong, intelligent woman. You could help in many ways. Think about what happened here and your part in it. Disregard what I say at your peril. You will not be warned again." He suddenly pushed her away with such force that she staggered backward a short distance. Without another word he turned and strode back into the encampment.

Unbowed and still full of fight, Frida glared at his broad back as he walked away. She rubbed circulation back into her tingling and bruised upper arms. She winced as the blood coursed back into her muscles. *Trouble?* she thought. *I have not even begun to cause you trouble. I will get even, you pig.*

* * *

Halfdan, Gudbjartur, and a group of men had assembled near the remains of the bear as the butchers dismembered the carcass. Halfdan already knew most of the story, except for a few details, and Gudbjartur provided them.

"The bear got the boy first, Halfdan. His mother ran in and tried to drag him away, but the bear hit her in the head and almost tore it off. She died instantly. The father, Ottar, fought the bear with his sword and cut him several times but the brute was so enraged he was hard to kill. He knocked Ottar down and crushed his skull. It only lasted a minute or two but Ottar fought like a Viking. His sword made these deep cuts in the bear's shoulders and chest," Gudbjartur said. He indicated the sword cuts with the toe of his shoe.

"He died with his sword in his hand," Bjorn said. "I put it there."

"The bear was slowed by the guard's two arrows and Ottar stopped him long enough for us to catch up and help kill him," Gisli said.

"Many more would have been killed if the bear had not stopped to tear up Ottar and his family." Thorgill glanced from Gudbjartur to Halfdan.

Gudbjartur listened silently. The other men repeatedly glanced at him expecting that he would enter the conversation. He locked eyes with Halfdan for a moment, but did not speak. The other men witnessed the wordless communication between the two but none interrupted.

Halfdan said nothing, his anger evident by his silence. Without a word to the group of men, he turned and walked toward the tents.

"We will get them ready for burial, Halfdan," Bjorn called.

Halfdan stopped and turned slowly around to face the men. He studied their faces as they watched him. "Prepare Ottar for a warrior's burial. His soul has already been carried to Valhalla by the Valkyries. We will honor him as a Viking warrior." Halfdan turned away again.

"And Ulfar? Will he, too, have a warrior's burial?" Gudbjartur called as Halfdan walked away.

Arrested in mid-stride by the question, Halfdan turned around once again. He gathered his thoughts as he regarded his lieutenant; he realized for the first time that Ulfar had slipped his mind in all the excitement.

The large group of men around Gudbjartur stood frozen in place, attentive, all eyes on Halfdan.

"I leave that decision to you, Gudbj. What do you think we should do?"

Taken aback by Halfdan's question, Gudbjartur frowned as his mind grappled for the right answer. "He made a serious mistake. As you said, he violated our law, the code we live by, and he died for it. He has paid for his mistake. He was a warrior. He died fighting but it was not the good fight. Had he killed Gizur it would have been a dishonor. Our honor is everything. He should be remembered as a good man and a warrior. I will remember him that way and I killed him. But, he did not die as a Viking and should not receive the same honor as one who dies in battle."

Halfdan regarded Gudbjartur, his expression pensive. His eyes shifted to the other men. He glanced from man to man; he paused on Vilhjalm, Ulfar's friend. The man returned his gaze for a couple heartbeats before he looked away. "So be it then. I agree with Gudbjartur's decision. Let Ulfar be given a warrior's burial, but he did not die as a Viking. The Valkyries will not carry him to Valhalla."

Halfdan's words were met with silence for a few heartbeats before a roar of agreement welled from the throats of those close enough to hear his words. He had called for the Viking burial ceremony to honor the slain warrior. He knew the spectacle would give his people something to think about other than loss.

Family and close friends of the dead and injured were stoic about death out of necessity. Life was hard. It required the concerted effort of everyone. Later there might be time for reflection. For now the business of life must continue. Men and women alike eagerly scattered to prepare for the age-old Viking burial tradition.

It was the hope of every man, as each went about his tasks, that he, too, would be chosen by the Valkyries to die a warrior's death; to be borne by them to Valhalla; to dwell with Odin in his Hall of the Slain for all time.

Halfdan's anger was obvious to everyone as he threw the tent's entry flap aside and stepped inside. He stooped to look more closely at the severely wounded Gizur. The man writhed in pain as Asa stitched up his wounds. To his credit not a sound escaped his lips while Halfdan looked on.

Those who tended Gizur and the people injured by the bear were loath to make eye contact with their chieftain as he watched the activity in the tent.

Everyone's attention fastened on Thorkatla as she entered the tent and began to chant. She walked slowly around the interior, paused at each of the injured people, and shook a large iron ring with iron rattles over them. She circled inside the tent to the entrance and Halfdan moved aside to give her room to pass. The girl paused in front of him, unfazed by his presence. Her dark eyes fastened on his. She shook the rattle once in front of the man who towered over her slight figure. With a lift of her chin, she continued on her way. She shook the rattle in every corner to ward off evil spirits. The loud metallic clatter of the rattle and the incantations that none but she and Asa understood riveted the attention of everyone. Not a person spoke, their minds filled with superstition. The girl finished the ceremony, glanced at Halfdan, and nodded.

All eyes shifted to Halfdan as he paced at the tent's entrance. "It is done, the fight is over. Good people died and were injured tonight because we all let our guard down. There will be no more trouble over Frida, or any other woman. Share her, do whatever you want with her, but the next man who fights over her will deal with me." He looked down on the prostrate Gizur.

The man said nothing, subdued by Halfdan's righteous anger and the pain of his knife wounds. They were all aware that Halfdan was right in his anger toward them, and himself, for allowing such a thing to happen.

Slow to anger usually, Halfdan was a berserker in a fight and not to be trifled with. Others had felt the caress of his unbound rage, and paid the ultimate price for invoking the beast that dwelt within. He was their leader and he had been chosen for his many abilities.

"All right then. Continue with your work." Halfdan turned and drew the tent flap aside to leave.

"Wait, Halfdan! We have concerns we want to talk to you about." Thora approached him.

Halfdan turned around and looked at Thora. *I was afraid of this. She is going to bring up her beliefs,* he thought. He folded his arms and waited in resignation. Halfdan was a traditionalist, a follower of the Old Norse ways, and he did not share her beliefs. But he resolved to allow her to spew them forth for a time. Thora was an outspoken convert to the new religion. He knew she would bring up her Christian beliefs because of the planned Viking ceremonial. "I am listening, Thora." He glanced at the other women as they joined her.

"We think Ottar, Gyda, and the boy Ari should be given a Christian burial." Thora glanced at the other women to elicit their support.

"Yes." Helga, another recent convert, joined in. "Gyda, Ottar's wife, was a Christian too. She would not want to be buried in a pagan ceremony."

The women recoiled slightly at the flash of anger in Halfdan's eyes at the veiled insult to his beliefs.

Thora continued nonetheless, her resolve up to the task as she confronted her chieftain. "It is not right to bury them without the proper ceremony. Many people feel the same way about this."

"No, not many people!" Ingerd stepped up in front of Thora. "You and a few others are Christian. The majority of us follow the old religion. And we are not pagans, Helga." She glanced pointedly at the woman. "We do not worship this new Christ because we do not believe in him." Turning her attention back to Thora, Ingerd pointed a finger at her. "Why, you are named for the great god, Thor." Ingerd tapped Thora on the chest. "You had better stay in this tent. What you have said may anger Thor and he will cast a bolt of lightning and slay you."

A look of superstitious dread crossed Thora's face as she glanced toward the tent entrance. She shook her head in denial. "No, I do not believe that anymore! None of us do." She glanced at her supporters.

They looked away. Their new beliefs were not strong enough to overcome their fear of the old gods.

"You do not look convinced to me. I would not want to be the one to anger Thor; he will not forget, and he is vengeful." Ingerd continued pitilessly, a slight smile on her lips.

Halfdan listened with growing amusement to the discussion.

"You can believe whatever you want, Ingerd. Some of us do believe that Gyda and her son, Ari, should have a Christian burial." Thora glanced at Halfdan, a question in her eyes.

"Have your Christian burial, Thora, for mother and son. Ottar will receive a Viking warrior's burial. Both ceremonies will be held in the morning," Halfdan said.

"Halfdan, there is one other matter to decide. We were discussing it when you came in." Ingerd waved her hand to include her companions.

Halfdan gave her his attention.

"Gudbj and I want to adopt Ottar's and Gyda's other son, Lothar. He is the same age as our son, Ivar. They are best friends."

"I know about that. Gudbj mentioned it to me," Halfdan said. "The council will make that decision after the burials. I have already spoken to them."

Ingerd nodded. "Thank you, Halfdan."

"Is there anything else?" He glanced at each woman. None responded. "No? Let us continue with our duties then." He turned to leave the tent and paused at the entrance. "We all have much to do before this day is over."

The women glanced at one another as he walked out.

"Well, I am glad that is over." Thora exhaled, relieved the matter was settled. She had not expected Halfdan to agree.

The others laughed at her relief. They were as glad as she that Halfdan had given in so easily. All were indeed satisfied with the way things had turned out.

* * *

After a restless night, people awakened to a soggy morning and began to move about the encampment. Light fog gave an opaque quality to the fjord. Moisture clung to every surface. Steam rose into the still air as the sun topped the ridge to the east and beamed warmth down into the fjord.

Gudbjartur stepped out of his tent, sniffed the still air, and surveyed the fjord to the limit of his vision. He always assessed the day to come and people valued his opinion on what to expect from the weather gods. *The sun will burn this fog off by midmorning and the Fog Giant will flee the fjord,* he mused. He turned at a slight sound from behind; his face split in a grin as Ingerd stepped from their tent.

"Good morning!" Ingerd always had a radiant smile for him.

He folded her into his arms and kissed her tenderly. "A fine soft morning it is, my love."

"Yes, it is soft. The fog always softens the hard edges." A look of concern clouded her face. She searched his face. "Are you all right now?"

"Now? What do you mean?"

"You know, the einvigi. What you had to do."

"Forget about that, Ingerd. Of course I am all right. Ulfar
made a mistake, and I killed him for it. I feel nothing. I did
my duty as I saw it, as Halfdan requested of me."

"I know. But you are different. You act differently than
before."

"No! You are mistaken."

"No, you are different. We all know of your bond with Halfdan, especially me. Sometimes you scare people, Gudbj. You
are so protective of him. Ivar and Lothar are in awe of you."

He held her at arms length, and his eyes searched her face.
"So, the boys are in awe of me. It is good for them to know of
honor and duty. It will make men of them." He paused before
he continued, his eyes locked on hers. "You already know of
my feelings, what drives me, Ingerd. I will speak of this now,
but never again. Halfdan is my chieftain, my friend. I would
die for him, and he would die for me. I killed Ulfar at his
order, before he could dishonor the einvigi or himself. When
Ulfar pushed Halfdan away, something snapped in me. He
dishonored my chieftain. And I killed him for it. That is all I
will ever say about the matter."

"All right. Thank you for your explanation. I will never
bring it up again. Are you hungry? Well, I am."

He watched her run toward the cook's fire. A slight smile
pulled at the corners of his mouth. He shook his head at the
antics of women, especially his wife, and headed toward the
smell of food. *She did not give me a chance to answer. Of course
I am hungry. She had the whole conversation with herself.* He
doubted he would ever get used to the speed and frequency
at which she could change subjects.

The soup bubbled in the kettles. The smell of fat, meat, and
barley drifted about on the moist air. The rich brew conveyed
a promise of something hot to drive away the chill, and people lined up with their bowls and spoons. The usual banter in
the line was not present on this day as everyone hurried to
finish. The task before them provided both a somber air to
dampen spirits and excitement to lift them at the prospect of
the ceremonies to come.

A single, drawn out horn blast pierced the ragged remnants
of the morning fog. The signal called everyone but the guards

to the burials. Every man came attired in full battle regalia. Women were dressed in their best finery and jewelry. Even the smallest children shone like new pennies. As the people assembled at the burial site, their colorful attire, the flash of jewelry, and the weapons and armor were a sight none would soon forget.

Gudbjartur and Ingerd, resplendent in finery that befitted their station, took up a position that afforded an unrestricted view of the grave site.

Ivar and Lothar stood at their side. Uncomfortable in their best togs, but on their best behavior, the boys tried to still the sense of excitement that simmered in their breasts.

Halfdan sought them out. Gudbjartur turned as his chieftain stepped up beside him. He greeted him with a nod.

Ingerd was not so reserved. "You look magnificent, Halfdan." Her glance took in his chain mail jerkin and his helmet, shield, and sword.

"And so do both of you." His eyes swept over his lieutenant. He took note of the helmet, chain mail jerkin, and the sheen of the axe at his belt, and nodded in approval. Their eyes held for a heartbeat. Words were unnecessary between them. His attention shifted to Ingerd. "I do not think I have ever seen you look so beautiful, Ingerd. The gods and your men approve." He indicated Gudbjartur with a lift of his chin.

Ingerd blushed to her hair roots and beamed at the two men. "Why, thank you."

They smiled at her pleasure. Halfdan turned his smile to include Ivar and Lothar. "Boys, you, too, look good." Both were fit to burst with pride that their chieftain would even notice them. "I am certain Gudbj has already spoken to you. I want to add my own thoughts. What you are about to witness is seldom seen these days. Two warriors are to be buried. One died without honor, but he is a warrior nonetheless. Ottar died as a Viking, in battle." His eyes fastened on Lothar. "We have gathered to honor him; to pay homage to him as a Viking warrior. You will hold the honor this ceremony bestows on your father in your heart for the remainder of your life." The boy said nothing, his eyes downcast. Halfdan squeezed his shoulder and looked over the crowd. "We are all here, I think." He waved to the men who stood by for his signal. The ceremonies began.

The four bodies, scrubbed clean of all signs of their violent deaths, were dressed in their finest attire. They rested near three shallow graves chiseled from the rocky, permanently frozen ground.

Thorgill and three helpers lowered the bodies of Gyda and her son Ari into a common grave. A small crowd had gathered out of curiosity as none had ever before seen a Christian burial. Most were women and children as the majority of men either had no religious beliefs or were lifelong followers of Old Norse religious tradition, and had no interest in the new religion. People shuffled closer to hear.

Thora led the brief Christian ceremony. She gazed pointedly over the small crowd, and waited for the shuffles and muted talk to subside. Then, in a clear, strong voice, she began. "Dear Lord, Jesus Christ, we beseech you to receive the souls of Gyda Egilsdattur and her son, Ari Ottarsson, into your realm. We commend their bodies to the ground in the certain hope and belief that they will rise again on the Day of Judgment to join with you in the Kingdom of Heaven for eternity." She glanced at her four assistants. "From dust, we come."

"And to dust, we shall return," Helga and her companions answered.

Thora paused as Lothar and Ivar walked up and looked into the grave. She glanced toward Ottar's grave at Ingerd, who stood alone watching her two young men. The two boys stood shoulder to shoulder gazing at the corpses. Lothar looked up at her. There were no tears; his expression conveyed a certain resolve. She thought he looked much older than she knew him to be. He and Ivar turned and walked back toward Ingerd. Thora watched them a moment and returned to the ceremony.

"In the name of our Lord Jesus Christ, we ask these things," Thora said.

"Amen," her assistants answered.

"Go, the ceremony is finished." Thora nodded to Helga, who placed a bit of cloth over each face, and then they stepped back. Thorgill and his men came forward, filled in the grave, and mounded it over with earth and large rocks.

A short distance away, Vilhjalm, Helge, and two helpers lowered Ulfar's corpse, attired in full battle array, into the second grave. Then they ritualistically killed his weapons so his spirit could not harm the living. They broke or bent knife and spear blades, snapped arrow and spear hafts, and pierced the iron boss on his shield. Then they arranged the weapons on either side of his body for his use in the afterlife. The grave was filled in and mounded over. Large rocks arranged in the shape of a ship were rolled into position.

Ottar was buried in the third grave. Driftwood filled the grave and rose above ground to waist level. The interlaced driftwood at the top of the pyre created a flat-topped parapet over which a blue and red woolen pall was draped.

Ottar's corpse rested atop an improvised litter of three iron-bound, wooden shields, laid bosses down, supported on heavy spear hafts, and covered with a tanned deer robe. The corpse wore a jerkin of thick, overlapped leather plates and an iron-reinforced leather helmet.

The ululating wail of the horns heralded the Viking burial ritual. The horns would sound at intervals until the corpse was consumed in the flames. The wail of the horns, each of a different pitch, caused chills to course through every breast as the six litter bearers, three on each side, picked up the litter and carried it to the graveside, where it was placed atop the pall-draped parapet.

Other men began the process of killing Ottar's weapons. They had pierced the iron bosses in the center of the three shields to release their spirits before they placed his corpse on top. Now they snapped or bent double his sword, spear, bow, arrows, and knives.

The sword, Neck Cleaver, rested atop his chest, and both hands enfolded the haft. The men arranged his other weapons to either side of the corpse.

Vilhjalm led Ottar's dog to the graveside. Thorgill grasped its snout in one hand, pulled the animal's head up, and cut its throat with one slash of his knife. The body still trembled when Vilhjalm laid it over Ottar's legs.

Two men arrived with iron scoops of live coals and thrust them into scattered piles of kindling and wood shavings at the base of the parapet. Eager flames licked at the wood. They spread quickly through the parapet, which supported the corpse. A roar rose from the many throats. Startled seabirds took flight. Dogs and unfettered livestock ran wildly about.

The fire spread through the wood of the pyre and increased in intensity until the heat caused those in the front ranks to recoil to a safer distance. The corpse slowly sank into the flames as the wood support burned away.

Ingerd stood between the two boys, her arms around each. She glanced at Lothar. His face was flushed from the heat of the pyre. Jaw muscles clenched as he stared through tear-filled eyes. A single tear coursed down his cheek.

The eager flames began to consume the body and everyone watched in fascination for the plume of oily black smoke that would tell them the corpse of Ottar ascended into the cold air. Another great roar came from the spellbound throng. Super-stition had it that the Valkyries, the handmaidens of Odin, would come for the warrior at this moment. Men and women would later swear they heard the song of the Valkyries as they carried Ottar to Valhalla.

Warriors shook their weapons in the air, banged on their shields, and shouted: "Odin!" The ancient, drawn-out war cry echoed through the fjord and across the landscape to alert the god of war to the arrival of another warrior in the Hall of the Slain.

The dreaded war cry of the Viking host was still heard throughout the Christian world. There beat in every breast that day a heart filled with a firm belief in the power of Odin. Pagan and Christian alike were overwhelmed as chills coursed through their bodies.

The crowd milled and shifted about while individuals exchanged muted acknowledgments of the events they had witnessed. Others simply stared into the coals of the funeral pyre, transfixed by the grandeur of the ritual.

"I heard the song of the Valkyries," one said.

"I saw them in the smoke bearing Ottar away on his shield to the Underworld!" another exclaimed.

Not to be outdone, Thorgill told them what he had seen. "I, too, saw the Valkyries bear Ottar away. Far in the distance, almost hidden in the plume of smoke, I thought I saw Odin, astride Sleipnir, his eight-legged horse. He fixed his one eye on the Valkyries as they bore Ottar away, and beckoned them to follow. As they joined him he wheeled Sleipnir and rode away to Valhalla." This statement ended further speculation. No one had anything to add; Thorgill's tale could not be bested.

After the coals of the pyre cooled enough to allow the site to be approached, the grave was filled in and mounded over with earth and stones. Large rocks were gathered and arranged in the shape of a ship, as with Ulfar's grave. That done, the crowd dispersed.

Ingerd walked away from the grave sites with the boys. Ivar and Lothar had not said a word, but Ingerd felt compelled to help Lothar if she could. Even Ivar, who, like his father, seldom showed emotion, had his arm around his friend's thin shoulders. Lothar's eyes were downcast and he scuffed his shoes at pebbles as they walked. Ingerd glanced at him again. *He is brave for one so young, but he has lost his entire family. He must mourn them sooner or later.*

"Let us be alone." Ivar stopped and looked at his mother. "Lothar will be all right. I am with him."

Her breast filled with pride and love for her son but concern remained nonetheless. "Lothar?" Ingerd bent toward him, a question in her eyes.

"I will be all right, Ingerd. My mother and father were brave. I am proud of them."

Ingerd swallowed the lump in her throat. "And well you should be proud of them."

The boys stood straight and tall, watching her.

She was almost overcome with feelings of pride. Before she lost her own closely reined composure, she decided to let them go. "Do not stray far from the encampment. I will keep a lamp lit for your return."

* * *

Ingerd intercepted Thora and Olga on their way to check the wounded before they turned in for the night. "I am glad this day is done," Ingerd observed as she joined them.

"Yes, we are all exhausted." Olga rubbed the small of her back, stretched her neck, and sighed.

"We would not be so tired if we were not better able to cope with misery than most of the others. Sometimes I think they are the smart ones. Why, we could be as drunk as the rest of them by now." Thora added with a chuckle.

Olga laughed. "I could do with a good draft of mead right now."

"Not me," Ingerd said. "All I want is my bed. I am proud that our disposition and skill is why we always help Asa and Thorkatla with the wounded."

"So are we, Ingerd. So are we." Thora sighed and stretched her tired muscles. "How is Lothar? We saw you walk with him and Ivar."

"He will be fine. Ivar is with him and I think that is exactly what the both of them need—each other."

"Lothar is tougher than he looks. He has lost everything," Thora said.

"No, not everything; he has us. We are his family now."

Her two friends simply nodded in agreement. There was nothing more to say.

"All right, sleep well, you two." Ingerd headed toward her tent. Gudbjartur was not in evidence but she did not expect him to be. He always had something to do, something to check on. As she walked through the encampment her mind filled with thoughts of her brave boys. *I hope the council allows Gudbj and me to adopt Lothar. He has always spent a lot of time with us. Now he is part of the family and we can raise him with Ivar.*

* * *

In many of the tents, in spite of the exhaustion brought on by hard work and the excitement of the burials, sleep did not come right away. People seemed loath to lie down and close their eyes. Many lounged on the benches and talked while they puttered with odd tasks.

One tent was occupied by a group of men. Oil lamps hung from the upright ends of the benches along both sides of the tent. Other lamps hung on waist-high iron lamp stakes thrust into the dirt floor. Sufficient illumination bathed the interior for the occupants to make equipment repairs, or whet knives, weapons, or tools while they participated in the conversation.

There were thirteen men in the tent. They had asked Gudbjartur to stop by before he turned in. They had questions for him.

Thorgill, the most forthright among them, sat hunched over the coals of an iron brazier on the dirt floor. He combed lice from his red hair and beard and dropped them into the brazier. He paused in his endeavors and looked at Gudbjartur. "Some do not think we should sail to the south from here. They would rather go to Leifsbudir as originally planned."

Gudbjartur did not answer for a moment. He examined the newly whetted edge of his axe. Setting the axe and whetstone aside, he regarded Thorgill thoughtfully. "Are you one of those, Thorgill?"

Not liking the direction his question had taken them, Thorgill answered. "Do not misunderstand me, Gudbj. I will do whatever Halfdan says. All of us will."

"He would not want to think otherwise." Gudbjartur interjected mildly. He glanced at each man in turn.

Thorgill continued in a slightly different vein. "We question if this is the right thing for us to do, Gudbj. We do not know what lies south of here, but we do know what awaits us at Leifsbudir."

"We sail south from here because we do not know what lies down there, and Halfdan wants to know. After much discussion the other captains and I agreed. The decision has been made. We sail south."

Thorgill was not satisfied. "I know you can not disagree with Halfdan. We are not asking you to. Some of us do not feel comfortable that such an important decision was made without our opinion being asked."

"I do disagree with Halfdan if I think he is wrong. He is not wrong on this. He is our chieftain. We owe him our loyalty. I will always make certain he has our loyalty. Does he?"

Several men nodded in agreement. They did not wish Gudbjartur to think they were part of a move against Halfdan.

Thorgill spread his hands. "We are loyal to Halfdan. We want to be certain before we sail so far into the unknown that it is the right thing for us to do. That is all I meant."

"I will tell him of your concerns. Or you can tell him yourself if you wish?"

"No, I will wait until he talks to all of us about it." Thorgill looked at his comb as he gathered his thoughts. "By Thor, I do not want to ask Halfdan such a question. You are better at it than I. He is less likely to get mad at you."

"That is the reason I do it instead of you—because I am better at it." He picked up the axe and tested the edge with his thumb. "I am certain he will want to clear the matter up for everyone. Until he does I think you all need to do your work and not discuss this matter further. Before we sail you will all feel we are doing the right thing. He will explain it or he will send me to explain it to you. Either way you will know why the decision has been made." He sighed as he got to his feet. "Now, I am tired and so are all of you. I am going to see if Ingerd is awake and will still talk to me after all that has happened this day." Chuckles and a ribald comment or two followed his attempt at humor.

"I will see you all tomorrow. Let us hope the drizzle stops so the meat and fish will dry and we can sail from this place." He placed his axe in the loop on his belt and stepped out through the tent flap. The men looked at the swinging tent flap for a moment.

Thorgill shook himself from his reverie. "I remember when Haakon forged that axe for him."

"And so do I." The memory was almost tangible as the voice came from the midst of the silent men as each relived the moment of violence they all shared and preferred to let lie.

* * *

Gudbjartur made his way toward the encampment perimeter to check the guard positions before he turned wearily toward his own tent. Along the way he ran into Ingerd.

"So, there you are. I did not expect to see you for awhile."

"I am finished. Where are the boys?"

"I do not know. They will be along soon, though." Ingerd glanced at her silent husband as they walked slowly, swinging their clasped hands like children.

She felt talkative. "Have you ever seen a Viking burial?"

"No."

"Is that all you have to say? No is not an answer."

"No is the answer to the question you asked, Ingerd. It means, no, I have not ever seen a Viking burial before."

"I want to talk about what we witnessed. Who knew how the ceremony should be?"

"All the men knew. It is passed down from our fathers."

"Well, I did not know. Why is it that only men know?"

He snorted at her difficult mood and stopped to watch her face. "Only men are warriors, and only warriors can go to Valhalla."

"That is not so, Gudbj. Frida is a warrior. Many women can fight. I, too, can fight."

"Frida is not a warrior, Ingerd. Oh, she is adept with a bow. Killing a deer is one thing. Killing a man who tries to kill you is different. And I know Norse women can fight. Life is a fight. But I do not ever want you to have to fight. Leave the fights to me and others like me."

She stood with hands on hips, one foot before the other, a broad smile on her face.

"What is so funny?"

"Nothing," she chuckled. "But I made you talk, and that is what I wanted."

He grinned back at her. "Sometimes I think you manipulate me."

"I would never do that, you great oaf." She smiled from under lowered eyelashes. "Come on, let us find our tent."

In the comfortable security of the tent, alone for the moment, he helped her fill the soapstone lamps with whale oil. She twisted new lichen wicks for the lamps that needed a replacement and dropped them into the open bowl of each. Then she searched through the top layer of ashes in a small iron bucket that they kept filled with coals and the ashes to preserve them. Finding what she sought, she carefully clamped a coal in her tongs, blew it to life, and lit the lamps and charcoal brazier. He watched her as she worked. A slight smile played around his mouth and the corners of his eyes. He caught her eye and patted the sleeping robes he lounged on.

She wiped her hands on her apron. With her eyes locked on his, she slowly untied her scarf and dropped it on the pile of dirty clothing. She took hold of the fat single braid coiled at the back of her head, unbraided it, and shook her long, blond hair loose. Then she disrobed.

He followed every movement; the slight smile remained fixed as she walked slowly toward his outstretched arms.

"What about the boys?" Her voice was husky.

"Never mind the boys." He drew her under their sleeping robes.

* * *

Gudbjartur awakened to a cold, clear morning. A light breeze blew from the northwest. After his morning ablutions he decided a short walk might remove the kinks of sleep from his muscles. He did not walk far before he came upon a small pond. A large, flat-sided rock near the pond's edge formed a natural backrest and seemed to beckon. He took a seat on the bed of lichen at its base. The morning sun reflected its heat from the rock and he leaned back to survey the countryside. Flushes of warmth coursed through his body. Normally unaffected by the weather in his environment, he realized how good the warmth felt as his eyes scanned the vista before him.

He chuckled to himself at the antics of a mother eider duck as she tried to keep two of her ducklings from running into the pond. They were too quick for her.

She had eight offspring in line astern as she waddled in Gudbjartur's direction along the pond's edge. Her other two ducklings happily paddled just offshore, chasing down water scooters on the pond's surface. She stopped and scolded them until they joined their siblings on the shore. In moments the same two ducklings quit the group again and launched into the water in a flurry. This caused a stampede of all the ducklings back into the water to join their troublesome siblings. Mother duck waddled back and forth along the water's edge as she tried to get her brood back ashore.

He laughed aloud.

Alarmed, the mother duck—she had not detected his presence a matter of feet away—squawked a loud warning and flew into the pond, quacking for her brood to follow. Her ducklings flapped their little wings and scuttled across the surface of the pond to their mother's side. Finally she had them in one place. She shook her tail happily and led her brood away.

Halfdan chanced to walk up at that exact moment.

"What do you laugh at?" Halfdan stopped and looked down at his friend.

"I have been watching that eider duck. She has had quite a time with her ducklings." Gudbjartur gestured toward the pond as he started to get to his feet.

Halfdan motioned for him to stay put and took a seat next to him. He leaned back against the rock. A contended sigh escaped his lips as the warmth coursed through his body.

Neither man spoke for a few moments as their eyes followed the progress of the duck family. Both appeared completely at ease. Gudbjartur had his hands folded in his lap and his legs crossed at the ankles. Halfdan sat with one leg drawn up. His arm rested loosely over his knee.

"This is relaxing." Halfdan's eyes surveyed the immediate area. "We should take more time to enjoy such simple things."

Gudbjartur glanced at his chieftain, a question in his furrowed brow.

Halfdan turned his head and made eye contact. "I have nothing special for today. Tomorrow I want you to gather the ship captains and meet me at my tent for a brief council. We have matters of importance to discuss."

Both men got to their feet. Their eyes followed the duck family as they rejoined a flock of their kind.

Gudbjartur stretched and glanced at Halfdan. "All right. I will tell them. Is midmorning all right?"

Halfdan nodded absentmindedly, his eyes on the pond. Gudbjartur shrugged and headed back to the encampment.

* * *

Before sunup the next morning, Gudbjartur quietly left his tent. He paused at a handy water bucket just outside the entrance, dropped the sealskin cloak that Ingerd had made for him on the ground, and leaned over to wash his face. He plunged his hands through the skim of ice and into the icy water, gasped at the sting, and scrubbed the sleep from his face and eyes. He ran the fingers of both hands through the tangled mass of his hair several times. As the water dripped from his beard, he looked around the encampment and found that all was well. He bent over to retrieve the sealskin cloak and shrugged into it. As he walked slowly toward the camp's perimeter he fastened the two ends of the cloak together over his right shoulder with a plain, iron ring pin.

The six guards had stationed themselves in the dark areas between each fire of the semicircular perimeter to avoid being blinded by the light. Gudbjartur walked the perimeter and talked to each man in turn.

At the last station, the guard, Gisli, spoke as he walked up. "Strangers have come in the night, Gudbj. Four boats, each with a single man." He gestured to the north shoreline of the encampment.

"Why was I not awakened?" Gudbjartur tone carried an edge.

"Because they have only been here a short time, and they have not moved at all. There are only four men, and I did not think there was any danger, or I would have sounded the alarm. I think they wait for the dawn."

Gudbjartur peered into gloom. "I can barely see them." He walked along the shoreline to a rocky outcrop, climbed atop it, and strained to pierce the semidarkness.

Within an hour the sky began to lighten with the coming dawn. The four boats emerged as distinct shapes as darkness retreated. Gudbjartur was able to see from his vantage point that they were similar to the Skraeling boats in Greenland. As he watched, he noted the rim of the dim yellow sun peek above the eastern horizon through holes in the clouds. A bank of fog and low moisture-laden clouds began to form over the waters of the fjord and the sea to the north. They promised rain later in the day. The air was cold and the slight breeze freshened. He could smell the smoke from the rekindled cook fire and hear early risers move about. He sniffed the air like the wild animal he was. Unconsciously he recognized each smell for what it represented and his brain registered no threat.

Gudbjartur regarded the changing conditions with distaste. He hoped the rain would hold off long enough for the women to finish smoking the meat. Most of it had already air-dried. The cold wind had sped up the process but the possibility of fog and drizzle made it necessary to build smudge fires to speed the cure. His mind wandered to the effort expended to finish the curing. He had had racks constructed of whatever wood and rope was not being used for some other purpose. The complete lack of wood this far north, except for driftwood, made it necessary to venture far afield to collect the necessary wood from the long shoreline. Ropes rigged between every imaginable impromptu prop supported vast quantities of meat and fish smoking and drying. The perimeter guards kept the smudge fires smoldering all night. The racks of meat needed only another day or so to be dried and packed away aboard ship. Thankfully, piles of seal and whale blubber had been reduced to oil and poured into barrels. As it solidified the barrels were stored aboard the ships, replacing some of the ballast stones. All that remained was the curing.

Gudbjartur could see the four boats distinctly now. He thought it best to go wake up Halfdan. He rose stiffly and stood for a moment longer to watch the boats. Then he strode toward Halfdan's tent.

He paused at the entry flap. "Wake up, Halfdan."

"I am awake. I will be out in a minute." Halfdan's sleep-blurred voice was barely audible.

Gudbjartur grinned in delight. Halfdan had been sound asleep, no matter what he said.

The man who suddenly threw back the tent flap and walked out seemed awake enough. "Is something wrong?" Halfdan asked.

"Strange boatmen came in the night. Gisli watched them for a while before I woke up. He decided they posed no danger because there were only four of them. I watched them for quite a while myself and they have not moved. They just sit there in their boats. They look similar to the Skraelings we have in Greenland."

"Where? Halfdan cleared his throat as he rubbed the last vestige of sleep from his face.

Gudbjartur pointed up the beach. Halfdan followed him to a small rise where they could observe the strangers beyond the beached ships on the encampment side of the river.

The boats blended perfectly with the shoreline. They were hard to pick out of the deep shadows as the light of early morning had not yet reached the shoreline. Halfdan cupped a hand to shield his eyes from the sun. As his eyes adjusted to the gloom he saw them.

Each long, low-slung boat held but one occupant who sat upright in the middle.

"They still have not moved," Gudbjartur said. "They gave no indication they saw me, but I know they did."

"How long have they been there? Halfdan asked, as he studied the boats.

"About four hours. Gisli said they were all towing something when he first saw them. They pulled it into the shore, just around that little point." Gudbjartur pointed to the uneven, rocky shoreline to the north. "Then they paddled down to where they are now. They have not moved at all since then."

Gudbjartur and Halfdan walked slowly toward the boatmen.

All four boatmen glided effortlessly from the shoreline with a few flicks of their paddles as the two men approached.

They stopped in a group about two ship lengths offshore and watched the Northmen's measured approach. The sun flashed on the blades of their double-ended paddles as they easily maneuvered around one another.

Halfdan carried only a belt knife, but Gudbjartur was armed with a spear and the ever-present axe. As they reached a point on the shoreline opposite the four boats, Halfdan spoke loud enough for his voice to carry to the boatmen. "Their boats are pointed at both ends and are covered with some kind of skin. If they are like the boats we see around Greenland, the hide will be walrus." He studied the men and their equipment with interest. "They all have lances or spears lashed to the boat deck in front of the hole they sit in. I do not see any bows and arrows."

"I did not see any, either. I do not think they want any trouble. They are hunters. I am sure they saw all the guards. They waited for the camp to begin to stir to see how many of us are here."

"You may be right. They seem to be as curious about us as we are about them. I would like to trade with them, to show them we are friendly, but it does not look like they have anything to trade. Maybe they will want to trade whatever it was they towed around the point. We will see."

He looked back toward camp as somebody shouted and he saw three boys run along the beach in their direction. "What is all the commotion?"

Gudbjartur saw his son, Ivar, in the lead. He walked toward them and raised his hands. "Stop! Do not alarm our visitors."

The appearance of the boys had exactly the opposite affect on the boatmen. Instead of alarm, the four men talked among themselves.

"Let the boys come." Halfdan waved the boys forward. "These men are not afraid. One of them even smiles."

Halfdan raised his hand palm out in the universal sign of peaceful greeting, and two of the boatmen replied in kind. He turned as the boys approached and chuckled at their appearance. They had no vests or coats in spite of the chill morning air. All three wore gray or brown woolen pullovers, tied with lengths of leather rope at the waist. Their legs were bare from the knee down, and their feet were clad in ankle-high leather shoes. Shoulder-length unkempt hair, held from their eyes with identical leather headbands, gave each a comical tousled appearance. No doubt the reason the boatman smiled. He chuckled to himself and shook his head. Each boy carried a small knife on his rope belt, thrust into a plain leather scabbard. At the front of the belt was the usual leather pouch to hold all the treasures picked up during the day.

Ivar and Lothar were almost identical in height. They were tall, well formed, and had blond hair and blue eyes. They looked so much alike they could be twins. The other boy, whose name Halfdan did not know, was shorter, sported a full head of curly red hair, a mass of freckles, and did not appear as sure of himself as his companions.

Each boy clutched a chunk of whale skin with oily blubber attached that he had grabbed before running off to begin the new day's round of adventure.

"Come here, boys." Halfdan dropped to one knee. "I want you to wave at those men and ask them to paddle ashore. Just talk to them in a normal tone; say whatever you want, but do not shout. Do you understand what I want you to do?

"Yes, Halfdan," Ivar said. "But do they speak our language?

Halfdan glanced up at Gudbjartur with a twinkle in his eye. "I doubt they do, but it will not matter. Just talk to them; that will be enough. We want to be friends with these men. You boys can help us do that. Go now." He urged them forward.

The boys moved up the beach. Halfdan and Gudbjartur heard noises from the encampment as curious early risers strolled toward them. The same thought occurred to both men simultaneously.

"I will tell them to stay back and pass the word to everyone else what we are doing." Gudbjartur said over his shoulder, as he headed back to the encampment.

Halfdan turned his attention back to the boys' efforts to communicate with the boatmen.

Ivar held his blubber out to the boatmen. "Here, come eat some of my whale blubber." Ivar spoke in a normal tone with no sign of hesitation or fear.

The boy's offer got the response Halfdan hoped for. The Skraelings slowly paddled toward the shore.

Halfdan did not wish to alarm the men with his imposing stature so he remained in a crouch.

"Come forward, you two." Halfdan gestured to Lothar and the redheaded boy. "Talk to these men. Offer them some of your whale blubber. I will not let them harm you."

Both boys approached tentatively, their faces stiff with fright.

"Lothar, come down here with Ivar and me. You, son, what is your name? He spoke to the smallest member of the trio.

"I am Yola," the boy squeaked.

"Yola. Very well. Come here son." Halfdan spoke gently, his hand extended toward the boy.

This exchange, observed by the boatmen, led them to believe they were in no imminent danger. At a word from one of them, the men beached their boats and stood grouped on the shore.

Similarly clad in knee-length, hooded, pullover parkas, the men had the same bowed legs, straight black hair, and narrow slit-eyes as the people Halfdan had traded with in Greenland. Their dress, down to the pants and boots, was almost identical. A ship's length separated them from Halfdan and the boys. They were not armed.

Halfdan turned toward the encampment and saw Gudbjartur. He walked back without the spear he had carried. He, too, had seen the Skraelings were not armed.

The three boys, urged on by Halfdan, walked toward the four men. They held out the whale blubber as they walked, much like they would to entice and catch an animal.

One of the boatmen said something to his companions and they laughed aloud.

Ivar continued forward, his hand still extended forward. Lothar and Yola stopped, intimidated by the boatmen's laughter.

One of the men smiled at Ivar as he walked toward him. He stopped and reached out slowly to take the blubber from the boy's hand. "Muktuk." The man held the blubber in such a way that there could be no doubt as to the meaning of this single word. He reached inside his parka and took out a short stone blade; then he grasped the blubber in his teeth and deftly cut off a mouthful. Oil ran from the corners of his mouth as he chewed expansively. He smacked his lips and offered the blubber and blade to Ivar, who took them. Ivar turned to Halfdan and Gudbjartur, a question on his face.

"He wants you to have a bite, Ivar." Gudbjartur gestured to his son. "Take a bite in your teeth and cut it off with his knife as he did."

"Watch your nose!" Lothar exclaimed. Ivar scowled at him as his father and Halfdan laughed.

The boatmen smiled at the laughter.

Ivar gamely took a bite of the blubber, locked his jaw, and proceeded to saw at the slippery material with the stone blade. Unlike the iron knives used by his people, the stone blade had no separate handle. The blubber yielded immediately to the razor-sharp blade. Ivar chewed the oily substance with the same exaggerated jaw movements as the boatman. He examined the stone blade with interest. A thick portion where the handle should be formed a depression for the thumb and index finger in the hard stone. This made the short wide blade easy to grasp and manipulate. Ivar smiled at the man and handed back the knife and blubber. "Your knife is sharp. The muktuk is good."

"Ummh." The man cut off another mouthful of blubber. He turned and spoke to his companions. The other men came forward and took the blubber from Lothar and Yola. They laughed at the boys' discomfort.

"These two boys are frightened of us. This one has no fear." The speaker, the first to eat the muktuk, gestured at Ivar.

Halfdan thought this might be a good time to enter the exchange. He stood and walked toward the group. Gudbjartur followed close behind.

All four of the boatmen fastened their attention on the Greenlanders. They recoiled slightly at the size and presence of both men.

Halfdan smiled and extended his hand. "I, too, want to try the muktuk." He spoke their word for blubber. The closest boatman handed him a piece of blubber. He took out his belt knife, cut off a bite, and handed the blubber to Gudbjartur, who repeated the process. Then Halfdan offered his knife to the man, handle first. The man reached for Halfdan's knife and extended his in return. Halfdan examined the stone blade, tested the edge with his thumb, and handed it to Gudbjartur. "Watch out. It is sharp."

The boatmen passed Halfdan's knife from man to man. One man managed to nick his thumb as he tested the edge, to the delight of his companions.

Both groups continued to be cautious. The whale blubber was soon consumed and the common ground established during its consumption subsided.

The boys, with Ivar in the lead, took the opportunity to continue along the shoreline on their daily quest to see what the tide had brought into the fjord. They left the adults to fend for themselves.

Halfdan pointed to himself and addressed the boatmen. "Halfdan." He tapped his chest.

Gudbjartur introduced himself. "Gudbjartur."

"Gudbj might be easier for them," Halfdan said.

Gudbjartur tapped his chest again, shook his head, and waved both hands in front of his chest to indicate what he had told them was wrong. "My name is Gudbj. Gudbj," he repeated with emphasis. He knew full well the men would not be able to pronounce his name.

"Gudbj." Halfdan held Gudbjartur's arm. "Halfdan," he said, indicating himself. "We are Greenlanders. Northmen."

The boatmen smiled and nodded as if they understood. The man who had offered his blade in return for Halfdan's knife tapped his chest and spoke in a clipped, guttural language. "Inuktuk." He turned to his companions. With a smile he pointed at each of them in turn. "Unanuk. Toodlejak. Kiakuk." They smiled and bobbed at the recognition.

"Tornit." Inuktuk swept his hand to include all of them together. "We are the Tornit people."

"Inuktuk must be their leader. He is certainly the friendliest. I think he meant his people are called Tornit. So they are the same as the people we have in Greenland. All the other words are their names," Gudbjartur said.

"I agree," Halfdan muttered.

Inuktuk recognized his name, although Gudbjartur's pronunciation was not exactly correct. He nodded expansively at Gudbjartur and his round, brown face wrinkled in an infectious smile.

Inuktuk pointed at Halfdan and spoke a few words in his strange language. His meaning escaped Halfdan but not Gudbjartur.

"I do not think this group has a leader." Halfdan smiled. "I suspect this man just has a good sense of humor and his companions defer to him."

"Maybe so, but I think what he means is he wants to trade for your coat." Gudbjartur chuckled and took a handful of the brilliant blue and red pullover Halfdan wore.

"Trade?" Gudbjartur asked Inuktuk. He almost laughed aloud at Halfdan's resistance.

"You are very free with my coat. Trade him your cloak. My coat is almost new." Halfdan got into the spirit of the exchange.

"He does not want my cloak. He likes the bright colors of your coat. No, it is your coat he wants." Gudbjartur laughed.

Sudden inspiration caused Gudbjartur to change tack. He pointed up the beach to the spot where the boatmen had cast their heavy tow loose. Gudbjartur conveyed his meaning with words and signs to Inuktuk. "What do you have there? We might trade you for it."

The four men talked among themselves for a moment before three of them made off to their boats. They paddled rapidly toward the small point. Their strange double-ended paddles flashed in the morning sunlight as they sped around the point and disappeared into the bay where they had left their burden.

"I will get a boat crew to go help them," Gudbjartur said over his shoulder, as he strode toward the crowd of Greenlanders who had gathered to watch.

A short time later, Snorri and his crew rowed toward the point, where they met the boatmen with their load already in tow and passed them a line to assist.

Excitement spread throughout the encampment as a hail from Snorri alerted the people to what they had in tow.

"It is a big bull walrus!" he shouted through cupped hands.

His announcement brought cheers from the throng, as this was only the second walrus harvested in Vinland.

The Skraelings retrieved their towropes and let the excited crowd have the walrus. Thorgill caught the towline from Snorri and with help managed to pull the carcass, tail first, far enough onto the sloping beach that it would not float away.

Halfdan, Gudbjartur, and Inuktuk joined the crowd gathered around the walrus. "That is a big bull," Gudbjartur said. "His ivory is long as my arm."

Inuktuk patted the wet hide of the animal and looked up at the two men. "Avik."

"Avik," Halfdan said.

Inuktuk smiled in acknowledgment and bobbed his head. "Avik," he repeated.

"Walrus." Gudbjartur patted the carcass. "We call it a walrus. Walrus."

Inuktuk mouthed the unfamiliar word without much success. Both Greenlanders smiled at his attempt.

"I think avik is easier to say than walrus in our language." Gudbjartur said. He glanced at Thorgill and a group of men who stood near the animal's tail. "Take care of him, Thorgill. Thorvard will be happy to get this hide. We need the rope."

He glanced at Halfdan with a smile around the corners of his mouth. Gudbjartur spoke directly to Inuktuk and gestured in the general direction of the encampment. "Follow us, Inuktuk, and we will see what you might want to trade for in addition to Halfdan's coat."

Halfdan snorted and smiled good-naturedly at Inuktuk as the three men went to collect the other three Tornit.

It took six men to drag the heavy hide to the river's edge and deliver it into the capable hands of Thorvard the Tanner and his crew.

"This bull hide will make the best rope. I hope we get many more before winter sets in." Thorvard examined the hide. "Stake it down right here; then we will scrape and salt it. After it dries a little, we will cut it into strips." He watched Thorgill and his men stake down the hide.

"His teeth are as long as my arm, Thorvard." Thorgill glanced up at the tanner as he drove a stake through the hide into the ground. "A ship loaded with walrus ivory like that, bales of hides, and barrels of walrus and whale oil would made the long, dangerous voyage to Iceland and Vestfoldland worth the risk."

Thorvard agreed. "With luck we will find them by the hundreds as they sun on their ice floes—enough to fill all our ships for a voyage to the homeland."

On the beach, all that remained of the walrus carcass was the skeleton. With the flood tide the crabs would soon pick it clean. The fresh meat would feed the people over the next few days; the remainder of it would join that already drying on the racks.

After considerable haggling, a trade was worked out. Inuktuk and his men traded their walrus for a roll of bright blue and red wadmal wool cloth sufficient for four parkas. A robe made from the hide of the bear that attacked the encampment—nobody wanted to keep it—and four leather bags of dried fish completed the deal. Inuktuk refused more goods lest their skin boats be overloaded for the long journey home. Altogether a good trade when one considered Halfdan kept his new coat.

Chapter Six

A heavy fog rolled in late in the afternoon and reduced visibility to a matter of feet for the next three days. The four Tornit stayed in their tents at the edge of the encampment at night. During the day, they provided the council with a wealth of knowledge about the land to the south.

Gudbjartur drew a map on the dirt floor of Halfdan's tent. He depicted the headland to the west of the fjord and as far south around the point as their knowledge extended. With sign language, the drawing, and more patience than they usually possessed, the Greenlanders slowly gained knowledge from the Tornit about this new land.

Gudbjartur and Inuktuk knelt on hands and knees. With guidance from Inuktuk and his men, a map of the coastline to the south of the headland slowly took shape. At times, their audience—Halfdan, the other five captains, and the other three Tornit—all tried to offer suggestions at once, in two different languages. Even reinforced with gestures and sign language, it presented difficulties.

"Wait, Gudbj," Halfdan said. "We are not going to accomplish anything this way. Draw that coast to the south a little farther and then curve back to the east, like the coastline would if it were an island."

Inuktuk understood immediately when the line Gudbjartur scratched curved to the east toward the depiction of the rising sun. He shook his head vigorously, erased Gudbjartur's east-bound line from the dirt, and drew the line farther to the south before he curved it gradually west and north.

Bjorn pointed eagerly. "Ha! This coastline forms what appears to be a very large bay, Halfdan. We do not need to explore it, there it is. It is not an island. We can not sail around it as we thought."

Ignoring Bjorn, Halfdan pointed at the southern end of the bay. "How far from here is the southern end of the bay?"

Gudbjartur mimed sunrise and sunset as one day and then pointed to the south end of the bay and counted off his fingers.

Inuktuk looked blankly at Gudbjartur until Kiakuk spoke to him. With an exclamation, he grasped the question. He spoke slowly and distinctly, as if that mattered to the Green-landers, and counted off all his fingers, twice, to indicate a long distance.

Silence followed this revelation as each man digested the significance of the new information. The four Tornit watched the Greenlanders without understanding.

Halfdan looked at each of the council members in turn. He spoke to all of them, but he looked directly at Bjorn. "Perhaps we had better discuss the trip down the coast in more detail now that we have this new information. The time they talk about," he indicated the boatmen, "is probably the distance they can paddle in one day. We are certain they do not travel at night. In open water, this time of year, when the bergs are gone, we do travel at night. Moreover, our ships are much faster than their boats. With the constant wind that blows outside this fjord it will not take long to sail all the way to here." He pointed to the extreme southern end of the bay Inuktuk had drawn. "I still feel we should explore this coast the gods have sent us to, so I have not changed my mind. We have all summer, if need be, to sail wherever we want to win-ter. For two moons we will explore this bay. After that, if we still want to sail for the east coast we will. Now, I want to hear what all of you think." He glanced at the council and his eyes came to rest on his lieutenant. "Gudbj?" Halfdan already knew what his answer would be.

"I have not changed my mind," Gudbjartur answered.

"What about you Bjorn?" Halfdan expected a continuation of his previous arguments.

Bjorn laughed. "Let us stick with our original decision, Halfdan. I have nothing further to offer except I am happy to know what lies ahead of us. I say we go."

Surprisingly, the other men agreed.

Halfdan chuckled as he looked at his men. "I never cease to be surprised at all of you. I thought you, Bjorn, would use this new information to reinforce your previous arguments."

Bjorn shrugged. A smile played about his mouth and the corners of his eyes.

Halfdan paused in thought while he studied his council. "When this fog lifts I will convene a *thing*. Normally we have them once a year. This decision is not normal, and all of you have told me that people have questions about our destination."

The men voiced their agreement.

"We are agreed," Halfdan said. "Now there is the question of Lothar's adoption by Gudbj and Ingerd. Gudbj, you cannot have a vote in this decision."

"I know."

"What say the rest of you?"

Each man spoke briefly and agreed unconditionally that Gudbjartur and Ingerd should raise the boy.

"Then the vote is unanimous. I, too, agree." Halfdan looked at his lieutenant. "Gudbj, from this time on Lothar is your son, to rear as you see fit in accordance with our laws and customs."

Gudbjartur nodded and stood from his place on the bench. "Thank you. Thank you all," he said with feeling. "Ingerd and the boys will be happy about your decision, as I am."

* * *

Snorri befriended Unanuk, one of the boatmen, during this period of weather-enforced association. He found Gudbjartur, and they showed him a special spear and the related equipment that Unanuk carried atop the foredeck of his boat.

"Gudbj, I think we can use this spear, or whatever it is called." He pointed to the long spear the man carried, along with a large coil of leather rope and four deflated sealskin floats. "He and I have talked about it and I wanted you to see how I think it works. They use it to spear every animal they hunt." He took the spear from Unanuk and demonstrated. "The haft fits in this socket of the head and is used only to thrust the point into the animal. Then it floats free or falls out of the head and leaves just the head and point in the animal. The leather rope connects the head and point to the four air bladders at the other end. They catch whales with this spear from those little, skin-covered boats!" he exclaimed. They spear the whale and then throw the rope and floats in the water. The drag of the floats exhausts the whale, and then they paddle in and kill him with a lance. I did not bring one of the lances because it is very similar to ours."

The three men stood in a tight group while Gudbjartur examined the cleverly designed spear. He turned it repeatedly in his hands, took the head off, and put it back on the haft. Gudbjartur looked at Snorri and nodded in appreciation. "This spear is definitely something we can use. Go find Halfdan and the smithies so you can show them what you have found. Good job, Snorri."

A short time later, Snorri returned with Halfdan and both smithies to find Gudbjartur engaged in conversation with the other three boatmen and a group of curious onlookers.

"Snorri has really found something here, Halfdan. This bone spearhead is very cleverly designed." He handed it to him.

Gudbjartur pointed to the various parts of the head as he demonstrated. "The half-moon-shaped bone point is pinned to the socket assembly. The cutting edge of the point aligns with the haft as the spear enters the animal's body. The point toggles on the pin and turns sideways to the direction of pull from the attached rope. This short line secures the haft and it floats freely out of the way. Before an animal stops struggling and is dead, the hafts of our spears are usually broken. The Tornit hafts do not break because they float away from the animal. I think theirs is a much better method. The head cannot pull out of the animal's flesh and you have caught him securely. Our people have always driven whales into small bays to kill them. This spear would allow us to kill them at sea. We would be more assured of success."

"Unless the rope breaks," Halfdan said.

"I do not think the rope will break. They do not attempt to hold him. They let the bladders exhaust the animal and they follow along until he is too tired to escape. Then they kill him with a lance."

"It is very well made," Halfdan said. He swiveled the sharp bone point as he examined the head assembly. He handed it to Haakon. "Can you make this head and point in steel?"

Both smithies examined the head assembly with interest, conferred with one another in the jargon of their trade, and Asgrim passed it back to Halfdan. "Aye, we can copy it if they will let us have it long enough."

For the remainder of the day the smithies were busy at their forge. They and their helpers heated iron bars to white hot and then shaped them into duplicates of the boatmen's spearhead. The boatmen seemed fascinated by the process and did not leave the area until a finished product emerged from the ringing anvils of the two smithies. Each boatman received a new steel spearhead for allowing a copy to be made of the bone spearhead.

* * *

People were ready for a change when late one afternoon a strong cold wind blew the last tatters of the of the Fog Giant's cloak from the fjord.

Work continued as before, and the steady wind soon dried out the last of the meat and fish. The walrus that the boatmen had traded lasted the people through all three days of fog.

The four boatmen made ready to depart. The men sat in their little boats just in front of the beach and grinned at the milling crowd come to see them off. They held their spears with the razor-sharp steel heads aloft in salute as the entire population of the encampment applauded and cheered their departure.

Halfdan and the council hoped the friendship forged with the Tornit men would ease life for all of them when they met again. This seemed likely, as the men had gone to considerable lengths to tell the Greenlanders how to find their village and where to hunt the avik.

Halfdan called the *thing* the next day. Every member of the expedition attended the important event. Although their numbers totaled little more than three hundred, the people were a social group in every sense of the term, sharing life or death together on a daily basis, dependent on one another for every aspect of their existence.

The *thing* represented a unique opportunity for freemen to voice concerns or complaints to their chieftain and the council before the entire community. The agenda covered all manner of social problems that affected the group as a whole. Traditionally, Halfdan and the council arrived at a consensus beforehand. The judgment or rule that they passed down in accordance to the established law and custom of the Northmen was final.

Halfdan had selected a knoll near the encampment for the *thing* to take place. He, Gudbjartur, and the five ship captains—Bjorn, Sweyn, Athils, Gudrod, and Brodir—sat atop this knoll in full view of the people arrayed in a semi-circle at its base.

As the last of the people settled themselves, Halfdan stood up to get everyone's attention. "Can you all hear me?"

Nods and a few waves satisfied him that all could hear. "As some of you know, I have called the *thing* to discuss the council's decision to explore to the south of this fjord in what we now know from the Tornit to be a huge bay. Before we discuss our decision and hear any concerns you may have, I want you all to know the council's decision regarding the adoption of Lothar by Gudbj and Ingerd. By unanimous vote, it is our decree that Lothar is now their son. He is to be raised as they see fit, in accordance with our laws and customs."

Applause followed this pronouncement and Gudbjartur and Ingerd gazed fondly at each other, a smile on their faces.

"Kiss her, Gudbj!" Thora shouted over the applause.

Happy to comply, Gudbjartur got up and walked down the knoll to where Ingerd sat with Ivar and Lothar. He took his wife's hand and helped her to her feet so everyone could see them kiss. The embrace and kiss lingered, to thunderous applause from his people. Even the council got into it.

Gudbjartur returned to the knoll and took his seat. There remained one final act to comply with the custom of the Northmen in an adoption. He called to Lothar. "Come here, boy."

Lothar came to stand before him. Gudbjartur reached up, took the boy by the arms, and seated him on his lap. By this simple action, taking the boy into his lap, Gudbjartur accepted Lothar as his son. He smiled at the boy and then he looked out over the raised faces of his people. He spoke in a loud, clear voice that all could hear. "It is done."

Ingerd jumped to her feet and yelled! "Yes, oh yes!" She held her arms out to Lothar. The boy looked at his new father. Gudbjartur smiled and winked. Lothar jumped up, ran to Ingerd, and threw his arms around her. Ivar grinned at his brother and punched him on the arm. Again thunderous applause rose from the throng of onlookers as people congratulated them.

After a few moments, Halfdan raised both arms high to restore quiet and order. "Let us begin the *thing*. The Tornit made a map for us of the bay that begins to the west of the headland some of us saw when we sailed into this fjord. It takes them many days to paddle their boats to the southern end of that bay. The Tornit have told us there are dense forests; the waters are full of seals and fish; the land is full of game; and there is grass for our animals. We unanimously decided to explore all the way to the southern end so others who come after us will know what to expect. We came here to find a better place to live and it is for that reason we must see what lies ahead. The god Njord sent a storm to bring us to this place for a reason. We will not leave until we know what that reason is.

The council has agreed to spend no more than two full moons on this quest. If we have not found that which we seek before the end of the second full moon, we will set sail for Markland. We will not sail to Leifsbudir because we have decided it is too dangerous there. The people who already live there are hostile to us Northmen because of mistakes made by previous expeditions. We cannot change that fact."

The mutter of many voices arose. Men had their heads together in muted conversation. He raised his arms to restore order. "The decision is final, for the reasons I have said." He looked out over the faces of his people. "Five moons remain in this summer season before another winter begins. We have ample time to explore the coastline of this great bay all the way to the south end, turn around and sail for Markland, and prepare for winter."

He paused to give them time to digest his words. "You have heard our decision. We will stay here until all who have concerns have expressed them and are satisfied that we have acted in the best interests of our people."

"Think carefully before you voice your opinion." His gaze slowly traveled over the crowd. "Speak one at a time after you are recognized by the council. Otherwise we will not have enough time left to explore before winter sets in."

He took his seat as laughter at his final remark rippled through the crowd. Halfdan and the council waited for the questions to begin.

As expected from Gudbjartur's previous discussion with him, Thorgill was the first to have a question. He stood to be recognized.

"The council recognizes Thorgill." Halfdan said formally.

"I understand the reason you think we should explore this bay. Nevertheless, I do not think we should because it so far from our original destination. Leifsbudir must be ten days' sail from here. I understand now why we cannot sail for Leifsbudir and I agree with that decision. But if we go south we will be even farther from Greenland."

Halfdan had his answer ready for the man. "The only reason we left Greenland is we all wanted to find a better place to live, where life might be easier. To find such a place we must explore. What is your concern? It is not the distance. What is it?"

"I am afraid winter will arrive and we will not be ready. It takes us all summer to get ready for the next winter without the necessity of having to build houses. All summer! I do not see how we can be ready in time. There are more than three hundred of us and we need to lay aside much food for that many. I am only concerned about the time, not the distance."

Some murmured agreement with Thorgill but they desisted when Bjorn rose to the occasion.

"I will answer that, Halfdan."

Somewhat surprised, Halfdan swept his hand toward Thorgill, indicating to Bjorn that he was to proceed.

"I also disagreed at first, Thorgill, but what Halfdan says about all of this has caused me to change my mind. We may find everything we seek down there, and that is reason enough to go. If we run out of time, we will build houses in the best place we find and spend the winter."

Gudbjartur entered the discussion with his own arguments to convince those who still harbored doubts. "The big difference between Greenland and Vinland is how much time it takes us to get ready for winter. In Greenland, we had to go far to the north, to Nordsettir or even farther, to hunt. The summer is shorter, too. Here there is game and fish everywhere, so it will take less time to obtain our winter stores; and we have a longer summer."

Several people made to enter the discussion, until Halfdan raised both arms to regain control before things got out of hand. He spoke to Thorgill. "I know you, man, and I know nothing scares you, so why let this bother you?" He appealed to the man's sense of masculinity. "Your concerns are justified and admirable but we have answered all of them. So what say you now?"

Thorgill chuckled at his own expense. "You are hard to disagree with, Halfdan. I only wanted to hear the whole plan. I wanted to know what all of you really thought about this, and now I am satisfied." With that, he took his seat on the ground once again.

And so it went: some voiced concerns; a few were in complete disagreement with the plan; the rest were in enthusiastic accord. After everyone so inclined had had a chance to speak, Halfdan called for a vote. Women voiced their opinions and had grievances heard, but they could not vote. A show of hands indicated a majority favored the original decision—to sail south.

* * *

Halfdan, anxious to begin the voyage to the south, pushed everyone to complete the work in progress. He and Gudbjartur stood atop a knoll that afforded a good view of the various activities in the encampment. Gudbjartur made his report.

"All the dried meat, dried fish, and oil barrels are packed aboard the ships. The boats have all returned and there are two more small whales and a good many auks that will provide us with fresh meat for about two days. They are being butchered now." Gudbjartur pointed toward a large group of people on the beach.

"I see Frida with Ingerd and the other women. I wonder if she learned something from the talk I had with her. Perhaps you will ask Ingerd about that." Halfdan glanced at his lieutenant, who nodded in assent.

Large flocks of flightless, black and white auks shared the coastal world of the Northmen. In the water, the swimming birds were symmetry in motion, but on land, they could not escape their hunters. The Northmen prized their meat, hides, and feathers. Thorgill and his men had cornered a large flock of the tall birds away from the water and clubbed them to death.

Ingerd, Thora, Helga, Frida, and several thrall women helped the hunters unload four boatloads of auk carcasses.

Thorgill seemed surprised to see Frida. "What are you doing here, Frida?"

"I am here to work, Thorgill. What are you doing here?"

"Same as you, working," he laughed. "We are not accustomed to have you join us for this dirty work."

"Well, get used to it. I have always worked, just not with others," Frida answered. She glanced at the other women. "How have you decided to butcher these birds today?"

"We are going to dress them and quarter the carcasses to roast for the evening meal," Ingerd said. All the women watched Frida to see how she intended to help.

"Then you want to skin them rather than pluck the feathers and down," Frida said.

"Yes. Some of us will skin and peel off the thick layer of fat, and others can quarter the carcasses for roasting," Ingerd answered. She watched Frida curiously, unused to her help or questions.

Frida pulled the knife from her scabbard, bent over a bird, and split the skin over the breast. She glanced up at Ingerd and the others with a smile on her lips. "Are you going to help or just stand there?"

Ingerd looked toward the other women, the beginnings of a smile on her face. "Why, help of course," she chuckled, as she flipped a carcass onto its back and split the skin at the breast.

The others pitched in too, and shortly a large pile of dressed carcasses had accumulated on the stony beach. Thora and the cooks quartered them and hung a large number on meat hooks to roast over the fire pit as they prepared the second and final meal of the day. The women gossiped and tended the browning carcasses, basted by their own body fat, as they twisted in the heat.

Near the riverbank, Thorvard and his crew of tanners continued to work over the various kinds of hides. When they finished the auk hides, the tanned, feathered skins would become warm winter garments. When plucked of feathers and down, the thick skins made durable bags and belt pouches. Remnants pieced together and stuffed with feathers and down became warm comforters.

* * *

"What about the hides, Gudbj? Are they about finished with them?" Halfdan looked toward the river where the large group of tanners worked.

"Thorvard said there was not enough time to tan all the hides so he selected only the best to be tanned into leather or cut into strips for rope. He has some rope finished. The remainder they intend to do aboard ship. The rest of the hides, including the auk hides, will be dry before we sail or they will dry aboard ship."

They were silent for a time as they watched the scene below. Halfdan suddenly chuckled. He gestured toward a young man and woman as they walked with studied nonchalance into the countryside away from the encampment. "I have heard people speak of that young Sigmund. I see he takes one of the women into the bushes."

Surprised that Halfdan knew of Sigmund and his popularity with many of the women, Gudbjartur stared at him. "How did you know of this?"

"Since you told me about Frida and the cause of the einvigi, I have paid more attention to what goes on between our men and women. I have listened to gossip and asked questions of certain people who seem to know all about these things. My own interest in women has increased consequently. I may need to select a woman for myself." Halfdan grinned foolishly at his lieutenant.

Gudbjartur looked at his friend and snorted. "I thought you did not have time for such things."

"I think I may take time." He saw the couple disappear into the scrub. "Is that a thrall with Sigmund?"

"Yes, she is the Celt, Genevra. Brodir owns her."

"Genevra, a pretty name. Do her looks match her name?"

Gudbjartur regarded Halfdan quizzically. "I have never seen you act like this."

"Well, do they?" Halfdan demanded.

"Yes, she is very pretty. She has the dark hair and dark eyes common to Celts."

"Umm," Halfdan replied, his gaze fixed on the spot where the couple had disappeared in the scrub.

Gudbjartur shook his head and grinned at this newly transformed Halfdan. "I hesitate to change the subject, but when do you want to sail?"

Halfdan seemed to be lost in thought, his eyes still on the scrub. "We sail with the outgoing tide tomorrow, as soon as we can break camp."

"I thought so. I will tell the captains. There is much to do before then."

"Umm," Halfdan replied.

Gudbjartur, a broad smile fixed on his face, looked at Halfdan for a moment as he gazed into the distance. He shook his head, turned, and walked away to begin preparations to sail.

* * *

A short distance away, Sigmund, with a willing Genevra in tow, stepped into a small amphitheater among the rocks and brush and turned with a slight smile on his lips. "How is this?"

She looked with anticipation at the bed of soft, furry skins nestled in the scrub brush, well protected from the cold north wind. She looked from under dark eyelashes at the tall blond youth. Her dark eyes smoldered with lust. She parted her full lips, moistened them with the tip of her tongue, and melted into his arms. Her voice gone husky with passion, she murmured into the warm hollow of his neck. "This will do very well. It looks like it has been used before."

"It has," he said. His hot breath fanned her face as he slowly lowered his parted lips to hers.

They locked their bodies together and swayed in the throes of desire. Their hands explored, their tongues wetly probed, as their need burned through the last restraints and eager fingers grasped and pulled at each other's clothing.

A sharp intake of breath came from Genevra as her eyes fastened on the rod-like projection of his manhood. A smile played across his face.

He gasped as her cold hands enfolded the engorged member. "Your hands are like ice!" he exclaimed.

"I will warm them for you." She stroked his long, thick member with one hand and cupped and kneaded his warm balls with the other.

A grunt escaped his lips as she gripped his member in both hands and rapidly pulled and stroked.

"Careful," he gasped, "it might go off."

"Not yet," she panted, falling to her knees. "We have only just begun." She took him into her mouth and sucked and stroked the throbbing member.

"Ohhh, by the gods, Genevra, I cannot stand much of that treatment. Unghh! I am going to release!"

"Oh no, you cannot, you sweet boy." She squeezed him tightly until he regained control and then pulled him onto the bed of skins. She smothered further comment with her mouth and covered his face and lips with kisses while guiding his free hand to her own hot wetness.

Stretched out side by side they pulled and probed at each other's sex until both were in a frenzy of lust. Sigmund kissed her large breasts. His tongue scribed small arcs and circles until his lips encircled her long, hardened nipples. Gently, so gently, he sucked each in turn into his mouth. Genevra writhed and bucked against the hand that cupped her womanhood. She shuddered and gasped as two of his fingers separated the lips of her sex and gently probed inside. He continued to probe deep inside her as his kisses and tongue trailed down her stomach. His nails scribed a gentle path down her side, over her hip, and down her thigh. Large, strong, work-roughened hands, one wet with her sex, gently pushed open first one and then the other leg as he continued to kiss, lick, and suck his way down her stomach and over her hip to her thigh. Her skin recoiled to his touch and the flicks of his tongue until her breath came in ragged gasps. His lips brushed the hair-covered mound. He sucked in the strong pungent smell of a heated woman and chuckled deep in his throat. His lips lightly brushed the drenched lips of her opening and his long, wet tongue flicked the end of her swollen button.

A sharp exclamation burst unbidden from the deepest recesses of her being at the brief pressure of his tongue.

Sigmund fastened his lips about the swollen button, sucked gently, and flicked the tip with his tongue. His efforts became more intense. Genevra bucked and squirmed against the relentless pressure. Her breath came in short gasps as her orgasm enfolded her like a warm blanket. He sucked in the hot viscous fluid of her orgasm. At the peak of her intensity, he rose to his knees between her legs, grasped a thigh in each hand, and thrust full length into her.

A high-pitched shriek burst from the rictus of her mouth as her orgasm flooded forth once again. Sigmund sheathed his manhood to its full length. He hit bottom deep inside her still pulsating womanhood. She bucked against his every thrust. Her womanhood pulled and sucked at his engorged tool. Finally, able to control himself no longer, he exploded deep inside her.

Both sweaty from exertion, they continued to match each other thrust for thrust. They reveled in the heat that washed over them, consumed them, until once again he grunted with effort and expelled another flood into her soaked recesses.

The spent couple laughed together, rolled, hugged, and kissed lovingly on the soft bed before they finally relaxed in each other's arms. Small talk followed until each became aware of another world, just a short distance away, as the din of the encampment penetrated their sex-fogged minds.

"Something is happening," Genevra said. She looked over the top of the brush toward the sound of activity.

"Something did happen," Sigmund laughed. "Have you already forgotten?"

She playfully punched him in the stomach, rolled atop his waist, bent forward, and kissed him deeply. "That dampness you feel running out of me is from you. I do not think I have forgotten," she said mischievously.

He pushed her off, scrambled to his feet, and looked toward the encampment. "Get up, woman; it looks like they get ready to sail without us."

She sprang up, threw her arms around his neck, and wrapped a leg around one of his. "Good, I will have you all to myself," she murmured into the hollow of his neck.

He pushed back from her embrace, bent over to retrieve her shift, and threw it to her. "Get dressed, beautiful, we have probably been missed. Halfdan will want to sail on the ebb tide tomorrow and there is much work to do before then. He would be unhappy if we do not do our part."

Chapter Seven

Gudbjartur told the ship's captains to prepare to sail on the ebb tide the next day. They gathered their crews and passengers and assigned the tasks to complete before departure.

Crews broke down the encampment and stowed equipment aboard the ships, except for the tents. They spent the final night ashore in the comfort they had come to enjoy. At the end of that day, all that remained of the encampment was the tents, the benches within, and the personal gear bags.

People arose early on the day of departure. An air of excitement pervaded the encampment as they completed last-minute tasks.

Thora, Ingerd, and all the other cooks prepared the remainder of their fresh meat for the last meal and apportioned the surplus to each ship.

Near the mouth of the river and down the beach a short way from the ships, Askhold of the Runes sat in front of a large, round-topped slab of rock. He scribed his art on the flat surface facing the beach. A group of children lounged around him in various positions and watched the precise movements of hammer and chisel as he put his final touches on the rune stone.

He cocked his head first one way and then the other as he studied his handiwork. He looked at his audience. "There, now others who come after us will know we stayed here for a time."

"What do the runes say, Askhold?" the pretty blond lass seated beside him asked.

He pointed at each rune incised in the face of the rock and recited the short history of their encampment. "Halfdan Ingolfsson and 315 people, with six ships, were storm driven here on winds sent by the god Njord. Eight people died here in Snorrisfjord and we buried them. We sailed around the headland to the west and far to the south toward the bottom of the bay. It is the end of the Sowing Moon in the year 1008. Askhold carved these runes."

Exclamations of wonder that he was able to make the runes speak to them came from the group of children.

"Why did you leave this story?" a small boy asked.

Askhold smiled at the boy. "Our people always leave a rune stone in special places we visit. Halfdan told me to put one here to tell others who come that people died while we were here and to tell them where we are going so that they may follow us."

"Will you teach me the runes, Askhold?" the blond girl asked.

"I will teach any of you who want to learn the runes. I will ask Halfdan if I can teach you after we settle for the winter. Until then there will be no time for such things."

Chattering excitedly over the prospect of being able to talk with the runes, the children ran off hither and yon. Askhold watched them for a moment and shook his head at their antics. He admired his handiwork one last time and leaned forward to wipe a bit of granite dust from the face of his rune stone. Finally, he turned and walked down the beach to board Athils' ship. He whistled tunelessly to himself, well satisfied with the morning. A low-lying cloud bank scudded in from the northwest. He nodded and thought, *what a fine day for a sail.*

The tide began to ebb in mid-morning and the last of the crew members and passengers boarded their ships. The crews retrieved all lines and anchors and the ships maneuvered away from the shore with their sweeps. Those not occupied with rowing stood wherever a vantage point presented itself and watched the shoreline slide by.

"I will remember Snorrisfjord with mixed emotions." Ingerd glanced at Thora, who stood beside her.

"We lost good people here, but at the same time I thank the gods for all the stores we have in our ships," Thora said.

Ingerd agreed. She looked toward the ships following astern. "I wonder what Frida is thinking?"

"She has changed since the einvigi and her contact with Halfdan afterward. I will wager she is sorry."

"Perhaps, but we will never hear her apologize. I think it is best to learn from mistakes and move on. I hope she does that, because I think we could be friends."

"Really! I am surprised, Ingerd. Frida has no friends, only herself. Gudbj does not like her. How will you handle him if you two become friends?"

"He does not like her because she caused trouble for Halfdan. Just a short time ago, Gudbj asked me how she acted when she helped us butcher the auks. I told him she acted fine and did her work. He will tell Halfdan what I said. If I am her friend, it will be because she has changed. Gudbj and Halfdan take people at face value. I predict they, too, will accept her if we become friends."

"Frida is responsible for the death of Ottar, Gyda, and Ari, Lothar's entire family. He is your son now. How can you accept that Frida caused the death of his family?"

Ingerd stood up from her place at the rail and locked eyes with her friend. "Now I am the one surprised, Thora. I would not expect this from you."

Thora made to interrupt, but she saw the warning in Ingerd's eyes.

"Frida is not my friend. What I said was, 'I think we could be friends.' To blame her for all the trouble here is wrong. She and the bear did not act in concert. The bear did the killing, not Frida. Oh, she certainly caused Ulfar's death and the maiming of Gizur. Our men have always fought over women, Thora. They have fought over both of us. No, I will not accept that Frida is directly responsible for the other deaths. The bear killed them, and that is that."

Thora looked into Ingerd's eyes and decided to drop the subject for now, perhaps forever.

The two women lapsed into silence as they watched the ship's progress toward the fjord entrance.

Just after Gudrod's wreck, two boats dragging a weighted line between them had finally located and marked the rocky spires that had snagged the ship. As Halfdan's ship passed abeam of the wooden float that marked the site, Gudbjartur alerted the ships that followed astern with a load blast of his ram's horn, and each ship gave the dangerous area a wide berth.

Halfdan nodded to Gudbjartur as their ship glided through the narrow exit from Snorrisfjord and the sea wind freshened from the north-northwest.

Gudbjartur cupped both hands around his mouth. "Hold the stroke! Toss your sweeps! Make sail!"

Sweeps clattered inboard to be stowed. The sail rose up the mast as six men walked the halyard aft. The ship heeled to the wind. The sheet tenders trimmed the sail and cleated the sheets. Gorm glanced aloft at the masthead's bronze weather vane and brought the ship's bow around to a more westerly course. Close-hauled on the port tack, to beat offshore and weather the headland, the Steed of the Sea charged across the swells, followed closely by the other ships in line astern.

Halfdan and Gudbjartur occupied their accustomed place on the bow platform. Spray dripped from their beards and beaded on their clothing. They grinned at each other like small boys, in ecstasy to be at sea once again.

A hail from Gauk drew attention. "Skerries on the port bow!" he cried from the masthead.

Halfdan looked aft in time to see Gorm bring the bow closer to the wind to allow plenty of sea room around the deadly, partially submerged rocks. He looked aloft at the trim of the sail and called to the sheet handlers, "Take a pull on the port sheet!"

Satisfied at the way the sail drew he turned his attention to the drinking horns of rich broth that Ingerd had just brought for him and Gudbjartur.

"Thank you, Ingerd." He smiled at her. Although cold, the broth was thick and delicious.

"There is enough for at least two days. We want to heat it for the evening meal if it is calm enough to light the charcoal braziers. The dried fish and meat would certainly taste better if washed down with hot broth." She looked from Halfdan to her husband.

"We will have the answer to that when we clear the headland and turn south." He gestured toward the headland, just visible through the sea mist off their port bow. "The wind will be from astern on the southerly course. With the ship on an even keel you should be able to light the charcoal. Gudbj will tell you, Ingerd."

She nodded, took the two empty drinking horns from the men, and made eye contact with Gudbjartur. She gave him a radiant smile and turned to make her way aft.

The men watched her weave her way aft along the crowded deck. Halfdan looked at his friend. "Yes, I think I will want a woman to keep me warm—before winter at the latest." He winked suggestively.

"They are very good to have around most of the time. However, you will need to keep her warm, not the other way around. That is the way of it. Most women have no extra warmth to share with you. But there are many other uses for them besides warmth." He smiled broadly.

* * *

Gudbjartur began to draw a chart of the coastline from Snorrisfjord on a thin square of leather, one of several provided by Thorvard. Northmen normally committed navigation details to collective memory rather than inaccurate charts. Halfdan and the council felt that this expedition and subsequent ones might have need of dependable charts. To that end Gudbjartur took on the task. Each time the ship changed course to follow a change in the coastline he took another bearing with a handheld, wooden dial and recorded the course change on the chart using an arrow to indicate direction of travel. In this way, he transcribed the general outline of the coast.

The courses noted in this manner corresponded to eight principal directions as indicated by eight notches cut around the top edge of the bearing dial: north, northeast, east, southeast, south, southwest, west, and northwest. To use the bearing dial, Gudbjartur aligned the device along the long axis of the ship. He then turned the dial until one of the eight courses on the dial face pointed in a known direction: east or west toward the rising or setting sun, or north toward the pole star at night. This served to orient the dial in the direction of travel.

The dim pole star was visible only in winter. Only the brightest stars were visible in the twilight of the summer nights. At this time the ship's course became guesswork. The helmsman maintained the course by reference to the ship's angle as she crossed the wave pattern. He knew wave patterns at sea changed little unless disrupted by a landmass or a violent storm.

Gudbjartur aligned the dial and then held it at arm's length by a handle that projected from the base. The shadow cast by the vertical, wooden center pin as it fell across a notch in the dial face indicated the course the ship sailed. Gudbjartur noted the new course and drew runic characters opposite that area of the coastline with a sharpened quill and black ink made from charcoal and whale oil. He completed his notation and extended the rugged coastline a little farther. He looked at the chart with satisfaction and sprinkled it with fine beach sand to blot and dry the wet ink. Then he shook off the excess and blew away the dust that lingered.

Halfdan stopped on his way forward and studied the chart for a time before he nodded in satisfaction. "You are better and better at that, Gudbj. I think anyone could follow us with a chart like you have drawn."

"It is hard for me to draw accurately. I cannot draw very well," Gudbjartur added ruefully. "Until we find someone who can draw, my chart will make it easier to sail these waters safely. We never know what lies around the next headland."

"That is the fun of being explorers," Halfdan said. "All of us want to know what new places will bring, and I hope there are others to come behind us one day. If we are to be alone here the charts will still be valuable to us."

"Yes they will, and it gives me something to do."

"When we sail closer inshore, put a man in the bow to take soundings of the water depth and include those on the chart."

"I will. But I am not that good with the runes."

Halfdan stroked his beard in thought. "Askhold is the best among us with the runes, but he is on another ship."

"He is on Athils' ship."

Halfdan glanced at him and nodded. "I will get him over here to help as soon as the sea state allows us to heave to."

The ships rounded the headland about midday and turned to a southerly course. Groups of islands were visible to the west; the new course took them between the headland and the two largest islands. A pod of large whales accompanied by a flock of gulls kept them company for a time. The Tornit had told them big whales spent all summer in the bay, and Halfdan felt there would be plenty of future opportunities to hunt them after they reached the southern limit of their exploration.

Halfdan decided not to land again for two full days. They made a swift passage until the first night.

Gudbjartur had set his chart making aside after sunset. The weather began to deteriorate and he sought out Halfdan for a conference. "We are in for another blow." He indicated the northwestern sky with a lift of his chin.

"I am afraid so. That island group off the steerboard bow will offer shelter if we can get there and anchor before the storm hits us."

"It will be a close race. Do you want to reef the sail?"

"No, there is not enough time. If we reef, the storm front will catch us out here and we will not be able to anchor." Halfdan studied the sail, strained to the limit in the wind. "It is new. It will hold."

"I agree. We have no choice in any case. We must win this race." Gudbjartur looked aloft at the wind vane and aft at the bank of black clouds that rushed toward them. "I will get the people ready and have the anchor crew standby. They will need to get the anchor set in good bottom as soon as you turn the ship into the wind."

"Good. Tell them to hang on when I make the turn; it is going to be rough."

Gudbjartur hurried aft. He stopped a moment with each group of people to brief them. By the time he rounded up the anchor crew every person knew what to expect.

"Gorm, steer for the lee shore of that biggest island. There is enough sea room to shelter the fleet." Halfdan glanced aft at the other ships that followed close astern. He squinted in the wind and rain and wiped his streaming face. Gorm guided the Steed of the Sea toward the downwind side of the rocky island.

It occurred to Gudbjartur, as he sat huddled below the rail in shared misery with Ingerd and the boys, that storms always seemed to come at night. The ship snubbed against the anchor rope as she plunged in the short choppy swells on the lee shore of the island. Suddenly the familiar sound changed, and the bow swung a little downwind. Gudbjartur jumped to his feet, ran over to the other rail, and grabbed Thorgill by the arm. He found it necessary to shout in the shrieking wind. "The anchor is dragging."

Thorgill lurched his way forward without a word, his head bowed in the wind. He chose two helpers from those sheltered below the weather rail. The three men let more anchor rode out and the anchor found a better purchase on the bottom. The crews aboard the other ships had their own fights with dragging anchors during the worst of the storm. The low islands afforded little protection from the pitiless wind, but the ships rode out the worst of the storm at anchor.

The rapidly moving storm front passed them by before morning and the ships regrouped on course. The cooks kindled the braziers and everyone aboard enjoyed drafts of hot broth to wash down their dried fish and dried meat. Askhold transferred to Halfdan's ship to help Gudbjartur, and the flotilla continued on its southerly course.

Steady progress continued. Their course took them past many bare, desolate islands that teemed with birds and seals. The coastline curved farther southwest before another headland passed astern. A course change to the southeast ensured the ship remained close inshore so Gudbjartur and Askhold could continue to record the coastline.

About midmorning of the second day, the ships sailed close together in line astern between a series of long barrier islands and the mainland. The islands and surrounding sea fairly teemed with birds of every kind. Flocks of auks and puffins dived out of the way at the last moment to avoid being run down. Immense pods of every known species of whale swam with the flotilla. Seals beyond count and of several species were everywhere. It was a dizzying sight.

"Deck there, a fjord off the port bow opens into a bay," Gauk shouted from the masthead.

Halfdan waved in acknowledgment, glad he had told him earlier to watch for a protected bay. "Let us have a look," he said to the helmsman.

Gorm put the helm over and the ship turned to port toward the mouth of the fjord that loomed in the near distance.

Gudbjartur alerted the first ship astern with a blast on his horn. The signal passed down the line as each ship signaled the next in line astern.

"Take the way off her, Gudbj, so we can coast in slowly," Halfdan ordered.

"Reef the sail by half," Gudbjartur called to the sail handlers. The ship's speed decreased slowly as they sailed from the barrier islands and into the fjord entrance. Copses of heavy evergreen forests were seen scattered about the lowlands. Fens, grassland, and rocky hills, dominated the shoreline and hinterland.

The fjord opened into a large bay. To afford some protection from the north wind Halfdan kept to the north shore. He guided the flotilla around a point and into a smaller bay that offered protection from the wind.

Except for the occasional sounds of the livestock confined aboard, and the cries of gulls that followed in the wake, the ship made a silent approach. People lined both rails as they passed the point and entered the small bay. Halfdan turned slightly and gestured further off shore. "Stay out of arrow range, Gorm."

The tiller bar came smartly aft as Gorm turned the bow sharply away from the shoreline. Sheet handlers trimmed to the new course.

This order drew the attention of every person in the ship, and they all scanned the edge of the tree line for a hint of danger. The ship slowly progressed into the bay.

"Do you see something, Halfdan?" Gudbjartur asked as he stepped up on the bow platform.

"Nothing yet, it is just a feeling. The hair stood up on the back of my neck." The two men studied the edge of the tree line. "I feel like we are being watched. I do not want to take any chances until we are sure we are alone." Halfdan turned to the passengers and idle crew who lined the rails. He spoke loud enough for his voice to carry the length of the ship. "Call it caution or a feeling of being watched if you want. I have not seen anything, but I want all of you to stay alert. If you see something that does not look like it belongs here, tell us immediately."

Without a word spoken to initiate the sudden change in attitude, women and children melted to the rear as armed men began lining the inshore rail of the ship.

Halfdan glanced aloft to be sure that the masthead lookout was alert and watchful.

"I do not see anything unusual," Gauk reported.

Halfdan waved in acknowledgment and turned and shouted to Gorm at the helm. "Steer for that flat beach away from the trees." He pointed ahead and to port.

Halfdan turned to Gudbjartur. "Man the sweeps, Gudbj."

Gudbjartur called to crewmen waiting amidships. "Lower the sail, out sweeps."

The sail came down the mast, and the sweeps came into play. The other ships followed suit. Steed of the Sea eased toward the beach, all aboard in a high state of readiness.

* * *

Other eyes on shore watched the strange ships approach with the same intensity. To the watcher, the ships were huge boats unlike anything in his experience. This man, unlike the pale-skinned men he watched, had brown skin and long black hair held in place by an animal skin hat. Clad in various shades of leather clothing, he blended perfectly into the landscape.

He lay stretched out full length in the low brush atop a high point of the promontory that the ships glided past on their way to the landing beach. He rested his chin on crossed forearms. In that position, he would have been difficult to see from a short distance and all but impossible to see from the ships. Lying beside him on the ground was an unstrung bow and several arrows that protruded from a quiver of the same nondescript leather as his clothing.

Thoughts of his own discomfort occupied his mind. He had lain immobile on the cold ground long enough that he shivered in the cold wind. Numbness had begun to creep through his limbs. A consuming curiosity about the strangers he had discovered made him endure the discomfort.

Animal sounds that came from the ships served to mystify him even further. The ships would pass his position soon. And then he would rise and steal away, provided his legs still functioned.

At that moment, he saw a woman with long hair the color of the pale winter sun join the two men who stood at the front of the lead ship. The voice of a young boy carried across the water to him. Until he saw the woman and heard the boy's voice, the watcher regarded the ships as intruders with enemies aboard. *But*, he now reasoned, *they could not be hostile. A war party would not have women and children with it.*

He watched with interest as the strangers guided their huge ships around the point and toward the beach below his vantage point. He studied every aspect of what he observed.

Having reached a decision to share this with his village, he crawled some distance away from his vantage point. He rose stiffly to a crouch and made his way into the forest far enough to ensure his presence would not be detected. He walked rapidly for a time. Pausing often, he watched his back trail for pursuers. Gradually he relaxed his vigilance. He broke into a ground-eating trot toward the bay's western shoreline.

* * *

The moment the ships ground ashore, armed men leaped to the beach and fanned out in all directions to secure the area. Everyone else remained aboard until Halfdan was satisfied that no danger existed.

Sometime later, Gudbjartur strode from the woods and reported to Halfdan, who walked impatiently back and forth on the landing beach.

"There was someone here. Ormiga found his tracks and where he hid while he watched us."

"Show me, Gudbj."

"We found his tracks on top of that hill." He pointed at the highest point of ground on the south end of the peninsula. "I have been up there. You can see far in all directions."

The two men walked rapidly through the brush in single file while Gudbjartur told Halfdan what his men had found. "He saw us before we ever sailed into this fjord."

"Was he alone?"

"I do not know yet. We have only found one set of fresh tracks. There are other tracks in the mud that are much older."

Gudbjartur stopped suddenly and pulled the brush aside. He knelt and pointed out the area as he described it. "The man lay right here. He watched us all the way around the point until we beached. You can see the imprints of his elbows and toes. He made himself more comfortable by moving rocks and sticks out of the way." Gudbjartur grinned up at him. "So he was here for quite some time, I think."

Halfdan was silent as he turned slowly to survey the land and seascape. He completed his examination of the area and sighed. "Post the perimeter guards and tell the people to unload. We will need to meet these strangers sometime. I do not seem to feel threatened by their presence. What do you think?"

"We have 250 fighting men and I do not think anyone would attack a force that size unless provoked."

"We came to settle somewhere in Vinland. We must be certain that the Skraelings will allow us to stay. Every effort must be made to get along with them. But we cannot do that until we meet them."

"I know. I will pass the word while we set up the encampment. How long will we stay here?"

"It depends on the Skraelings. I want to see what happens when they all find out we are here. Tell our people what you found and that we want them to be alert. Also tell them to carry on as always, that we expect nothing unusual."

"I will tell them that." Gudbjartur walked back toward the beach.

Later that day Halfdan and the council decided to remain in the bay until scouting expeditions into the interior and along the coast in both directions were completed.

Halfdan watched the activity along the landing beach for a time. Then he walked toward a group of men returning from the north.

Thorgill, the first in a line of men threading their way through the scrub, stopped in front of Halfdan. "We found where the man launched a boat. He had pulled the boat up on the beach in plain view. We think he did not expect unfriendly visitors."

"Good, I want them to know we come in peace." The other men gathered around him. "I want you all to pass the word to the other men who are still out. Do not provoke these Skraelings. We must try to be friends with them. We will remain here until contact is made with them." He talked to the men for a time before he picked two of them to accompany him on his own reconnaissance to the hill atop the promontory. He exchanged his sword for a bow and quiver of arrows and he and his companions set off toward the top of the promontory.

* * *

"Gudbj, are we going to stay here for awhile?" Ingerd called from the press of people on the beach.

Gudbjartur nodded and motioned the people to gather round. "We have found the tracks of a man who watched us sail in here and beach our ships."

A cacophony of voices rose from his listeners.

He raised both arms to quiet them down. "Just listen to what I have to tell you. I will answer any questions you have when I have told you what we know." He waited a moment for people to stop talking. "A single Skraeling watched us for quite some time before he left to the north. There are many sets of man tracks here but his are the only fresh ones. Halfdan wants to stay here until we make contact with them. He wants all of us to make every effort to befriend these people because we cannot remain anywhere in this land if they become our enemies."

Thorgill and a large group of scouts joined the crowd on the beach. Gudbjartur expected Halfdan to be among them. "Where is Halfdan?"

"He took Thorkell and Skeggi with him on a sweep to the north," Thorgill said.

"Tell us what you found." Gudbjartur ordered.

Thorgill stood beside Gudbjartur and faced the crowd of expectant people. "The man was alone," he said in his deep rumbling voice. "We tracked him to the north along this same shoreline and found where he launched a boat and paddled away. There are many other tracks along the shore, so they come here often in their boats. They live somewhere to the north in this big bay. Halfdan hopes to see some sign of them from the top of that hill." He pointed toward the highest hill.

Again, Gudbjartur had to restore order as people tried to be heard. "That is all there is to hear for now. There is much work to do so let us get at it. This is a good site for our purposes. You all know what needs to be done."

He assigned men to all the everyday tasks. The encampment rapidly took shape as the many chores associated with life on the move proceeded. He designated a safety perimeter and posted guards as before. "Ormiga, you and five others take the first guard. Everything is the same as our last camp, and you all have the same tasks to perform. Find me if there are problems, but I expect you can work them out yourselves. If somebody wants off guard duty, find me and I will find a man to trade with you."

The men scattered to their various tasks. Gudbjartur watched the encampment take shape. The guards moved out to secure the perimeter. Gudbjartur gazed out over the countryside. He noticed a flash from atop the promontory, and just barely picked out Halfdan and his men as they returned from their reconnaissance.

Some time later Halfdan sought Gudbjartur out as he moved about the encampment lending a hand where needed. Halfdan pulled him aside to where they had privacy. "We saw smoke to the north, Gudbj, quite a lot of it. I believe the Skraelings may have a village up there along the shore somewhere. The smoke is a long way off but I would not be surprised to receive visitors, perhaps today or tomorrow."

"They have probably watched us for some time, even before we sailed into this bay. That man who watched us sail in here has surely told his people of our presence, so I agree with you. I will tell the guards we expect visitors."

"Tell them not to sound the alarm. Let the Skraelings through the perimeter unless there is a large group of them. If they seem hostile, the guards are to sound the alarm and fall back to the encampment. We will deal with the problem then."

After Gudbjartur's departure, Halfdan reflected on the suitability of the beach he had chosen for their encampment. He walked about making mental notes. The area seemed ideal. Game abounded, a freshwater rill flowed from the fen and into the bay nearby, and timber for firewood and building material grew on two sides of the landing beach. He watched the ships' crews secure the ships' beams to the beach. They rigged gangplanks, and lines of people unloaded all the equipment necessary for life ashore. All the livestock followed, and he saw the herders scatter them over the grassland and the edge of the fen. Within a short span of time, the encampment assumed the bustle and order he had come to expect of his people.

* * *

With the encampment's immediate needs taken care of, women and children gathered at the water's edge to wash the accumulated dirty clothes.

Ingerd sat with her sons on the gravel beach basking in the sun. She let the laundry go for the moment. The three of them watched several women wade into the knee-deep water and begin to wash their clothes while they caught up on the latest gossip.

The boys made eye contact with their mother. "We do not want to be here, mother. We do not wash dirty clothes. That is for women and girls," Ivar said.

Ingerd looked from one boy to the other. "So, you do not wash dirty clothes, huh?"

They shook their heads.

"Oh all right, go do boy-like things if you must. I thought we might take a swim; you two need a bath," she called after them as they tore down the beach.

"The water is too cold!" Lothar shouted back as they ran away laughing.

She grinned, got to her feet, stooped to pick up her basket of dirty clothes, and walked into the water. An involuntary intake of breath confirmed what she already knew. The boys were right. The water was cold. She passed through islands of soapsuds floating on the surface as she waded toward the group of chattering women.

"Have I missed anything important?" Ingerd made eye contact with Frida, who looked up from her washing when she heard Ingerd's voice.

"Not yet," Frida said.

The women passed gray lumps of lye soap—prepared by boiling down a mixture of fat and the liquid remaining after water leached through wood ashes—back and forth as they did their washing.

"The boys did not seem to want to join us." Rannveig stooped over and sloshed a tunic up and down to rinse out the soap.

"No, they did not want to be here at all. They informed me that this work is for women and girls." Ingerd laughed with her friends as she washed and rinsed. Even Frida smiled. Ingerd felt good about that for some reason.

"Well, it would not hurt them to know how to do the washing," Gudrun said.

"I might be able to teach Lothar, but not Ivar," Ingerd said. "He would never stoop to this work. In many respects, he is already a man. Lothar has a ways to go yet." Ingerd finished her laundry quickly, picked her basket out of the water, and carried it to the beach.

"Are you finished already?" Rannveig asked.

Ingerd walked back into the water as she stripped off her clothes. "Not quite, I still have these." Stripped naked, Ingerd sat on the silt bottom and washed the clothes she had been wearing, herself, and her long blond hair. She stood, waded out until the icy water reached her waist, and dove under to rinse. She surfaced beside Frida, sputtered and gasped for air, and deliberately splashed her.

"Come on in Frida, the water is great!"

An involuntary whoosh of air escaped from Frida's lips as the cold water hit her bare back. "So, a water fight you want, is it?" She leaped to her feet, threw a soapy shift at Ingerd, and churned through the water in pursuit.

A wild, good-natured melee ensued that involved everyone already in the water. Many joined from the beach as the fun progressed.

"Oh, by the gods that is cold!" Gudrun shouted as a wet apron wrapped around her head from behind. She tore off in pursuit of Rannveig. Water and silt flew everywhere.

The water was so cold few people remained long. Most were content to watch from the beach while they scrubbed circulation back into their limbs with course scraps of dry wool and shouted encouragement to the hardier souls still in the water.

Frida caught Ingerd, pushed her under, and then tried to escape. She hollered and screeched like a banshee as she plowed through the water with Ingerd in close pursuit.

"Look out, Frida, she is right behind you!" A voice shouted from the crowd on the beach. Too late, Frida tried to dart to the side. Ingerd cut her off, leaped on her back, and both went under in a welter of spray.

A short time later Ingerd and Frida stumbled out of the water, their arms around each other's shoulders like old friends. Lips blue and teeth chattering from the cold, they laughed like girls and almost ran into Halfdan and Gudbjartur, who stood among the bystanders.

Both men had big smiles on their face as they gazed at the two naked women.

Unabashed by her nakedness, Frida looked Halfdan straight in the eye. "So, you came in time to watch us bathe?"

"And I am glad I did." His eyes traveled up and down her body.

Ingerd and Gudbjartur watched the exchange with more than a little interest.

"Do you like what you see, Halfdan?" Frida pushed the mop of wet red hair out of her face.

"I do, Frida, yes, I do." He looked from one naked body to the other. "Both of you look very good, even if you are a little blue."

Ingerd watched this exchange with an openmouthed smile. She glanced at Gudbjartur in time to catch a subtle wink. "I thought you two did not like each other." She looked from one to the other, a mystified smile on her face.

Frida fixed Ingerd with her wide green eyes. "I would not say that. We hardly know each other." She made eye contact with Halfdan again.

Halfdan seemed transfixed by her, a stupid smile on his face.

"Whew! You could use a bath too, Halfdan. I think your hike to the hilltop got you pretty heated up." Frida smiled mischievously from under arched eyebrows.

Gudbjartur laughed as he looked at Halfdan. "Something has him heated up. Even I can smell him."

Halfdan just stood there, smiling.

"Both of you stink. Take a bath and get some clean clothes. Come on, Frida, before we freeze." Ingerd took Frida by the arm and pulled her away.

"Ingerd is right. Both of you need a bath," Frida threw back over her shoulder as the two walked away arm in arm.

Halfdan and Gudbjartur turned to watch them, their eyes riveted on the swaying hips of the two women. They lost sight of them after the two women stopped to pick up the clothes they had washed and disappeared into the encampment. They looked at each another. Halfdan sighed and with a shake of his head began to peel off his clothes. Gudbjartur looked around to see who might be watching, shrugged, and stripped. Whooping like small boys the two men ran into the water.

Frida and Ingerd returned a short time later with clean, dry, warm clothes on, to find the beach taken up by bathers who lolled about or bobbed like corks in the shallows. Half the population, or at least those not still at work, swam, waded, or dawdled about in groups on the beach or in the shallows, visiting or simply relaxing. The two women found Halfdan and Gudbjartur stretched out full length, naked, napping on the warm sand. They seemed oblivious to the activity around them. Both women stood a moment looking at the men. Neither had ever seen them relaxed together, and it took them by surprise. It gave them pause to watch these two hardened, tough men sleeping naked side by side on the beach without visible concern.

"I have never seen them naked before." Frida studied the two bodies. "Both are covered with scars."

"They are men, Frida, warriors. Gudbj has collected those scars all his life. They are the marks of his honor, as are Halfdan's scars. I have always felt safe when I am with them. They would die to protect us, you know?" She spoke in low voice, glancing at Frida to see her reaction.

"I guess I never thought of them that way. I did not realize, or even take the time to consider, their importance, because I have always known I could take care of myself. They were just men to me. I wanted them on my terms, and I never considered what they might think of me, nor did I care. Oh, I knew they all wanted to have their way with me. And I wanted some of them to have their way. But always on my terms."

Ingerd looked at her new friend with interest. "Well, maybe you had better give it some more thought. Halfdan is a man among men. Gudbj loves him like a brother. Halfdan is a lonely man because he is our chieftain. He holds himself above the normal wants and desires of other men. However, he has those feelings nonetheless. He needs a woman, a strong woman. A woman such as you, Frida, with fire in her loins;

fire that waits and wants a man such as Halfdan to quench it. Sagas would be told of the both of you. A union of equals; he would tame you and you him," she concluded.

Frida laughed self-consciously. She studied the other woman. "You surprise me. I like trouble, Ingerd. And men. You give me too much credit, I think."

"No I do not. I know you, because in you I see myself. We are young, you and I. The difference between us is you are still wild because you have not been with the right man. I have found the man to still my wild nature, to quench my thirst, in Gudbj. You, my friend, will find the same in Halfdan, mark my words. I saw how you looked at each other." She watched Frida closely. "I see things and know things about you two that neither of you see for yourselves, but you will. You will."

Speechless, a condition she was unused to, Frida stared at Ingerd, a look of confusion on her face.

"I have things to do, Frida. Moreover, so do you. I will see you later when everyone gathers for the evening meal." She left Frida nodding dumbly at her back.

"Now, where do you suppose those boys have gotten off to?" Ingerd mumbled to herself as she walked away.

Frida turned her attention back to the two sleeping men. She stood thus, lost in thought, when the blast of a warning horn and a single word jerked her from her reverie.

"Skraelings!"

Halfdan and Gudbjartur leaped up. All movement and speech hung suspended as every eye sought out and fastened upon the group of men who stood at the edge of the promontory overlooking the encampment, in full view of the semicircle of watchful guards.

"Easy!" Halfdan shouted. His eyes fastened on the group of Skraelings.

He and Gudbjartur suddenly realized they were naked, as Frida handed them the clothes they had discarded on the beach.

"You may need these," she said, a slight smile on her lips.

Halfdan took his clothes from her outstretched hand. His eyes mirrored the intensity of his feelings at the arrival of the Skraelings.

"Thank you," he said. He and Gudbjartur strode rapidly through the encampment toward the Skraelings, donning their clothes along the way.

Eleven Skraeling men stood loosely grouped on the rocky point above the encampment.

Halfdan, Gudbjartur, and the five ship captains approached the base of the promontory and began the short climb to where the natives waited.

The Skraeling at the forefront of the group turned his head slightly and said something to the men behind him. Apparently, they found some humor in the remark he made, as many of them laughed quickly or smiled.

Bjorn followed closely behind Gudbjartur. He was the first to realize the levity in what should have been a more serious situation. He, too, thought it comical that his leaders donned their clothes as they walked toward the Skraelings. He commented dryly. "I think they find it humorous that you two are getting dressed as we walk to meet them, Halfdan."

Halfdan spoke without turning or slowing the pace. "Humor may prevent trouble."

Halfdan had only a belt knife, while Gudbjartur carried his belted axe and a knife. The five captains all carried spears or bows and quivers of arrows. The Skraelings carried an array of similar weaponry. Neither group had any weapon at the ready.

The Greenlanders stopped several feet in front of the Skraelings and not a word or gesture passed between them as the two disparate groups examined each other.

The Skraelings had brown skin, long black hair, and well-formed bodies of medium height. Their faces were hairless, their black eyes intent. Dressed in leather attire from head to foot, they were different from the Tornit farther north. They were taller, their eyes more rounded and open. They were a different people, a different tribe.

The seven Greenlanders were at least a head taller and had hairy faces. Most had pale eyes, light-colored hair, and very large muscular bodies, especially the two men at the forefront. They wore brilliant blue, green, and red clothing.

The mutual examination was brief and perfunctory. Neither missed anything of importance. Each noted the other's weapons. They had slowly fanned out during their silent examination of each other. The silence was thick enough to cut with a knife.

Halfdan raised his right hand, palm toward the Skraelings in the universal sign of peace. "We come to your land in peace."

The instant he spoke the eyes of all eleven men fastened on him as though the sound of his voice had awakened them from slumber. The Skraeling who had previously spoken to the others spoke a single word of command. Then he, too, raised his palm toward Halfdan. "I greet you in the name of the People."

Although neither knew the meaning of the other's words, they understood and accepted the gesture of peace. Both groups relaxed somewhat and conversation began within each.

"If they were not brown they would look just like us." Bjorn smiled as he spoke.

"They smell different. They do not stink. It is a smell like an animal. They smell wild. That is it," Gudrod said.

"Aye, they do smell wild," Gudbjartur agreed.

The Skraeling leader spoke to his men and one of them produced a pipe and leather bag. He and his men shuffled into a semicircle and sank into comfortable sitting positions on the ground. He gestured to Halfdan and his men to follow suit.

"It appears they want us to smoke that pipe with them." Gudbjartur said as he took a seat on the ground with the others.

"Aye. If they did not want to be friendly I doubt they would offer to smoke with us," Brodir added.

"I hope that proves to be the case," Halfdan said.

Another Skraeling reached into a small pack he carried over one shoulder and drew forth a tiny bow and drill which he began working with. He wrapped the bowstring around the drill and placed the rounded bottom end into a notch cut into a flat piece of wood with a small bit of tinder underneath. The top end above the bowstring he fitted into another piece of wood he held in the palm of his hand. He applied downward pressure on this assembly and sawed the bow back and forth vigorously. The drill rotated rapidly. Tendrils of smoke rose from the tip of the drill a moment later as drill tip and notched wood heated up. He set the bow and drill aside, cupped the tinder between the palms of his hands, and blew softly into it. His efforts almost immediately produced a tiny blue flame that he transferred into the bowl of the pipe held forth by one of his companions. The man puffed mightily until clouds of acrid smoke issued from his mouth and the pipe's bowl.

"Look at that!" Bjorn exclaimed. "I do not think I could have made fire any faster with flint and steel."

"Nor I," Sweyn agreed. "I have never seen fire made that way before."

"I saw the Tornit make it that way once. Their bow was even smaller than that one," Gudbjartur said.

The Skraeling leader started the pipe around the circle. He drew on it briefly and passed it across to Halfdan, who took a puff and passed it on.

The pipe made it about halfway around the circle when the material within was consumed and it went out. Gudrod attempted to puff it back to life.

The Skraelings laughed and the man who had the bag of tobacco gestured for him to return the pipe for a reload.

"What is that?" Bjorn gestured at the material the Skraeling tamped in the bowl.

The Skraeling leader answered. "Knickanick, we call it knickanick." He rose to his feet, walked a few steps away, bent over, and broke off a sprig from a low, ground-hugging shrub. He returned and offered it to Halfdan as he sat down. "Knick-anick." He pointed to the sprig in Halfdan's hand.

"Knickanick." Halfdan repeated the word for the tobacco perfectly.

"Knickanick." The Skraeling leader nodded and smiled as he looked from man to man.

"Well, knickanick it is then." Brodir spat on the ground. "It sure stinks. My tongue and eyes burn from the smoke."

"Mine too." Gudrod coughed as he looked at the smiling Skraelings. "But I think they want us to keep smoking their pipe anyway."

Most of the Greenlanders had never before smoked and they laughed at Gudrod's comment. The laughter was infectious and everyone joined in.

"Here, let me show them our flint and steel." Gudbjartur gestured at the man about to relight the pipe with his bow and drill.

The man passed a small bit of tinder to Gudbjartur, who placed it on the ground. He smiled at the group of Skraelings. They watched his every movement. Gudbjartur reached into the pouch on his belt and removed his flint and steel. He held them up for all to see, took the steel in his right hand, the flint in his left, and struck the steel smartly against the flint. A shower of sparks flew into the tinder. Smoke rose from the tinder immediately as the sparks caught, and Gudbjartur cupped it in his hands and softly blew the sparks to a flame. He twisted the tinder tightly in his fingers and thrust the tiny flame into the pipe bowl while the Skraeling puffed it back into life.

The Skraelings gestured and exclaimed.

"They must think it is magic," Gudbjartur said as he passed his flint and steel to the leader. This comparison of fire-starting methods served to melt the last reservations of both groups of men. Through words and gestures a conversation of sorts developed.

"Halfdan, why not take them into the encampment. They cannot harm us. The women and children may work with them the same way they worked with the Tornit," Bjorn said.

"I agree, Halfdan. We are limited in what we can talk about here. The people's activities might save a lot of time in establishing friendly relations with them," Gudbjartur said.

Halfdan rose from his seat on the ground, and all the other men followed suit.

"Gudbj. You, Bjorn, and Sweyn alert our people that we are coming down with these men. I want everyone to continue with his or her work. Act naturally and friendly." The three men walked down ahead of the main body to tell the people what Halfdan expected of them.

A few moments later, Halfdan beckoned to the Skraelings to follow. He and the four remaining council members led them down to the encampment.

Chapter Eight

When Gudbjartur, Bjorn, and Sweyn returned without the others and told the people the Skraelings would be visiting the encampment and what Halfdan expected, the word spread like a wildfire.

Not surprisingly, the Skraelings showed signs of nervousness as they entered the encampment. They were few in the midst of many. They walked in a tight group for a time but began to spread out and relax among the friendly settlers.

The council led the visitors slowly by the tents and the men building the fire pit so they could see groups of people busy at normal everyday tasks. The Skraeling leader paused to examine a tent's fabric. He and his men peered inside curiously.

Thora and Gudrun sat on a bench inside. Both were spinning wool when the men stopped at the entrance.

"Come in." Thora smiled and motioned for them to enter.

Their leader said something to his men. He and two others walked inside with Halfdan. The rest of the men watched from the entrance.

The two women went on with their spinning while the Skraelings watched. Their leader pointed at the wool yarn and asked a question. Thora glanced at Halfdan quizzically.

"I think he wants to know what the yarn is used for," Halfdan said. "Just talk to him. He will not understand so show him what you mean."

Thora nodded, set her spindle aside, took a skein of yarn from her basket, and stood. "This is wool yarn. We call it wadmal. We make our clothes from it." She held her apron out to him. He rubbed the material between his fingers and spoke to his men. Thora continued. "This tent is made of wadmal." She touched the tent's sidewall. The Skraeling leader spoke to his men again and made eye contact with Thora. He spoke a single word to her, smiled, and turned to Halfdan.

"I think he understands, Thora. You did well," Halfdan said.

"Thank you," she answered with a broad smile. The Skraelings smiled back.

Halfdan beckoned the leader to follow, and he and his men filed from the tent. The tour continued through the encampment to the landing beach.

The Skraelings gathered on the beach in a tight group in front of the ships, talking among themselves.

"You are all too quiet," Halfdan said to his men. "Talk to each other. These men are nervous, so try to relax them by acting natural. Laughter might help."

Gudbjartur slapped Bjorn on the back and laughed.

"What did you do that for?" Bjorn asked. Then he, too, laughed as realization dawned on all of them at once. Gudbjartur's slap on the back started them talking.

"Come aboard." Halfdan walked part way up one of the gangplanks of Steed of the Sea and gestured for the Skraeling leader to follow.

Hesitantly the man followed as Halfdan stepped down into the ship.

The other Skraelings watched Halfdan and their leader walk the deck from end to end. The two men stopped several times while the Skraeling leader examined the sweeps, sail, ship's boats, the huge anchor, and other equipment. The large animal pens still held the ship's livestock. The Skraeling leader halted in midstride at the sight of these animals. He called out to his men on the beach and gestured for them to join him.

Down in the holding pens chickens scratched in the dunnage and animal droppings. As luck would have it, a rooster picked that moment to crow. The Skraelings exclaimed in surprise at the noise made by this colorful bird. The Greenlanders laughed at their surprised expressions, and the Skraelings joined in.

One of the ewes had given birth to a pair of lambs during the voyage south, and the bleats of these small creatures dispelled the last reservations of the Skraelings. They plied Halfdan and his men with a multitude of questions about the animals. It was impossible to understand what they asked, but with sign language, they conveyed much of their meaning. Despite the crudeness of these attempts, a method of communication evolved.

"Gudbj, unload the horses and show them what we use them for," Halfdan said.

They unloaded the horses and the chattering Skraelings tried to help. Bjorn and Sweyn each bridled a horse, leaped to their backs, and galloped down the beach to the delight of the Skraelings.

"I think they thought the horses were food," Gudbjartur laughed, as some of the Skraelings ran down the beach in pursuit of the mounted men, laughing like small boys on a lark.

"I think so, too, Gudbj," Halfdan said.

With a lift of his chin, he indicated a group of four men who stood together, stern and unsmiling. "Not all of them accept our friendship with the same enthusiasm."

"I have been watching them, too. They do not want to be here. They have not participated at all."

"Keep an eye on them and alert the other captains that we may still have a problem."

"I will." He moved away unobtrusively.

Bjorn and Sweyn pulled their galloping mounts to a stop in front of the group. The horses blew and pranced; the Skraelings recoiled at the antics of the powerful animals.

The Skraeling leader, noticing that four of his men had not joined the group, strode toward them. He gestured toward the Greenlanders and the ships. Heated words passed back and forth as the Skraeling leader berated them. The discussion ended when the Skraeling leader gestured to the north. The four men marched away without a word to or glance at the Greenlanders.

With a lift of his chin and a slight inclination of his head, Halfdan motioned for Gudbjartur to follow the four Skraelings. Gudbjartur tapped Brodir on his way by and the two men separated from the group without attracting the attention of the remaining Skraelings.

To distract the remaining seven Skraelings, Halfdan and his men led the group back into the encampment. He pointed out the activity around the smithies' forge. Haakon and Asgrim forged tools while their helpers finished the temporary smithy. The Skraelings watched the smiths transform iron bars into various tools. Although they had no understanding of the process, the Skraelings grasped the significance of what they witnessed almost immediately, as evidenced by their excited chatter. The ringing blows of hammer on anvil and the sparks that flew from the white-hot metal as it was forged into recognizable shapes seemed to awe them.

Haakon forged the familiar shape of a knife blade, and as the group watched him, he drew the flat tang of the handle out of the white-hot steel. Sigmund, one of the helpers, skillfully punched two rivet holes in the tang and then shoved the knife blank back into the fire. Another helper pumped the large, leather and wood bellows to reheat the metal. When the blank glowed white hot again, Haakon grasped the glowing steel with his tongs and carefully shaped the blade into a double-sided edge. He plunged the roughed-out blade into a bucket of cold water beside his anvil to temper and cool it. A loud hissing pop followed by a great cloud of steam brought exclamations of wonder from the Skraelings.

Haakon and Asgrim enjoyed their captivated audience. Caught up in the moment, Asgrim handed the knife blade to one of the Skraelings. The man examined it carefully then passed it on.

The Skraeling leader, the last man to examine the blade, turned to Bjorn and pointed to his belt knife. He pointed to himself, spoke a few guttural words, and then pointed at

Bjorn's knife again. Bjorn passed his knife to the man handle first. The Skraeling held the finished knife beside the newly forged blade.

Through sign language and speech, Bjorn made the Skraeling leader understand that the smithies had forged both blades. "Here, I will show you." Bjorn took his knife back, laid it on the anvil, and mimed hitting it with a hammer. Then he pointed the knife at Haakon. "Haakon forged my knife."

The Skraeling nodded. He pointed to Bjorn with the knife, then to himself. "Trade?" he asked.

"He wants to trade for my knife." Bjorn glanced at Halfdan.

"No weapons." Halfdan shook his head. "We will not trade any weapons to you."

The Skraeling leader's face clouded. His personality underwent an immediate change for the worse. Clipped speech and abrupt signings conveyed the extent of his displeasure.

"Haakon, do you have a new fire steel you could give him?" Halfdan asked.

"No, but it will take only a short time to make him one," he said.

"Make it then." Halfdan turned aside to talk to the Skraeling leader.

Halfdan mimed his intention to have Haakon make a fire steel for the Skraeling leader. He produced his own fire steel from his belt pouch and showed it to him. Then he pointed to the white-hot bar Haakon and Asgrim had just drawn from the forge and made him understand it would be for him.

Understanding came to the Skraeling gradually as he watched the fire steel take shape under Haakon's hammer. The smith bent both ends of the short steel bar around until they almost touched. This shape created a handle for the flat striking surface on the bottom of the steel. The partially enclosed shape also protected the user's hand against sparks. Haakon produced the implement in one heating of the iron bar. He dropped it in the bucket of water to temper and cool the steel. Haakon retrieved the new tool, examined it, and handed it to the Skraeling.

"Here, let me show you how it works." Halfdan crouched on the ground over a bit of tinder he had removed from his pouch. Using his own flint, he struck the fire steel sharply against the flint. Sparks showered into the tinder. He cupped the smoking tinder in his hands and blew it into a flame. Halfdan dropped the flaming tinder to the ground, stood, and handed the fire steel to the Skraeling leader. "This will produce fire for you and your people for the rest of your life." He pointed at the Skraeling's belt knife and his own flint he held in his hand. "The flint we use to make sparks is the same as the flint you use for knives and arrow heads."

The man nodded and muttered a few guttural words of his language while he examined his newly acquired fire steel.

To complete the set, Asgrim handed him a good piece of flint from the supply the smiths kept on hand. The Skraeling looked at Asgrim and nodded his thanks.

One of the Skraeling's men handed him a handful of tinder at his request. He crouched on the ground and tried out the unfamiliar fire steel as he had seen Halfdan do.

The Greenlanders gathered around him, offering advice as he made several abortive attempts to strike a spark.

"He is not striking the flint and steel together hard enough." Gudrod joined the Skraeling on the ground and demonstrated the proper technique to him. "Hold the flint at an angle like this. Strike the steel against it hard like this." A great shower of sparks flew into the tinder. The Skraeling looked up at his men, grunted something, and they all laughed.

Halfdan and his men laughed with them. "I wonder what we laugh at," Brodir said.

The Skraeling leader glanced at Brodir and said something to him. His men found whatever he said to be hysterical. A couple of them slapped their legs as the group dissolved in laughter.

"Maybe the joke is on us." Halfdan laughed along with the rest of his men. "It does not matter. They are laughing and that is the object of all this."

The Skraeling leader took the fire steel and flint from Gudrod and produced a shower of sparks as if he had done it all his life.

"That is the way to do it!" Gudrod slapped the Skraeling on the back.

* * *

Gudbjartur and Brodir returned from following the four Skraelings who had left in a huff. As they rejoined the tour group, Gudbjartur spoke conversationally to Halfdan so as not to arouse the other Skraeling's suspicion. "All four of them got into a boat and paddled along the shore to the north, in the direction of the smoke you saw earlier. We watched them until they were out of sight."

Halfdan nodded but made no comment. The Skraelings continued their examination of the strange encampment, unaware of the content of Gudbjartur's report.

They approached the camp perimeter. The Skraeling leader turned to face Halfdan. He extended his hand with a few words that Halfdan interpreted to be in farewell and friendship.

Halfdan smiled and nodded as he shook hands with the man. "I am happy that we are friends. We look forward to a long friendship with you and your people."

The Skraeling leader made a short speech as well. He held his new flint and steel and gestured with it to encompass the entire encampment. Then he turned and swept his arm to the north and looked back at Halfdan and his men. "I want our two peoples to meet at our village to trade and become friends. We will wait for you to come. We welcome you in peace, and I give you this talisman as my word that there is peace between us." He handed a talisman to Halfdan, a neck amulet made of leather and decorated with porcupine quills.

Although none of the Northmen knew exactly what the Skraeling said to them, they took his speech, facial expressions, and sign language as an indication of his sincerity.

Halfdan, somewhat taken aback by the man's obvious sincerity, held the gift up for all to see. "He wants us to come to his village to trade, I think." Halfdan smiled and nodded his acceptance to the Skraeling.

The council agreed with his assessment and Gudbjartur spoke for them. "We think that is exactly what he said."

The two groups nodded, smiled at one another, and parted company.

The Skraelings walked away in single file to the north without a backward glance.

"I am gratified. I think that meeting went well." Halfdan and his men watched the Skraelings until they passed from sight.

His men agreed. The captains went to their separate tasks, and Halfdan and Gudbjartur walked back into the encampment.

"That went very well indeed. I did not expect our first meeting with them to be that easy," Gudbjartur said.

"Neither did I. Tomorrow I will select a party to visit their village to trade. Then we shall see if we can really have a peaceful relationship with these people." They parted company near the encampment center.

After the Skraelings departed, activity around the encampment assumed a state of watchful normalcy as word passed that the first meeting with the strangers had seemed friendly and open. Gudbjartur told each of the perimeter guards the current situation and established a permanent lookout atop the promontory, so they could give ample warning of any further visits from the north, just in case the first contact had been a ruse. He and Halfdan thought it prudent to be in a high state of readiness until they were certain the Skraelings were indeed honorable and open.

As he walked back from posting the guard on the promontory, Gudbjartur observed the activity on the beach around Halfdan's ship. Crewmen readied the ship to put to sea. He walked up to Halfdan as he knelt on the sand and stuffed gear into his sleeping bag. "I suppose you want me to stay here."

Halfdan stopped what he was doing and looked up at his lieutenant with a slight smile. "Once again you have anticipated me. Who else but you would I leave in charge?"

"Any one of the captains can be in charge." Gudbjartur's lips thinned in disapproval. "I do not think you should do this thing without me."

"Nor do I, but we have little choice in the matter. I want you here in case of trouble. I trust no man as I do you. There will be trouble with these Skraelings, of that I am certain, and while I am gone I do not want to worry. With you here I will not worry. That is the way of it, the way it must be."

Gudbjartur gritted his teeth in frustration but said no more.

Halfdan knew his lieutenant did not like the decision. "I will be gone two days at most. We will sail on the flood tide in the morning and return the next day. I take my ship because she is the largest. I want to impress these people with our power. Several women will be going with us. We will call the people together and ask for volunteers. I want the Skraelings to view the women as a peaceful gesture on our part."

"Good idea. I see you are taking plenty of trade goods with you." Gudbjartur watched men carry bags and barrels up the gangplank. "They wanted to trade. If they all feel that way, maybe there will be no trouble with them."

"Let us hope so. Trading often forges a bond between peoples who have nothing else in common."

Gudbjartur watched the men load the ship for a time before he took his leave. He strode off into the encampment, his mind occupied with the security of his people.

* * *

After the evening's communal meal, Halfdan and Gudbjartur called everyone to a meeting.

"As most of you know, I sail for the Skraeling village tomorrow on the flood tide. I expect to be away two full days and one night. I will take a crew of fifty volunteers—forty men, and ten women. The presence of the women will show them we are peaceful." Halfdan knew his comment would cause laughter, which it did.

"They do not know our women." Thorgill hollered from the rear of the crowd. "They are not always peaceful."

Several others offered similar comments. Halfdan let them laugh and joke for a time before he raised his arms to restore order.

"All right. All right. You may be correct, Thorgill. I would not know." Good-natured jeers and whistles followed his comment. He gestured once more for silence. "Now then, back to the matters at hand. Nobody need volunteer, including my regular crew. Anybody can go who wants to, up to a total of fifty. Those who want to go raise your hands, and Gudbj and I will count you off."

Frida, to the surprise of everyone save Ingerd, who accompanied her, was the first to volunteer. "I will go, Halfdan," she shouted from the forefront of the crowd.

"And I," Ingerd shouted.

Both women grinned at each other like girls who had shared knowledge of a plot.

"Why do you want to go, Ingerd? What about the boys? Who is to care for them?" Gudbjartur asked.

"I am going because Frida is going. We want to go together on this adventure," she said, her arm over Frida's shoulder. "The boys are big enough to take care of themselves. Everyone will watch out for them as they always do."

Halfdan watched Gudbjartur closely. He expected a reaction to Ingerd's new independence.

"If I do not want you to go, you will not go, no matter what you and Frida want to do," Gudbjartur said.

Ingerd looked at the ground for a heartbeat. "You are right. I should have asked you first." Then she asked hopefully, "So, can I go with them?"

Frida snorted in disgust and started to say something until warned by Ingerd's sharp intake of breathe and quick shake of her head.

The crowd watched in anticipation as Ingerd stood before Gudbjartur, hands on hips, her chin raised in the most defiant pose she could muster. Gudbjartur glanced from her to Frida to Halfdan, and over the sea of faces. His eyes came back to his wife. His unblinking eyes bored into her. Then his glance traveled down her taut body. He noted the hands on hips, the clenched jaw muscles, and the look of resolve on her beautiful face. *Why, she is doing everything but tapping her foot,* he thought, amused.

Not a sound came from the crowd. The wind soughed through the pines; a dog barked.

Gudbjartur suddenly threw his head back and laughed. He grabbed Ingerd around the waist, lifted her off her feet, and crushed her body to his chest.

"I guess I would have you no other way, woman." He held her close to his face and looked into his wife's pale blue eyes. "You have always had your own mind. It is one of the many things I like about you. You may go, Ingerd, with this trouble-maker of a friend." He fixed Frida with a feigned baleful look as he put Ingerd down. "But only because you go with Halfdan."

Frida sniffed and tossed her luxurious red hair in her own small act of defiance. She winked mischievously at Ingerd. "Thank you, Gudbj. I am certain we will be safe with Halfdan. And the break from our normal everyday duties will be most welcome, not to mention the chance of adventure." She smiled and looked directly at Halfdan. Her glance covered him from head to foot.

None of the intrigue was lost on the crowd, especially those in front. All waited breathlessly for Halfdan's reaction.

Halfdan just smiled foolishly at Frida. He recovered quickly though and tore his eyes from her. "Who else volunteers for this two-day adventure to the lair of the Skraelings?"

A moment of bedlam followed as most everyone tried to shove their way to the front or shout for Halfdan's attention.

Ingerd pulled Gudbjartur aside before Halfdan could make his selections from the crowd. "Halfdan is smitten with her, Gudbj." She looked into his eyes.

Gudbjartur looked toward his friend, who pointed out his selections from the press of people. He reflected in silence for a moment. "He has been acting strangely of late. Time will tell. He is lonely; he wants a woman to share his life, but he will do nothing in haste. They would make quite a team, I expect." He looked at Ingerd. "Give it time. They will figure out what is best for them." He moved away to join Halfdan. Ingerd watched her husband rejoin Halfdan and the crowd of volunteers.

* * *

The volunteers boarded Halfdan's ship after the mid-morning meal and prepared to sail. The ship floated free of the bottom suction after the flood tide began. The mixed crew maneuvered her away from the beach with sweeps. They hoisted the sail the moment the wind had purchase as the ship distanced itself from the blanking effect of the land. The flood tide provided a good push as they sailed toward the north end of the bay.

* * *

Activity around the encampment was normal for late afternoon. Gudbjartur tried to keep busy so he would not watch the promontory for a signal that he did not expect until tomorrow. He shook thoughts of Ingerd and Halfdan from his mind. Bending forward, he freed the carpenter's axe he had stuck in the log's butt end. He tested the edge with his thumb and, satisfied with its keenness, he directed his attention to the log he had started to square for the carpenters.

Logs were skidded to the site with teams of horses. Gudbjartur and several other men hewed them into squared balks from which they split planks. The timber hereabouts was too small for most of their needs, but the narrow planks were useful nonetheless. Pine predominated in the thick forests. But only yesterday, hunters had found stands of good birch hardwood close by. Some timber, selected for its shape, the men adzed smooth for replacement ship's ribs and knees. Straight logs they split into thin planks and smoothed to replace the planks used to repair Gudrod's ship.

Gudbjartur drove wedges into the ends of a straight birch log until it started to split. He coaxed the split carefully down the length of the log with additional wedges until the second quarter-round slab split cleanly away. Now he had a birch balk with two flats from which he split thin boards. He finished splitting the balk into planks, left the work of adzing to another, and walked over to watch a bowl take shape under the skillful hands of Jorundr the Carver.

The man had selected a large, oval-shaped, birch-wood burl that he split from a standing tree. He shaped the burl round with a hatchet. Then he used a specially designed, two-handed, curved drawknife to scoop wood from the inside.

"Who is to get this one, Jorundr?" Gudbjartur took a seat on the ground across from the man. He removed the battle-axe from its belt loop as he took a seat and laid it on the ground at his side.

"Thora has needed a new one for some time. She told me so at Snorrisfjord but, until we came to this place, I had no wood suitable for a bowl. I laced her old bowl together with rawhide, and it has lasted until now." Jorundr glanced up as Gudbjartur watched the bowl take shape, stopped carving, and set his work aside. He studied Gudbjartur's troubled face. "They will be all right, Gudbj. Tomorrow will be here before we know it. Halfdan's ship will sail back around the point, and it will be as though they never sailed away."

Gudbjartur laughed at his own trepidation. "I am that obvious?"

Jorundr nodded. "We all know you are worried. You have helped do many things today that you do not normally do, to keep busy." Jorundr smiled.

Gudbjartur glanced in the direction of the promontory lookout. He chuckled again, shook his head in resignation, and slapped Jorundr on the back. "Perhaps you are right. All of you are right." He raised his voice to include the others. "I appreciate your concern."

Jorundr turned his attention back to the bowl. He kept glancing at the now silent Gudbjartur, who watched with a faraway look in his eyes.

"By Hel," Gudbjartur said, in acceptance of the situation. "She is only a woman, and if she does not come back, I will simply get another."

The men offered several off-color remarks. They all knew Gudbjartur did not mean it.

"You had better hope Ingerd returns. Many men are without women. The waiting line is long. You would be at the end of it," Jorundr said.

Gudbjartur knew he fooled none of these men with his lighthearted remark about Ingerd's return. He just smiled in acknowledgment, sat for a time watching the Jorundr work, and thought his own thoughts. "You are very skilled with your tools, Jorundr." He watched the shavings accumulate as the bowl took shape. He examined an assortment of carving tools the man stored in the ornately carved box at his side.

"We are fortunate you and the others from Iceland arrived in Greenland in time to join our expedition. You have brought many skills with you that we neglected in Greenland. I see that your tools are much used. Many are unknown to me," Gudbjartur said.

"I made this box." Jorundr rubbed his hand over the ornately carved toolbox. "Most of these tools belonged to my father and his father before him. We are from Vestfoldland. I arrived in Iceland last Slaughtering Time and spent the winter there."

"Why did you sail to Greenland?" Gudbjartur asked. "With your trade you would have found ample work in Iceland and made a good life there."

"That is true. I already had more work than I could do. However, I soon found that others had taken all the good land. Iceland was too crowded for me. When I heard that Sweyn sought settlers for a voyage to Greenland, and that good land was still available there, I volunteered."

"You have had quite an adventure. My life has been dull by comparison. I have been to Iceland on many voyages to trade, but never to Vestfoldland. I was born in Iceland. My father moved the family to Greenland when I was a little boy. I am the only one left. My family is all dead. Before I married Ingerd and we came on this voyage, my life was spent just trying to survive through each winter and lay aside enough walrus ivory, rope, and blubber to trade with Iceland for goods we could not produce at home."

"Where did you meet Halfdan?"

"I sailed on hunting and trading voyages with him from Brattahlid, the farm of Eirik the Red, at Eiriksfjord in Greenland. He came from Vestfoldland as a boy. His family lived in Iceland for a time until his father moved to Greenland with Eirik the Red. His father is still alive, but the rest of his family is dead, too. We met two summers ago. We have been together since."

"Your loyalty to him is a legend among the people, Gudbj. It was one of the first things I heard when we joined this expedition—the bond between you two."

"He is my chief, my friend," Gudbjartur said simply. He riveted Jorundr with a direct glance. "I would follow him into the Underworld."

"I, too, follow him. He is a great chieftain," he said.

Gudbjartur stood up and motioned at the toolbox. "The smithies would be interested in seeing those tools. They might want to copy some of them to provide to others."

"Haakon made wooden patterns of several of them just the other day. He told me he will make samples when he has the time."

"Good. I will see you at the evening meal then." Gudbjartur unconsciously hung the axe in its belt loop.

He nodded to the other workers near at hand, glanced once again toward the promontory lookout, and moved off into another area of the encampment.

Jorundr watched him walk away. He chanced to glance toward the nearest of the woodworkers and saw that he, too, watched Gudbjartur walk away. The man glanced at Jorundr and shook his head once; the gesture conveyed as much meaning as a spoken word. Jorundr watched Gudbjartur as he disappeared behind the nearest of the tents. His thoughts came into focus. *Yes, he is respected and perhaps a little feared. Not a man to cross unless one is willing to accept the inevitable consequence. Halfdan is lucky to have such a man beside him. We all are.*

Chapter Nine

Halfdan's ship beat against a brisk northwesterly wind. Progress to the north was slower than he wanted as he tacked his ship back and forth across the eye of the wind. He had directed Gorm to keep to the center of the large bay to avoid the many skerries and small islands they saw along their course. The expected ranks of serried swells associated with relatively shallow water slapped at the hull as the ship's bow sliced them asunder. He stood at his accustomed place on the bow platform, oblivious to the large school of dolphins playing in the water ahead of the bow wave, the cries of following seabirds, the sough of the wind in the rigging, and all the other familiar sounds of a ship underway. Thoughts of what they might expect at the village of the Skraelings occupied his mind. *I do not expect to be welcomed with open arms. Perhaps a truce of sorts might result because of the women aboard ship and the possibility of trade.*

The smudge of smoke on the northern horizon began to separate into the columns of many cooking fires as the ship drew nearer the village. He reflected on his decision to heave to near one of the many islands they encountered to kill seals to present to the villagers. He looked aft at the four towed seals that bobbed in the wake. He hoped they provided a common ground that would forge a bond between the two peoples.

The northwesterly wind held steady. As they drew nearer the northern shoreline the land's influence caused eddies and gusts. Halfdan glanced out over the rolling, tree-covered hills, squinting in bright sunlight under the cloudless sky. *It looks like a good day to trade*, he thought. His eyes swept the northern horizon; then he focused attention back toward the village.

He watched keenly as details of the village began to emerge. Dwellings warmed by a southern exposure were nestled along the base of a tree-covered ridge. Protected by the ridge's proximity from the north wind, the village meandered along the sandy north shore of a narrow east-west inlet. The landscape looked similar to that surrounding the encampment. Rolling hills and a vast tundra opened out to the northeast. A river flowed into the inlet from the tundra.

A loud horn shattered the quiet of the ship's approach. Although they had expected it, people jumped in surprise and then chuckled at their own reaction. At Halfdan's orders, the masthead lookout began to sound his signal horn at intervals to alert the village of their approach. He wanted them fully prepared for visitors.

Halfdan turned and looked at the trim of the sail and decided to slow their approach. He cupped his hands and shouted aft. "Loose the sheets a little, men. Gorm, bring her head into the wind a bit to slow us down."

Gorm pulled the tiller a little upwind to allow the sail to luff, and then he steered toward a new point of reference on the shoreline. The speed bled off as the flapping sail slowed the ship.

"Good, hold her so!" Halfdan shouted.

Halfdan briefed the crew on what he expected when they arrived at the village. "Everyone gather round." He waited for the shuffling to stop. "I want no surprises ashore. I expect trouble. Everyone aboard is to be armed when we get there. You all wear chain mail or leather jerkins and helmets. There is a shield for every crew member hanging on the outside of the ship's rails. Our final approach will be with sweeps. If they greet us in friendship, continue to row toward the beach. Be alert for my orders. If anyone sees an arrow or any other missile come aboard, and I have not seen it, warn me and I will give the order to shear off. Get the sail on her as quickly as possible. Continue to row until the sail draws well. Then stow the sweeps and take up your weapons. If they attack in a mass, leave the sweeps. The sweeps may keep them from boarding and give us more time to shoot. Forget them and shoot arrows. When we come about, whoever is closest should cut the towline. Maybe the seals will distract them long enough for us to get away. If they attack us, I want every Skraeling in the closest boat killed with the first flight of arrows. Hurt them! All of you are good archers. That is why we chose you. We do not want them to board this ship. Hold them off at all cost. If they get aboard, we are doomed. They have us outnumbered at least four to one." He paused and looked from face to face. "Do you all understand what I have said? Are there any questions?" There were none.

"If I fall, Thorgill is in command. Now return to your places. Be alert. Perhaps we can be friends with them and all this preparation will prove to be unnecessary."

He had told Thorgill earlier that he wanted to wait as long as possible to lower the sail and deploy the sweeps. He wanted the Skraelings to see the orderly maneuver.

A man stood near Halfdan in the bows casting the weighted plummet forward of the ship to sound the water depth. "No bottom on the line," the man said after each cast. So far, the weighted fifty-foot line had not reached the bottom, indicating plenty of depth for the ship's three-foot draft amidships.

A large crowd of Skraelings gathered on the village beach. Several boats filled with men put out from the shore.

A whistle came from the masthead lookout. "Boats putting out from shore with armed men, Halfdan. Some of those who were in our camp are in the first boat. I think their leader is one of them."

"I see them now. It is time for you to come down from there." Halfdan did not want the lookout to remain in his exposed position until he knew what the Skraelings intended.

Halfdan nodded to Thorgill. He turned to the waiting crew. "Lower the sail, out sweeps!"

Within moments, the crew stowed the sail. The ship lost little headway as the sweeps came into play to the measured boom of the stroke drum. Women worked right beside the men on this voyage and they manned some of sweeps in pairs. Frida and Ingerd were two of them. They sweated and grunted with the effort.

"Are you pulling?" Ingerd asked.

"Of course," Frida said. "I was wondering the same about you."

"Save your breath. Pull."

Frida managed a snort as the two women strained into the backstroke.

Halfdan stood on the bow platform with part of the crew and watched the approach of the Skraeling boats. The gap between ship and boats closed rapidly. He slung a quiver of arrows over his shoulder, selected a bow from the pile of weapons forward of the mast, and strung the powerful weapon as he watched the boats approach. He reckoned they were almost within arrow range.

"Everyone try to relax. Look normal if you can." A nervous laugh or two came to his ears. He turned to the man at the stroke drum. "Slow the stroke."

The ship gradually slowed to the lowest speed that the helmsman could maintain steerageway.

Halfdan watched the flotilla of small boats, now less than two ship lengths forward of the upswept bow. "Easy! Continue the stroke."

A Skraeling stood erect in one of the boats nearest the front, raised an arm above his head, and called out in greeting.

Halfdan recognized him as the leader of the contingent that had visited the encampment the previous day. He raised his arm in greeting.

"Hold the stroke, back sweeps!" Thorgill shouted to the crew.

A solid phalanx of boats blocked forward progress. The ship slowed to dead in the water with half a ship length separating the two groups. The sweeps remained deployed; their blades floated on the water's surface. The crew rested at the ready.

For a moment, not a word passed between them as each group looked the other over. The erratic buzz of a fly, the bark of a dog in the village, the cry of a bird in the distance, and the slap of a fish's tail were the only sounds to hear. A palpable tension hung thick in the air.

"We have come to trade with you." Halfdan held a roll of bright red and blue wadmal aloft. The loose end blew in the wind. He gestured toward the seals, clearly visible bobbing astern. "We have brought meat."

Although neither understood the other's speech, the gestures helped. The Skraeling gestured toward the four seals and asked Halfdan something. Then he said something to the men in his boat. Halfdan understood. He turned and called aft. "Bring those seals forward."

Two crewmen towed the seals as far forward along the ship's side as the deployed sweeps allowed, and threw the coiled line to a man in the nearest boat. This man stood and hauled in the line hand over hand. Because of the dead weight of the carcasses in the water, his efforts drew his boat to the seals rather than the other way around. Laughter and hoots erupted from his fellows.

The laughter spread to the Northmen.

"They sound just like we do," Frida said.

"I have an idea they are very much like us," Ingerd said. "Let us hope they really are as friendly as they appear."

Frida smiled at her friend. "This seems almost too good to be true."

"Maybe, but I do not think so. We shall see." Ingerd looked out over the massed boats toward the village, trying to take it all in.

The seals provided the hoped-for diversion as several boats maneuvered around the floating carcasses. The occupants chattered in animated fashion. The prospect of fresh meat transferred attention from the Greenlanders to the seals. Individual boats took a seal in tow and headed for the village beach with a flurry of flashing paddles.

One boat separated from the others and paddled swiftly toward the ship. This caused quite a stir among the Greenlanders as everyone's attention focused on the possible threat. Thorgill shouted from the bow. "They are bringing our towline back!"

The boat closed to within throwing distance and the Skraeling in the bow heaved the coiled line aboard the ship. He uttered a few clipped, guttural words and gestured to the men that watched from the ship.

Vilhjalm, who chanced to catch the coil of line, held it aloft. "You are welcome. And thank you for bringing our line back."

The Skraeling nodded and smiled up at him. He and his companions paddled back toward the press of boats.

A few witty remarks followed from crew members along the ship's rail.

"You act as though you know what he said." Frida's rowing station happened to be where the exchange took place.

"I do not know what he said, Frida, but somebody needed to say something. I would rather try to talk to them than fight them."

"So would I, Vilhjalm. I am glad you said the right thing." Her green eyes locked on his.

Vilhjalm shifted his attention to Frida momentarily. He did not want to appear friendly with the woman responsible for the death of his friend, Ulfar. The unaccustomed note of sincerity in her tone struck him nonetheless.

He nodded and studied her for a moment through narrowed eyes. She returned his look without sign of intimidation or fear. *There may be more to her than I thought. Perhaps she regrets having caused the einvigi,* he mused, turning toward the milling boats.

The Skraeling leader shouted above the din of conversation. He gestured at the closely packed boats in the ship's path. In response the boats scattered somewhat and began paddling toward the beach. Their leader beckoned for the ship to follow.

"It appears we are allowed to proceed," Halfdan said.

Thorgill turned to the crew. "Give way together, slow ahead." The stroke drum took up the beat of dead slow as the ship gathered way for the beach.

The ship gathered speed; many of the boats were overtaken. It became apparent to Halfdan that even at dead slow the ship was considerably faster. The gaggle of boats pulled out of the ship's path. A sort of race to the beach developed, with much shouting between boats.

Men, women, and children milled about on the beach. Willing hands hauled the seal carcasses up on dry land.

Halfdan held his arm aloft to signal Thorgill. "Hold the stroke! Let her drift until her way is off, then drop the anchor."

His orders passed aft from man to man. Halfdan returned his attention forward as the ship lost momentum.

Two men in the bow wrestled the heavy anchor over the side. It plunged to the bottom; the ship payed off downwind and the anchor rode came up taut as the hook snagged. The ship swung downwind on the anchor line to lie parallel to the beach.

Halfdan watched the people on the beach and in the many boats offshore. He knew his first inclination to anchor rather than beach the ship was the correct choice. He still did not trust these people. Until he could trust them, the ship would remain at anchor.

"Stay alert!" he called to his crew. "I will take three women and three men with me to the village. The rest of you will stay aboard." As he spoke, several men worked to launch one of the two ship's boats over the leeward side, out of sight of those on the beach. Halfdan waited impatiently while they rigged the gin pole from the mast base to swing the boat over the ship's side. He watched the shoreline while he gathered his thoughts.

The boat splashed into the water. He gathered the crew amidships to make his selection for the landing party.

"This is a mission of peaceful trade. There is a risk for those of you who go ashore with me. We do not know if all of them are friendly. Until we have been among them we will not know the answer to that question. I will take volunteers only for this first trip. If things work out with these people as I hope, all will have an opportunity to come ashore later. Thorgill is in command of the ship during my absence. Now, who wishes to go?"

The entire ship's company raised their hands. Halfdan called off the chosen few. "Ring, Vilhjalm, Helge, Ingerd, Helga, and—" He paused for a moment, looking over the many expectant faces before he made his final selection. Almost as an afterthought, he finished. "Frida."

An audible sigh went around the group. Frida shot Halfdan a fiery look, as if in admonishment for seeming to forget her.

A smile spread over his face and he winked at her. "Gather a sampling of trade goods and get them loaded. Bring your weapons. Make haste; everyone into the boat. From the activity ashore they are getting impatient." Halfdan glanced at the dust cloud stirred up by the crowd milling about on the beach and climbed down into the boat.

"Their leader's boat has put out from shore, Halfdan. He is standing in the bow and beckoning for us to beach the ship, I think," Thorgill said from the bow platform.

Halfdan stood in the boat and held onto the ship's rail. "Remember what I told you. If something happens, you are to save the ship and the rest of the crew. We are on our own now, as far as the ship and the rest of you is concerned. If you hear a horn sound from shore and see me standing on the beach, it means it is safe to beach the ship; otherwise, I will send our boat out for more of you when I feel it is safe." Halfdan motioned to his crew as he pushed away. They began to row and he turned the boat inshore as they cleared the ship's side.

Thorgill nodded and waved. He looked toward the beach. "He has you in sight now," he reported, as Halfdan's boat pulled around the ship's bow. "They are returning to the beach."

Halfdan waved at him as they sped by. He stood erect in the stern, tiller in hand. He grinned at the surprise of the people on shore as they became aware of the speed achieved by the six oars that drove his boat toward the landing beach. "We have their attention with our speed," he said, chuckling. He locked eyes with Frida as she strained at her oar. "Easy all, boat your oars." He watched with pride as the oars rose smartly to the perpendicular. Inertia carried the boat into the beach.

The ship's boat was both longer and wider than the Skraeling boats pulled up on the beach. Considerably heavier than their boats, it did not seem to hinder the group of chattering Skraeling men who waded into the shallow water and grabbed the boat along each side of the bow to draw it up on the beach.

The six oars clattered as the crew stowed them across the thwarts along the inside of the boat. The occupants vaulted over the sides and onto the gravel beach.

For a brief moment, open curiosity held both groups back. Then they merged without conscious thought or effort. The Greenlanders saw a sea of leather clothing in various shades of brown.

"All this brown clothing is pretty drab," Ingerd said.

"Yes, it is, but it is well made. I cannot see a stitch showing in the seams," Frida answered.

A continuous buzz of conversation rose from the large throng around the Greenlanders, as people took a closer look at these strangers who had come among them.

"Sling your bows," Halfdan said. He pulled the string of his own bow far enough out to put his head and arm through, allowing the bow's limb to settle comfortably across his back beside his quiver. "I do not think we will be needing weapons after all." He smiled in greeting as the Skraeling leader strode up to him with a smile and words of welcome.

The slinging of their bows, a universal sign of peaceful intent, had an immediate effect on the way the Skraelings acted. The curious crowd surged around the Greenlanders, touching them and fingering their colorful clothing.

* * *

Back at the encampment, a warning horn blasted suddenly. Ormiga, the guard who sounded the alarm, ran down the hill from his place on the perimeter. "Skraelings! Skraelings attack! To arms! To arms!" Several arrows from a source unseen from the encampment zipped around the man as he zigzagged down the hill. One slammed into his lower back. He faltered, and fell wounded. He crawled to continue his flight.

Gudbjartur whirled in time to see Ormiga fall. "Gudrod, Athils!" Gudbjartur shouted, looking wildly around the encampment. "You and Athils take over here," he said, as Gudrod ran up to him. Without waiting for an answer, Gudbjartur hurried through the encampment gathering his men. "Bjorn, Brodir, Sweyn, and half of you men come with me." He and a little more than a hundred men grabbed their weapons and converged inland on the wounded man at a dead run.

"Form a cordon between Gudbj and the encampment." Gudrod gestured with his spear as the rest of the men spread out to repel an attack.

Near the camp's center, Thora shrieked, "Ivar, Lothar, to me!" She and the other women armed themselves and gathered the children together. The two boys, both armed with spears, joined the ranks of women and older children. They faced inland, a grim set to their faces, and arrayed themselves in front of the little ones. If the enemy broke through to the encampment center, the final resistance would be from them.

Gudbjartur shouted, gesturing with his axe. "Spread out along the ridge!" He dropped to a knee beside the now still Ormiga. He saw the arrow low in his back and laid a hand on his shoulder. "The women will get you to camp, Ormiga. How many, and where are they?"

"Four attacked me. I saw many more in the distance." He grunted in pain.

Gudbjartur jumped to his feet to survey the area to make certain his standing orders were followed. His people were ready, well versed in their individual duties in the event of attack. He glanced down at Ormiga, and then looked back down the hill to see two men running toward him from camp. "Here you men, get Ormiga down to Asa; he has an arrow in his back."

Up the hill, his men had spread out in a large, semicircular defensive perimeter, and he ran to join them. He stretched full length on the ground beside Bjorn and looked down the inland slope of the small ridge above the encampment. He saw a large group of Skraelings at the edge of the forest conferring among themselves.

"They may have us outnumbered," Bjorn said, as they lay watching the Skraelings. "It is hard to tell because there are more of them scattered throughout the forest."

"I see that. Before they get set, I want to give them a taste of our steel. Bjorn, gather about twenty men with bows and circle around this ridge to get as close as you can before they see you. As soon as you are in position, shoot into that large group at the edge of the forest as fast as you can put arrow to bow. We will wait until you send your first flight of arrows into them. Then we will attack from here."

Bjorn set off in a crouch, gathering men as he went.

"Pass the word." Gudbjartur spoke to the men beside him. "We attack when Bjorn and his men have shot their first flight of arrows."

Rapidly his order passed down the line from man to man. The Northmen readied edged weapons and spears, nocked arrows to bowstrings, and mentally gathered themselves for the attack.

The Skraelings saw them and began to spread out a little, but the largest group remained at the edge of the forest shouting and gesturing.

Gudbjartur watched this group. He spoke to the men at his side. "It appears they are in disagreement."

Sweyn said, "And well they should be. Perhaps they regret their attack on us."

"They should have planned more carefully then. In a moment it is going to be too late for some of them."

As if in answer, Bjorn and his men sent their first arrows into the Skraelings, and several went down, dead or wounded. Flight after flight of arrows followed with the same result.

"Odin!" Shouts of the war cry burst over the field of battle as Gudbjartur and the rest of the yelling Greenlanders attacked in a wall of shields and flashing weapons.

Gudbjartur held his axe at the ready as the shield wall smashed into the enemy. He danced nimbly through an enemy line stunned by its collision with the massed shields.

A painted warrior loomed in front of him. A vicious backhand swipe of his axe cut through the man's raised arm and cleanly decapitated him. Gudbjartur followed through with an upper-cut under an enemy shield that eviscerated another warrior. The bearded axe head struck left and right. The crunch of the razor edge through flesh and bone went unnoticed as he sundered all who stood in opposition.

With a quarter of the Skraeling warriors killed or wounded in Bjorn's attack, the opening round of hand-to-hand combat saw the two groups numerically equal. The surprised and disorganized Skraelings proved to be no match for the ferocity of the Norse methods of warfare. Their line recoiled as groups of desperate men crashed together. Those in back had difficulty shooting arrows through the packed front ranks without hitting their own men. The melee fragmented into pitched battles between small groups or individuals. The Skraelings recovered rapidly from their disarray during the Greenlander's initial onslaught and proved to be dangerous adversaries. They had little choice but to fight for their lives. And fight they did.

Norse battle strategy called for the axemen to lurk to the rear of the line of spearmen and swordsmen. When the shield wall smashed the enemy aside they darted forward on the attack. Gudbjartur and the other axemen, armed only with the two-handed battle-axe, wreaked havoc among the Skraelings. They had no effective defense against the heavy axe. Beheaded and sundered bodies dotted the field of battle, grim testament to the path of the axemen. Warriors missing arms or legs staggered or crawled away. Blood jetted into the dust.

The noise and confusion of battle spread throughout the large clearing and into the forest verge. The two lines surged back and forth. A pall of dust kicked up by the struggling combatants hung in the still air. The crash of weaponry and the strange mutters and grunts of conflict filled the air, punctuated by shouts of victory on the one hand and cries of anguish on the other.

The Skraelings were adept at hand-to-hand combat. Their weapons were light, especially suited to hit-and-run battle tactics. They customarily attacked after taunts were hurled back and forth. The Northmen did not join combat gradually; they attacked immediately. These giant, heavily armed white men came in a screaming mass, crashing into their adversary and crushing all who stood before them. The Skraelings had never faced such crazed men in battle.

"Brodir, Sweyn, flank them! Cut them off before they get into the forest!" Gudbjartur shouted, gesturing wildly with his axe from the backside of the shield wall. At his command, both captains rallied their men and swept around the struggling line of warriors to cut off escape to the rear.

The pressing shield wall, on a shouted command from Gudbjartur, suddenly smashed the opposing force aside, and the axemen, screaming like demons from the Underworld, surged forward, once again cutting a bloody path through the Skraelings. Individuals nearly ran one another down escaping the arc of the battle-axes. The largest and strongest Greenlanders wielded the fearsome weapon. The power transferred to the cutting edge by their physical strength alone ensured the axe cut through the puny, hide-covered shields of the Skraeling warriors and severed the arm of the holder or cleaved his body in two.

The battle raged back and forth until Skraeling losses made the outcome inevitable. The last attack of the axemen broke their will to fight. The bloodied survivors broke and retreated as best they could. Those warriors unable to run because of crippling wounds, or cut off from escape into the forest, were chopped down or impaled on the spears of their merciless foes.

Hotly pursued by the Northmen, who were overcome by bloodlust, few made good their flight. The untidy heaps of their dead and wounded liberally sprinkled the path of escape and were scattered over the field of battle and far into the forest.

Gudbjartur called all the able-bodied men to him. He sent Bjorn and Brodir with a fast moving body of men after the retreating warriors. "Take ten men each and go after the Skraelings that got away. I do not want those men to forget what happens to those who attack us. They must have come in boats so you will find them heading toward the bay or the river. Let none escape."

Each captain gathered the men he needed, supplies for an overnight, and set off in pursuit of the enemy. They split into two groups as they disappeared into the forest.

Gudbjartur and Sweyn surveyed the carnage of battle, both blood spattered and breathless from exertion. Not all the blood spattered over the two men came from the enemy. Both had several minor cuts. Sweyn did not sustain a disabling wound. Gudbjartur was not so lucky.

Stooped over somewhat, Gudbjartur rested both hands for support on the upright handle of his grounded axe. He glanced at Sweyn. "Thanks for cutting down the Skraeling who almost got me with his spear. I did not see him until he thrust at me from behind. I think he only nicked me." He stretched his left arm over his shoulder and tried to reach the source of pain in the area of his right shoulder blade.

"He got you good, Gudbj. I would not call that a nick," Sweyn clucked as he poked at the edges of the wound with his finger. Gudbjartur flinched away. "You have a hole in your back. I see your shoulder blade through the blood. The spear point cut a groove across it. The gods smile on you. If he had not hit your shoulder blade, the hole would be in your lung. There are no bubbles so the point missed your lung. It is too bad we did not have time to don our chain mail. You would have been protected from that wound."

Gudbjartur responded with a short grunt.

"Yes," Sweyn said, "I think you will live. We will need to burn that hole closed pretty soon before all your blood leaks out."

Gudbjartur grimaced when he moved the shoulder. He glanced at the headless body of his assailant. "At least I am not like him. I doubt he felt your sword remove his head."

Sweyn rolled the detached head face up with the toe of his shoe. "Oh, I think he knew. Look how wide his eyes are. He looks surprised." He chuckled.

The Skraelings got the worst of the battle, losing all but a few of their complement, but the victory was not without cost for the Northmen. Several of them walked over the battlefield among the dead and dying from both sides.

"Gudbj, there are several wounded Skraelings. What do you want to do with them?" Tostig walked up to the two men.

Gudbjartur's eyes traveled over the blood-spattered man. His voice was flat, emotionless. "Kill them. Every last one."

Tostig nodded shortly and walked away to do his bidding. Gudbjartur and Sweyn watched him walk slowly through the battlefield. He paused briefly at each wounded Skraeling he encountered and thrust his spear into the man. Other men nearby saw what Tostig was about and helped him with the grim task.

Gudbjartur felt Sweyn's eyes on him. "They attacked us without provocation. We cannot talk to them, so we do not need them for anything." He looked out over the battlefield. "If I could learn why they attacked I would question the wounded and then kill them. But we cannot speak to them and sign language is too cumbersome to question prisoners."

"I agree with you. We cannot take prisoners while we are on the move." Sweyn watched Gudbjartur. "Now, I will kindle a fire to sear that wound closed." A note of concern tinged his voice.

"Someone else will kindle a fire. I need you to find out how many we lost. Get me a tally of the dead and wounded."

"I will get you the tally. You had better sit down before you fall down."

"Do not cluck over me like a mother hen, Sweyn. Go." Gudbjartur's weak smile followed him as he walked away. A wave of dizziness and nausea swept over him. Abruptly he sank to the ground. He knew that he had lost a lot of blood. *Wound dew, some would call it. I feel my wound dew running down my back,* he thought vaguely.

The able-bodied men helped the wounded to a fire kindled nearby. Several irons heated in the coals. Asa, Thorkatla, and several other women arrived to take over the work with the wounded. Asa or Thorkatla worked their magic to put the men's wounds to rights with stitches and hot irons. Most took the intense pain stoically. Some, not so inured to it, cried out or fainted when the iron seared their flesh. Thora, Olga, and the others prepared poultices, helped with the irons, applied soothing salve, and bound the wounds. The stench of burned flesh hung heavily in the air. After on-the-spot first aid, the women helped or carried the wounded to the encampment and made them as comfortable as possible.

Gudbjartur chaffed at the inactivity his wounds forced on him. He worried about the men he had sent in pursuit of the Skraeling survivors. When his turn came to have his wounds repaired and dressed, Asa found cuts he regarded as only a nuisance.

"They are minor cuts. Do not bother, Asa."

"They are not minor. I do not tell you how to do your work, Gudbj. Do not tell me how to do mine."

"They are only small cuts and scratches," he insisted.

"I will decide what needs to be fixed. This is what I do. I am good at it. That is why you let me do it."

He gave up, stopped arguing with her, and tried to sit stoically while she stanched with a hot iron the blood weeping from each wound. He gritted his teeth. Other than several sharp intakes of breath, he made not a sound. The long cut over his right shoulder blade proved to be particularly troublesome. She stitched the edges together and trimmed away excess skin with her scissors. He braced himself against the wave of pain from the iron.

"I am finished now, Gudbj." Asa patted him on the other shoulder. "This salve will cool the cut a little, but it is a bad one. It will hurt for a long time. You will have a terrible scar." She carefully smeared the burnt, ragged cut with her magic paste.

By the time she finished, his normal firm resolve was diminished. The face he turned toward her as he offered his thanks was drained of color.

Her dark eyes held his for a moment; she shook her head and clucked softly. For her it could mean anything. "Our people suffered from this attack. I hope we do not have more trouble with those men."

"We all hope that, Asa. Those men will never trouble us again for they are all dead."

She shook her head again, stooped to pick up her bag of magic, and turned to leave.

"Asa," he said, "thank you for all you do for us."

She nodded and walked from the tent.

After Asa applied the iron and dressed his wounds, the pain progressed from searing to a heavy throb. He sat for moment gathering himself, got carefully to his feet, and swayed as a wave of dizziness and nausea swept over him. It passed, and he walked slowly from his tent.

Sweyn found Gudbjartur restlessly moving from tent to tent checking on the wounded. He took him by the arm and led him back to his own tent.

"Gudbj, you must lie down for a little while. You are pale from loss of blood. And so weak that I can easily overpower you," he chided.

"I will be all right, Sweyn, and I will not be weak for long."

"I know, Gudbj, I know, but we need you in one piece."

"Enough about me, how many?" He looked at the man.

"It could have been much worse. They put up a good fight. We had ten killed and fourteen wounded, including you. Two of the wounded may not recover. Ormiga is one of them. If the arrow in his lower back missed his guts, he will live. The other man, Gunnar, got an arrow low on the right side of his chest. We will know about both of them soon. Every man received cuts and bruises. About what you would expect in any battle." He paused to give Gudbjartur time to respond. "We counted eighty-two Skraeling dead and the men think at least thirty got away. Bjorn and Brodir should have no trouble tracking them by the bodies along the way. Skeggi, our best tracker, is with Brodir. They will get all of them." He paused again. Gudbjartur remained silent. "Something else has come up. These men are not like the other Skraelings that Halfdan went to trade with."

"I noticed that, too. They are a different tribe. We may know more about them by the time Halfdan returns. For now, we have enough concerns. Besides, they are all dead. It does not matter who they were."

"It matters not, especially to them." Sweyn gestured toward the bodies that littered the field of battle.

"Have those bodies cast into the water. The tide will carry them into the bay. They will become food for the fishes and crabs. The ravens, the eaters of the dead, can have the rest." He gestured at the big, black birds waiting in the treetops.

Sweyn's eyes narrowed as he watched his leader closely. *Gudbj's approach is a simple solution,* he thought.

"Make arrangements for our dead to have a Viking burial. They died in battle. We will honor them." He glanced at Sweyn. "I cannot do this thing now. I depend on you and the other captains to see it is done in accordance with our customs."

Sweyn peered approvingly at Gudbjartur. "It will be as you order. The ceremony will be after the evening meal."

Gudbjartur flexed his shoulder. He sighed, and shook his head. "I hope the Skraelings learned something from this and leave us alone. We cannot afford to lose many people in battle. If we cannot get along with them, Halfdan will leave Vinland to protect those of us who remain. A fight is acceptable but we cannot have a war with these people. Perhaps I should not have called for an attack on them."

"You had no choice, Gudbj. We would have lost many more if we had merely defended ourselves. Defense alone will get us picked off one by one. We all know that the only way to win a battle is to attack. No, you made the correct decision. Everyone thinks so."

"It is too late to change anything anyway. We put them to flight. Bjorn and Brodir will get the stragglers if they can. If nobody returns from their war party, perhaps they will leave us in peace. I hope Halfdan is not trading with the same tribe of Skraelings. That would be a bad thing after all this."

The two men paused in reflection. People began moving toward the cook's awning for the final meal of the day. All would think about what happened on this day, and their part in it. Those who had fought the battle would be thankful they had survived. Others mourned the loss of a friend or loved one. Perhaps some good would come of it. They were a close-knit community, tied in life and death to each other. Of the two choices available for his people, Gudbjartur hoped for life. Accompanied by Sweyn, he painfully made his way toward the fire pit to join his fellows. *Some food will taste good,* he thought.

Chapter Ten

"**T**his is exciting! I have never been in any villages other than ours." Frida's enthusiasm infected all of them.

"Nor I," Ingerd said. "I already see trade goods I want. Look at those baskets!"

Halfdan's face split in a grin. "I think this visit will work out well for us. I am glad you women are with us. You are just what a first contact like this needs to be successful." Halfdan and Frida made eye contact.

The Skraelings' leader and tribal elders seemed appreciative of their visitors' enthusiasm. The leader gave a short talk and indicated that the Northmen were to accompany them through the village.

"I think he just welcomed us to their village," Halfdan said.

The overpowering smell was the first thing they noticed. Black biting flies filled the air; they could not open their mouths wide without a few gaining entrance. Without the steady wind, the flies would soon overpower all living things.

Large, wolf-like work dogs roamed throughout the village. Many lay about, as dogs will. Several dogs dragged two-legged, rawhide-bound travois loaded with deer quarters, fresh hides, and all manner of supplies. The first pups of the season followed along behind their working mothers.

They stopped to examine the cleverly designed, well-made travois and winter sledges scattered about.

Helge picked up a travois. "Look how well this is made. The legs are held apart with this framework that fits over the dog's shoulders." He indicated the rawhide binding the frame together at the top and holding the crossbars in place behind the dog's rump. "The narrow end of the frame is laced to the dog's harness; the harness attaches over his shoulders and around his chest." He held up the top end of the travois with the harness attached.

"It looks like they leave the harness attached to the travois." Vilhjalm inspected the clever harness attachment that Helge held. "The bindings and harness are rawhide. They should last a long time."

"The frame ends are rawhide bound, too, to cut down on wear." Frida squatted at the wide end of the travois.

Halfdan's eyes shifted to her moist lips. He quickly looked away when Ingerd offered a comparison of the Norse and Skraeling dogs.

"Their dogs are much bigger than ours," Ingerd said. "They can easily pull these sledges and travois. I do not think ours could. Both are too big and heavy."

Halfdan's face softened as he looked at her appreciatively. "These dogs are at least twice the size of ours. They are part wolf and have the long legs and big feet of the wolf."

"Why not trade for a pair?" Vilhjalm asked.

"If we had a pair of their dogs we could breed them with ours. Eventually we would have a breed of dog with the best of both," Helge said.

"If we trade for some dogs, you could have them throw in a travois and sledge," Ring said.

"We can use them. It depends on how the trading goes," Halfdan said. A plan began to take shape in his mind. "We will wait until they make known what they really want to trade for. Then I will see if we can do just that."

The Skraelings allowed them free rein as the tour continued slowly through the village.

Unable to ignore the common distraction any longer, Helge voiced their collective concern. "By Thor, Halfdan." Helge grunted in distaste. "The smell is foul."

"Do not say anything further," Halfdan said. "We will only be here overnight. We can stand it that long."

"I wonder why there are no bears in this village. They can smell it for a long way." Ingerd addressed her comment to Frida. But they all heard and laughed softly among themselves. A glare from Halfdan silenced them.

The reason for the smell and clouds of black flies became apparent as they moved through the village. Decomposing deer carcasses lay everywhere. Fortunately, the flies were more attracted to the fresh smell of bloody meat than they were to the people.

Most of the meat hung from drying racks, but the waste still lay wherever someone had dropped it. They stopped to watch women cut strips from fresh haunches and front quarters and then hang them on the drying racks.

"They do that just like we do, Ingerd," Helga said.

"I do not think they use salt though."

"I do not see any, but I will bet that is saltwater they rinse the strips in before they are hung up." Helga bent over and dipped a finger in a leather bucket of water and held it to her lips. She nodded. "It is salty."

The Skraeling leader smiled, took a strip of meat from the bucket, and offered it to Helga.

"He thinks you are hungry," Frida laughed.

"No, no, I am not hungry now," Helga said, waving her hands in front of the offering.

The Skraeling chuckled at his own joke and dropped the strip back in the bucket. The women smiled shyly and continued to work on the meat. Other people arrived with fresh quarters as fast as the animals were dismembered.

"It looks like the women cut off portions for daily consumption until nothing is left but bones. Then they cast the bones aside instead of removing them from the village or throwing them in the fire like we do," Frida said. "That accounts for most of the smell."

"No doubt. It all looks so haphazard. They have no plan for the location of their houses or drying racks, like we do," Ingerd said, as they stopped.

There seemed to be no order to the village at all. "Their methods have worked a long time for them. Judging from all the old deer bones lying about, this is a permanent village." Halfdan stopped at the entrance to one of the houses that had been partially taken apart. A large group of women chatted as they made repairs. The area around the house hummed like a beehive with all the activity. Groups of women carried in bundles of willow limbs and branches while others took the outer covering off the house, exposing details of the interior structure to the Greenlanders.

"They build their houses of long, closely spaced, upright pine poles arranged in a large circle. The top ends intertwine to form a cone." Ingerd shaded her eyes as she pointed out the various parts of the structure.

"Look how adept they are at weaving willow branches through the upright poles. By the time they weave them all the way to the top, they will have a good stiff surface to support the covering," Helga observed as they watched.

"That house would support a covering of mud, like ours. It could not be any heavier than those green hides they are working on." Ring pointed to a group of four women who attached green hides together with sharpened wooden pins. Another group arranged the joined hides around the outside of the pole framework from ground level.

"They have plenty of hides to work with. I think enough mud to seal the house might be too heavy for those poles," Halfdan said, pointing out the sagging walls of the closest complete house.

"You are probably right. This soil is so rocky they could not get enough clean dirt to make our daub-and-wattle walls," Ring said.

They watched the crew of women overlap and lace the rows that followed above the first course of hides. The final course at the top closed in the house and made it water tight. At the very top, the interlaced ends of the support poles protruded above the last layer of hide covering. When the women finished they installed the smoke vent system on top of the house at the smoke hole. Notched poles did double duty as ladders and smoke-flap props.

"Their ladders seem to work well," Helga observed, "but I do not think I could hang on one of them like they do." She pointed to a woman at the top of the house. The woman had one foot in a notch and a leg wrapped around the pole ladder, leaving both hands free to work.

"Nor I. I am afraid of heights. You will never see me up on one of them," Ingerd said, shielding her eyes from the sun as she watched the woman lace a section of hide in place.

With so many strange sights, smells, and sounds, the tour through the village prompted frequent discussions. "That hide attached to the top of the support poles is a smoke flap. Those two notched pole ladders spread the flap to catch the wind and they can adjust it to the wind direction so the smoke is sucked from the house." Frida pointed as she told her companions how she thought the smoke flap worked.

"I am impressed with the smoke flap. I will wager it is not as smoky in there as it is in our houses," Vilhjalm said. "Maybe we can adapt their idea to our houses."

"We will keep it in mind," Halfdan said. "Their houses are well built, too, but the poles sag from the weight of the hides."

"Maybe they spring back after the hides dry," Helge said.

Ring tapped one of the dry hides. "They are too hard."

"I do not think it is a concern for them so long as the weight does not break the poles," Halfdan added.

The completed house was round with a pointed roof. At ground level, around the outside, other women dug a ditch and mounded the dirt over the bottom skirt of the house. This kept out the wind, and the ditch drained snowmelt and rain away so it did not soak under the bottom edge of the skirt. As the green hides dried in the wind they conformed naturally to the curvature of the house and lent rigidity to the structure.

The houses were quite large. The seven Greenlanders and the Skraeling elders all stood together in the leader's house. Halfdan and his people examined every aspect of the structure and its contents. Personal possessions hung from the poles on the inside. Skin bags of goods hung in similar fashion. Beautifully made baskets, both round and rectangular, held foodstuffs and cooking gear. They lay grouped against the circle of the interior house wall, where they would not be underfoot.

"They think it amusing that we find their houses interesting," said Frida. She pointed to a circular piece of deer hide laced tightly across the support poles, just below the peak of the roof. "I wonder what that hide is for."

Their gaze drawn aloft by her gesture, the Skraelings launched into animated conversation. Their leader, by way of demonstration, took hold of one of the support poles and shook it violently while he made a sound like the north wind. One of the elders spoke a few words and pointed at the centrally located fire pit. He repeated his words and mimed smoke rising and rain falling from the sky.

The Greenlanders watched all this with blank looks on their faces. Except for Frida. She gestured excitedly and explained each part of the riddle. "They just told us the circular hide strengthens the house so the wind will not blow it down. Smoke from the fire goes up around the narrow opening at the edges of that circular hide and out. It also keeps the rain or snow from coming in and putting out the fire." She held her arms open toward Halfdan and the others. "See, it is so clear to me! You must have understood."

"You understood all that from what they just said?" Halfdan asked.

"Yes, I did! We can communicate with them, Halfdan. It came to me suddenly. I understood everything they told us."

Halfdan shook his head and looked at her. The lines in his face softened. "Good, Frida, you stay with me and translate until I learn to communicate better. I certainly did not understand all that you did." He glanced at the others.

"I will stay with you too, Frida," Ingerd said, tongue in cheek. "I did not get all of it either."

"We all will. Now that I know the meaning of what they just told us it is clear what they were trying to say. But it was not clear when they said it," Halfdan said.

The Skraelings were amused by the conversation and soon all were either smiling or laughing aloud at what they considered a joke on their visitors. The Skraeling leader tapped his chest with a thumb and spoke to Halfdan. "I am called Essipit."

Halfdan understood. He pointed to himself. "Halfdan. My name is Halfdan." He extended his hand in friendship.

The Skraeling grasped his hand and shook it vigorously, his lips curved in a broad smile. Essipit waved his arm to encompass the others of his group and the village in general. "Thalmiut, we are the Thalmiut, the People of the Deer."

"Did you understand?" Frida asked. She looked from Halfdan to the others. "Did all of you understand?"

Without waiting for confirmation she looked at the Thalmiut leader with a friendly smile. She tapped her own chest with a thumb. "Frida, I am a Greenlander." She pointed to the others and introduced each in turn. "We are Greenlanders, people of the north, Northmen." She looked at Halfdan; a quizzical expression furrowed her brow.

Halfdan, between gritted teeth, cut her off. "We understood most of it, Frida. You can be the most maddening woman, especially when you have the upper hand. Why not surprise us someday and win gracefully?"

"I will try, I really will," she said mischievously.

Ingerd and Helga both snorted in unison at this obvious untruth. They all knew she would not be what she was not: graceful in anything. To charge forward without fear of consequence—that was her way.

"What did Essipit call his people?" Halfdan asked.

"They are called Thalmiut. He said something after that, but I do not know what his words meant," Frida answered helpfully. Her answers usually were clipped. She had always had a sharp tongue, but not this time. Halfdan gave her a curt nod.

One old gray-haired man had not spoken a word during the tour of the village. Nor had any of the Thalmiut spoken directly to him.

Halfdan's curiosity was roused and he turned toward the man. "What is your name, old one?"

The question caused an immediate reaction among the Thalmiut. They clustered protectively around the old man as if Halfdan's question posed a threat of some sort. His intention was just the opposite.

Essipit launched into a long speech with copious gestures to make the Greenlanders understand. It became apparent to all of them that to acknowledge the presence of the old man was forbidden. To address him directly might even be taboo.

"I guess they do not want us to talk to him." Halfdan felt contrite and somewhat subdued by Essipit's outburst and the changed attitude of the Thalmiut.

"It is deeper than that, Halfdan," Frida explained. "I watched his gestures carefully and this old man may be a shaman or a priest to the Thalmiut. Whatever he is, all of them, including Essipit, have a deep respect, almost a reverence for him.

Essipit and several others nodded, as though they understood and agreed with Frida's explanation. Then Essipit began anew until interrupted in midsentence by one word from the old man. Essipit acceded and stepped aside. The old man turned toward the Greenlanders. He extended his hand in greeting and spoke to Halfdan in a shaky voice. "I am called Natsheku, Halfdan."

Halfdan laughed in spite of himself and shook the old man's hand with a broad smile on his face. Slowly, the wrinkled old face split in a wide grin, and the other Thalmiut clustered around the Greenlanders. They all tried to talk at once after this final act of acceptance.

Without Natsheku's acceptance, Halfdan thought as he smiled and bobbed his head, *we might have had trouble with these people.*

Natsheku's exact status was unclear but it was obvious to all concerned that he was most certainly important to the Thalmiut people.

"He knows my name. I thought he was not paying attention." Halfdan felt relief over their rapid reversal of fortune.

"He said your name better than Essipit, at least it sounded better to me," Ring said. "Why, even I have begun to understand what is said." He grinned at the others.

Frida spoke to all her companions. "If we listen carefully and watch their hand signs we can understand them. Their spoken language does not have very many words, so some words can mean several different things, like our language. It depends on how the word is used and what hand signs go with it. They always use hand signs when they speak. I think the signs are as important to their communication as words."

The others seemed somewhat taken aback by the extent of her understanding.

"What is it?" she asked sharply. "You do not believe me?"

"Yes, Frida, we all believe you." Halfdan's stern visage softened as he looked into her pale eyes. He glanced at the others. "It is just difficult for us to accept that you are so good with this strange language. I, for one, am happy that you are. I have difficulty understanding much of what they try to tell us."

The agreement of the others mollified Frida. The Thalmiut watched the exchange.

Introductions continued for everyone in the house. Most did not understand nor would they remember, but the effort had been made. All seemed satisfied at this first step.

The group left the house, and the tour of the village continued. The village felt friendlier, more open, as word spread of the Greenlanders' acceptance by Natsheku.

The Greenlanders stayed in a group and talked among themselves. "Halfdan, when the old man, Natsheku, spoke to you, the Thalmiut accepted us. Before that they only tolerated us. Essipit is their chief or a leader of some status, but his is not the final word. That belongs to that old man." Frida explained as they walked along.

"I agree, Frida. I do not know if we will ever understand their language well enough to know what his position is. To them he is essential in some way and that is good enough for me."

"I see those four men that came to our encampment with Essipit, Halfdan. The ones who left after Essipit sent them away." Vilhjalm indicated a group of men and women with a lift of his chin.

"I see them," Halfdan said.

Essipit recognized his name in spite of Vilhjalm's poor pronunciation. Understanding Vilhjalm's words and gesture to be a reference to the group that obviously preferred not to be a part of the general activity, he strode over and confronted them. Another argument ensued, with the same result.

Essipit returned and spoke to Halfdan. "They are of a different band of our tribe. They live on the banks of a big river, two days south of here by boat. They will return to their own band during the next full moon. For some reason they do not wish to be friendly with you." He shrugged his shoulders.

Halfdan glanced at Frida. "He told us that they are from far away, but that is all I understood."

"I think he meant they are from another band entirely. But you are right to say they come from far away, I understood that also." She looked at Ingerd and the others for their opinion on the matter.

"Wherever they come from they do not like us. That is hard to understand. They do not even know us." Helga watched the group of four men and four women walk away into another part of the village.

As Halfdan watched the almost hostile Thalmiut he rubbed his chin thoughtfully. "I will attempt to learn more about these people from Essipit"

Trade with the Thalmiut has gone well, thought Halfdan. He and about half the ship's contingent enjoyed a meal with the Thalmiut while the trading continued. A boatload of crew members, finished with their trading, had just left for the ship. They would change places with their fellows so everyone had an opportunity to do some trading on their own before it became time to depart. *This load will be the last,* he mused. *The remainder of the crew can come ashore when they beach the ship.*

Each freeman customarily traded goods they themselves had fashioned, or previously traded, for whatever they fancied from the other parties to the trading. Tightly woven baskets and prime furs from all manner of furbearing animal had become the most sought of the Thalmiut goods. Groups of both peoples were busily engaged in trading for these and whatever else individuals took a fancy to.

Unable to resist the lure of trading, especially when it involved strange new articles, the unfriendly group from the other band finally joined the rest of the populace.

Halfdan, Frida, and Essipit stood a little apart from most of the activity. They watched the group's hesitation become open interest.

"I am glad they decided to join in. I was afraid there would be trouble with them later," Halfdan said.

"Their women talked them into it. I have watched them. The men would not have changed had it not been for the women." Frida glanced at Halfdan and Essipit. She used sign language so Essipit would understand the exchange. "We women have a great deal of influence over what men do and think." She smiled at the two men. "You just think all your ideas are yours alone. Actually, many of them are what we want you to do."

"Really!" Halfdan laughed. "Essipit and I are very happy to know that."

Essipit laughed too, although it was uncertain if he actually knew why. He indicated he wanted Halfdan and Frida to accompany him to meet the four men and their women.

The women were all smiles after the introductions. However, the men remained aloof.

From Halfdan's expression, Frida knew he had doubts. "I think it will be all right. Someday we might even know why they do not completely accept us."

"Perhaps," he said. "For now let us forget about them and go on trading. I do not want to call attention to them. It could cause trouble with the others."

"All right." Frida beckoned for Halfdan and Essipit to follow, and she walked toward the nearest group of traders. Halfdan and Essipit trailed behind, talking and gesturing as if they actually understood each other. Frida's lips curved in a smile as she glanced back at them. *That is a good start. At least they are trying to communicate.*

Random lengths and small rolls of gaily colored wadmal and odd lengths and thin pieces of beaten copper were the items most sought by the Thalmiut. The copper strips provided the Thalmiut with an easily worked, shiny material from which jewelry and other ornaments could be fashioned. Copper baubles decorated with colorful glass beads proved to be the most sought after commodity the Greenlanders traded.

Helga and Ingerd demonstrated the various uses to several women and young girls. "See, each bead has a hole in it for the string." Ingerd reclined comfortably against a Thalmiut backrest facing her audience. Her legs were crossed at the ankles and she held a supply of beads and thread in the hollow of her apron. With elaborate pantomime, she opened her beautifully carved, walrus-ivory needle case and selected a steel needle. She held the needle up for all to see, wet the end of the thread in her mouth, and fed it through the eye. Then she began to string the blue and green beads. The needle and thread caused quite a stir among the Thalmiut women, who had never before seen the like. The sharpness and cutting ability of the flat pointed needle mystified them.

"They want to see our needles and thread." Helga handed her needle to the nearest women.

Ingerd handed the skein of wool thread to another woman. Excited chatter followed the items as they were passed around. "The thread's strength is what they are excited about." Ingerd watched as the thread made its way around the circle and each person tested it for themselves. While the women enthused over the thread and needle, Helga cut a copper sheet into several thin strips with her scissors. She formed a spiral bracelet from one of the strips and twisted others into various decorative shapes. Ingerd pierced the soft copper easily with her needle and interspersed each with glass beads as she strung them. The Thalmiut women, many with hands to mouths in awe of the skill demonstrated by Ingerd and Helga, broke into applause and animated conversation as the necklace took shape. Ingerd finished the necklace by knotting the two ends of thread together. Slowly and carefully, so as not to cause alarm, she reached out and slipped it over the head of a pretty young woman seated to her front. The woman squealed in delight and held it out for all to see. The other women clamored to see the necklace firsthand, and the young woman reluctantly took it off and passed it around to her friends. Each had a need to finger it, turning it over and over to examine each bead and shiny bit of copper.

The pretty young recipient of the necklace gave Ingerd the beautiful fox pelt she had been holding in her lap.

"Why, thank you!" Ingerd exclaimed, smiling at the young woman. "I did not expect a gift in return. I will always remember you when I look at this pelt."

The young woman bobbed and smiled in happiness at Ingerd's appreciation. She turned to her friends and began a conversation that, judging from the gestures, was about Ingerd. It soon became clear that all the women wanted necklaces and bracelets in trade for goods they proffered to Ingerd and Helga. The trading activity for all manner of Thalmiut goods became hectic as women vied for a particularly desirable piece of jewelry. Ingerd and Helga worked feverishly to stay abreast of demand. Small mounds of furs, baskets, and various culinary items accumulated. Helga traded another necklace for a finely stitched, pale beige, pullover dress. The leather had been uniformly scraped to a pliable thinness, tanned, and worked until it felt as soft as fine cloth.

"Well done, you two!" Halfdan said, as he, Frida, and Essipit looked on. "I doubt any of us could have pleased so many people that quickly with anything else."

Scenes such as this were played out throughout the village until everything the Greenlanders had brought to trade had been carted away by the Thalmiut.

* * *

Halfdan and Frida lounged comfortably against two wooden, rawhide-reinforced backrests they had traded for. Several others had been acquired by their shipmates. Essipit had wandered off into the throngs of milling people some time ago. Halfdan and Frida were left alone for the first time since coming ashore.

Halfdan chuckled.

Frida looked at him; the beginnings of a smile twisted the corners of her mouth. "What is it?"

"Oh, a thought about Gudbj and his weather predictions just jumped into my mind. With conditions like this he would tell me there will be fog tomorrow morning."

"Fog!" She glanced out over the countryside and the waters of the inlet. "Why, there is almost no wind, and the sky is so blue it hurts my eyes to look at it."

"I know, but he would still tell you there will be fog in the morning."

Frida snorted. "If he was here I would wager there would not be fog in the morning or anytime tomorrow."

"He is never wrong about the weather, Frida. He has a sense about it. I have seen him sniff the air on a day just like this and tell me, 'There will be fog in the morning.' I would never wager against him about the weather."

"You love him, Halfdan. It is more than friendship."

"Love him? I do not know about that. I have never loved. I will save that for the right woman." His eyes shifted to her when he said it. "We are men, and men do not express love for each other. I respect and admire him. He is my only friend. We are loyal to each other. That says it all for me."

"And me." Frida's face softened; her lips curved in a smile. They held each others eyes for a heartbeat.

Small talk between them ebbed and flowed for a time. A silence settled. They watched the activity in the village. Frida rose to her feet.

"I am going to see what I have missed."

He watched the sway of her hips as she walked away. *By the gods, she is beautiful*, he thought.

Chapter Eleven

The day after the battle, Gudbjartur visited the wounded. His own wounds gave him considerable pain but he wanted to look in on every man nonetheless. Each time he stepped from a tent his eyes swept the forest verge to the northeast. Impatience for the return of the men he had sent after the surviving Skraelings ruled his thoughts. Several people had tried to engage him in conversation but his response to their attempts had been perfunctory at best. His mind dwelled on the battle, its aftermath, Halfdan, Ingerd, and the others. Thora had fussed over him for a time before she, too, left him to his thoughts. His sons sensed his mood better than most. He was aware that they watched him. He silently offered thanks to the gods that they had decided not to intrude. Maybe Thora had talked to them, he did not know. The pain of his wounds diminished his normally outgoing personality to a glimmer. His stoicism made unimportant chatter impossible.

"Gudbj, please sit down and have some of this cod chowder." Thora stood next to his high seat holding a steaming bowl.

He sighed and sat down. "Thank you," he said, catching her eye as she handed him the bowl. He had enjoyed about half the chowder when the blast of a lookout's horn made him lurch painfully to his feet. The bowl of chowder spun to the side, forgotten.

Finally, he thought, *they return!* A long column of men filed down the hill from the northeast. As they came closer he saw they had a prisoner, in spite of his orders.

The column scattered throughout the encampment as individuals sought hot food and the company of other friends or family. Bjorn and Brodir, followed by Tostig, who was dragging a prisoner on a tether, walked directly to Gudbjartur.

"There were twenty-three of them, Gudbj. With the exception of this man here, all the others are dead. We caught up with them just as they were launching their boats. We allowed one boat to be paddled away by two wounded men. Every man in the boat was hit with our last flight of arrows." Bjorn watched Gudbjartur closely for his reaction.

Gudbjartur nodded wordlessly. He glanced briefly at the trussed prisoner. Then he fastened his eyes on the two captains. "I am interested to know why you spared two Skraelings you could have killed, as I ordered, and why this man stands before me now?"

Bjorn made to answer him but Brodir interrupted. "Let me answer that." Bjorn stepped aside and waved for Brodir to continue. "The two that we allowed to escape were in a boat with five others. As they paddled from shore, all were hit by several arrows. They were either dead or dying. Bjorn left his men to deal with other boats farther down the beach. He ran up to me just as the last flight of arrows hit the Skraelings in the boat. He convinced me to let the boat go and I did."

"I thought the two left alive should escape to take the story back to their people that they lost over one hundred warriors when they attacked us. It might give others pause before they attack us," Bjorn said.

"And this man?" Gudbjartur lifted his chin toward the prisoner.

"He stumbled out of the forest after we had killed all his fellows and allowed the one boat to escape. He was addled by the battle or that head wound and he just stood there, unarmed and bleeding," Bjorn said, pointing at the prisoner's head wound. "We all watched him. Brodir and I decided to take him prisoner rather than kill him."

Gudbjartur stood to examine the prisoner more closely. The man swayed weakly. He stood trussed with a stout branch that passed through his bent arms and across his back. His hands were tied tightly together across his stomach. Tostig held the tether looped around the man's neck. Blood from a deep head wound seeped down the right side of his face and congealed over his eye, cementing it shut. The other eye stared defiantly at Gudbjartur.

"Addled he may be, but that look tells me he will recover," Gudbjartur said. "I respect bravery in an enemy. Tostig, take him to the landing beach and stake him out in the open. Have Asa or Thorkatla tend his wounds. And have somebody feed him. We will see if he can provide some information to us after he recovers somewhat." He turned to Bjorn and Brodir. "I agree with your decision, you did the right thing. You were there and I was not. You made a decision based on the situation, and I approve of that. So would Halfdan."

The men accepted his words without comment. Brodir looked Gudbjartur over. "It will take your wounds a while to heal," he said. He and Bjorn examined the long gash on Gudbjartur's back.

"You are lucky it glanced off your shoulder blade," Bjorn said, "whatever it was."

"It was a spear. Sweyn beheaded the Skraeling. If he had not been close the man might have finished the job. They fought well. We all respect that. But I would like to know why they attacked us. Maybe your prisoner can tell us."

"If not, we will have no use for him. Unless it is decided to let him live anyway. We can always use another strong slave," Brodir said.

"That decision will be made at a full council meeting when Halfdan returns." Gudbjartur glanced toward the prisoner staked on the beach. "You two must be hungry. Let us go get a bowl of Thora's chowder. I did not finish mine before you arrived."

The three men joined the crowd at the fire pit.

* * *

After Frida disappeared from his sight, Halfdan's thoughts wandered to what he had learned from this visit among the Thalmiut. It appeared the Thalmiut did not eat meals at regular intervals, as did his people. Stew or roasted meat was available whenever one was hungry. It occurred to him that this arrangement might not entirely be a bad idea. Like his people, the Thalmiut subsisted almost entirely on meat or fish. Deer meat and a few fish seemed to be their mainstay, rather than the seal meat he had provided them on arrival. But the seal meat disappeared first.

The sound of a step at his back caused him to turn. A flush of pleasure coursed through him when he saw Frida. "I thought you wanted to see what you were missing."

"I changed my mind; I am a woman, after all. And I decided I would rather be with you."

"Good! Sit down; I saved your place." He waved at her backrest.

"What were you in such deep thought about when I walked up?"

"When you left, I thought of you."

"That is a good thing." Her lips curved in a smile. "I like a man to think about me. But what were you thinking about the moment I walked up to you?"

"These people and what I have learned by being among them." He waved a hand to encompass the village. "I thought about what they eat and how like us they are."

Frida nodded and launched right into the discussion as though she had never left. "Their food is unappetizing to look at because of their lack of cleanliness, but it is surprisingly good to eat."

He turned his head toward her. "That is exactly how I would describe their food. Their roasted meat and stew include large amounts of deer hair, which they take no notice of."

"Yes, and I have seen clots of hair floating on top of the stew."

They chuckled together at the thought.

Frida continued. "With the exception of Vilhjalm and Helge, both of whom eat vast amounts of stew, our people seem to prefer the roasted meat. Most of the hair burns away over the fire."

"Yes, I tried the stew and it is delicious but after I choked on a gob of hair I gave it up and stuck with the meat. Vilhjalm told me to spit the gobs out and swallow the rest."

They both laughed at Vilhjalm's method of handling the hair. They were quiet a moment as the various scenes they had witnessed came to mind.

"The Thalmiut crave fat like we do. They render it down for winter and also eat it with their daily fare," Frida said. "I watched some women butcher a deer and they eat some of the organs as they butcher. But they manage to save most of the heart, liver, tongue, and sweetbread to roast later or chop into the stew."

Halfdan waved toward a column of steam that rose into the cold air from a pile of roasted marrow bones just pulled from the fire. "Have you eaten some of their deer marrow?"

She nodded as they watched two women crack bones open with a rock and feed the hot, greasy cylinders to their children. "Ingerd, Helga, and I had our fill before they started to make their jewelry. It is delicious."

"I have never seen people eat so much at one time. To the Thalmiut the object of eating is to fill oneself, rest awhile, and begin anew."

"I think they do that because starvation lurks always in the shadows," she mused. "It is eager to claim a few or all."

"I suppose that is so. They cannot hunt like we do. Without ships they must wait for the deer to come to them. That seems like a risky way to live."

"I am sure many Thalmiut have died over the years, waiting for deer that never came." She paused a moment as a pensive mood seized her. "To these people the vast herds of migrating reindeer are life itself. Reindeer hides cover their houses and deer leather covers their bodies. Deer meat, fat, and a few fish provide their only food. They eat it fresh during the summer migration. In winter I am told they eat dried meat, as we do. They store the deer fat in bark containers in the permafrost to add to their stew in winter."

He considered her knowledge of the Thalmiut to be thorough given their short association, and told her so.

"I have become a careful observer recently," she answered, turning toward him. "I have learned much and I hope to learn more. You are responsible for that, Halfdan."

"I made you a careful observer?" He looked perplexed.

"No, but you woke me up. I have become a careful observer, among other things."

He looked at her, not understanding, but he let the subject go for the time being.

A poignant silence settled over them. Neither entirely understood the feelings they engendered in each other.

Halfdan took a new tack. "I think the tribal name for these people is especially important. We called them Skraelings because that is what we Northmen originally called the short, ugly people encountered in Greenland. We now know them as Tornit. Although they are ugly compared to our people, you for instance, it does not really describe them." That got him a smile from those luscious lips. "That opinion of them is what I came here with, and it is wrong. Without Inuktuk and his men we would not have known what to expect further south."

"Nor would you have been given the toggle-headed harpoon."

"Aye, you are correct. We could not hunt whales in open water before Inuktuk gave us the harpoon."

"Essipit's people do not look like the Tornit at all. Except for their skin color and shorter stature they are more akin to our people," she said.

"Yes, they are. You told me Thalmiut means "the people" in their language."

She nodded. "They also call themselves the People of the Deer. They are nomads that follow the reindeer in their annual summer migration out of the forests and into the barren tundra of the hinterland. Essipit told us that his village is one of several permanent winter towns that tribal bands of Thalmiut people occupy through the winter months while they wait for the reindeer herds. These bands are scattered all across this peninsula to the east as far as the great salt sea. In response to the change of seasons from winter to summer, the deer gather in their vast host and travel north in search of fresh lichen exposed as the snow melts. The first of the northbound herds just passed this town a few days before we arrived. The fresh meat scattered around the village came from those deer."

"I am glad to know all that, Frida. You have done well." A slight curve of her lips held his attention. He found himself to be mesmerized by her mouth.

"The Thalmiut are gripped by excitement at the prospect of the plenty they will soon enjoy as the migration reaches fever pitch." She paused to look at him. "If we had waited a short time before we sailed to this village, it would have been almost abandoned, except for the very old and very young. The rest of the Thalmiut would have loaded their dogs and trekked off to kill as many of the deer as possible before the host passed them by."

"Aye, Essipit showed us the huge deer traps his ancestors constructed," he said. "He and his people maintain them to drive the herds into for the mass slaughter. The trap is almost invisible, a part of the countryside, so the deer will not be spooked away. Once the deer are within the funnel, people hidden behind the little hillocks of the funnel spook them into the trap where the hunters await them."

She paused a bit and took a long drink of water from a water skin. He took it from her extended hand and drank his fill.

She licked her lips and continued her tale. "On the hunt they abandon their winter villages and shelter in deer-hide tents each night. When sufficient meat has dried and fat stored to insure their survival for another long winter, the hunters return to their permanent villages. Essipit told us that the system has worked for untold generations of the people. They will survive in this place as long as the deer come in their thousands each year."

He had no comment when she paused; his thoughts were of the Thalmiut. *If the migration does not come one year, without another food source available—and they have no other—these people will starve during the time of darkness. The few fish they catch will not sustain them. And it is the same for us,* he thought grimly.

They sat and watched the activity around them.

He chuckled to himself as he thought of their arrival at the village. Her red hair had caused exclamations of awe when she took off the confining leather helmet and shook it loose.

"What do you laugh at?"

"I thought about the reaction when you took off your helmet and they saw your hair."

"They are fascinated by all the bright colors we have shown them. Bright colors are not a part of their culture. Compared to our skin, hair, and clothing, theirs are pretty drab."

"Color is not important to me either, so I understand why it is not part of their culture. Color is important to you women, and now their women, too." He grinned at her.

"So that is what you think. I noticed you liked that colorful new coat one of our women made for you."

"Of course, but I would have liked it just as much if it was brown like the Thalmiut coats."

"All right, you win." She got to her feet and stretched. "I am stiff from sitting. Let us take a walk."

They walked side by side through the village toward the beach. Each stole a glance at the other, unobtrusively, as they strolled along with their hands clasped behind them.

"I want to watch them build one of their boats and examine one that is completed."

"It looks like Helge, Ring, and Vilhjalm want to watch as well." She indicated the three men with a lift of her chin. "I will go find Ingerd and let you men look at your boats." She smiled at him and turned away with a toss of her hair.

He watched her until she was out of sight in the village, shook his head, muttered under his breath, and turned toward the area where the Thalmiut built and repaired their boats.

"You arrived in time to watch them sew the rawhide on this new frame, Halfdan. They make a good boat." Helge

motioned toward a group of Thalmiut men that had just centered the boat frame over its rawhide cover.

"They look plenty stout and capable of carrying heavy
loads," Halfdan said.

"We watched them finish this framework," Ring explained.
"They use birch and pine laced together with rawhide thongs.
As the thongs shrink and harden each joint is rigidly secured
in place. Some women just dragged this rawhide covering
over here. They pick the best dehaired rawhide for their boats.
As the women sew them together they carefully repair knife
nicks and grub holes. Look at how close these stitches are."
Ring held a seam for his inspection.

"What do they use for thread?" Halfdan asked.

"Deer sinew. The women hold the thread in their mouths
and chew it until it is soft." He pointed at a large circle of
Thalmiut women in time for Halfdan to see one of the women
pull a thread from her mouth and lace it through holes
punched along an edge of a hide.

Halfdan shook his head as he watched one of several sew-
ing sessions close by. The women went about their ceaseless
tasks as they gossiped, joked, and laughed.

"They do not look any different at their work than our
women, do they?" Vilhjalm asked.

"No they do not," Halfdan made eye contact with him.
"Ingerd told me just a short time ago, 'They are just like us.'
And they are just like us. She and Helga gave several steel
needles away, and they should help when these women get
used to using them."

"Here, you men, let us give these fellows a hand with this
covering," Ring called to them as he helped pull one side of
the covering up and secure it along the top of the boat's rail
with rawhide thongs.

Halfdan grabbed the edge of the slippery hide, and with
the help of a mixed group of Thalmiut and Northmen, pulled
the other side up to the rail and laced it in place. After the
covering was secured along both sides of the boat's rail, the
men whipstitched long thongs of rawhide close together
around the entire rail and secured it in place.

Halfdan stood back and admired their handiwork. "Not bad for our first time." He handed his deer-antler awl to one of the Thalmiut. The two men grinned at each other. "I believe we have made friends here," he said, the satisfaction clear in his voice.

As the cover dried, it would shrink rigidly over to the boat's internal framework. When fully cured, both inner and outer surfaces were smeared with melted deer fat. This effectively waterproofed the hull. The process could be repeated as necessary.

"Halfdan, Ring, and I want to trade for two of these boats. There is plenty of room aboard Steed of the Sea for them and we think they will make excellent fishing boats," Vilhjalm said.

"What do you have to trade? They are going to want something special to part with a boat," Halfdan said.

"I have a number of combs, in both walrus ivory and antler," Ring said. "And Vilhjalm has fishing gear to trade."

"Make your trades," Halfdan said. "I agree with you. These boats will be useful." He watched the two men as they began to make their pitches to the boat builders.

Ring demonstrated how his combs came apart for broken tooth replacement. The combs were beautifully made and highly polished, with animal heads incised in the two wide top pieces that held the teeth. The crowd of Thalmiut men and women quickly traded him out of every comb he had brought. Vilhjalm threw in a long fish net, steel fish hooks, and several cod jigs, and the deal was made.

* * *

Halfdan and his shipmates awakened to a heavy wet blanket of fog the next morning. They had slept aboard ship to satisfy his nagging safety concerns. He climbed from his sleeping bag, splashed cold water from a bucket over his face, and stepped to the rail to take a wet. He lost sight of the stream before it hit the water's surface. Nothing could be seen toward the shoreline, but he heard voices so he knew the Thalmiut stirred as well. The rigging was festooned with water droplets, like a pearl necklace, that jiggled from the vibration of his step on the deck. He smiled when he recalled telling Frida that Gudbj would have predicted this fog. A soft step caused him to turn. His face split in a grin and warmth flushed through his body when Frida's smile swam through the mist as she stepped up to him.

"I knew you would be here, enjoying the soft morning." She stepped close; her eyes searched his face.

"The gods brought you to my mind, just now; I thought of what I had told you about Gudbj and fog."

She laughed happily. "I am glad he was not here. I would have lost the wager."

"Aye." He pointed at the shrouds beside them. "Look at the droplets. They remind me of a string of pearls."

She looked at him, and her face softened; a slight smile curved her lips. "You surprise me. I would not expect that of you."

"And why not? I see everything around me."

Before she could answer, Thorgill appeared out of the mist.

"Thorgill, good morning," Halfdan said. "I feel comfortable enough about these people that I want you to beach the ship later this morning. Bring it ashore when you hear the signal horn."

Thorgill glanced from Halfdan to Frida. "Good, it will be easier to load that pile of goods stacked on the beach."

"Aye, it will. I still have a little trading to do, but I think the others are done. Now, let us round up two boatloads of our people and go ashore."

Frida disappeared into the fog without a word. He fastened his eyes on the spot where she disappeared. Her passage caused small eddies. His hand felt along the rail for a painter as he thought of her. He grasped the painter and drew one of boats to the ship's side so his people could board. The mood was broken; their feelings would wait for another time.

* * *

Sometime later that morning a horn blast, the signal to beach the ship, carried far and wide through the eerie dampness. People surged toward the beach as realization spread that the ship was coming in. The fog accentuated the sounds of many voices.

Halfdan and some of his people lounged with Essipit and the tribal elders under a lean-to. They dined on roasted reindeer meat from a communal trencher. Trading had been mostly completed and they talked while they watched for the ship to materialize from the fog. Until the horn had passed the signal to Thorgill and the crew to beach the ship, she had been invisible from shore, and many of the villagers had no doubt forgotten she was still out there somewhere. To see her gradually appear ghostlike from the swirling mist, accompanied by the eerie creaking sound the long sweeps made, caused a stir of superstition among the Thalmiut. People close to the beach stampeded in fright until some among them realized the apparition was the giant boat of the Greenlanders rather than a spectral visitor from the Underworld.

Conditions on this morning proved to be ideal to beach the ship. The still air and cloaking fog made her all but invisible from a short distance away. The crew secured her parallel to the shoreline. The Thalmiut were curious about the ship and clustered on the beach to watch as well as they could in the mist. Thorgill and the crew rigged gangplanks and then allowed the curious aboard. After almost the entire population had a look aboard, the loading began.

The ship's crew that had not yet been ashore scattered throughout the village to look at the sights and enjoy their turn at the feast. Halfdan supervised a shore party of Thalmiuts and Greenlanders and together they made short work of loading the trade goods.

The one item the Thalmiut would not trade were their excellent soapstone cooking pots. Frida's questions had revealed that the soapstone came from a quarry many days to the east, on an island in the sea.

"The Thalmiut trade with the Beothuk, who live on the island, and they have a secret place where the soapstone is quarried." Frida could not pinpoint the exact location, given the communication limitations.

"Who are the Beothuk?" Halfdan asked.

"I do not know exactly. Apparently they are a small tribe that lives only on the island."

Halfdan contemplated her answer. "Perhaps someday we will know where to find this important trade item."

One final trade remained. Essipit avoided mention of it until he thought the Northmen were preparing to depart. He knew that Halfdan had already told him no, and at the time he could think of nothing his people possessed that might prove able to change his mind. But, by dint of careful observation one possibility came to him. The Northmen all showed an interest in the big dogs of the Thalmiut. Essipit thought he would try to trade Halfdan a pair of dogs for that which he coveted above all else: the axe of iron. An opportunity presented itself while the ship was being loaded. He had arranged to have two dogs brought to Halfdan while he sat relaxing with his crew. A group of Thalmiut, including himself, thought it might provide a trading advantage while Halfdan was distracted by the dogs.

The friendly animals caught bones thrown by crew members, and Halfdan found himself drawn to the dogs as he scratched the ears of a big male. He saw that both animals were restrained by lengths of rope held by the man who had brought them. Essipit sat beside him with a smug smile on his face, pleased about something. Halfdan sensed an undercurrent of humor. "What is it, Essipit?"

Essipit got to his feet, took the tethers from the man, and dragged the animals forward. He gestured toward the dogs and began to speak.

Halfdan looked quizzically at Frida and Ring. "He wants to trade the dogs for the battle-axe, does he not?

Frida nodded. "I think so."

"I will not trade weapons," Halfdan said. "Ring, go to the ship and get me a couple long-handled work axes and a hand axe, good ones mind you, and bring them back here. I will trade him iron tools."

Essipit watched the exchange carefully.

"Essipit, Ring is going to the ship. He will come back." Frida's explanation seemed to satisfy him.

"He will have to be satisfied with tools instead of weapons, Frida. I will not change my mind on that."

"I know, and I agree, but will he agree?"

"Good question, we will soon know the answer. Here comes Ring with the other axes."

"These are the best that we have aboard ship." Ring handed the axes to Halfdan as he got to his feet.

Halfdan examined the long- and short-handled axes. He took note of the bright sharp edges and tight hafts, stuck the haft of the hand axe in his belt, and handed one of the axes back to Ring. He turned toward Frida.

"Help me out with this. If he does not understand me, you make him understand."

She nodded to him, turned, and spoke to Essipit briefly.

Halfdan spoke to Essipit when Frida finished. He held the axe before him. "I will trade you this axe for the pair of dogs, Essipit." He saw the man's reluctance as his brow furrowed. I will have to sell this to him. He wants a battle-axe, not this carpenter's axe. Halfdan stepped toward a nearby log from which the Thalmiut women had split firewood. He turned toward Essipit and gestured with the axe for emphasis. "This axe is a tool. We use it to build our ships, split straight logs into boards, and split dry logs into firewood." Then he began to chop the log in half. Chips fairly flew. The crowd of Thalmiut exclaimed in wonder. He cut all the way through the log, and it fell into two pieces. He split off slabs from one half and then split the slabs into smaller pieces perfectly suited for the cooking fire. Purposely he left half the log in one piece. He gestured to Essipit and extended the axe toward him haft first. "Here, you try it."

Essipit hefted the unfamiliar axe in his hands, as he had seen Halfdan do, raised it over his head, and delivered a rather timid blow to the log. The blow did not drive the edge of the blade in deep enough for it to stick upright, and nary a chip flew from the log. Howls of laughter and hoots of derision rose from the gathering throng of Thalmiut, much to Essipit's embarrassment. He smiled self-consciously at the crowd of onlookers. His succeeding efforts produced a satisfying shower of chips as he gained a level of aplomb with the unfamiliar tool. A ripple of appreciative applause, with everyone now entering into the spirit of the event, rushed through the group as more and more new arrivals craned to see what was happening.

Essipit finished splitting the firewood in short order—for a novice—and stood regarding the tool with a new appreciation of its utility. He nodded and indicated to the man holding the dogs that he was to give them to Halfdan. He handed the long handled axe to another Thalmiut and pointed at the axe that Ring held. "I want that axe too, what will you trade for it?"

Halfdan's original plan had been to acquire a pair of dogs, a sledge, and a travois in return for the two axes. He pointed to a nearby sledge and travois. "I will take them for this axe, Essipit."

Essipit agreed. He pointed to the hand axe in Halfdan's belt. "I want to trade for that axe, too."

"This axe?" Halfdan pulled it from his belt. "I want you to have this axe as my gift to you." Halfdan handed the axe to him and indicated with a wave of his hand that it was his as a gift.

Essipit beamed. He beckoned one of his men over and whispered in his ear. The man trotted away, and Essipit smiled and nodded to Halfdan.

"I think he is about to have the last word, Halfdan." Frida's lips curved in a broad smile. The other Northmen present nodded and nudged one another as though they shared a secret, when in fact they had no more idea what was happening than did Halfdan.

The man that Essipit had dispatched trotted up leading a magnificent female dog with four pups doing their level best to keep up.

Essipit gestured and spoke one word to the man, and he handed Halfdan the dog's tether. "I give you, Halfdan, this bitch and her whelps." A huge grin split his face. He had the last word.

The simple trade for the dogs in the Thalmiut village that foggy morning was to eventually produce for the Norse settlers the large, heavily muscled, working breed of dog they enjoyed for generations. The dogs domesticated by the Norse, beyond the memory of any living person, were smaller than those acquired from the Thalmiut. The cross of the two breeds produced a strain of animal whose desirable characteristics— size, strength, courage, and loyalty—passed from one generation to the next. Many times in the coming years the saga of the wolf dogs was to be told and retold around the fires and in the longhouses of the Northmen. And all for the price of three iron axes.

* * *

The fog and incoming tide delayed sailing until early afternoon. Sailing on the slack or ebb tide was preferred to battling the flood tide. The heat of the sun, aided by a freshening breeze, began to move the last tatters of fog from the bay. The big ship backed slowly away from the beach. She wheeled majestically to the beat of her sweeps; the colorful red- and white-striped sail rose up the mast, filled, and she gained headway.

The entire village population stood on the beach waving and shouting. The people lining the ship's rails displayed the same exuberance. Soon the village and its environs were but specks in the distance.

Halfdan watched with satisfaction as his ship gathered speed. The breeze increased to the strong wind he expected as the masking effect of the loom of the landmass astern lost its influence. His glance automatically took in every detail of his ship and its crew: Thorgill near the helm with Gorm, Gauk at the masthead, other members of the crew busy with the business of the ship or engaged in personal projects while sitting about the deck conferring with shipmates. Nothing out of the ordinary.

On a broad reach with a steady wind from the steerboard quarter, the ship fairly flew downwind on a nearly even keel. The clear blue water creamed from her bow. The ride was exhilarating. *At this speed the return voyage promises to be short indeed,* thought Halfdan. He took a final glance at the set of the sail, and finished the greasy deer joint he had been tearing at as he leaned comfortably against the bow rail.

The male dog had bonded with him, for some reason known only to the dog. The animal now sat patiently at

Halfdan's feet. His long bushy tail scribed arcs on the bow platform as he watched every movement of the deer joint. Drool dripped from the dog's mouth as he smiled up at Halfdan. The tip of his tongue protruded, forgotten in his anticipation, from his slack lower lip.

"You want this?" Halfdan asked, taunting the animal by holding the joint out above him. "What will I call you? Dog? No, I will call you Wolf, for that is what you look like." Still holding the bone above the dog's head, he raised his voice so that others might hear. "I will call this dog Wolf!"

No doubt believing this to be his cue to claim the bone, Wolf sprang at it. His jaws snapped closed over his target as he fell back to the deck. The web of skin between Halfdan's thumb and first finger chanced to be in the way as the jaws snapped shut over the bone.

"By Thor," Halfdan exclaimed. He shook the injured hand and laughed at his own misfortune. "He has bitten the hand that feeds him!"

Attempts to playfully wrestle the bone away from Wolf, who was stretched on the deck with the bone clamped possessively in his jaws and between his front paws, met with a series of growls from deep within the great chest. Halfdan stood with hands on hips and watched the dog gnaw the bone. He looked at the bite laceration in his hand. He chanced to look up directly into the pale eyes of Frida. She had walked up unobserved and stood leaning against the other ship's rail watching his antics with the dog.

"I do not think Wolf is an appropriate name for your dog. Wolf Fang or just Fang might be a better choice," she said, tongue in cheek.

"Maybe you are right. I would call him Wolf Fang, it fits him. But I do not like long names for animals. Everyone, including you and me, would shorten it to either Wolf or Fang anyway. So, to acknowledge my wound I will call him Fang." He grinned at her.

"Fang it is then." She glanced at the dog and then fastened her eyes on his; a radiant smile dominated her face.

He recognized their short conversation about the dog as the opportunity he had sought for private contact with her.

They were never entirely alone. He stood for a moment and just looked into her eyes before he shared his thoughts.

"You have been very helpful, Frida. I wanted to tell you I appreciate the way you were able to understand the Thalmiut and help the rest of us understand. I also wanted you to know that I have seen a change for the better in you since our talk after the einvigi. Both of us were angry at that time, but we both got over it. I sensed you wanted to kill me as I walked away."

Frida made to interrupt his train of thought.

He stopped her with a raised hand. "Let me finish, please. That was then, this is now. I spoke my mind as the chieftain of our people. It is over, done with, because you heeded what I said."

He paused to collect his thoughts before he plunged on. She stood within arm's length of him. His eyes fastened on hers. Both were conscious of naught save each other.

"The rest of what I want to say is hard for me. It has to do with feelings that I have developed toward you since that day. Let me get it all out without interruption. All right?"

Her heart soared on fluttering wings. She simply nodded meekly.

"I have watched you. In the beginning, I did so because I did not trust you to heed my words. As time went by, I found I watched you because I liked to. I am not certain how or when the reason I watched you changed for me, but it did without my being aware of it. Gudbj knew it before I did. So did Ingerd. And I suspect so did you."

She had been immobilized by the simple sincerity of his words. Beyond crossing her arms she could have been carved from stone. She felt incapable of movement, afraid the moment would be borne away on the wind.

"I am only a man, Frida, a lonely man. I am certain I have missed much of what you three already know of all this. As chieftain, many things are expected of me. I must hold myself above the feelings others have and not involve the people in my personal feelings. But I have them nonetheless. I have strong feelings for you. I have need of a strong woman to stand beside me in all things. I yearn for a mate, a friend, a partner to warm my bed in winter."

Her hand rose unbidden to rest lightly on his chest. Wordlessly she looked into each of his eyes in turn; her breath came in shallow drafts. She stilled herself to catch every word, every inflection.

"That is all I have to say now. I wanted to say these things to you so you would know my heart. I guess it is my heart. I have never taken the time to think on it before. All I know for certain is I have never experienced feelings such as those I have whenever I look about for you and catch sight of you." His eyes searched her face. He waited in anticipation for her reaction.

Now both her hands rested lightly on his chest. His right hand had risen to rest on her arm. They stood thusly for a moment, unaware of all else. The aura of their beings entwined, silent and still, save the fluttering of each heart.

Her words, when they came, were preceded by a deep breath. She rose to the occasion as one returning from a trance.

"I have come to act the same as you, Halfdan. I watch for you, and I have the same feelings when I catch sight of you. But I did hate you after our 'talk,' as you call it. I would have killed you had the opportunity come." Her eyes flashed. "When I had those thoughts, I knew it could not be done, because you are too aware of danger. I also knew that if I did somehow surprise you and deliver a death wound, Gudbj would kill me with that axe before the Valkyries bore your spirit away to Valhalla. Nobody would be able to stay his hand. And I was only angry, not crazy."

He had been smiling slightly as she spoke. He started to interrupt her. She shook her head, warming to the occasion.

"No, it is my turn to talk now. And you must let me 'get it all out,' Halfdan. Ingerd has said that you and I are made for each other. At the time she told me that, I was still a little angry with you. To be fair, I realized you were correct in what you said to me. I was a troublemaker. Since then I have tried to change my behavior. It is difficult because I like to make trouble." She smiled coyly up at him.

Once again he tried to take part in the conversation, without success.

"I am not finished." She pushed on his chest with both hands.

He rolled his eyes and allowed her to continue.

"Ingerd and I began our friendship about this time, and she helped me see what I had been doing better than anyone else could have. Without her, I would not be at this place now, and you would not like me as you do.

"I have been with many men, Halfdan. For that, I do not apologize. It is the way of our people. It has nothing to do with you and me now, at this time. Once everyone knows you and I are to be one, no man would dare think or say anything about the past. You would kill him. If Gudbj heard it before you, that person would die without your even hearing what he had said. Besides, everyone fears both of you, so it will never be an issue."

She paused to let her words sink in. In a low voice, gone husky with the depth of her feeling, she asked the question she dreaded. "My past is not a problem for you?"

His immediate response was a return of the foolish grin. His arms encircled her waist. At the same time both her arms slid up his chest and around his neck.

He shook his head slowly. Her firm breasts contacted his chest, and he tightened his grip. He savored the moment. "No, Frida, I have no problem with the past. It is just that, past. I look forward only to the future. We have much to learn about each other. I am ready for this, so ready."

"And I, Halfdan." The invitation on her face was plain to see.

He slowly bent his head down toward her upturned face, his eyes locked on hers until the moment their moist lips met for the first time. The titillating contact caused a contented sigh to escape from each of them. A low moan escaped Frida's lips as their mouths opened and their tongues explored. Halfdan's manhood swelled erect. Unrestricted by their loose-fitting clothing, their groins lustfully ground together. The lingering contact of their lips, finally broken, left both breathless and wanting more. They remained still entwined, faces inches apart, as each regarded the other silently, breathless in their need to preserve this moment of bliss.

"Whew!" Halfdan exclaimed. He threw his head back and shouted at the sky. "I knew your lips would taste good! I just knew it!"

Frida laughed in delight. She hugged him hard and rested her head against his chest. As chance would have it, her eyes focused on their all-but-forgotten shipmates.

Everybody on board had watched the entire exchange with rapt attention to every detail.

"Oh!" Frida exclaimed.

Turning his head, Halfdan, too, saw that they were the center of attention.

"You were correct, Ingerd, we are made for each other. And I want all of you to be the first to know." He held Frida at arm's length, picked her up, and swung her wildly in a circle. "This is my woman. I am in love with her!"

"It is good you have decided to tell us, Halfdan." Ingerd laughed with everyone else. "I doubt we would have known otherwise."

Laughter swept the ship as the crew congratulated the couple. Everyone milled about the deck enjoying the light moment. Although he said nothing, a slight smile played over Vilhjalm's face as he watched his chieftain and Frida.

A horn blast from the masthead alerted the crew that something needed their attention.

Halfdan looked aloft and then aft toward the helm. Gorm shouted loudly enough to be heard the length of the deck. "Gauk and I did not know any other way to get your attention, Halfdan. First of all, congratulations, I hope you and Frida can be happy." He pointed forward, a wide grin on his face. "Gauk has our fjord entrance in sight. It is time to attend to the ship."

Halfdan waved in acknowledgment. He glanced aloft at Gauk, who had enjoyed a bird's-eye view of the drama from his perch atop the sail yard. He waved to the grinning man and turned his attention to the rest of the crew. He had eyes only for Frida. But duty called. "Let us be about our duties. Our people might think something is wrong with me if I allow the ship to be driven ashore with the sail set."

Chapter Twelve

A long horn blast, accompanied by a short blast, the signal for a returning ship, reverberated from the hills. "Halfdan comes!" The lookouts shouted.

The tall mast of the ship came into view above the headland; Steed of the Sea rounded the point and turned into the fjord. An answering horn sounded from the ship.

Every person not encumbered in some way made for the landing beach to greet the arrival.

"I am happy to see them," Gudbj said, grinning at his two companions as they walked down to the beach. "It seems like they have been gone longer than two days. I am anxious to hear how the visit with the Skraelings went and to tell Halfdan and his crew what has happened while they were gone."

"He will be very concerned about the attack, Gudbj. We may leave this place tomorrow on the ebb tide," Bjorn said, as the three men stood at the forefront of the crowd. Sweeps propelled the ship slowly toward the landing beach.

The crew took advantage of the light onshore breeze and turned the ship parallel to the beach so she came to rest beam to the shoreline. Lines were heaved from bow and stern to waiting hands ashore, gangplanks clattered over the side, and the crew began unloading the trade goods.

Gudbjartur watched Halfdan as the ship beached. He saw him look at the tethered Skraeling and he could not help but notice that his lieutenant and several others were wounded. It came as no surprise to Gudbjartur when Halfdan was the first person down the gangplank.

"You have been busy in my absence," Halfdan said, as he carefully examined his three officers. "What happened?"

"We were attacked about midday yesterday. There were over a hundred of them. One, maybe two men we let escape. The rest are dead, except him." Gudbjartur gestured toward the Skraeling staked out on the beach.

Halfdan looked his lieutenant over again. "How bad are your wounds, Gudbj?"

"The spear cut in my back will take some time to heal. The others are just minor cuts. I am all right."

"I see that," Halfdan said, his hand on Gudbjartur's shoulder. "I am glad you are in one piece."

"And you, Brodir?" Halfdan had seen the telltale smears of Asa's healing paste.

"Just a few small cuts, nothing serious," the big man rumbled.

With a nod at the welcome news, he glanced at Bjorn.

"I did not get a scratch, Halfdan. I tore off a thumbnail and skinned my knees gouging out a man's eyes."

"You should have seen them rolling on the ground," Gudbjartur said. "Both had lost their weapons. Bjorn finally killed the Skraeling with his bare hands."

Halfdan looked them over once again, just to satisfy himself that they were all right. He did not share his thoughts with them as his glance swept the encampment. He then turned back to them and nodded his satisfaction. "Good then, you all did well."

Halfdan and Gudbjartur made eye contact and Halfdan turned away, his attention drawn elsewhere.

Gudbjartur had kept an eye out for Ingerd. He had seen her stay aboard with the others to give him and Halfdan time to report to each other before she came to him. Now she strode purposefully toward him, her eyes on him alone. He knew she would accept no further delay, so he turned to meet her.

Halfdan and his captains walked away when they saw the determined set of her jaw, preferring to leave the two alone. Halfdan called back. "I will want to talk more, Gudbj. It has started to drizzle so we will meet in my tent after you and Ingerd are finished."

Gudbjartur answered out one side of his mouth as the three men walked into the encampment, his eyes on Ingerd as she approached. "I will meet you there shortly, Halfdan. This will not take long."

"Shortly," Ingerd exploded. "I have not seen you in two days. I return to find you wounded and you have no time to talk to me."

Gudbjartur tried to placate her. "Easy, Ingerd, we cannot go into it now; there is no time. I will tell you all about it later. We were attacked, and we have had losses. I am not badly wounded. It is painful and my shoulder is stiff, but I will heal quickly. I am all right." His hand rested on her arm. "Now I must join the council. We have things of grave importance to discuss."

"What about the boys?" She looked around the crowd for them.

"They are fine," he said.

"Where are they?" she asked.

"I do not know. They are here somewhere. I must go, Ingerd, now." He turned away.

She called after him. "All right, Gudbj. Go to your council." Her anger was plain to see as Frida walked up and put an arm around her shoulder. She shouted at his retreating back. "We have something to tell you too. We may just keep it a secret since you are too busy to talk to us."

* * *

Gudbjartur pulled the tent flap aside and entered Halfdan's tent to find the council members gathered and waiting for him. He nodded to Halfdan and the captains and took a seat on the platform next to the entrance. He felt a tearing sensation and his right shoulder burned every time he moved. Determination ensured he gave no outward sign of his pain and discomfort.

Conversation ceased after Gudbjartur's arrival as the men waited for Halfdan to begin.

Halfdan shifted his eyes to Gudbjartur. "I have been told of our losses. You do not need to speak of that any further." He looked at the other council members. "I want a complete discussion of the battle. I want to hear from those involved—why you allowed two to escape and why a prisoner was taken contrary to Gudbj's orders. I have already been told what happened. This discussion is to ensure we all have the same facts."

"I have agreed with their decisions." Gudbjartur looked at Halfdan, his agitation at the perceived slight apparent.

"I know that, Gudbj. I do not question the decisions made. This is not a hearing to attach blame; it is a discussion so we all know what happened and why it happened."

Mollified, Gudbjartur waited in silence for him to continue. Over the next hour Gudbjartur, Bjorn, and Brodir related the details of the battle and the pursuit of the Skraeling survivors. The men unanimously agreed with every decision Gudbjartur had made. There was little discussion of the battle itself. Instead the talk moved to other areas of interest.

"I saved twelve of their boats, two for each ship, and a large number of paddles," Athils said. "The boats are very light and strongly made. I thought they might prove useful to us. The others we destroyed."

"Ring and Vilhjalm traded for two Thalmiut boats. They, too, are sturdy and well made," Halfdan told the men.

"Thalmiuts, what are they?" Gudbjartur looked at Halfdan, his brow furrowed.

"That is what the men I have been trading with call their people. They are Thalmiut. It means People of the Deer, or just "the people" in their language. No more can we call them Skraelings."

The council members looked from one to the other. "Thalmiut they are then. I wonder how long it will take before everyone stops calling them Skraelings." Athils looked from man to man, the slight smile partially concealed by his beard.

"Habits are hard to break. I will wager it takes a long time." Bjorn found no takers among his fellows, so he went on. "We also collected some of their weapons." He pointed at the pile of bows, arrows, spears, hatchets, clubs, and knives he had dropped in the middle of the floor. "They are well made. Except for the flint or chert points and blades, they are similar to our weapons."

"And what does that tell you?" Halfdan asked.

"We are almost equal in battle," Athils said.

"Aye, almost equal. But our advantage is the way we fight." Brodir examined one of the bows with interest. "Their weapons are similar but not as good as ours. This bow is weak compared to ours."

"They could not stand against our attack," Sweyn said. "Our battle cries confused them. The fighting ability of our men overwhelmed them."

"The axes, more than anything, are what overwhelmed them." Gudrod glanced at Gudbjartur. "They had no defense against the axemen."

A rumble of agreement followed his statement as they passed the weapons back and forth. Halfdan and Gudbjartur did not take part in the small talk as the men examined the weapons.

Halfdan spoke up during a lull in the conversation. "Gudrod, have Tostig bring the prisoner in here. Find Frida, she will interrogate him."

"Frida?" Gudbjartur said, as they waited. "What has she got to do with this?"

His question caused the others to watch Halfdan expectantly. None knew the reason he had requested her participation.

Halfdan regarded his lieutenant for a moment, a slight smile on his face. "Much has happened since we sailed from here two days ago. Frida has a natural ability to communicate with these people. She understands almost everything they say."

"She can speak to the Skraelings?" Athils's question reflected everyone's astonishment.

"Not exactly. She uses a combination of our language, theirs, and sign language. The difference between her and the rest of us is she understands what they are trying to tell us in their language. Not part of what they are telling us, all of it. And remember, they are not Skraelings. We will call them

Thalmiut from now on. We have established a very good relationship with them. The trading was a success for everyone
concerned. You have seen the dogs we brought back to breed
with ours. We also have traded for one of their sledges and a
travois they harness their dogs to. Their dogs haul all manner
of goods with these travois during the summer. Someday our
dogs and the Thalmiut dogs will produce a breed of larger
work dogs for us that can pull the sledge and travois. In the
meantime, we will cut our travois down to a size our dogs can
pull and then build others like it. We also have acquired many
baskets, wicker containers, and bales of prime furs from last
winter. When we finish here you can examine everything we
brought back. I think you will agree everything we traded for
will be very useful for our people and for trade with Greenland and Iceland."

Frida entered the tent, nodded a greeting to the council
members, walked directly to Halfdan, kissed him on the lips,
and sat down beside him. She placed a hand on his knee and
smiled at the looks of surprise on the faces of every other man
in the tent. She looked at Halfdan. "Tostig and Thorgill are
bringing the prisoner. They told me you wanted me to be here
for his interrogation."

Halfdan put his hand atop hers on his knee and smiled at
her. "I do, Frida. I hope you two will be able to understand
each other." He smiled at the council members. "From the
looks on your faces, none of you knew about Frida and me."
He laughed out loud. "How could you know? We did not
know ourselves until we sailed back here from the Thalmiut
village. We have decided we like each other well enough to
try to make a life together." He punched Athils, who sat on
his other side, in the arm. "Come on you men, somebody
speak or I will think you do not approve. Your silence is
unlike you."

Athils rubbed his arm in mock pain and glanced at
Gudbjartur, but said nothing.

Gudbjartur sensed the others' hesitation and answered for
all of them. "We all approve. I, for one, am happy for you.
You two have just surprised us. We do not know what to say."
He looked at Frida. "So this is the secret you and Ingerd

laughed about? I should have known." He grinned at the happy couple.

The council members added their congratulations. Suddenly both tent flaps opened and Thorgill and Tostig entered with the prisoner. Thorgill shoved him into the center. "Here he is."

The council members sat or lounged comfortably on the benches. Nobody moved and not a word was spoken as they stared at the prisoner.

The prisoner stared back at them. The man's face was finely formed, rather thin, almost wolfish in profile. His narrow, hooked nose imparted a cruel cast to his countenance. His head was shaven, except for a scalp lock of black hair that extended from his forehead to the nape of his neck. He was of medium height. The exposed parts of his well-muscled body were stained a uniform red from the remains of a greasy mud he had spread on his skin. His legs were encased in leather leggings that attached to a belt at his waist. The belt also supported a breechclout that covered his crotch, an empty knife scabbard, and a pouch. A beaded vest and leather shoes completed his attire. The man's head wound had been dressed and most of the dried blood associated with it was gone. His bearing was proudly aloof and conveyed a total indifference to his predicament. He defiantly returned the stares of his captors.

"Look at him glare at us," Sweyn said with a chuckle. "I do not think I would be quite so hostile if I was in his position."

"Oh, yes, you would, and so would the rest of us. He is a warrior and I do not think we can make him talk unless he wants to," Gudrod observed.

Thora and Genevra pushed through the tent's flap and interrupted the council's discourse. They carried a large trencher piled high with joints and chunks of roasted meat, fish, and boiled eggs. Halla followed close behind with a bucket of soup and bowls.

They set the trencher on an open space of the bench. Halla set her burden on the ground near the prisoner. "We thought all this talk might make you hungry and thirsty," Thora said. "It is almost time to eat so I decided to feed you here."

The men crowded around the trencher and each selected their particular favorite. Frida and Gudbjartur hung back while the others made their choices.

The three women examined the prisoner from head to foot. Sidelong glances were cast in Frida's direction.

"All right girls, we had best be about our business so they can continue with their meeting," Thora said.

Halla and Genevra walked from the tent. But Thora paused a moment while she continued to look at the prisoner. To get a better look in the dim light she stepped closer to him. "He is a good-looking man. I will take him if nobody else wants him, Halfdan."

The prisoner's black eyes were fastened on her face.

"Your sharp tongue would have no affect on him, because he would not understand you." Bjorn's comment brought a few chuckles. "Look at him, Thora. The scowl on his face and the hate in those black eyes has not changed. I do not think he likes you."

"Oh, he likes me well enough." Her smile at the impassive prisoner did not alter his facial expression.

"That is enough," Halfdan said. "We have matters of importance to discuss. Thank you for the food. Now be off with you."

Thora glanced toward Frida questioningly.

"Frida stays because I want her here. That is reason enough. To satisfy your curiosity, Frida is a good interpreter, much better than any of us."

Thora glanced at Frida and then back to Halfdan. She nodded to him. "Thank you, Halfdan." Her eyes again met the expressionless black eyes of the prisoner. Then she turned away and walked from the tent.

The prisoner stood as before. His facial expression never changed as the other occupants of the tent ate their meal.

Halfdan watched his face for some sign that he, too, might be hungry. But he saw not a flicker of emotion. The man just stood impassively, hands tied together in front, while the normal conversation associated with a meal went on around him. Halfdan gestured to Bjorn. "Cut him loose."

Bjorn looked somewhat askance but got to his feet and cut the bonds from the prisoner's wrists with a flick of his knife. The two men made eye contact. The prisoner rubbed the circulation back into his wrists, his eyes expressionless.

"He is a cool one. We will not scare this man." Bjorn sat back down and began tearing at his meat joint again.

For the first time the prisoner focused a moment on each one of his captors as they watched him closely. He glanced briefly at the pile of weapons near where he sat. The tableau froze in expectation. His cursory examination correctly assessed his situation. He would not make it out of the tent alive. His glance settled on Gudbjartur, seated next to the entrance. Gudbjartur's baleful eyes were fixed on his face. Intuitively he knew this man would stop his bid for freedom should he make the attempt. Across the man's lap rested the wicked axe he vividly recalled from the battle he and his fellows had had with these strangers. No, this is not the time to escape, he thought.

Halfdan gestured with a joint of meat. "Sit!"

The man sat down on the ground as directed, crossed his ankles, his arms, and waited stoically.

Halfdan gestured again with his joint of meat, this time toward the heaped trencher. "Eat, if you are hungry. This may be your last meal."

The prisoner did not move.

Irritated, Halfdan repeated himself in a more commanding tone of voice. "Eat!"

The prisoner looked at him a moment. Then he reached over and selected a meaty joint from the trencher. His eyes did not leave Halfdan's face.

"I admire his courage," Halfdan laughed.

"I do not think he is very smart to act like this," Frida observed, as she watched the man gnaw on the tough meat. Juice ran unnoticed down his arms and dripped off each elbow onto the dirt floor.

The meal continued in silence for a time. Frida raised her eyebrows at Halfdan over her bowl of soup.

Halfdan indicated the prisoner with a lift of his chin. "Go ahead Frida. See if he will talk to you."

She got to her feet and bent over to refill her bowl from the soup bucket. Instead of returning to the bench she sat down on the ground directly in front of the prisoner. The man's flinty black eyes followed her every movement. Frida arranged herself a little more than arm's length away and watched him over the rim of her bowl as she slurped her soup.

The other occupants of the tent continued as if the prisoner did not exist. They occupied themselves by honing a knife or other weapon. Some combed lice from their beards or hair. When they captured one, a satisfying, almost inaudible pop rewarded them as they absentmindedly crushed the little pest. The men were content to let Frida establish communication with the prisoner on her own terms.

Finished with her second bowl, Frida belched contentedly and tossed the empty bowl on the pile of dirty utensils collecting next to the soup bucket. She got the prisoner's attention by extending an open palm toward him. Then she tapped herself on the chest. "Frida. I am called Frida."

All movement ceased when she spoke. Everyone waited to see what affect her attempt had on the prisoner.

No understanding registered on the man's face. He watched her. Then he turned his head to look at the others.

Frida watched his face expectantly.

His eyes turned back to Frida. He spoke the first words to pass his lips since his capture. "Frida," he repeated clearly. He tapped himself in the chest. "I am called Deskaheh."

"Let me talk to him, please." Her raised hand quelled the murmurs. Her eyes never left the prisoner's face.

Although he had spoken in his native language, Frida understood his words. She nodded slowly and repeated his name. "Deskaheh."

The man waited impassively for her next move.

She swept her hand to include the council and then pointed to herself.

"We are Greenlanders. Green-land-ers," she repeated clearly and slowly. Exaggerated hand movements accompanied each word. "I am Frida, a Greenlander. We are the people of the north, Northmen. What are your people called, Deskaheh?"

The man's expression did not alter for a time. Frida sat quietly and waited for a response from him, her facial expression friendly and inquisitive. He glanced once again at the silent men seated on both sides of them. Then he directed his attention back to his inquisitor. He spoke at length, slowly, emphasizing each word and phrase with an illustrative sign.

"I am called Deskaheh. I am Haudenosaunee." He swept his arm to include the area far to the south and east. "My band is from one of the five tribes of my people." He held up his right hand with the fingers spread and swept his other hand slowly over it to indicate each finger represented one of a whole group of people. "We are all called Haudenosaunee. It means People of the Longhouses."

Frida smiled in understanding. She repeated the key words. "You are Haudenosaunee. Your people are called the Haudenosaunee." She said it well enough that the man almost returned her smile. He nodded instead.

"Did any of you understand what he told us?" Frida asked, glancing at each man in turn.

"I understood his name, Deskaheh." Halfdan looked at the others. Several of them nodded in agreement. "We did not understand his other words."

"I understood him to call his tribe the Haudenosaunee. That is a long, difficult name. I did not understand the rest of what he said." She repeated what she had learned, purposely shortening the name of his tribe. "Haudeno, Deskaheh? Your people are Haudeno?

He canted his head slightly in assent. "Haudeno."

"Ask him why they attacked us." Halfdan's patience wore thin with the preliminaries.

"I will try." She began an elaborate pantomime of battle: The Haudeno attack on her people, the defense mounted by the Northmen, their attack on the Haudeno, the dead and dying, his capture. He watched her efforts closely for a time before he began to respond. Once he began, each question laboriously presented by Frida was answered in detail. Over time a clear picture of what had transpired in the immediate past became apparent to her.

"I understand, Deskaheh." She nodded her understanding to the prisoner and turned to Halfdan and the council.

"I do not want to continue asking you if you understand. How about I tell you what I think he means. If you disagree we can talk about it." She spoke to Halfdan directly.

Halfdan nodded.

She stood and stretched, then stepped to a water bucket for a drink. She offered the full ladle to Deskaheh. He took it from her hand and drank. The dark eyes never left her face.

Frida walked slowly back and forth as she organized her thoughts. "Deskaheh is a war chief among his people. He led a war party into the land of the Thalmiut and the Naskapi, their traditional enemies. We have not made contact with the Naskapi yet; their villages are inland around the rivers and lakes. He and his warriors have watched us since we arrived in this place. They would not have attacked us had we not befriended the Thalmiut. He did not want to attack us because he thought we were too many and too strong for his warriors. The young men wanted to attack, and they were still arguing when Bjorn—he pointed at Bjorn when he told me, so I know I understood him—attacked them."

"That is true, Halfdan." Gudbjartur's eyes shifted from Halfdan to Bjorn. "Frida has it right. A large group of them were arguing when Bjorn attacked. They had already attacked and wounded Ormiga, so I sent Bjorn and a bunch of men to attack them before they got organized."

Pleased with Frida's interpretive ability, Halfdan smiled and gestured for her to continue.

"Deskaheh told me of his part in the battle up to the time he and his men retreated into the forest. After that he does not remember anything until sometime after Asa and Thorkatla dressed his head wound and cleaned him up. He has no memory of his capture, only of fighting a big, red-headed man with a sword. Thorgill maybe, I do not know. You could ask him if you want to know, I guess. Not that it matters who almost cut off his head," she chuckled.

"That is correct, Frida, it does not matter. We did not start this fight, they did," Halfdan said.

She nodded, her eyes on Halfdan. "He does not know that just he and one, possibly two others, are the only survivors. Do you want me to tell him?"

"No. Not now. If we decide to keep him alive he may know what happened someday," Halfdan said. He turned to Gudbjartur. "Get that map you have been working on. Let us see what he can tell us about the coast south of here."

Gudbjartur got to his feet, pushed the tent flap aside, and went to get the map. Halfdan looked at Frida. "Ask him where he comes from."

By the time Gudbjartur returned with his map, Frida had encouraged Deskaheh to speak of the home country of his people by drawing a map of the bay, as the Greenlanders understood it, on the dirt floor of the tent. Halfdan and the council offered assistance as the drawing took shape. Knowledge of the coastline, gleaned from talks with the Tornit, extended only to a point south of their present encampment, where the coastline began to curve away to the west and north. The interior areas were unknown to them. But not to Deskaheh, as became abundantly clear when Gudbjartur joined them on the floor with his map.

The council members gathered around to look at the map Gudbjartur had drawn on a square of tanned hide and the drawing on the dirt floor. Deskaheh drew a large river and connecting lakes that flowed into the great salt bay they had been exploring. He explained to Frida that his party had paddled their boats from his village on the shore of a lake far to the southeast. His village's lake was located north of a very large river that flowed to the east and emptied into a long, narrow, saltwater bay. The trip by boat from his village, including the time required to transport their boats around rapids and over a divide, had taken him and his warriors seven days before they had paddled out of the mouth of the river several days ago. By dint of skillful questioning, Frida determined that this river delta lay about one day by ship, or five by their boats, south of their present encampment.

Frida repeated what Deskaheh had just told her. Before she finished her narrative a pervasive air of excitement gripped the council.

Gudbjartur looked at Halfdan as the enormity of what Des-kaheh had just revealed became known. "When we sail into the south end of this bay we will be about seven days by boat from the sea." Excitement sharpened Gudbjartur's voice.

"It will make no difference. We cannot sail the ships up that river," Brodir said. "Our only way out of here with the ships is still back the way we came."

"I know that, Brodir, but the sea is much closer than we first thought. I believe this land is a wide peninsula. If need be we could trek overland to reach the sea."

"You may be right. One day we will know for certain." Halfdan looked thoughtful.

The others agreed. A general discussion followed.

Halfdan let them talk. He caught Frida's eye and winked at her. She answered with the warm smile he sought.

Deskaheh squirmed uncomfortably while the council deliberated on the information he had provided them. His discomfort became more pronounced.

"He must be uncomfortable from sitting so long. He probably needs to relieve himself." Frida pointed out.

"Tostig, take the prisoner to the pits." Gudbjartur responded.

"Prisoner, Gudbj? He has a name." Frida took her former seat beside Halfdan.

Gudbjartur looked at Frida. "He is no friend of mine. I do not care what his name is. We fought him and his men not long ago and killed all but two of them. As far as I am concerned he should join them when we are finished with him. I will not be friendly with my enemies."

"You are right, Gudbj. I did not mean we should be friendly with him. But he did give us much valuable information. We may have more questions. I cannot get him to cooperate unless I am friendly or neutral, which is what I have done." She glanced at Halfdan but his eyes and expression revealed nothing to her.

"And you have done well." Gudbjartur spoke in a flat tone. "But you will not kill him when we have no further need for him. I will. That makes it different for you and me."

She nodded in understanding, her eyes downcast. She had no wish to get on the wrong side of this man.

A noise at the tent entrance caught everyone's attention as Tostig pushed the flap aside and came in with the prisoner. Tostig motioned for the prisoner to sit. Deskaheh sat down on the ground and crossed his ankles as before.

The council waited for Halfdan to speak.

"I have made my decision. We will continue our journey to the south tomorrow unless one of you wants to talk about it some more." Halfdan looked from face to face.

"I agree." Gudbjartur looked at the others. They agreed without dissent.

The prisoner had another go at the few meaty joints that remained on the trencher.

"That looks like a good idea." Sweyn got to his feet and picked through the remains before he selected a suitable joint. The meat had long since gone cold, its fat congealed in grayish blobs. Sweyn tore at it with gusto. The others watched.

"By the gods, Sweyn, how can you eat any more?" Athils asked.

"Want some? There are still a few juicy pieces left here." Sweyn talked around a mouthful.

Athils snorted and waved a hand at Sweyn. Everyone laughed.

The prisoner watched his captors while he wolfed down chunks of meat he had torn from his meaty joint.

"I told Essipit and his Thalmiut that we would be sailing south to explore the bay, so they expect us to be gone," Halfdan said. Halfdan noticed a widening of the prisoner's eyes at mention of the word 'Thalmiut.' His eyes shifted down the bench to Gudbjartur.

"I saw him. He recognized the word." Gudbjartur leaned against a tent support at the entrance, facing the interior.

Halfdan continued. "I did not tell Essipit exactly when we would sail. They will probably never know we have a prisoner from an enemy tribe. They will find the battlefield, but even then they will not know about him."

"There is little sign that a battle took place, beyond a few arrows here and there. We destroyed everything else, including his friends." Brodir gestured toward the prisoner with the sword he whetted.

"I hope they do not ever find out because we have made friends with them and I want to preserve that. I do not think they will, because they are on their summer quest for next winter's meat supply. They will not return to the village for some time. By then this area will be overgrown." Halfdan sat silently in thought for a time, his hand resting on Frida's knee. He gestured toward the prisoner. "He has answered all our questions, unless someone has something else they want to ask?"

No one spoke.

"No? So be it then. Frida, tell him we will let him live. Tomorrow afternoon we sail on the slack tide. We will take him with us until we no longer have a use for him. After we are aboard ship I may turn him loose; it depends on him alone. Any trouble from him at any time and he dies. Tell him that too. If I turn him loose he can help Gudbj with his map while we sail south. Tostig, when Frida has finished telling him what is to happen, take him out by the fire pit and tie him to one of the awning supports. Give him water and a sleeping robe."

"What about a guard?" Tostig asked.

"Gudbj will take care of that." Halfdan looked at his lieutenant. Gudbjartur nodded.

"After we sail tomorrow it will not be necessary to guard him. He will be thrown overboard to feed the crabs if there is any problem," Halfdan said. "It has been a long day. My sleeping robe beckons."

The tent emptied rapidly as the prisoner was led away. The council members scattered to alert their ships' crews to tomorrow's departure. As the last man pushed his way through the tent flap, Halfdan glanced at Frida, the lust in his eyes plain for her to see. Alone at last. If only there is enough time, he thought as he reached for her.

* * *

Not far away from the encampment, a canoe with six dead bodies, and another about to join them in death, slowly drifted toward the south shore of the bay.

It was the canoe that contained the seven men Brodir and Bjorn allowed to escape from the battleground. Three of the seven had still lived when they made their escape, the others were dead. All had been transfixed by the last flight of arrows from Brodir's men. One died soon after, the other finally bled out the second day, dying of his wounds. The third man, although seriously wounded, managed to paddle the canoe toward the bay's distant southeast shore. His effort made no difference to his situation but he had gotten away.

He had slumped forward only a short time ago. His life's blood continued to slowly seep from the arrow wound in his chest. The powerful bow of the Northman had driven the arrow completely through him. Just nicking one shoulder blade on entry it sliced through the bottom of his left lung. Its path missed the heart and liver. The shaft exited his chest between two ribs to the left of his breastbone. The bloody shaft buried itself to half its length in the middle of a man's back directly in front of him. He realized the blood matted and drying on the feathers that fletched the arrow shaft was his own.

He watched both of his companions slowly bleed to death from their multiple arrow wounds. Not a word had passed between the wounded men. Now the lone survivor was truly alone. He realized his wounds were mortal as his strength slowly ebbed away. He looked at the bodies of his erstwhile companions and realized he should have shoved them overboard to lighten the canoe. Now he no longer had the strength.

He felt weak, his limbs leaden. He rested for a time. His paddle lay athwart the canoe. His eyes traveled slowly over his surroundings. A fog claimed his mind. He chanced to glance down at the arrow's exit wound in his chest. For the first time he noticed the bubbles. Bubbles were not good. From somewhere in the dimming recesses of a brain that slowly died from lack of oxygen, he remembered bubbles always came from a pierced lung.

He willed himself to paddle some more. The effort proved to be short lived. His arms grew impossibly heavy. Random thoughts of his life passed through his mind. He was unaware of outward physical sensation. His chin slowly sank to his chest. His torso bent slowly forward at the hips. The vibrant life force that controlled muscle rigidity ebbed; his body relaxed. The paddle gripped in his right hand trailed in the water. A light breeze drifted the canoe toward the tree-lined shoreline.

* * *

Some distance from the canoe, a large, hump-shouldered, male brown bear ambled slowly through the forest. He paused occasionally as a faint blood spoor passed into his flared nostrils. The silver guard hairs along his neck and over both shoulders stood erect in response to the smell.

He stopped for a moment as he neared the water's edge. The great head moved slowly from side to side as his nose tested the air. He dropped his head to the surface of a rill that flowed into the bay. His long, purple tongue lapped at the water's surface. His wet nose moved from side to side; the whiffs of the blood spoor tickled his nostrils.

His tongue continued to dart in and out of the water. Suddenly the breeze shifted and a strong smell of fresh blood flooded his senses.

"Whoof!" The loud expiration of alarm came from deep in his chest as his brain registered the smell. He jerked his head from the surface of the water so quickly his tongue lolled from slack lips. His senses came to full alert. The smell came from close by. Noiselessly, he withdrew both front feet from the rill and pivoted his upper body fluidly on hind legs in the direction of the smell. The pads of his front feet made not a sound when he dropped to all fours. He crept toward the bay's shoreline. His small rounded ears probed for the slightest alien sound. But there was none to hear. Natural sounds of birds and insects of the forest and water were all he heard. His weak, little eyes probed ahead. He stepped carefully through the detritus of the shoreline without a sound. In tune with his high state of angst, the long, silver guard hairs along his neck and hump remained rigidly erect.

Mere feet away an almost inaudible moan passed the lips of the lone survivor in the canoe. The bear stopped in mid-stride. The hated human smell mixed with the overpowering smell of blood came on a puff of breeze off the bay. He detected a slight movement from the form slumped in the canoe.

The great muscles bunched. The long hair of his coat fairly danced as the animal ran to the side. Fear momentarily overcame the aggression inherent in his kind. He stopped so suddenly a shower of dirt and small rocks sprayed from under his feet. Without pause he wheeled and charged the canoe; the roars of his rage filled the air. The figure in the canoe did not move. The animal skidded to a stop.

He stretched out his neck and turned his head from side to side. His roars shook the forest and shoreline. He girded himself for the final charge. The great muscles bunched and propelled him at the figure slumped in the canoe. Water, mud, and gravel flew from his feet. The long claws of his right paw tore away most of the side of the man's head. The body shuddered and convulsed from the impact. His slathering jaws tore off what remained of the head. He crunched up the bones of the skull and swallowed the remains. Tearing at the bodies, he satiated his hunger.

He dragged the remains from the canoe and covered the mangled meat with sticks and dirt, as was the way of his kind. When finished, he ambled away on his interrupted rounds.

As he made the circuit of his territory, his prey would rot. The meat would become more tender, more to his liking. He would soon return to feed again. When finished, all that would remain of the bodies of the Haudeno warriors, the cream of their nation, would be a few scattered and broken bones.

* * *

Southeast of the bear's cache, on the banks of a lake, a lone woman shielded her eyes from the setting sun. She looked up the long axis of the lake into the northwest. Another day had passed and still the war party did not return.

Others members of the large Haudeno band had also watched and wondered. As time passed all knew for certain that one war party of their men would not return to the comfort and safety of the wigwam hearth.

Squaws hacked off their hair and slashed their arms in grief. The enormity of their loss settled over all of them. Such a thing had never before happened. It was hard to comprehend.

Superstition won out. Demons or devils had taken their men.

Fear sat on the shoulders of every warrior who ventured out. Darkness, the time when demons and evil spirits walked the earth, was especially fearsome.

* * *

Some distance to the northwest, in the encampment of the Northmen, the twilight of a summer morning changed to the dawn of a new day. The rising sun peeked above the eastern horizon and drove the grayness before it as the people began to stir.

Halfdan awoke at first light, as was his habit. For a moment his thoughts were unfocused in the semi-dark interior of the tent. A pile of luxurious red hair that belonged to the woman snuggled beside him lay on his outstretched arm. He smiled at the memory of their first night together. He blinked and swallowed a few times to clear his mind of sleep. Gradually he began to emerge from the torpor induced by his first night of lovemaking in ages. He did not remember the last time. One thing was certain; it had not been anything like last night. A sigh escaped from his lips. He thought of the intensity of his feelings for this woman. A vast erection rose from his loins. Its appearance surprised him given the past night's debauchery. It screamed for attention. He felt as though he would burst, as Frida stirred beside him.

She grasped his straining manhood. "Umm, did he wake you up?" she purred sleepily as she stroked the rigid pole.

She made him feel like a boy again. Until last night he had not realized how deprived he had been. Nor what he had missed. My morning hard may not be only because I have to take a wet, he thought. The up thrust of his hips opposed the down thrust of her hand. "Easy, Frida. Stroke it slower!"

In answer she threw the auk-down quilt aside with her other hand and took him into her mouth. Halfdan's groin convulsed as she pulled and sucked at him. A deep groan escaped his lips and he exploded in her mouth.

"Ohhh, by the gods, Frida!" He thrashed on the bed.

She continued to suck and pull at the sudden tenderness of his manhood. With a final kiss she released his now flaccid member. Her blue eyes fastened on his. A mischievous grin split her face. "Good morning, my love." She bent forward to kiss him. They melted together and explored each other's lips and mouths with their tongues. Completely contented they purred the little bed sounds people made at such times, as warmth and happiness washed over them.

After a time, Halfdan stretched out to his full length on the bed beside her. He tensed his muscles to their maximum. His body went rigid as an iron bar, vibrating in warm sensuousness. He slowly relaxed, a thoroughly spent man. "I am not certain I can stand. You have drained my last reserve of strength."

"Good, I want everyone to know that you are the most loved man among us." She poked him in the ribs. "Now, maybe we should think about getting up. A wash will feel good. I want to comb my hair and then go eat some food. I am starved." She swung her long legs off the sleeping bench.

"I do not hear a sound out there." He listened intently, his head propped on one hand. "Maybe it is too early to have something to eat."

"It is not too early. If you do not get up we will be the last to eat."

He gazed fondly at her beautiful body while she brushed her long red hair. His eyes traveled over the swell of her buttocks and paused on her large breasts as they swung to the movement of her arms.

"You are beautiful, Frida. I love you."

She laughed happily, stepped to the sleeping bench, and bent over to kiss him tenderly on the lips. "And I love you, Halfdan. Now please get up. I am starved."

A quizzical look crossed his face. "I still do not hear anything out there. Where is everyone?"

"They are all out there. Gudbj has told everyone to stay away from here and leave us alone. He would allow nothing to disturb us."

"Oh, I had not thought of that. I guess he would." He grinned.

"As long as he is beside you, concern yourself with nothing. He will take care of whatever comes up."

"Of course he will." He lurched out of bed, slapped her across the buttocks, and stepped up to the night bucket to take a wet.

They finished with their ablutions and donned clean clothes. Halfdan threw the entry flaps aside. His eyes swept the area. They strode from the tent arm in arm, laughing together as they made their way to the fire pit.

A large crowd had already gathered for the morning meal. Gudbjartur and Ingerd scooted aside to make room for the new arrivals.

Halfdan and Frida greeted everyone close by. They grinned happily at the seated Gudbjartur and Ingerd. "Good morning," they said in unison. Halfdan looked down at his friends. "How is the shoulder, Gudbj?"

"Every day it is better." They looked at each other.

"Thanks, Gudbj," Halfdan said simply.

Gudbjartur looked away, embarrassed to be thanked in front of the others by this man he loved above all other men.

Frida and Ingerd bore witness to the moment they shared.

"Gudbj." Frida caught his eye. "Me, too."

Gudbjartur smiled at the two of them and pulled Ingerd onto his lap. He kissed her fondly. "We are very happy for the both of you. Ingerd has told me you are made for each other. I think she is right." He swept his arm to include everyone watching. "Everyone is happy for you. They have talked of little else since you returned. You two are the main gossip around the encampment, at least for now." He grinned.

Chapter Thirteen

Halfdan watched his people as they basked in the sun under the clear blue skies of the southern bay. He felt a sense of satisfaction and thankfulness to the gods for this fine day and the possible end to the journey. It had been two days since the flotilla sailed from the bay of the Thalmiut and the scene of the battle with the hostile Haudeno. He turned his attention back to his ship.

Steed of the Sea coursed along on a broad reach, with a brisk northwest wind over her stern quarter. She rolled through the steep, close-set ranks of swells, the gurgles and swishes of her passage reminders of her communion with the elements of the sea. Several rock strewn islands, scattered with clumps of sparse brush and teeming with nesting seabirds, fell astern as the course took her toward the entrance to a wide bay.

"Turn to the southeast and steer toward the far end of the bay, Gorm." Halfdan called to the helmsman. The new heading brought the ship close aboard a single, large, tree-covered island centered in the wide approach to the bay.

As mainland shore features became more distinct, Halfdan reflected that Bjorn must be happy about all the trees. Heavy evergreen and hardwood forest could be seen on the mainland. Willow, birch, and scattered evergreen covered the larger islands. Seabirds, seals, and small whales beyond count were seen on or near every island they sailed past. Seabirds of every description followed astern and wheeled overhead. At least two different kinds of small whales, along with different species of dolphin, swam back and forth between the ships as they continued into the bay. Halfdan turned and signaled to the helmsman for a turn closer inshore. Then he waved his hand forward over the bow to indicate he wanted Gorm to parallel the shoreline. He shielded his eyes from the glare of the sun off the water's surface and looked aloft. "I want a beach with a river, Gauk, protected from the north wind."

"All right, Halfdan, I will look for another like Snorrisfjord," the lookout answered from the masthead.

A flurry of disturbed water from the port side near the stern announced another successful seal kill by Tostig and a group of men. The men shouted and scurried out of the way as they pulled the fifth harpooned seal over the side of the ship. The seals attacked as soon as they were hauled aboard. The men quickly clubbed them to death before any damage could be done by the animal's sharp teeth. Halfdan was amused to see the prisoner, Deskaheh, in the middle of the activity. He had quickly become a part of the crew. Everyone aboard attempted to converse with him, and he with them. Halfdan observed a struggling seal being pulled over the side of the ship following astern. *We will eat well tonight,* he mused.

Gudbjartur had completed his map now that arrival at their destination was assured. He rolled it up and went to show it to Halfdan. Another struggling seal was dragged over the ship's rail just as he started to walk forward. He turned to watch. This seal was still full of fight and it wheeled this way and that as it tried to bite its tormentors.

"Look out, Helge!" Askhold of the Runes shouted. Men scattered before the large bull's lunging charge. Tostig delivered a tremendous blow with his club to the back of the seal's head as the animal lunged toward Helge.

"That got him. You cracked his skull, Tostig." Helge stood at the dead seal's head and watched the dark blood run from the animal's ears and nostrils. He looked at Tostig. "Thanks. He almost got me."

Tostig gave a nod and looked down at the still trembling animal. "He is a big one. He must weigh as much as five men. He is the last. It looks like Halfdan is heading inshore." He pointed toward the shoreline to port.

Gudbjartur continued toward the bow. He smiled and winked at Ingerd as he stepped around a group of women seated at the foot of the mast. She looked up from her mending and her lips curved in a smile.

Halfdan rested both hands on the portside bow rail as he looked at the distant shoreline.

Gudbjartur stepped onto the bow platform beside him. "Those harpoon heads the Tornit gave us are better than anything we have ever had. Tostig told me we have not broken a single haft since we began to use them."

The two men looked aft to watch Tostig's crew dip buckets of salt water from the sea to wash the blood from the deck. "Aye, they are cleverly designed. I am glad we have them. I see you have the map." He indicated the roll in Gudbjartur's hand with a lift of his chin.

Gudbjartur nodded. "It is finished to the entrance of this bay." He stepped over and unrolled the map on the upturned hull of one of the ship's boats. They studied it together. "Deskaheh helped me with this, as you know. He learns very quickly and most of the drawings are his. He is better at it than I am."

"So, he is your friend now, Gudbj?" He was amused at his lieutenant's acceptance of their prisoner's presence among them.

"I did not say he is my friend. He is useful, and he seems willing enough. If you decide we do not need him anymore, it will not matter to me."

"I know, but as you told Frida a while back, it would not be easy to kill him once he is no longer your enemy."

"Maybe, but that would not stop me."

He watched the play of emotion across Gudbjartur's face. "We are several leagues south of the river he and his warriors paddled down from their home country. He pointed it out yesterday morning as we sailed by. If he knows this country here we will have use for him. Of that I am sure." The two men continued to study the map.

Gudbjartur pointed out several map additions. "Askhold added the runic bearings. I am not so good with numbers. The details of this bay will be added later—the shape of the bay, the islands, water depths, and bearings to key features."

"The animals and birds we observed on the voyage are a nice touch."

Gudbjartur shook his head; a slight smile drew at the corners of his mouth. "Deskaheh drew them. We decided they were useful to have on our map."

Halfdan's reply was cut short by a hail from the masthead.

"A landing site is off the port beam. Just beyond that island." Gauk's outstretched arm pointed the direction.

Passengers and idle crew crowded along the inshore rail to have a look. From the deck the island blocked their sight of the river.

"There are two islands. There is a sound between them. The islands block your view of the river. I cannot tell for certain yet, but a good landing beach may be on both sides of the river mouth," Gauk called.

"Steer for the island, Gorm," Halfdan called aft to the helmsman. He and Gudbjartur turned and stepped back onto the bow platform to better observe their approach. Gudbjartur twisted the map into a tight roll and stuck it in his belt.

"Tell Askhold and Deskaheh they did a good job on the map. For a man who cannot draw and who has never seen a real map, you, too, did a good job." Halfdan looked at his friend.

"I already told them they did a good job. Copies can be made and given to each captain. I think the map will be useful for us. I am well pleased with how it turned out."

Halfdan nodded at him, and the two men turned their attention to the new course.

The ship came around to port as Gorm pushed the tiller bar away. He set the ship on a course close-hauled on the steerboard tack for the island.

The other five ships of the flotilla altered course to follow.

"Stand by the sweeps!" Gudbjartur called to the crew.

Passengers dutifully shuffled to positions amidships to leave the ship's sides free for the rowers. Crewmen moved to their rowing stations with the long sweeps held upright at the ready. Others prepared to lower the sail when they received the order.

Land features became distinct as they drew nearer. Both islands were covered with boulders. Scraggly pine and willows survived in copses over the craggy surface of each. The islands appeared to be separated by an inlet or sound. Seals sunned on the outer island. Gudbjartur and Halfdan keenly watched the approach.

"There are too many boulders to land a ship on either island," Gudbjartur observed. "But the passage between them might be a possibility."

"Let us hope for either a mud or sand bottom at the river's mouth." Halfdan looked aft at the other ships and aloft at the trim of his sail. "Slow the ship, Gudbj. You bring us in." For the first time, he relinquished command entirely to Gudbjartur.

Gudbjartur glanced at Halfdan. "Aye." He turned aft and called through cupped hands to the helmsman: "Bring her into the wind a little, Gorm. Let her luff."

The helmsman pointed the bow into the wind until the sail began to quiver and flap. The sail lost some of its thrust and the ship began to slow.

Each maneuver of Steed of the Sea was quickly duplicated by those that followed astern.

Gudbjartur looked aft for the man with the plummet. He nodded to him, and the man stepped to the bow platform to cast the line into the ship's path. He called out the depth. "No bottom on the line." He coiled the line for the next cast.

"Good," Gudbjartur said with satisfaction. "I want to close the shore as near as possible under sail."

As the ship slid by the nearest island the bottom began to shelve. But the depth remained deep enough that Gudbjartur continued as before.

"Thirty feet," the man called.

The island passed to port without the water depth changing significantly. The ship's company observed the features of the place of intended landing with interest. Enthusiasm increased with each slap of the short waves against the hull.

"Both sides of the river's mouth look good from here," Gauk called from the masthead.

"Gorm," Gudbjartur called aft, "steer for the right side of the river. That looks the best to me, Halfdan." He glanced toward him.

Halfdan turned to look at him. "It is your decision. If I do not think it is safe I will tell you."

"I am certain you will," he said with a grin. The ship eased toward the shoreline. Gudbjartur knew he had sailed about as close inshore as he could. The land would soon blank the wind. He watched the wind streaks on the water's surface. His eyes shifted back and forth to either side of the course as he looked for the telltale sign of the first area of slick water. The slick would indicate the wind had died to nothing. Shelter from the north wind was what they always sought. Finding it meant the end of sailing. *Knowing just the right time to drop the sail— that was the trick,* thought Gudbjartur. He chuckled to himself.

Halfdan heard the slight chuckle and looked at him. "What is it?"

"Oh, I was just thinking about when to drop the sail. I know when I am going to do it, but it is just a guess on my part."

Halfdan smiled. "Do not tell anyone. They all think their leaders alone know these things. That is why we are leaders. We do not want to disappoint them, do we?"

Gudbjartur laughed aloud, and slapped Halfdan on the shoulder. "Whatever you say, Halfdan. Just in case, I think I will give myself a little extra room for a mistake since this is my first landing." He pointed toward an area of slick water about six ship lengths ahead. He turned aft and cupped his hands. "Out sweeps! Lower the sail!"

"Twenty feet," the man on the plummet called.

Gudbjartur turned toward the man at the stroke drum. "Slow the stroke."

The stroke drummer began the slow beat.

"Ten feet on the line." The man coiled up the plummet for another cast.

Gudbjartur held his hand up. "That is enough for now. We will beach the ship."

The ship crept at a speed of dead slow toward the beach. Gorm barely had steerageway. He managed to maintain a straight course with frequent corrections to the big steerboard. He waited to feel the keel make contact as the bottom shelved. His free hand held the thick leather keeper strap for the steering oar. He would have to jerk the strap loose from the slots cut in the rail before the forward half of the keel contacted the bottom. If he waited too long, the steering oar might not pivot out of the way quickly enough.

Gauks was right. The beach appears to be mud and sand, about what one would expect at the mouth of a slow moving river, Gudbjartur thought.

Halfdan echoed his thoughts. "This may be the place we are looking for, Gudbj."

"I had similar thoughts."

One ship length from the beach he turned and cupped his hands. "Boat your sweeps!"

Sweeps clattered inboard. They had reached the end of the journey for the present. Crew and passengers prepared to disembark.

The big ship drifted slowly ahead as the way went off her. The deck canted as the keel rode onto the muddy bottom. She came to rest with the raked bow hanging over the beach.

Gudbjartur waited until the other ships slipped ashore before he gave the order for the armed men gathered in the bows to go ashore. They trotted up and down the beach and far into the forest to secure the area.

The passengers waited and watched as the security force checked the beach and the countryside inland.

Halfdan and Gudbjartur stayed aboard with Ingerd and Frida and talked about this new place they had discovered.

"I am not certain why, but I feel like we just came home." Frida looked up at Halfdan.

"I hope that is not just wishful thinking," he answered, as his eyes swept the countryside in the near distance.

"We feel like we have found a new place to build a home, too. He has not said anything yet, but I know my husband.

He feels the same as I." Ingerd looked at Gudbjartur. A nod was all she got, but the smile that went with it answered the question for her.

"I hope so. After we have been here for awhile and scouted the hinterland, we will have enough information to make a decision." Halfdan took hold of Frida's hand, and they stood with their friends and gazed at the beauty of the new land.

The beach combined a mix of coarse sand and smooth stones. To the west, a rocky cliff wound its way along the water's edge until it joined the slope of the highest hill to be seen. At the east end of the landing beach, forest and scattered rocky outcroppings at the water's edge extended into the distance. Visible through the scattered trees above the beach, a panorama of gently rolling hills, covered with grass, willow, and stands of timber were interspersed around a large fen through which a river meandered to the bay. Grassy meadows dotted with copses of trees were seen in the distance. Evergreen trees predominated, but large areas of birch, maple, willow, alder, butternut, and aspen were also seen. People exclaimed excitedly at sight of large oak trees scattered throughout the forest. Directly in front of the landing beach, through openings in the forest verge, the large fen extended out of sight in the distance. Small lakes and ponds dotted the low areas. In the nearby lakes were several large deer, some with palmate antlers.

"Moose!" Frida cried. "I have not seen one since I was a young girl in Vestfoldland."

"I have never seen one before. He is so big," Ingerd said excitedly.

Others caught sight of the moose.

"What kind of animals are they?" somebody shouted from the ship next to Steed of the Sea.

"Moose!" Frida shouted back. The word passed down the line from ship to ship.

A short distance from the ships, a large bull was feeding in the nearest lake. His whole body, except for the tips of his antlers and his back, was underwater. He raised his head above the water's surface and chewed contentedly on the clump of rushes that hung from his mouth. Water cascaded from his antlers and head. He looked comical. Shrill laughter from the women and children soon made him aware that he was not alone. He gazed stupidly at the six ships on the beach. He became alarmed. With a loud snort he wheeled and ran from the lake in a flurry of water and mud.

"He is bigger than a horse," Ingerd said.

"It is because of the long legs that he looks so big," Frida said.

"He is big, not counting the long legs." Ingerd and Frida watched the bull's alarm spread to the other moose nearby. Soon all were headed at a gallop for the concealment of the forest.

As luck would have it, two cows and two young bulls ran into a contingent of the security force. A well-placed flight of arrows brought them down.

"More fresh meat!" Thora shouted from Steed of the Sea. A cheer rose from the onlookers. The bowmen acknowledged the shouted accolades as they gathered around the fallen moose. All four animals dropped within a few feet of each other.

Halfdan and Gudbjartur climbed over the ship's bow and dropped to the beach. Gudbjartur passed the word to the others aboard the six ships to wait a while longer before disembarking.

Men crowded around the two, and group leaders gave their reports.

"The area is secure. There is no sign of people at all. Not a single track, fresh or old. It is hard to believe, Halfdan." Thorgill gestured as he emphasized his points. "Game is everywhere. Besides the moose we have all seen caribou, geese, and ducks on every pond, grouse, rabbits, and black bear. The women will be happy to know there are all kinds of berries in the fen. The butternut trees are loaded with nuts."

Each group gave almost identical reports. Halfdan issued his orders and dispatched men to find a suitable place for the encampment. "Secure the ships, Gudbj. We will stay here to explore the interior and send expeditions up the rivers. The people can disembark and stretch their legs. After they have a look around, unload the ships."

Deep in thought, he watched Gudbjartur walk away.

With what little we know, it looks favorable, he mused. *I will send scouts out tomorrow. I must have more information before a decision can be made about staying here.*

Gudbjartur returned after a short time. "The ships will be moored beam to the beach. After the gangplanks are rigged, the people can disembark. They will unload the ship after they have a look around. Tostig and his crew are quartering the moose so the meat can be carried to the cooks. Thora, Ingerd, Frida, and their helpers are butchering the seals now. Every ship killed at least two, so there will be plenty of meat. As soon as we have a campsite picked out, I will have the fire pit built. The cooks tell me they will cook the fresh meat for the evening meal. So there is plenty to do, as always." He grinned.

"Good." Halfdan folded his arms and looked at his lieutenant. "You did a good job bringing the ship in. One day you will have your own ship. You deserve it."

"I am happy as your lieutenant. But I will do whatever you want me to do. That will never change."

"I know that. I have been thinking while you were away. I want your opinion on some things."

Gudbjartur waited for Halfdan to continue while they watched the activity along the beach.

"Lambing Time is about to begin in earnest. We will remain here until all our livestock have had their young. Regardless of what is decided about the permanency of this place. Build pens within the encampment. It is the best way to protect our animals from bears and wolves. This bay is much further south so it will be dark at night, not the twilight we are accustomed to this time of year," Halfdan said.

Gudbjartur thought about that. "The time of darkness should be short, though. We are still in the high north. Camp guards will be posted by nightfall. Firewood is plentiful and they will keep fires burning through the night. The men told me there are black bears here and tracks of wolves are all about. No white bear tracks have been seen yet."

"Maybe they do not come so far south."

"I would be surprised if they are here in summer. It is too hot during the day. But with all the seals we saw during the sail down here there will be white bears when the bay freezes this winter." Gudbjartur observed.

"You are probably right. Have our tents pitched in a quadrangle. The livestock pens can be built at one end. With the guards, the fires, and our dogs, they will be safe."

They were silent for a time. "After people have a chance to explore and form opinions about this place, I will call a council meeting. The final decision will be made then. Tell the captains this. They will soon know what their people want to do."

"It will be done." Gudbjartur agreed.

They strolled down the beach toward the ships and the hub of activity, talking as they went. People nodded greetings to them but continued with their appointed tasks.

All six ships were warped into the beach beam to. Gangplanks led down onto dry ground. Men, women, and children scurried back and forth unloading the ships.

Brodir and Athils intercepted the two men.

"We found a good site for the encampment." Brodir pointed inland. He led the way to an elongated, flat-topped rise that commanded a view of the beach; the upper and lower bay stretched out before them.

"This is the best site close to everything." Athils pointed out features. "Brodir and I have walked this whole area and it is high and dry. Fodder and building materials are close at hand. The river is down the slope there. A peat bog is nearby and a good layer of sod covers this whole area."

"A steady breeze will help keep the bugs to a minimum," Brodir added.

"You think so?" Gudbjartur said with a chuckle. "We should be so lucky."

Athils laughed too. "Deskaheh's greasy red mud seems to be the only thing that keeps the bugs at bay. The rest of us have little protection except smudge fires and clothing that covers as much skin as possible."

Brodir gestured toward the two men and their helpers kneeling on the ground at the far end of the knoll. "Haakon and Asgrim have peeled the sod back and found a bucketful of bog-iron lumps. Haakon told us they will build a smithy and smelter right there with the blocks of sod." He paused a moment. "This looks like a good place to stay for a while. What do you think?"

"We will see," Halfdan said. "After we send out scouts and the people have time to think about it, we will make our decision. But for now, I agree. This place seems to have everything we need."

The men stood for a time looking out over what had been a pristine rise or bluff that was rapidly being transformed into a comfortable encampment. Smoke rose from the newly constructed fire pit. They could see women making the necessary preparations to turn the fire pit into a workable kitchen area. Crews of workers were building the animal pens at the opposite end of the tent quadrangle from the fire pit. People already referred to the area as the town commons. The site was particularly suited to such an arrangement. It overlooked the beach, the fen with the river, the many lakes and ponds, and much of the countryside.

"If we remain here it will be easy to convert this site into a permanent settlement," Halfdan said. "Longhouses can be built over the summer to gradually replace the tents."

"The materials to build them are right here," Gudbjartur said. "As trees are cut for the longhouses and palisade, the forest verge will be pushed back, giving us more security and room to expand."

"Brodir and I watched the smithies turning over sod. The soil is rich but fairly shallow. It looked like the soil depth was at least the length of a spade blade. After that they started running into loose rocks. We think it will grow a good crop of barley from the seed grain the women horded from last season's trade with Vestfold. Providing the weather is cooperative," Athils said.

"That is good news. It will be good to live in a place where grain grows. Perhaps this Vinland will provide everything we need." Halfdan seemed pleased.

The men made no further comment, but instead they watched the various areas of the encampment take shape. Tostig could be heard shouting at some unfortunate while the livestock was unloaded.

"He should let the herders unload the livestock. I do not think he has the temperament for it," Gudbjartur observed with a chuckle.

"Like the rest of us, eh?" Athils said.

They laughed again.

"Before we go, this is what must be done tomorrow," Halfdan said to the three men. "I want each captain to leave in the morning with a boat crew and explore this land for at least two days in all directions. Gudbj, you assign them their areas of coverage. I will take a boat crew and explore the bay to its eastern limit, including the river that probably flows into it. I will return before nightfall. Have the five captains explore the rivers and bay shoreline." He pointed toward the highest point, a hilltop up the coast to the west. "The men who scout the hinterland can start their circle from that hill. Everything for many leagues in all directions will be visible from the top."

Gudbjartur looked at the hill, his eyes slits in the glare of the pale red sun as it peeked from behind a bank of clouds to the southwest. "After I assign the areas to be scouted, what do you want of me?"

"I want you here to see to the encampment's security and to organize the hunting and fishing. Also, I do not know how many people remain after our losses. We knew the total number when we left Greenland, but not how many we had in each group: families, children, young adults, single men, single women, that sort of thing."

"I will tell the captains to give me a tally of everyone aboard their ships." Athils and Brodir nodded when his eyes shifted to them. "So be it then." He glanced out over the bay. "It is cooling off, and the Fog Giant stirs in his lair. Soon this day will be done. I will give the other captains your orders."

With that, the men went their separate ways. The mouth-watering smell of roasted meat wafted through the encampment. Everyone would soon gather for the final meal of the day.

* * *

The four moose and six seals provided forty upper leg joints of rich meat and fat. The cooks hung the roasts on treble meat hooks suspended on chains from the tripods over the fire pit. The meat basted in its own melting fat as the roasts turned back and forth in the heat rising from the deep bed of glowing coals.

Succulent slabs of red meat carved and hacked from the roasted joints provided everyone with their fill. All that remained of the roasts on the sideboard trenchers were a few fragments of meat swimming in juice and congealing fat.

After people stripped the meat from the bones they dropped them into kettles of boiling water. The broth that resulted formed the base for the next day's soup and stew.

Satiated by food and drink, people lounged in groups or walked about visiting, content to allow the prodigious quantities of half-raw meat to settle somewhat before festivities began.

The coming dusk found everyone in a jovial mood fueled by the dwindling stocks of mead and the last of the beer. They were thankful to have reached a place of safety and optimistic about the future.

As was customary, the children ate together in small animated groups segregated by choice as to sex and company. Some consisted of both boys and girls while others were either one or the other. Best friends were always together, while certain ages, because of shared experience or common feelings, gravitated to one another. Inevitably the older boys and girls who approached puberty took special notice of one another. As a consequence, much of their group conversation revolved around the opposite sex, especially the conversations of the groups of giggling girls.

Gudbjartur's sons, Ivar and Lothar, with their friend Yola, sat to the side of a large group of boys, their heads close together in secret conversation.

"Come on Ivar, which girl do you like best?" Lothar elbowed Yola in the ribs as the two bent forward to watch Ivar's reaction.

"I have no interest in girls. All they do is giggle and talk about the rest of us." Ivar's voice was tinged with a hint of disdain.

"We know all that. But which one do you like?" Lothar pushed for an answer.

Ivar's eyes shifted between his brother and Yola. "That pretty blond, I guess." He pointed her out with a lift of his chin as he struggled to suppress the smile that tugged at the corners of his mouth.

"You were right, Yola. It is Vigdis." Lothar slapped Yola on the back, and the three boys laughed together.

Vigdis sat with a small group of female friends, and they all noticed the boys' attention. The girls put their heads together when the three boys erupted in laughter.

"Go talk to her, Ivar," Yola said.

"I do not want to talk to a stupid girl. Now forget it, both of you," Ivar said between gritted teeth.

"She does not look stupid, Ivar. I think she has you figured out," Lothar said with a chuckle.

Ivar glared at his brother and got to his feet.

"Come on, I want to move closer to the front so we can hear the stories better." With a final glance toward Vigdis and friends, he turned and threaded his way through the crowd. His brother and Yola followed.

* * *

Tonight was a special time for all of them. After the story-telling, they would dance in celebration of the end of their voyage. Everyone would participate.

The sagas of the people had been told many times. But when the tellers changed so did the story. It was this aspect that made it fun for everyone. After all, well-told lies and boasts of personal involvement in chivalry, bravery, and love were the stuff of which legends were made. The tellings offered a very rare opportunity to relax and be entertained. For the children especially, it was the only time the adults descended to their level, and they sat waiting patiently, facing into the quadrangle in watchful anticipation.

Jokes and mimes of humorous aspects of everyday life tra-ditionally began the storytelling. As people warmed to the occasion, and mead or beer eliminated personal inhibition, stories became more humorous or serious.

Tales of trolls, dwarfs in the earth, the helpers of the gods, the slaying of dragons by the heroes of old—the favored stories of generations of Northmen were told.

Thora, one of the most gifted storytellers among them, became the center of attention. She began in a deep voice. Her words came with a singsong lilt tinged with an eerie quality intended to scare her audience. It worked. "I have a tale of Njord, god of the wind, of his visit one dark night. A tale of terror, cold, hunger, and death in the deep I will tell you. Njord came at us on his ill tempest, in the company of Thor, who threw his lightning bolts at our frail ships over the many dark days and nights." She told of the big storm at sea to a rapt audience. She told all: the fury of the tempest, the minds numbed by cold and terror, stomachs churned by the heart-stopping plunges of the ship, the icy sting of the rain on bare flesh. Many of her listeners squirmed at their places as each relived the fury visited upon them by the gods.

She finished as abruptly as she had begun. A silence hung over the throng. Gradually the applause began. Thora grinned and bowed to her audience. Her eyes sought Deskaheh. He leaned against an awning support, impassively watching the proceedings. The moment their eyes made contact, his face underwent a transformation. He did not smile exactly, but the slight inclination of his head spoke volumes to Thora. She nodded in return, her lips curved in a broad smile as she took her seat to thunderous applause.

Thora was a hard act to follow, but the audience listened attentively to the telling of a few more stories before the mood turned to music and dance. Five-finger wooden flutes and stringed instruments appeared. The songs of old—tales of bravery, love, sorrow, and death—continued the theme of the sagas. What people lacked in skill was more than made up by boisterous exuberance, all but drowning out the simple instruments. But nobody seemed to notice. The entire assembly joined in song until the favorites known by all had been sung.

Two lines formed in the quadrangle: women on one side, men on the other, and children mixed throughout. Illumination by the flames of the fire pit and the torches spiked around the area lent a surrealistic quality; the swaying forms appeared as darkened shadows. Disembodied faces flashed in the flickering light.

To the flute and strings were added a stroke drum and a couple signal horns. The rhythm of the dance began to manifest itself. The primal tempo of the music aroused in every breast the ancient need of all peoples to move together to a beat in accordance with something perceived.

Ivar placed himself opposite Vigdis. She greeted him with a shy smile. They watched each other self-consciously as they swayed to the tempo. The dance brought about a heightened awareness of one for the other. Talking would come later.

Thora, swept up and inspired by the music, boldly approached Deskaheh. She held out her hand and gestured toward the dancers. "Come, Deskaheh, dance with me."

His dark eyes fastened on her friendly and open face. He took her hand, and they jostled through the throng of onlookers to join the dancers. More than a few heads came together in whispered conversation. Facial expressions of acceptance dominated, however, for enjoyment was the purpose of the evening.

The dance had no beginning, no end. It just was, as long as the participants deemed it so. By some unheard and unseen signal, a shuffle took place in the female line as a few of the women positioned themselves opposite the man they wished to claim as their mate in the jumping-across ceremony.

Two of those so positioned were Halfdan and Frida.

Halfdan stepped up to Frida. "Are you ready to become my wife, my mate, Frida?"

"Oh, yes. I am so ready." Her luscious lips curved in a smile as she looked up into his eyes.

"Aye. And so am I." His eyes traveled over her body before he turned to take his place among the men.

An eagerly awaited union, formalized by the woman simply leaping across the intervening space between herself and her man, was about to take place.

As the two lines swayed to their closest proximity, Frida made her leap toward Halfdan. He crushed her to his chest, then swung her in a great arc, scattering people left and right. A great booming laugh came from the depths of his being.

Others followed in similar fashion. When it was done, all had made their choice of mate. They were joined in accordance with the laws and customs of the Northmen.

* * *

Thora and Deskaheh danced themselves out. They claimed a spot under the fire pit awning and sat warming their backsides at the fire. Thora had found him a cloak to ward off the chill of the night air. They were quiet for a time, seemingly content, and oblivious to the occasional stares of passersby.

Thora shifted toward him and looked into his eyes. "I do not know how much we can talk, Deskaheh, but I want to try."

His black eyes searched her face.

"Do you have a woman, a mate? Oh, how can I make you understand?" Sudden inspiration came to her. She pointed to a woman walking by, then to him, clasped her hands together, and repeated the question. "Do you have a woman?"

Suddenly he chuckled. A grin crept over his face, and he said a few words she did not understand, but she understood the shake of his head.

A flush bloomed on her cheeks and a heat rose in her breast that had nothing to do with the fire at her back. "You do not have a woman," she whispered.

He pointed to the same woman, held up a single finger, and shook his head. A slight smile pulled at the corners of his thin lips.

"You do not have a woman. Or you want only one woman. Which is it?"

Again he said something she did not understand. He watched her closely, leaned toward her, and took her hands in his. Their faces were but inches apart. He slowly shook his head; a wide grin split his face, and he uttered a single word.

She squeezed his hands. "You want only one woman, and you do not have a woman. Is that right?"

He responded with a nod, as though her thoughts had entered his head.

"Well, you have a woman now, Deskaheh, you have me." Her face felt hot.

He took her chin in his hand and wiped the sheen of sweat from her brow with a finger, his dark eyes on hers.

She swam in his eyes. It was hard for her to breathe. She had never been so aware of another person.

The fact that neither spoke the other's language posed no difficulty as they continued their conversation. Words were emphasized with signs that both understood.

Their regard for one another would furnish fuel for gossip around the encampment for some time to come.

* * *

The scouting parties were ready to depart with the dawn. The captains had each chosen six or eight men to accompany them. Individual portions of dried meat and fish, sufficient for two days, had been doled out to each scout. The men carried bows or spears in addition to the ever-present belt knife and pouch. Their dried rations were rolled in a sleeping robe looped over a shoulder. Some carried water skins; most did not, relying on the many lakes, streams, and rivers for water.

"Bjorn, take the prisoner, Deskaheh, with you," Halfdan said, as he handed his bow and arrows to one of his crewmen. "He might provide some insight into whatever you discover on your journey into the interior."

"What if he tries to escape?" Bjorn glanced toward the prisoner.

"If he escapes, so be it. He can tell his people about us; perhaps they will leave us in peace." Halfdan helped his crew push their boat into the water.

"I do not think he will try to escape," Gudbjartur said. "Thora has her hooks in him."

The men laughed.

"Helge, go get a Haudeno bow and quiver of arrows for him. He will have use for them whether he stays with us or goes back to his people." Gudbjartur beckoned to Deskaheh, and the man walked over to him. "I want you to go with Bjorn." Gudbjartur made signs as he spoke.

Deskaheh nodded. Helge handed him a bow, arrows, a knife scabbard, and a rolled robe of rations. He accepted them and turned to Gudbjartur, surprise on his face.

"Take them, Deskaheh." Gudbjartur gestured. "You might have need of them."

The two men regarded each other for a heartbeat. Gudbjartur turned away and walked to where Halfdan stood.

Without a word about what he had witnessed, Halfdan looked at his friend; then his eyes swept over the large party of men gathered on the beach. "Let us be about it. I will be back by nightfall." A slight nod to Gudbjartur was his only sign of approval regarding the prisoner.

The six boats rowed from the landing beach and hoisted their sails. Halfdan set a course for the southeastern end of the bay, and the others split into two groups to cover the north and south shorelines.

Bjorn and his party strode away toward the hilltop to the west. They were soon lost to sight around the first headland.

Gudbjartur watched the boats as they stood out from shore and scattered into the bay. He remained on the beach for a time. His eyes slowly swept the horizon toward the south shore. It appeared as an indistinct dark gash between the blue of water and sky. He combed his fingers through his beard while plans for the day's activities went through his mind. Occupied thusly, he slowly turned in a circle until he faced the hilltop to the west. A flash near the summit got his attention. Another flash followed. *There it is again,* he thought. *It is probably off a spearhead. Bjorn is almost to the top. He and his men will be able to see the whole countryside from up there.* Movement in the near distance caught his eye. A black shape moved along the edge of the granite cliff above the bay at the western end of the landing beach. He watched it closely. From its movements, he figured it to be a black bear. Its shambling gait in its eternal quest for food was easy to spot. He smiled, shook his head at the simple things of life, and turned away to walk into the encampment.

* * *

The sound of a lookout's horn, before the face of the sun disappeared below the horizon, told Gudbjartur that Halfdan had returned. He compared the copy of his map with the original while he wiped the ink from his quill's nib. Carefully he dusted the copy with dry sand, shook it off after it had blotted his new entries, rolled it loosely, and stowed the charts and his supplies in Ingerd's trunk. He dusted the sand off his hands and bent over to retrieve another rolled skin from the trunk. *Halfdan should be about to land,* he thought, walking from the tent. He caught sight of the boat's sail as soon as he had a clear view of the bay. She was beating into the landing beach, sailing close-hauled to a brisk northwest wind.

The land's dampening influence began to still the wind; the oars came into play, and the boat closed on Gudbjartur and Frida standing side by side on the beach.

Halfdan jumped over the boat's low side into the knee-deep water and waded ashore into Frida's open arms. A smiling Gudbjartur hung back until they finished.

Halfdan's crew hauled the boat up on the beach and began to unload their gear.

"Here, Frida, take my gear to our tent." Halfdan handed his bow and quiver to her. "I will join you at the fire pit after I talk to Gudbj."

"Ingerd and I will be waiting for you both." Her mouth curved in a smile, and she headed back to the encampment.

"I think I will like having a mate." Halfdan and Gudbjartur watched Frida's hips as she swayed up the path toward the encampment.

"There are many advantages you will grow accustomed to," Gudbjartur said with a chuckle.

Halfdan grinned. He noticed the tightly rolled piece of hide in Gudbjartur's hand. "What have you there?"

"I have the tally you requested. The captains gave me their tally of those aboard their ships before you left this morning. I divided up those totals on this list." Gudbjartur unrolled the square piece of hide. Halfdan took it and looked over the runic inscriptions.

"There are 206 men, forty-two women, and fifty young people counting small children; thirty-three of these are boys and seventeen are girls. There are eleven families including you and Frida." Gudbjartur smiled at this last. "That leaves thirty-one unmated women spread among 195 single men. This tally includes those who jumped across last night. The scarcity of women will cause more trouble one day. I think at least half of the young girls will be available for mates by next summer. That may help. Right now we have a total of 298 people. Seventeen people have been killed outright or died from wounds. Ormiga, Gunnar, and Gizur are still crippled from wounds but can do some work. Ormiga and Gunnar are lucky to be alive. Gizur heals as well, but he will never fully recover from the wounds he received in the einvigi."

Halfdan looked up from the tally. "Good, Gudbj! This tally will be helpful for our future planning. We must try to do a better job of keeping track of these kinds of things. Before you gave me this I had no idea about age groups or how our people are divided up. Hopefully the woman shortage will work itself out. Not all the men want a mate." He rolled the tally back up and handed it to Gudbjartur.

"True, but the trouble we have had was caused by the other thing men want from women. It has nothing to do with a mate."

Halfdan snorted. "You have a way of getting right to the heart of the matter. You are probably correct. It will not work itself out without a little help from the gods."

"I hope a friendly native band has a man shortage, Halfdan. Or someday there will be another einvigi."

"Ever since Iceland was colonized, a shortage of women has been a problem for our people. The problem only becomes worse with time." Halfdan eyed his friend again. "I think finding a native band that needs a few new men is the best idea I have heard. Maybe that will happen if we settle in this land."

"I hope so." Gudbjartur looked at Halfdan. "What did you find in the east end of the bay?"

"I found more of what we have here. There are many sites to settle. We passed several large islands as the bay narrowed down at the southeast end. Both shorelines are heavily forested with the same mix of trees as here. But there are more hardwoods, I think. A big river flows into the bay just beyond the two biggest islands. We turned back there in order to get here before the darkness came. On the way back my crew could talk of little else. They like this Vinland. I think the people will want to stay here through this next winter, maybe longer. We will not know for certain until the other scouts return. But, in anticipation of good reports, I think we can keep the men busy cutting four shiploads of logs. If we stay here, they will be used to build longhouses. If not, they can be transported to Greenland for trade."

"Good idea. I, too, think we will stay here. This place seems to have everything we need, and it is about the same distance from Greenland as Leifsbudir. The winter will be shorter and warmer than Greenland and game is abundant close by, unlike Greenland. Which ships do you want to send, if it comes to that?"

"I will leave that up to the captains. It depends on who wants to make another voyage."

Gudbjartur thought over the idea. "On the way back they could stop at the Tornit village of Inuktuk and hunt walrus. Two shiploads of walrus hides, ivory, and meat for winter would be most welcome. By spring, the hides will have been made into rope. The extra rope, ivory, and furs we will accumulate over the winter might make a voyage to Iceland worthwhile." He looked at Halfdan, a slight smile playing about his lips.

Halfdan regarded his friend quizzically. "It seems you have given this some thought, Gudbj."

"Of course, I am your lieutenant."

"Good suggestions," Halfdan said. "Regardless of whether we settle here or not, that is what we will do. All four ships will sail to Greenland with timber. There is plenty of time for the round trip. Two ships can stop at Inuktuk's village on the way back here to hunt walrus and trade with them. We can decide later what the other two ships are to do on the return voyage. If they leave before the next moon, they will be back before winter loaded with enough walrus meat, hides, ivory, and other trade goods to feed and occupy the people most of the winter."

"So be it, Halfdan. I will get the men started cutting trees tomorrow."

Halfdan laid a hand on his friend's shoulder. "How is the shoulder doing? You never say anything about your wounds."

"I am all right." Gudbjartur flexed his right arm and shoulder muscles. "It is stiff and sore. I keep working to loosen it up."

"At least you are not like Gizur. I saw him this morning, and I think he will be permanently crippled by his wounds. He still cannot move his right arm over his head."

"Did you talk to him?"

"Yes, we had a talk. I wanted to make certain he did not harbor a grudge about Frida."

"And?"

"He told me he is all right with it." Halfdan saw a sudden change in Gudbjartur's demeanor. His friend's relaxed posture suddenly stiffened like a bowstring. He became agitated at the mention of Gizur.

"I have watched him since he recovered enough to move around," Gudbjartur said. "I do not trust him. I think he might try to kill Frida after he has recovered his full strength."

"He would not do that, not now that she and I are together."

"I think he would. I will continue to watch him. Ingerd and Frida are seldom apart. I have told Ingerd of my concern. You had better tell Frida as well."

Halfdan's eyes narrowed as he contemplated this change in his future outlook. Their future. "I will do that. If I get the least indication he poses a danger to Frida, I will kill him."

"You will not get the chance, for he will already be dead." Gudbjartur's eyes conveyed the intensity of his feeling as he looked at his chieftain. "Gizur will be among the tree cutters tomorrow. He cannot wield an axe, but he helps where he can. I will tell him how it is to be."

Halfdan looked at his friend. He placed a hand on the man's shoulder. "Come on." His cheerful tone belied his inner feeling. "It is time to join our women. I am starved. How about you?"

"I can eat," Gudbjartur said shortly.

The two men walked up the path from the beach toward the flickering light of the fire pit. Both were silent as they mulled over the substance of their discussion.

* * *

Over the next three days, two large crews selected and felled pine trees. They limbed and cut the trees to length, then skidded the logs to the beach with teams of horses, where they were stacked above the high water mark. In two day's time, enough timber for shipment to Greenland had been stockpiled. The heavy, green logs were specially cut in random lengths to replace all ballast stone low within the hull of each ship. The men clear-cut the forest. They harvested every tree regardless of diameter. All would be used for something. Goats and sheep would eat the remaining leafy brush. They left select hardwood trees that would be harvested when needed. Cleanup crews piled pine tree limbs with other unusable slash for later burning. The open ground of a new field for next year's barley crop began to emerge from what had previously been the verge of untrammeled forest.

Frida, Ingerd, and several other women moved about in the animal pens feeding and checking on the pregnant females confined there.

"I will go check the sow we thought was about ready," Frida said, as she climbed over the low wall of the pig pen.

Ingerd did not answer as she stooped to look into a loafing shed.

Both of the large pens, finished by the men the previous day, were divided into four smaller pens across one end. The females about to birth and the females with newborns were confined in them to protect the young. Each small pen included a simple loafing shed, a pole framework covered in pine bows woven through roof and sidewall supports to provide shelter for the birthing females from the frequent drizzle and rain showers.

"Look Frida!" Ingerd called to her companion. "Two calves, four lambs, and two kid goats were born last night."

"This sow has birthed six piglets. She is still lying down, there might be more to come," Frida answered from the next pen.

"With the young birthed at the last encampment and aboard ship on the voyage south, our livestock numbers are increasing daily," Ingerd enthused.

"Yes, most of the young will arrive over the wax and wane of this full moon," Frida answered, as she bent over the sow. "The Lambing Time moon is the most hectic time of year but I always look forward to it. I have two more piglets over here."

"Is she finished?" Ingerd called to Frida.

"I cannot tell. Maybe—she just got up and is cleaning her piglets." Frida beat a hasty retreat from the pen.

Pigs, being almost impossible to confine because they either dug out or knocked the pen down, wandered here and there rooting in the droppings of the other livestock and crunching up the bones and debris thrown out by the cooks. In this way refuse was kept to a minimum around the encampment. This arrangement worked fine until a sow birthed her new young. For the first day or two she needed somehow to be kept confined, because she presented a very real danger to other livestock and any person who might alarm her or her new piglets.

"I see you are not too proud to run from that sow." Ingerd leaned on the top rail of the fence.

"Only a fool would risk the wrath of a sow." Frida grinned as she slogged through the mud of the pen toward Ingerd.

"If you are finished with her, I can use some help mothering up these ewes and their lambs," Ingerd said. "Two lambs have not suckled yet and the ewe is not doing anything to help. Two other ewes just went down so they are about to birth."

Frida climbed into Ingerd's pen. She looked back at the pigpen in time to see the sow's snout pushing at the rocks under the bottom pen rail. "Thora," she called. "Send somebody to throw some scraps into the pigpen, the sow is digging out."

Halla soon arrived and dumped a basket of refuse and scraps into the pen.

"That should hold her," Halla said, as she watched the sow root happily through the garbage.

The herdsmen dried up the female grazing animals about a month before they gave birth to the next generation. The first fresh milk of the season came from the females after they birthed their young. Out of necessity newborns always suckled their fill of their mother's first rich milk. When the heavy birthing milk thinned the milkmaids began milking the animals twice a day. The young were allowed to strip the remainder of the milk out, getting their share in the process. This method ensured the female continued to produce the maximum volume of milk possible. Herdsmen penned milking females away from their new offspring, or they were driven out without their young during the day to crop the lush grass of the meadows. The milkmaids saved the bulk of the milk for the people's consumption. During hard times, and sometimes by preference, mare's milk was added to the daily volume.

Cheese and butter from the last of the milk earlier in the spring had only recently run out. People eagerly anticipated the first fresh milk of Lambing Time. All the cream was made into butter. Skyr, fermented sour milk, was produced from the buttermilk. As skimmed milk accumulated crews of women and children began making a new supply of cheese. These three dairy products were dietary staples of the Northmen.

Frida tied one of the fresh ewes to a fence rail and knelt next to the animal on the ground to direct twin streams of her rich milk into a small wooden pail that just fit under the animal's distended bag. Ingerd milked a nanny goat beside her, while other women were similarly engaged in other pens. Both women finished about the same time.

"Here Ingerd, do you want a swallow?" Frida wiped the milk from her mouth and held her pail toward Ingerd.

Ingerd dumped her pail of goat milk into a large bucket that hung from a fence post. "Thank you." She took Frida's pail and drank directly from it. "Ummh, fresh warm milk, I have missed it." She added the remainder to that already in the bucket and handed the pail back. Then she walked with her milk pail to catch another animal.

"We should have a full bucket by the time we finish," Frida said. She caught another ewe and repeated the process.

The milk from the sheep and goats gathered in the little pails began to accumulate as the milkmaids poured it into the large buckets of cow's milk until all the animals had been milked. Then they set it aside for the cream to rise.

Two shearers leaned on the fence nearby. They watched Ingerd and Frida as they finished the milking.

"Have a drink, you two," Frida offered.

"Thank you, we will. As soon as you are finished milking, we will shear those three, and that will finish it up. We have fifty-seven prime fleeces." Finbar the Celt was one of Halfdan's highly regarded thralls.

"With the fleeces you will get from this autumn, there will be more than enough to keep us busy all winter," Frida said.

"Aye, even though half the fleeces will be from spring lambs and kid goats. Frida, young Ewyn here asked me if I thought he might get enough of the long-haired goat fleece to make a winter coat." With a lift of his chin, Finbar indicated the tall, taciturn young man who had helped him with the shearing. "I told him to ask Halfdan, but he is too bashful."

Finished with her milking, Frida walked up to the two men. "Ask Halfdan, Ewyn. You might be surprised what you can get from him when you use a direct approach."

Blushing, the young man stammered in confusion. "I would never ask him for anything, Frida. I am sorry to bother you." He glared angrily at his companion. "Why did you have to say anything, Finbar? I do not need a new coat."

Frida stuck a finger in one of several holes in the young man's threadbare coat. "It looks like you do. But you will get nothing if you do not ask. Come with me. We will go find Halfdan."

"Please," the wretched Ewyn pleaded. "I am sorry to bother you with this. I certainly do not want to ask Halfdan for a new coat."

"Come with me, Ewyn." Frida took his arm and looked him in the eye. "We will go find him together. You must never hesitate to ask something of Halfdan, or tell him something. Important or not, let him be the judge of its merit. He is our chieftain. If Halfdan is not available, take the matter to Gudbjartur."

"We will return shortly, Ingerd." Frida smiled and winked at her friend. "You and I need to sort through those fleeces before everyone else picks over them."

"Good, I will meet you in the storage tent. If you see Gudbj, tell him I want to see him."

Frida waved in acknowledgment. With Ewyn in tow, she headed off in search of Halfdan.

* * *

Gizur watched Frida closely through red-rimmed, sleep-deprived eyes as she strode through the encampment. Her curly mass of red hair made it easy for him to follow her progress from his hiding place at the edge of a cliff that overlooked the encampment and landing beach.

His hatred of her had become an obsession since the ein-vigi. He well remembered Gudbjartur's warning, but he heeded it not. Only Frida's blood would quench the boiling cauldron of his thoughts.

The pain in his body and the poison in his mind caused him to wander alone through the night. He seldom slept beyond fitful snatches as he lay hidden away in the brush shunning his fellows.

As the savage knife wounds healed, his arm and shoulder muscles drew up and twisted his upper body out of alignment. He could no longer stand up straight. As he witnessed Frida's and Halfdan's happiness, his mind festered and twisted as surely as the knife wounds twisted his body.

Tonight, he thought. Spittle ran unnoticed from the corner of his mouth. *I will get her tonight when she and Halfdan least expect it, just as they enter the tent. Even Halfdan cannot stop the stroke of my axe.*

His last thoughts ended abruptly when the heavy arrow slammed into the back of his head, tore through his brain, and exited from the corner of his right eye. His body folded to the ground like a wet hide, the man dead before the shaft exited his skull.

Gudbjartur walked slowly up to the inert form. The limbs still quivered and jerked as the final impulses from the brain registered in the muscles. He stood for a moment and looked out over the bay. Then he laid the powerful bow aside and watched in disgust as the tremors subsided in the body. He bent down, jerked the knife from the belt scabbard, and threw it in the direction of his bow. Then he took hold of Gizur's belt and hair, picked him up, and heaved his body over the cliff. He watched the body turning loosely in the air before it plunged into the sea. *He should have heeded my warning*, he thought, spitting in the direction of the corpse as the tide carried it out to sea. *Now he is just so much garbage, food for the crabs.*

Without a backward glance he retrieved his bow. He briefly examined the knife he had taken from the corpse and then made his way down the cliff in the direction of the encampment, whistling softly to himself, satisfied that another problem had been solved.

Chapter Fourteen

A stiff south wind, heavy with the salt smell of the sea, kept the mosquitoes of the fen at bay as they awakened in their hiding places and began to search for prey in the long shadows of early evening. The sun still burned brightly from its position low on the western horizon, but its daily plunge from view would soon bring closure to another hot, cloudless day.

With the coming sunset, the biting flies sought the shelter of forest and bush for the period of darkness and lethargy brought about by the chill night, thereby relinquishing their prey to the hordes of mosquitoes and repeating the endless daily summer cycle in the far north.

The hot days and chill nights of summer instilled in all living things a frenzy to procreate and reach a level of maturity that would ensure the survival of their species before the onset of another harsh winter. Gradual changes in the weather and the shortening hours of daylight after passage of the summer equinox were a harbinger of the changing season. From the tiniest green plant to the myriad insects to the largest whales, all reacted to this primal urge. So, too, did man.

Gudbjartur and Halfdan sat on their high seats enjoying the evening meal with some of the boat crews and talking over the day's events. It was early evening of the second

day in the new encampment on the north shore of the big
southern bay.

Three of the twelve boat crews who had been sent out to
hunt and fish sat on benches or cross-legged on the ground
in a group near Halfdan and Gudbjartur. The hungry men
gorged on muktuk and blood-rare steaks. The cooks, Frida,
Ingerd, and Thora among them, replaced the fare on the trestle tables as fast as the men could eat it.

"I sent twelve boats out today, including six of the native
boats we acquired. Half I sent to hunt whales, four went after
seals, and two emptied and reset crab traps," Gudbjartur said.
"We are eating about half of the daily catch. The rest goes into
the larder until we have sufficient stores for winter. At the rate
the men are going it will not take much longer. The drying
racks sag with the weight of meat and fish. Never has there
been so much game and fish close at hand."

"I hope this weather holds. So far it has been perfect,"
Halfdan said.

"Aye, the warm south wind has kept the Fog Giant away
and made it easier to work this bay and the coastline hereabouts," Gudbjartur said. "If the gods continue to bring this
steady warm wind, we will soon fill the larder."

The conversation ebbed back and forth as the remaining
boat crews straggled in to join friends and family at the final
meal of the day. Boat captains and single crew members without attachments joined the group with Halfdan to make their
reports.

"Sea conditions in the hunting grounds were rough later
today. We sheltered in the lee of one of the seal islands and
snuck up on them." Snorri chuckled at the memory. "All we
brought back were meat and hides, and we had a boatload."

"We saw so many sea and land animals it was hard to pick
out one to kill," Helge said. "We had harpooned a lone seal
and were following our line floats while he bled out when
Vilhjalm sounded his horn inshore. I left the seal for later and
went to see what Vilhjalm wanted. Everybody with earshot of
his horn headed inshore. He and his crew had trapped a big
pod of beluga whales in the narrow neck of a river delta. In a
short time seven boats came in to Vilhjalm's signals and sealed

the fate of the whales. Between us we killed all thirty-four of the animals driven to ground in the shallows. A few escaped to deep water for another day."

"This is the first time we have driven whales into a beach here. All the others were killed at sea," observed Vilhjalm between mouthfuls.

"Why did you not harpoon them? I thought you liked the Tornit harpoon head," Halfdan said.

"We do, but today it was easier to drive them ashore, as we have always done," Vilhjalm answered. "We will use the harpoons on the big whales we have seen farther out in the bay."

"We were lucky to kill the belugas early in the morning. It took half the daylight time just to tow them here to be butchered. Two whales in tow is a heavy load for our boats," Vilhjalm added. The others agreed.

"Halfdan, I think a ship with four to six boats should sail out into the bay until large whales are sighted. Then the boats could be launched to hunt down the whales. After they make their kills, the boats can be reloaded on the mother ship for the return here. The mother ship would have no difficulty towing the carcasses in here to butcher. A couple big whales would be very welcome," Gudbjartur said.

"Do as you see fit, Gudbj." Halfdan intentionally fortified his lieutenant's considerable authority before his men, knowing that word would pass rapidly through the encampment.

Gudbjartur stood to stretch. "I will send Gudrod on the mother ship for the whale hunters and fishermen. His hull must still have some damage from that grounding in Snorrisfjord. He told me yesterday that his ship leaked a little too much on the voyage here. We will need to careen her later and check for more sprung planks. This work will not pose a danger to him or his ship. But he does not want go to sea again until we have time to fix it right." Halfdan had a mouthful, so Gudbjartur continued. "The scouts must return soon if they are to be here before darkness." Gudbjartur gazed out over the bay as he strode toward the trestle table for more meat.

"With all this noise to guide them, they should have no trouble finding the encampment. Get me some more meat too." Halfdan called after his friend.

Gudbjartur waved his empty trencher in acknowledgment. He carefully sorted through the new pile of still-smoking meat with the blade of his belt knife. He stabbed four perfectly grilled steaks for himself and Halfdan.

Ingerd arrived with another heaping trencher of steaks, followed by another cook who bore an equally large trencher of oil-fried codfish fillets. Gudbjartur made his final selections.

"The fish is delicious," she said, smiling at her husband.

He leaned over and planted a kiss on her sweat-dampened forehead. "You take good care of me. It looks like you have plenty of help." He lifted his chin in the direction of the crowd at the fire pit.

"Yes, and it is fine with us. It is so hot around the fire I needed a break anyway." She fanned her flushed cheeks.

"You look very sexy, all flushed and sweaty, Ingerd," he whispered. He bent close; his hot breath fanned her ear.

"Go on, finish eating," she said in a husky voice. "I am very gamy with all this sweat and need to bathe before bed tonight."

Not to be deterred, he remained close to her. The tip of his wet tongue flicked at her ear.

"I like you gamy, Ingerd, and well you know it."

"By the gods, Gudbj, leave before I throw you down right here and mount that rod that rises under your tunic."

"All right, all right, later then." He laughed lecherously as he walked back to his high seat with the loaded trencher.

Ingerd watched him walk toward the men. Hands on hips, a smile on her lips, she shook her head, her mind a jumble of thoughts, all sexual in nature. *I love to watch his buttocks when he walks. He makes my mouth water with anticipation. And, my mouth is not the only thing that is wet.* She chuckled to herself as she turned and picked up an empty trencher from the trestle table. Swinging it back and forth in an arc, she strode back to her duties, whistling a lively tune.

The evening meal developed into a community affair. People lined both sides of the fire pit, grilling their own meat.

Ring took the long-handled, flat grilling iron from Frida's hand. "You three need some time away from the cook fire." He motioned to Ingerd and Thora as they bent over the edge of the fire to flip steaks. "The thralls can do this hot work by themselves for awhile."

"That is a good idea, Ring. Come on you two, it is time for us to relax awhile and eat." Frida took a long-handled fork from Ingerd and handed it to Ring, her lips curved in a smile.

"Halla, we are going to join the men. Call me if you need help." Thora gestured as she called to the thrall. Halla waved.

Ring dropped two thick whale steaks on the hot, greased end of the grilling iron and set the iron on the coals. He liked his meat hot, half raw, and so tender it melted in his mouth.

The sounds and smells of sizzling steaks filled the air, to mix with laughter and conversation as people milled about cooking their meat. Most used a handy belt knife to flip the meat over to sear both sides, sealing in the juices, because there were not sufficient long-handled forks for everyone.

Helge and Vilhjalm joined Ring at the fire pit as he finished grilling the first steak.

"Let me have that iron if you are done with it." Helge took the grilling iron from his extended hand and Ring took a seat on a bench to eat his steak while the men cooked theirs. Soon both men sat down with him to enjoy their steaks. They balanced their wooden trenchers on their laps, cut off mouthfuls of steak, and popped them into their mouths. Beyond a grin or burp they made no attempt to talk. They were busy chewing. The three repeated this process until they had their fill of the rich meat.

All the men and most of the women ate prodigious quantities of fresh meat, fat, and the bounty of the sea daily. This feeding frenzy would continue as long as the weather allowed the hunters and fishermen to provide it fresh.

Ring finished first. He lay back on the ground, his hands clasped under his head. "Too soon, the teeming masses of land animals, whales, and the huge flocks of birds will begin their annual migration south before the onset of winter. Then we will no longer eat like this, I think." He looked at his companions.

"Let us hope that seals remain through winter. We can hunt them when they surface at their breathing holes through the ice." Helge picked his teeth with a wood splinter.

"That works for the Thalmiut of Essipit," Vilhjalm said, "and for us Greenlanders too."

"Aye, Essipit and his people only take seals through the ice. They do not hunt them in summer; they are too busy hunting the reindeer," Ring said.

"I think we will hunt seals through the ice this winter ourselves, as we have always done." Helge trimmed another splinter with his knife.

"Any fresh meat is better than dried rations from the larder. We will see what is here if we stay through the winter," Ring said.

The men were silent for a time as they picked their teeth. Lethargy took hold as they relaxed by the fire.

"Let us take a walk before we go to sleep. I need to shake down all the meat I ate." Helge chuckled at his gluttony as he lurched to his feet.

His companions followed suit. The three men strolled toward the beach, always drawn to the water's edge, any water.

"You know, I liked Essipit and his people," Helge said, as they walked down the path. "I could live with them."

His companions gazed at him in surprise. Then they looked at each other.

"Ring and I talked about that only yesterday. We, too, could live with them," Vilhjalm said.

"Well, none of us want to leave our people here, but the Thalmiut and the Tornit might solve the woman problem we have always had." Helge grunted as he bent over to pick up a smooth stone, his belt coming up tight against his distended belly. "I am stuffed like a roasted duck full of watercress." He skipped the stone over the smooth surface of the bay.

"Aye, so am I." Ring skipped another stone. "Seven, I beat both of you."

The three men selected stones and threw them low over the water's surface, counting the skips unconsciously. None, including Ring, bested the seven skips. Soon tired of the game, they ambled back toward the encampment.

None of the men asked the question on everyone's mind: do we stay here or sail for the east coast?

Instead, they lounged around after the meal and talked about things they knew and had some control over: fishing, hunting, women perhaps, and other things of like nature. Their trust in their chieftain was unequivocal. Now they had but to wait patiently for Halfdan and the council to make the decision. It would be made after the scouts returned and Halfdan called a council. This they knew.

Unknown to these men, Halfdan and Gudbjartur had already made the decision to remain based on people's daily activities alone. The people had prepared elements of a permanent settlement without conscious thought. Construction crews took extra pains in building the animal pens and loafing sheds. Others carefully prepared the barley field with rotted seaweed and wood ashes, and the encampment assumed an order out of keeping with an on-the-go camp. The breeze of change blew through the encampment.

* * *

A single long horn blast, followed by a short blast, announced the return of the scouts.

The first group was led by Bjorn, who made directly toward Halfdan while his men scattered to join the crowd around the fire pit.

"How did the trip go, Bjorn?" Halfdan asked as the man approached.

"It went very well, but I am glad to be back. The interior is very rough going on foot."

"I see Deskaheh has returned with you." Gudbjartur watched Thora greet the man, handing him a trencher of steak.

"Without him our journey would have been much more difficult. He has not been here before, but this country is similar enough to his home that he was a great help to us."

"Thora is certainly happy to see him," Halfdan said. "I suspect he is the cause of the change in her lately."

"Perhaps we will not kill him after all," Gudbjartur said. The beginnings of a smile played about the corners of his eyes.

"It is worth having him around just to keep Thora quiet," Halfdan said.

The men laughed at the jest.

Frida walked up with a trencher of smoking steak. "What is so funny?" She handed the trencher to Bjorn.

"Nothing, Frida, it is just man talk," Halfdan said.

"Man talk?" she asked, hands on hips.

"All right. All right." He waved a hand at her. "We thought it humorous that Thora has changed almost overnight from a sharp-tongued gossiper to a rational, helpful, calmer woman." Halfdan gestured in the general direction of the couple seated on the ground consuming their steaks, heads together in conversation.

Frida studied the couple for a moment. "It looks like love to me." She looked directly at Halfdan. "And we know what that is like."

"Aye, we do, Frida. You have transformed my life."

She tossed her mane of curly red hair, winked at him, and turned away without a word.

The men watched her stride away.

Bjorn cleared his throat loudly. "Well, I may need to look for a mate. I never gave it much thought before."

The men laughed aloud.

"I wish you luck in your quest, Bjorn. All the good ones are already taken, leaving most of us without women," Gorm said ruefully, from his seat on the ground.

Halfdan and Gudbjartur made eye contact at the remark, both aware that the woman problem would continue to rear its ugly head until a solution presented itself. *Gudbj may be right,* thought Halfdan. *The native women may be the answer, provided we can be on friendly terms with them.*

Another sentry horn announced the arrival of another scouting party. At short intervals other sentry horns sounded as the remaining boats returned, racing one another to the landing beach.

"Bjorn, tell the other captains to go ahead and eat. We will call a council in the morning to get your reports and talk over the situation together. This day is done, so go and enjoy yourselves." Halfdan lolled in his high seat, his legs thrust out and crossed at the ankles. The group of men around him and Gudbjartur began to move off as they finished eating.

The echoing cry of a loon came out of the fen.

"I love that sound. I do not know what bird or animal makes it. But I think it is a bird." Gudbjartur stood and surveyed the fen. "It reminds me we have come to a new, wild land that we know very little about."

"And I, too, love the sound. It is so wild. Like the cry of the Valkyries when they ride across the sky to bear the slain to Valhalla."

A superstitious shudder shook Gudbjartur at the mention of the Valkyries.

"With time we will know what kind of animal or bird it is. We do have much to learn as we build our home here in this Vinland." Halfdan watched his friend closely. "Are you all right, Gudbj?"

"I am fine. I was just thinking about what you said."

Gudbjartur left Halfdan to wonder as he continued as if nothing untoward had transpired. "The people grow weary of travel. It is time to stop and build. We have journeyed far. They will be happy to hear our decision tomorrow. I predict it will occasion a feast of some sort."

Halfdan stood and stretched cramped muscles as his eyes swept the encampment. "Every day is a feast here. We have never had so much to eat. All of us will grow fat."

"We work too hard to grow fat. I, for one, prefer not to be hungry when I work. It is time to go to our mates. As you said, this day is done."

He gazed out over the bay and far to the west. He tipped his head back to sniff the air. The smell of the sea and the drying seaweed exposed by low tide were heavy in his nostrils. "The Fog Giant may come in the night." He looked at Halfdan. "I will see you tomorrow morning."

"Tomorrow, then," Halfdan said.

The two men made eye contact. Gudbjartur went off in search of Ingerd.

Halfdan watched his friend walk away. He looked out over the bay and sniffed the air. *I should have made a wager with him,* he thought. *I do not smell any sign of fog.*

* * *

True to Gudbjartur's prediction, the following morning the encampment awoke to dense fog. Water droplets covered every exposed surface and clung to the clothing of those who moved about.

Gudbjartur was sitting on a shaving horse fashioning a new haft for his axe. His hair and beard fairly dripped moisture. He turned at the sound of a step.

Herjulf the Bowyer materialized from the mist. "Good day to you, Gudbj. What kind of wood is that?" He bent closer to inspect the length of wood Gudbjartur was shaping with the drawknife.

Nodding at the greeting, Gudbjartur took the wood out of the shaving horse and handed it to Herjulf. "I do not know, Herjulf. It is some kind of berry wood. The wood is close grained and tough so it will work well for an axe handle."

"It is not mulberry. I think it may be chokecherry." Herjulf handed it back. "And you are right; it is a very tough wood. I wanted to show you what I found out in the fen." He held out a long stave of straight-grained, knot-free wood for examination.

Gudbjartur turned the wood in his hands, admiring the feel of the stave. He recognized it as a bow blank and he glanced up at Herjulf. "Good bow wood?"

"The best, it is yew. Very similar to what we had in Vestfold. I found several yew trees scattered through the fen and the forest. Supply will never be a problem for us. I have bundles of bow blanks like that one curing. My helpers have split off many slabs that they are splitting into arrow blanks. The blanks will be shaped and sanded to round shafts. As they accumulate they will be tied in bundles until they cure. Until then I have sufficient wood for our needs already cured."

"You are a Vestfoldmanni?" Gudbjartur asked with interest.

"Aye, I am. I left Vestfold for the same reason Jorundr did, it is too crowded. As you know, I, too, came with Sweyn.

Jorundr told me you have never been to the homeland. Perhaps one day you will make a trading voyage there."

"I doubt it. It is here I am needed. I would have liked to see where it all began, but the gods have dictated otherwise."

"The gods always know what is best for us and they usually have their reasons. It is beautiful there but very rugged and difficult to farm. I will miss my family for a time, and they me. But I am the youngest of three sons and had no chance for my own land, so here I am. I am happy to be a part of this adventure. It is beautiful here too. I think life will not be so difficult in this place."

"Good! I, too, am well-satisfied with what we try to do. Life is already easier here than it was in either Greenland or Iceland." Gudbjartur handed the bow stave back to Herjulf. "Since we are discussing bows, I think it is time for me to trade you out of three bows and three quivers full of blunt arrows for the boys. Ivar and Lothar have already killed several small animals with the Haudeno bows I gave them. So has Yola. But I want them to have bows and arrows made by our master bowyer."

Herjulf flushed at the complement. "I will select special blanks of cured wood from which to fashion them bows. Ivar and Lothar are about the same size so their bows will be identical, but their small friend, Yola, will need a shorter bow."

Gudbjartur went back to shaping his axe handle while he waited for Herjulf to continue.

Herjulf paused for a moment to consider his task. "I guess you will want this to be a surprise?"

"Aye. Ivar has a birthday during the next moon. We do not know when Lothar's birthday is, nor does he, so we decided to celebrate them together. Their 'small friend,' as you call him, Yola, will receive his bow at the same time. I am certain his mother will not mind because I will teach all three of them the proper use of a real bow. The bows you will make are weapons, not toys. They must be taught the correct usage of them. After I have given them their new bows and arrows I also want them to watch you and your men make bows and arrows. It is good for young men to know these things."

"We are always making bows, arrows, and spear hafts. Send them over to me when you want. Helping with the work for a time is the best way to learn."

"Good idea. I will send them over to help you after you are finished with my order. I especially want them to know how to make arrows. I remember being fascinated when I was a boy watching our bowyer turn square arrow stock into rounded shafts, and so will they be."

"I will have them ready by the next moon. We can discuss the trade when I give them to you. Is that all right?"

"It is, Herjulf. I will trust you not to cheat me." He smiled at the man.

"Good, I would not want you to think I would cheat you or anyone else."

"All of us try to make the best possible trade. I know you would not intentionally cheat me. I also know that you will try for the very best trade for yourself."

Herjulf chuckled. "I will tell you when I have finished with your order."

Gudbjartur stood to stretch tired muscles.

Herjulf looked aloft. "I hope this fog burns off soon. I almost did not find you." He turned to go. "I will be about my work."

"Go ahead and include two arrows with sharp iron points for each boy, Herjulf. They may want to kill something bigger than a rabbit one day." Gudbjartur called to the man as his figure began to diffuse in the wetness.

"All right, Gudbj, and two sharp arrows apiece it is." The answer came from a swirl where Herjulf disappeared into the gray cloak of the fog.

Pleased with himself over the prospect of the gifts he had ordered for his sons and their friend, Gudbjartur whistled tunelessly to himself as he pulled the drawknife toward his chest. At each pass he ran his hand over the wood's surface. Then he carefully scraped the last of the excess wood away.

A slight onshore breeze stirred the fog around him. A short time later it lifted enough for Gudbjartur to see as far as the fire pit. He could barely make out the women going about their morning chores, but he knew one of them was Ingerd.

When she had left their tent earlier she had tried to place a perfunctory kiss on his cheek as she hurried away. He grabbed her and gave her a proper kiss, deep and lingering.

"Gudbj, how can you after last night? There is no time. I am already late, and the boys might come back," she appealed earnestly, but without conviction.

"There is time. I have a want for you. And the boys will not come back. It does not matter who comes into the tent. I need you now." He grinned at her as he picked her up easily and walked into the tent.

She threw her arms around him and complained because he was getting her all wet. But the brief complaint was soon replaced by murmured words of surrender into the hollow of his thick neck. She realized there was always time to join with her man.

Chuckling to himself at the memory of their recent love-making, he sniffed his fingers and savored her scent as he watched the indistinct figures move around the fire pit. Lost in thought for a moment, he continued to stare into the opaqueness. The hollow feeling in the pit of his stomach and the smells of cooking borne on the damp, heavy air reminded him that it was time to eat.

He selected a piece of rough sharkskin to smooth out the nicks left by the drawknife. Turning the haft in his hands he admired his handiwork. Then he began to rub the beautifully grained handle with a soft piece of leather dipped in hot seal oil from a lamp he had left burning in the tent. *A few coats of oil will bring out the grain and leave it as shiny as the sunlight on still water,* he thought. He critically examined the haft once again. His hand rubbed the surface lightly for nicks. *I will finish it with a couple coats of warm beeswax to waterproof the surface and fill any tiny voids. No cracks in this one. Better than the haft I have now. I will have it finished today, providing I have time to work on it a little longer.* He rubbed the oiled haft rapidly with the heel of his hand until the heat of friction forced the oil into the wood. He examined the haft one more time before laying it inside the tent and away from the moisture of the fog. Later he would heat the wood until the surface almost scorched. This drove the first layer of oil into the wood and hardened and set the grain. He would repeat the hot oil treatments and heating until the handle was sufficiently cured. Then he would mount the axe head and apply the warm beeswax.

He stood to stretch his cramped muscles and then stepped into his tent. He shrugged out of his wet cloak and tunic and then dried his hair and beard with a bit of wool cloth. After he brushed and combed his beard and hair, he gathered all the loose ends of his unruly hair and pulled it neatly back into a queue, securing it in place with a length of leather thong. He donned a dry tunic and sealskin vest and walked from his tent. As he made his way toward the fire pit awning he felt this was the beginning of a great day. *There is much to do before sunset. But then, that is the way it is every day,* he thought as he approached the people gathered around the warmth of the fire.

"You have the look of a satisfied man, Gudbj." Bjorn grinned as he spooned stew from a large wooden bowl.

"Right now I may be the happiest man here." His eyes shifted to Ingerd's nicely rounded buttocks. He had a full view of her as she bent over to stir one of the kettles suspended over the coals.

Bjorn stole a quick glance at the object of Gudbjartur's attention, but always mindful of the unpredictability of his lieutenant, he cleared his throat and changed the subject. "The captains are gathered in Halfdan's tent for a council. Halfdan sent me to find you."

"I will get a bowl of stew, a plate of scrambled eggs, and join you there," Gudbjartur said.

Ingerd turned in time to observe her husband talking to Bjorn. She watched Gudbjartur appreciatively; her tongue moistened her lips as she stood in contemplation of him. In one hand, she held a long-handled spoon on her hip. A slight smile played at the corners of her mouth. When Bjorn walked away, Gudbjartur turned toward her. Their eyes locked; their thoughts melded into one. He approached her. She remained as before, hipshot, hands on hips, one foot slightly ahead of the other. A come-hither smile curved her lips and lit her face. Her blue eyes smoldered. His eyes traveled up and down her body. A flush of hot blood coursed through her. The animal maleness of the man always awakened a primal urge deep within her loins. The wet heat of her womanhood flowed immediate and intense. Although recently quenched by the fiery drive of his need, the sight of him always affected her in the same way. She chuckled deep in her throat as he stopped in front of her. "By the gods, Gudbj, you look so good to me. Feel my heart." She pressed his hand to her breast.

"Feel my heart, Ingerd." He pressed her hand to his crotch.

"That is your brain," she said, laughing. "Not your heart."

They laughed at themselves.

Suddenly serious, Gudbjartur placed his hands on her shoulders and drew her close. He blew gently in her ear. "I must attend a council meeting now. Otherwise—" He left the obvious unsaid. "Please get me a bowl of stew and a plate of those scrambled eggs Genevra is cooking and I will be on my way."

The raven-haired beauty smiled at Gudbjartur as she handed him a plate of scrambled eggs. He nodded his thanks.

Gudbjartur thrust a spoon in his belt and balanced the plate of scrambled eggs atop the bowl of stew. He winked at his wife. "I love you, Ingerd." He gestured with his morning meal. "And thanks for the food."

"And I, you, Gudbj. And you are welcome," she said.

He turned and walked toward Halfdan's tent, mindful of the full vessels of food balanced in his hands.

Ingerd watched him until he disappeared into the tent. A single expiration of breath escaped from her lips. "Whew!" she exclaimed softly.

Thora and the other cooks had observed the exchange between Gudbjartur and Ingerd. Thora walked over to her friend and placed a hand on her shoulder. "It is wonderful to have a mate. And to have one you love and who loves you is even better. Is it not?"

"Yes, Thora, it is. We are very fortunate, you and I. We are all pleased for you and Deskaheh. It is as if the gods sent him to you."

"They did, and for that we, too, are thankful. He is all man and he is mine. I thought I would never find a man. I knew he was the one the first time I saw him, Ingerd. He did too."

"He speaks our language well. I understand you can speak his language too."

"Yes, we converse better all the time. We have worked hard to learn each other's languages. Frida has helped when I asked her. She has a natural ability with languages, as you know."

"Yes, she has kept me informed. You two have replaced Gudbj and me as the camp gossip." Ingerd smiled at Thora.

"Good, we want people to gossip about us." Thora looked across the encampment until she saw Deskaheh and Bjorn walking toward Halfdan's tent.

"I think Deskaheh has been called to speak to the council," Ingerd said.

"I guess so. I did not know until now. I am proud of him, Ingerd. We think that having him as a member of our community and our ability to speak each other's language will be useful to our people one day."

"Let us hope so, Thora. Our future here may depend on that ability."

"I think it will." Thora watched the morning crowd begin to thin out. "Let us get some eggs and stew for ourselves, before it is time to clean up."

"I could eat some of those scrambled eggs," Ingerd said. They joined the other cooks to catch up on the latest.

They ate sparingly and then busied themselves cleaning up the mess. Halla and Genevra carried a tub of leftovers to the pigs and returned to wash the cooking and eating utensils. Ingerd and Thora added meat and chopped seaweed to the stew.

"Are you going with us for mussels and periwinkles among the rocks and tide pools?" Thora asked Ingerd.

Ingerd sniffed the air. The smell of newly exposed seashore came to her on the breeze. "Yes, I will be on the beach as soon as I find Frida."

"Good, the more the merrier," Thora said with enthusiasm. "It smells like another low tide has come to our shore. So everyone grab your buckets and baskets. We will not have long at the water's edge before the flood tide roars back in."

* * *

"You were right about the fog, Gudbj. At the time I wished I had offered a wager, now I am glad I resisted the urge." Halfdan chuckled at the memory of their parting last night as his lieutenant entered the tent and took a seat on the platform with the others.

"I thought the Fog Giant would visit us," Gudbjartur said. "He returns to his lair with the heat of the morning sun. The fishermen were sailing away from the strand as I came in here."

Bjorn arrived with Deskaheh at that moment. As the two men pushed the tent flap aside and entered, conversation ceased as all eyes fell on the visitor. Although he was becoming an accepted member of the community, he was not a Northman. He never would be, to some.

Halfdan watched Gudbjartur. His lieutenant considered Deskaheh's presence an intrusion, judging from the hard look in his eyes. "I told Bjorn to bring Deskaheh. He is the only man here who knows what we face from those who already claim this land. He has been most helpful to us, as all of you know." Halfdan looked pointedly at his lieutenant.

"As you say, Halfdan." Gudbjartur's pale blue eyes did not leave Deskaheh's face for a heartbeat. Without another word he began to eat his morning meal.

"We had been watching Gizur. Gudbj felt he was a danger to me or Frida. I have not seen him lately. Has anyone seen him?" He looked from face to face before his eyes came to rest on Gudbjartur. He already knew what the answer would be, but he wanted the others to know the outcome of any perfidy.

A palpable silence settled over the five captains as all eyes shifted to Gudbjartur. Halfdan saw the indrawn breaths, the rigidity of their postures that spoke of a tension that settled over his men like a mantle of thick northern fog, impenetrable.

Gudbjartur fixed Halfdan with his pale unblinking eyes. His face was devoid of expression. "Gizur was about to make a serious mistake. The Fog Giant ate him."

Halfdan's eyes conveyed his appreciation to his friend. He would never again broach the subject, nor would any of the others. Halfdan saw his men take a full breath and look away. The rigid postures relaxed. He saw a universal acceptance. Theirs was a violent life fraught with danger. Savagery and swift death often came for a visit, to sit on the shoulder of the unwary. Gizur had been such a man. He had killed himself. Gudbjartur had been but the instrument of his demise.

Halfdan's glance swept the room. The face of every man turned openly toward him. His eyes came to rest on Brodir, who combed his fingers through his shaggy beard as he gathered his thoughts.

"This land has everything we wanted, Halfdan." Brodir began. "We were able to sail most of one day farther into the bay and up a big river. The wind direction became variable because of the forest so we dropped our sail and rowed until nightfall. We camped on an island in midstream. At dawn the next day I put two men ashore on each riverbank to explore downstream. We picked them up at midday yesterday to return here. They all reported no sign of other people. But they saw game everywhere. There are herds of deer, moose, and many brown bears fish the river's edge. But there is no sign of the great white bears. Meadows full of grass are at every hand, close to the river's edge. Boat crews can scythe the grass when it matures during the Harvest Time moon and a ship can transport the cured hay here for winter fodder. Several rivers flow into this bay from the north, south, and east. This bay here narrows into a fjord one day's boat sail to the southeast. At the bottom end, the fjord narrows farther into the big river we sailed up. Our ships can sail up the river as far as we went without difficulty. We encountered rapids and slack water, as you would expect, but we were still able to proceed. There are many islands in the fjord and the river, just like around here. The river water is clear and deep, full of giant fish, some as long as I am tall."

Some of the men laughed at the mention of such large fish in a river.

Sweyn came to Brodir's defense. "Brodir is correct. Those fish are called sturgeon, and they get much bigger than any man. I have seen them in Vestfold, and the lands of the Gotar and Svear, where they are hunted for their meat and eggs. During the early summer, the fish migrate from the sea into the rivers and collect in large numbers near the shore to spawn. That is why Brodir saw so many of them; they are spawning. They are very easy to catch at this time. Our men can use the new harpoon heads or nets to catch them."

"I, too, have heard of them, but I have never seen one before," Halfdan said.

"And I," Athils said.

"I will send boats to hunt them. The smoked meat and their eggs will be welcome this winter," Gudbjartur said.

"Each big female will have enough eggs to fill a tub," Sweyn added. "Salted and stored in barrels, the eggs can be fried in oil or eaten right from the barrels. I have had them both ways and they are delicious."

"Good. See that we have plenty of both in our winter stores, Gudbj," Halfdan said. "Now, let us hear the reports of the other captains."

Bjorn's report of his overland route made it clear that transport for any distance must be by water. "After being wet to the knees for a couple days, all of us were ready for the journey to end. It is possible to walk, but not in anything close to a straight line. It would take many days to go a relatively short distance overland." He called attention to Deskaheh, seated beside him, with a lift of his chin. "Deskaheh led the whole way. I told him what I wanted and he stepped right out. He sets quite a pace. We would have blundered into bogs and dead-end areas if he had not led us around."

"Does he understand our language well enough for me to ask him questions?" Halfdan asked Bjorn.

"Yes, Halfdan. I understand your language better than I speak it. I am still learning."

The councilmen were surprised when Deskaheh answered for himself.

"Thora has helped you in this I am certain," Halfdan said.

"Yes, we are very valuable to each other. Frida helped us in the beginning."

"Good. I understand Thora speaks your language well."

"She does. Haudeno is difficult to learn because one word can mean many things depending on how it is used."

Without preamble, Halfdan asked, "How are the people called who live in this land?"

"They are called Naskapi. They are the traditional enemies of my people. They call their land Nitassinan. It means homeland."

"How many are there?"

"I do not know. They are many, I think. Bands of their tribe are scattered throughout the land; from this place all the way to the great salt sea to the east."

"Can we live here in peace?"

"I do not know. They distrust strangers. They regard all these lands as their hunting grounds. That is why my people fight with them every summer. Our wars have always been over the hunting grounds."

His answer brought a period of silence to the councilmen. The men thought over the importance of what had been revealed.

"How will we be able to get along with them if they think we are stealing food from their mouths?" Gudbjartur echoed the other's thoughts.

Deskaheh responded. "The Naskapi are like my people. They are people of the forest, lakes, and rivers. They do not hunt the whales and seals. They do not venture onto the great waters. They hunt only land game and the fish of the lakes and rivers. I think that if you convince them you will not deplete their game but will hunt mostly from the sea, and trade with them fairly in the products of your people, they might allow you to stay in their land. We already know they do not live within two days of this place. There may be enough room and animals of the sea and land for everyone."

Halfdan slammed Gudbjartur across the back. The spoon full of stew he had been directing toward his open mouth flew in all directions, mostly down his front. "Hah!" Halfdan laughed aloud. "I told you he would be useful. And you wanted to kill him."

A rumble of laughter swept through the men. Deskaheh joined in, for the laughter was infectious and it soothed the anxiety he felt at being with these men.

Gudbjartur scooped the mess off his lap and licked it from his hand. He eyed Deskaheh as he wiped his hands on his tunic. "It appears I was wrong about him. I am certainly willing to admitting it now that he has come forward with all this intelligence about the Naskapi." He paused a moment in appraisal of the Haudeno. Gudbjartur saw that the man had allowed his hair to grow from its original scalp lock to shoulder length and Thora had replaced his clothing with the attire of the Northmen. Except for his sharp, distinctive features and the color of his skin, he could almost be one of us, he thought. He set the remains of his morning meal aside. "Do you speak the Naskapi language, Deskaheh?"

"No, Gudbj. But our language is similar enough that with signs I have no difficulty communicating with them."

"What do you think they will want to trade for?"

"Cloth, beads, walrus rope, fur seal hides, iron tools and cooking utensils, and of course weapons, which I know you will not trade them."

"No we will not." Gudbjartur glanced at Halfdan. "Iron tools perhaps, but no weapons."

"They will be interested in everything you make here. Much of it will have trade value, especially the things I mentioned."

Gudbjartur crossed his legs and clasped his big hands together around his knee.

"And what do they have that we might find useful?" Gudrod asked after Gudbjartur lapsed into silence.

"Like my people, many of their bands cultivate gardens of squash and beans. They would trade some of this produce, the herbs, magical potions of forest and fen, leather clothing, pemmican, prime furs in winter, and very fine baskets and boxes of willow and birch bark. Like my people, they make excellent ash and birch snowshoes."

"What is pemmican?" Bjorn asked.

"It is one of our principal trail and winter foods. The women make it in the time of falling leaves with dried deer or bear meat, dried berries, and melted fat. It is all mixed together and poured hot into long birchbark molds. They cut it into cakes after the fat hardens. These cakes are stored in bark boxes for later use."

The taciturn Sweyn looked at the group of men silenced by what they had heard. He guffawed loudly and voiced everyone's opinion of pemmican. "It sounds delicious! I cannot wait to eat some."

General laughter swept through the tent.

"It does sound like a disgusting mess." Bjorn slapped his knee and laughed.

"I wonder if it smells like Asa's potions when they cook it." Brodir chuckled at the thought.

Deskaheh bobbed his head appreciatively. He realized his candor and humor had won him a place among these hard men. *Pemmican is delicious and very filling. One day I am certain they will know its value, for I will make them some,* he thought. He felt Gudbjartur's eyes. He smiled at Halfdan's lieutenant, although the smile was not returned. He recalled their first meeting. *I was correct that first time I saw him. This is a very dangerous and unpredictable man. They all are. But this one! I hope we can truly become friends one day,* he thought.

Halfdan dismissed Deskaheh with their gratitude for his insight. He called for a council vote. Halfdan and his lieutenant already knew what their answer would be, for they had seen how the people accepted their new surroundings.

"Based on what you found and what Deskaheh has told us, what say you? An aye means stay; a nay means we sail to the east coast." Halfdan looked from man to man. The vote was a necessary formality. "Gudbj?"

"Aye."

"Bjorn?"

"Aye."

"Athils?"

"Aye."

"Gudrod?"
"Aye."
"Brodir?"
"Aye."
"Sweyn?"
"Aye."
"Good. The ayes have it; we are unanimous." Halfdan looked at his men again. "We will build our settlement here. Hopefully, given time and the cooperation of the Naskapi, it will prove to be the success we all yearn for. I want to tell you why we are here in this place, why I insisted we sail down here." The men leaned forward on the benches, attentive. "Gudbj and I meant to tell you that I had changed my mind as soon as we found a bay along the Markland coast, but the storm changed everything, and I did not need to tell you until now. I was bothered by the hostility of the east coast natives. I felt they were too hostile to risk settlement at Leifsbudir and especially all the mainland south of there. The Icelander, Karlsefni, failed at both Straumfjord and Hop, due entirely to mistakes made with the natives by prior expeditions. To be successful, I knew we must find a new land entirely. This Nitassinan, of the Naskapi, is such a place. We must live in peace among the Naskapi or die in the attempt. There is no other option, no place left for us at this point. I wanted you to know these things. Someday, after our two peoples know each other, perhaps other settlements will be built. Perhaps our peoples will someday become one, I do not know. When contact is made with the Naskapi, we must ensure that our people treat them as friends, always. We have already befriended the Thalmiut and the Tornit of this Vinland. Other native peoples will follow. Maybe even the Haudeno one day. Deskaheh can help with that." Halfdan's eyes moved over his council. Beyond a nod or two they had nothing to question, nothing to add. "I have been told some of you think we should call this river inlet settlement Halfdansfjord. I thank you for that. I was going to suggest Straumfjord, but since the rest of you prefer Halfdansfjord, so be it."

"How could we have named it Straumfjord? I thought Straumfjord was on the east coast, south of Leifsbudir." Brodir said.

"It is, but it would not have mattered. In a few years there will not be anyone left alive who remembers where the original Straumfjord was or that it even existed," Halfdan said.

Halfdan moved the conversation on to the plan for the settlement. Over the course of the next couple of hours, a plan took shape around a drawing on the floor of his tent.

"With the abundance of building material we have here, I think we can build seven traditional peaked-roof wattle-and-daub longhouses like those in our homelands. This will give everyone plenty of room." Halfdan said.

Gudbjartur thought it over a moment before he spoke. "Seven will allow for an increase in population. We should build them on stone foundations. That will prevent later rot on the bottom of the walls."

"The longhouses can be arranged in a quadrangle around a central common area. The animal pens and shelters will be at the far end as they are now." Bjorn used an arrow to scratch the seven longhouses into the drawing. "The seventh building can close the upper end of the quadrangle. We can leave enough room on each end to walk around to the palisade."

"I like that idea," Halfdan said. "One or two gates can be built into the palisade wall right here at the back of the seventh longhouse, to make it easy to walk inland without having to walk all the way around to the main gate." He bent forward and scratched the two gates in with his knife point.

"The three houses on each side of the town square can be the same. The seventh longhouse should be twice the length of the other six to close off the top end of the town square. Half or more of the floor space can be walled off for a council and social room. You, Frida, and your thralls could live there." Sweyn addressed Halfdan and then changed the drawing to show the added length of the seventh longhouse.

Gudbjartur looked at Sweyn and chuckled. "Sweyn, you do not say much, but I have learned to listen when you do have something to say."

The others smiled and nodded in agreement.

"In winter we shelter the livestock in our houses. Each house will need a barn at one end, walled off from the living area for our animals and hay storage," Brodir said.

"Aye, and the inside barn wall should have a door to the living area." Gudrod paused a moment. "While we are thinking about doors, each house will need two outside doorways to open into the central common area: one for the livestock and another double door under a protected entryway for the people."

"Like this?" Bjorn scratched in the additions.

Gudrod nodded. "I have built horizontal sapling walls interlaced on vertical support posts and beams before," Athils said. "Wattle walls, plastered with a thick daub, a mixture of mud, dried grass, and manure, take extra time, but you have a much stronger and longer-lasting house as a result."

"Has anyone else used this building method before?" Halfdan asked.

The men shook their heads.

"Nor I," Halfdan said. "Athils, you are in charge of construction."

Athils nodded. "We will build each house with a rammed-earth floor, rather than stone. It is smoother, warmer, and easier for the women to keep clean. With use, the rammed-earth floor becomes hard and shiny. Stone hearths for the cooking of food and winter warmth will run down the central floor. Smoke has always been a problem in our houses. Rather than roof holes for the smoke to find its way out I will try to build square wooden chimneys into the peaked roof above each hearth, with a cap to keep out rain and snow. I saw them the last time I was in Gotland."

"How do you keep the wood chimney from catching fire?" Gudbjartur asked the obvious question.

"The chimney is in the roof peak, well above the hearth." Athils answered.

The men thought over the plan.

"We will need walkways, with ladders from the ground, around the inside of the palisade wall so we can move men back and forth to fight off attackers," Brodir said.

"And, two main entrance gates through the palisade wall should face the landing beach," Sweyn added.

"Agreed," Halfdan said.

"Two large, rectangular windows in the wall that faces the village square will ventilate and illuminate the inside," Gudbjartur said. "It gets stuffy without fresh air."

"A smaller window on the barn end will do the same thing for the livestock. The thralls can prop it open when they do the morning chores," Bjorn added.

"All right, it looks like we have a plan." Halfdan studied the drawing. "That leaves the roof. Any suggestions?"

"Aye, a sod-covered roof is the warmest and driest." Athils sketched a roof cross section while he talked. "You start off with split logs laid athwart inside support timbers. Follow that with a thick layer of well-cured grass. The outer layer is overlapped sod. The grass in the sod will continue to grow. The sod seals and insulates the roof from the heat of summer and the cold of winter. It is snug and comfortable inside." He glanced at his attentive companions.

"Two walled and roofed guard towers, one facing the bay and landing beach, the other facing the fen and forest, with ladders from the palisade walkway, will ensure village security," Gudbjartur said

"Any attacker will face an uphill battle against our defenses. The guards will be able to give warning long before the attackers come up to our palisade," Gudrod said.

"Good, I think that covers our village." Halfdan looked at his captains. "I want our four biggest ships, including mine, to sail for Greenland with timber. Take only enough crew to work the ships and perform the tasks ashore. I leave that to you men and Gudbj to decide. Trade for anything they have in surplus including more settlers for here. Gudrod, your ship is the smallest and Gudbj tells me she is leaking. There might be damage from your grounding that we do not know about. Gudbj and I think it best for you to stay here this time. That is why you were chosen to be the mother ship for the whale hunters. After we haul our ships out for winter you can rebuild her for the next season." Halfdan knew Gudrod wanted the benefit of a trading voyage. But he also knew Gudbj had told

Gudrod to send his trade goods with one of the other captains to trade for him. *Gudrod's ship has leaked more than normal ever since the grounding,* Halfdan thought. *Gudrod admitted to me that his ship seemed sluggish to rise to the wave crests.*

"As for the rest of you, our future as traders in this land is in your hands," Halfdan said. "Bjorn, take my ship and leave yours here for me or Gudbj. On the voyage back here, I want you to stop at Essipit's Thalmiut village. Take my crew and Thorgill with you. They know where the village is, and the Thalmiut will recognize my ship and crew. You will have a better chance of success that way. Blow your horns; make noise so they know you are coming. Treat them fairly, Bjorn. We made a trust between us, and I want that relationship to continue."

"I will, Halfdan. You should know that."

"Aye, I do, but it needs repeating." After a short pause he continued with his orders to the other captains. "On the return voyage, two ships will find the Tornit, Inuktuk's people. He told us their village is next to a big river mouth in a big bay to the east of Snorrisfjord. Take them and their boats into northern waters until you find the walrus herds. Hunt and trade with these people. You know what we need and what they have to trade. Trade fairly, our products for theirs. Take them a few more iron harpoon heads. Cement our friendship with them, for they are important to our success in Vinland." Halfdan paused. "Trade or give them all the walrus meat they can use. We have so much here we can do without the meat so long as you bring back plenty of hides and ivory for trade with Iceland next year. We need enough hides to keep the rope makers busy through the winter. The fourth ship will return here direct from Greenland with the traded goods. Make barley a priority of trade. We are almost down to seed for next year's crop." He paused. His eyes shifted from face to face as he thought about what he had asked of them. "Gudbj, any of you, do you have anything to add?"

Gudbjartur shook his head.

"What if Tornits or Thalmiuts want to come down here with us after we spend the remainder of the summer among them?" Brodir asked.

"Bring them. Women would be especially welcome." Halfdan grinned.

They all laughed.

Athils asked the question Halfdan and Gudbjartur had talked about. "Speaking of women," Athils said, "many men are still without them. Those of us in this council without a mate have no such interest. Most of our men do have such an interest. What if somebody wants to stay with either the Tornit or Thalmiut?"

"You cannot lose your small crews. It could compromise the safety of your ship." He pulled at his beard as he thought over the prickly subject. "They are freemen; they can stay if they wish. But try to talk them out of it because we need every man here."

"That is difficult when you are a randy young man," Sweyn said with a laugh.

Halfdan laughed with the others, and then sobered.

"I think we have talked over every concern. If there is nothing else, our people are waiting. After I have told them of our decision, select your crews and load your ships. You will want to sail on the outgoing tide tomorrow."

* * *

Halfdan and the councilmen watched as word swept through the encampment like wildfire. Halfdan made eye contact with Gudbjartur and nodded. Gudbjartur raised his signal horn to his lips. The long, drawn-out wail of the horn called the people to assembly.

All work ceased as the people gathered.

The leaders stood atop a hillock to the west of the common area, so they could be seen by the people milling about in response to the call.

The dog Fang sat at Halfdan's feet. Tongue lolling to the side, he watched the gathering throng. Occasionally his eyes darted to other lesser members of his kind as they loped about the fringe of the crowd yipping in the excitement.

Halfdan waited for the noise to subside. Gudbjartur beckoned for the crowd to form a semicircle and gather close. A silence settled. Halfdan began to deliver his carefully thought-out speech. "As most of you already know, the council has decided we are to stay here." He raised his arms after a moment to quiet the cheers. "By a unanimous vote, our settlement is to be called Halfdansfjord." His eyes swept the uplifted faces of his people as more cheers came from them. Halfdan smiled at their enthusiasm and waited for the noise to subside. "Six longhouses one hundred feet long and thirty-five feet wide, and one two hundred feet by fifty feet will be constructed. There will be plenty of room for future expansion. Each longhouse will house forty to fifty people. Athils will supervise their construction. Gudbj will assign who is to live where and these assignments can be changed as need be."

General laughter and the usual ribald comments followed his last.

He continued, his tone forceful, his eyes intent as his gaze swept the assembly. This was the part of his speech he wanted to drive home. "Everything about this venture depends on the native people hereabouts, whether they are Haudeno, Thalmiut, Tornit, Naskapi, or whatever else they are called; it all depends on them. We must, and I want to emphasize this point, must get along with them. Our survival in Vinland depends on it. This is contrary to our nature, our people love war. To die in battle is every man's dream, but this is a different place. These people were here long before we came. We are outnumbered. If any of you cause trouble with these people, and I learn of it, that person will suffer my wrath under our law." He gazed out over the upturned faces.

"The scouts saw no sign of other people. Deskaheh has told us they are here, and sooner or later they will know we are here among them. Guards will be posted as always, but only a few, and they will be comfortable and secure from attack in two guard towers that will be a part of the palisade walls. Our entire village will be behind these palisades. One double main gate will face the landing beach. There will be two wide walk-through gates in the north palisade wall. The first building completed will be the smithy." He gestured toward the sod walls enclosing the forge and work area. The roof support timbers were already in place. "Other tradesmen can locate as they wish. I will not tell you how to do your work, but everything must be within the settlement walls for security, including the charcoal kiln. Tomorrow morning the ships of Brodir, Athils, Sweyn, and Bjorn with my ship and crew sail on the outgoing tide for Greenland with timber to trade. They will load their ships when this assembly is finished. On the return voyage two ships will find the Tornit of Inuktuk and the crews will hunt walrus with them. Bjorn will trade with the Thalmiut of Essipit. The fourth ship will return direct to Halfdansfjord with goods traded in Greenland. I expect the voyage and trading will take the remainder of this summer. If you have specific needs or trade goods to include with these ships, contact the captains. Gudrod and his ship and Bjorn's ship and crew will remain here with us. Now, I know questions will occur as we build our settlement, but for now let us get busy."

The four captains picked their crews and selected a large group of men to load the Greenland ships. The rest of the people scattered to their work.

Halfdan and Gudbjartur watched them for a time and then went their separate ways.

Chapter Fifteen

Heavy morning fog delayed the departure of the four heavily laden ships for the Greenland settlements.

A throng of well-wishers had assembled on the beach to watch the ships put to sea on the long voyage. The ships' crewmen visited among them, waiting for the fog to thin before they boarded their ships.

Halfdan, Gudbjartur, and Gudrod stood on the beach with the four captains. They all kept an eye on weather conditions and the dwindling surge of the ebb tide.

"The heat of the sun will soon start the breeze to blow the Fog Giant from the bay," Gudbjartur observed.

"I hope it happens soon." Bjorn gestured at the short ripples that slapped at the water's edge. "We want to sail on the ebb tide and it will stop before long."

"Aye, it will, but you will have slack water long enough to put to sea." Halfdan paused for a heartbeat. "We have high hopes for this voyage. This is the first of the annual midsummer trading voyages to Greenland."

"With the ivory and rope from your walrus hunt with the Tornit on the return voyage, and the furs that we trade for this winter, at least one ship of the trading flotilla next summer will be bound for Iceland," Gudbjartur said.

"I would like that voyage." Gudrod looked at Halfdan. "My ship will be good as new, and a trade with Iceland will make up for missing this year."

"I imagine the only fair way to assign such a voyage would be to draw lots," Halfdan answered.

"I suppose so," Gudrod said.

A period of silence followed.

Gudbjartur laughed aloud at the captain's impatience. "Relax! You have at least five hundred leagues to sail. Unless you are on a long beat into the wind the voyage should take about eight days. If you are on a beat all the way it might take half a moon to reach Eiriksfjord. Either way, I doubt this fog delay will make much difference."

Bjorn, by consensus in charge of the voyage, spoke for all of them when he answered. "You are correct. But when the decision is made to sail, we are always anxious to get underway."

"I know. I wish I was going with you." Gudbjartur looked from the men to Halfdan.

"We all wish to go. Our people have spent many lifetimes on the sea. The fog thins so be off with you. We will eagerly await the sight of your sails before winter." Halfdan shook hands with each captain.

"Load up. Stand by the sweeps," Bjorn shouted as he and his companions scattered to their ships.

The four ships backed from the strand and turned into the bay. The rhythmic creak of the sweeps as the long blades slashed into the water carried to the watchers ashore. The ships became at first spectral and then faded from view in the mist. Cries of farewell came out of the mist and from the throng of watchers on the strand. A sound of sails flapping carried ashore as the freshening breeze blew at the tatters of the Fog Giant to move him from the bay.

The lookouts' horns heralded the departure. To the many people scattered throughout the encampment and surrounding countryside, the call of the horns gave them pause as each paid tribute to the departing men in their own way. The cooks under the fire pit awning looked up from their work. "They are away." Thora said, as she gazed toward the beach.

"Look, I see the masts above the fog." Ingerd pointed toward the beach. The top of the ships' masts alternately appeared and disappeared.

* * *

"That is the first time I have seen my ship sail away." Halfdan watched Steed of the Sea sail into the mist.

"It is only the second time that I have seen it sail away," Gudbjartur mused. "I imagine this will happen frequently over the years. She cannot make you a wealthy man unless she is kept busy trading."

"I know, but it is sobering to see the ship I built sail away without me, even if, as you say, it will make me wealthy. I had not considered that before."

"Well, consider it. You are a married man and Frida has certain expectations. They always do, you know."

"Do they now?" He chuckled; his hand came to rest on his friend's shoulder. "Come; let us be about our work."

The two men joined separate groups of workers as skilled carpenters staked out the location and size of each longhouse and the palisade walls that would enclose the village.

* * *

Crews of woodcutters continued to clear-cut the forest verge for building materials, gradually pushing back the forest as the work progressed.

It became necessary to relocate the tent encampment in a tight group just outside where the main gates would open onto the landing beach. The new site for the tent encampment, the very end of the bluff the settlement would occupy when completed, enjoyed a steady onshore breeze that helped keep the clouds of insects at bay.

The position of the livestock pens at one end of the central common area fit perfectly into the layout of the settlement. Birthing would continue through the waning half of the Lambing Time moon.

The forest verge continued to recede from Halfdansfjord proper as the woodcutters harvested every usable tree and sapling. The goats and sheep took care of the remainder.

Limbs from felled trees were added to the brush piles that had accumulated, and all were set ablaze. As the land was cleared, the barley field was prepared by the workers. They scattered ash from the fires, rotted seaweed, and chopped green grass, and plowed all of it into the soil to enrich the earth for next year's barley crop. The field would lie fallow under the snow until the Sowing Time moon in the spring. The workers told their leaders that, barring a calamitous accident, they expected a bumper crop of grain.

The thin crescent of the Midsummer moon began to wax. The settlement took shape as the new moon became visible in the night sky. Days were a constant succession of light redolent breezes with a subtle scent of forest, sea, or fen under clear blue skies. The sounds of insects filled the hot humid air. Fog Giant gradually ceased his daily visits to the waters of the bay. Except for an occasional passing rain shower, which served to wash off the accumulated dust from the construction activity, the weather could not have been better.

Halfdan and Gudbjartur were well satisfied with the progress thus far. Both men worked side-by-side with various work crews. They lent a hand wherever one was needed and handled planning and construction issues that arose.

All seven longhouse structures were essentially complete. Men swarmed over the roofs, placing the outer sod layer. They wove wattle exterior walls, made of saplings about the diameter of a man's wrist, horizontally through buried support posts. Every available man, woman, and child smeared layers of daub on completed walls. Men spread daub with trowels fashioned from a section of short plank with a handle attached. They worked the sticky mess into the wattle with semicircular strokes to spread it evenly over the surface, imparting a finished look to the walls. The sticky daub came from a large pit within the quadrangle, that later would become the communal steam house. The work became a game and many of the children were already covered with the mixture. But that was the fun of it.

* * *

Gudbjartur and Halfdan were discussing the size of the steam house when Gudbjartur spied his sons and laughed at their antics. Both were virtually unrecognizable under their covering of daub.

Halfdan laughed too. "I did not recognize them until you pointed them out. What a mess they are."

"Aye, they are that. But at least they have figured out how to have fun doing the hard work. Ingerd may have to throw their tunics away or send them into the bay fully clothed after this."

Their attention was drawn to a man running from the forest verge, waving his arms and shouting. He came to a breathless halt in front of Halfdan. "You had best come see what we have found."

The three men trotted off in the direction the man had come.

"What is it?" Halfdan asked the man.

"Nothing is wrong, but wait until you see what we found. It is unbelievable."

"Come!" Ingerd exclaimed to her companions. "We do not want to miss whatever this is." She grinned at Frida as her friend joined the group. Before they got to the forest verge, a crowd followed close behind as they made their way into the forest.

Halfdan and Gudbjartur broke out of the dense forest into a natural clearing dominated by a small grove of misshapen oak and birch trees devoid of underbrush, which stood alone within the surrounding pine forest. An immense ash tree, the only one they had seen in this land, stood in the center of the grove. Off to the side, under one of the three main roots of the giant ash, a spring bubbled beneath a large boulder into a lichen-edged pool at its base.

"Yggdrasil!" Gudbjartur's voice was filled with awe. "It is Yggdrasil, the world-tree!" He looked at Halfdan, his eyes wide. "The Sacred Grove is here in this land!"

Halfdan said nothing for a moment. He turned to the throng of people spreading out behind them. "It would seem so, Gudbj. It is definitely Yggdrasil."

The crowd formed a semicircle in front of the sacred world-tree of the gods.

"It is Yggdrasil, the Sacred Grove of Odin!" Halfdan shouted and extended his arms over his head. Chills coursed through his body.

The cry was taken up by the throng. Finding Yggdrasil, the Sacred Grove and the world-tree, here in this new land that was to become their home validated their desire to settle here. The world-tree was the stuff of myth and none had ever before seen it. To find Yggdrasil here was their miracle, the affirmation of all their beliefs, and they embraced it wholeheartedly.

Halfdan called the woodcutters together. He issued orders as to how they must cut the forest back from the Sacred Grove, leaving it alone to stand in full view of the village.

Before another day was done, the people had carried his orders out, and the Sacred Grove stood in full view of Halfdansfjord, a majestic symbol of the religious fervor that swept through the populace. Ingerd made it a point to brace Thora over the discovery of Yggdrasil. Thora and the few Christians among them were affected in the same way. The people regarded this sign from the gods as too powerful to deny.

The Lambing Time moon passed without the loss of a single newborn, an unheard-of thing. The Sun Time moon rose early in the morning darkness and was visible into midday as it continued its journey across the northern sky. Days grew increasingly hotter, but chilly nights persisted in the long days of midsummer. The Greenlanders gradually struck down and stored the tents as people moved into their new longhouses. With completion of the final section of palisade wall, workmen installed the three gates. The people of Halfdansfjord would now sleep securely within the stout walls behind closed and barred gates each night, rather than exposed under the flimsy sides of their tents. Life was good and the people were well contented.

* * *

With the end of another day at hand, a group of tired men and women enjoyed the comforts of the steam house, an integral part of communal life among the Northmen. The low circular dugout was built over the daub pit left over from building the longhouses. The little sod-roofed building comprised a waist-high, daub-chinked fieldstone wall around internal support timbers, and a flat stone floor. Rocks were heated in a hearth just outside the doorway, tonged into an iron basket, and pulled into the steam house by a thrall. Her job was to tend the fire and keep the rocks hot.

An air of comfort and relaxation permeated the interior. Clouds of steam rose from the hot rocks in the rectangular iron basket on the stone floor as Ingerd poured another dipper of water over them. Steam condensed on every surface and dripped onto the flat stone floor to drain into the earth underneath. Two dozen naked people sat on wooden benches around the periphery. Halfdan, Frida, Gudbjartur, and Ingerd were among them. They occasionally whipped themselves with small, leafy willow branches, to promote circulation. Conversation was minimal. People sat in attitudes of relaxation and held council with their own thoughts, as they stared into the opaque, steam-laden air.

"There must be a better way to produce steam than hot rocks," Gudbjartur said.

Nobody said anything for a time while they considered his statement.

"Why change it, Gudbj? We have always done it this way," Jorundr said from the other side of the room.

"Life changes every day," Gudbjartur answered. "I think we should have found a better way to produce steam."

"A great deal of steam rises from water boiling in a kettle, Gudbj," Frida said. "But we cannot build a fire in here to keep the water boiling. The smoke would choke us all to death."

Several people laughed aloud. Then an air of consideration descended over the sweating occupants.

"I believe you may have a point, Frida." Gudbjartur realized that Frida might have stumbled on the solution to generating steam without someone having to tend the fire and haul hot rocks in and cooled rocks out.

"I propose we all think about a solution to what is apparently a dilemma. If you have an idea about this, talk it over with Gudbj," Halfdan said.

The group lapsed into silence after his announcement, sitting quietly as before, enjoying the swirling gouts of steam as Frida dribbled more water on the hot rocks.

Gudbjartur wiped sweat from his eyes and flung it in the general direction of the pile of hot rocks. He looked around the interior dimly lit by flickering oil lamps. "I have had enough. I am almost light-headed from the heat. It is time for a run into the cold water of the bay."

Ingerd lurched up from the bench beside him and jumped for the deer hide that closed off the doorway. "I will race you!" she called, as she and Frida disappeared from view.

A mass exodus followed them out the low doorway. Gudbjartur realized too late that the race was on. The two long-legged women led all the way down to the beach where they ran into the icy water and dove under.

Gudbjartur strolled into the water in time to proclaim the race between Frida and Ingerd to be a dead heat.

"No, I won by a nose," Frida proclaimed to her laughing companion.

"You did not, I won." Ingerd leaped on Frida and pushed her under.

People sputtered and splashed in the neck-deep shallows until each reached their personal limit of endurance.

"That is it for me." Halfdan staggered from the water gasping for breath. He and Frida clasped hands and walked toward their longhouse. Gudbjartur, Ingerd, and the others followed.

* * *

Herjulf the Bowyer delivered the three bows and arrows to Gudbjartur in time for the birthday celebration. Ingerd wanted to make a ceremony of it and Gudbjartur gave in to her.

Gudbjartur hid the three bows and quivers of arrows in the edge of the forest beside Yggdrasil. He wanted to give the three boys their weapons in Odin's grove. He saw Ingerd walk through the gate of the palisade with the boys in tow and turn toward Yggdrasil.

The boys had not been told what was to occur, but Ivar saw his father sitting at the base of the world-tree, and he walked closer to Lothar and whispered in his ear.

Gudbjartur observed the byplay between his sons, and he grinned to himself. It is hard to fool that Ivar, he thought proudly. They know something is up, but they do not know what it is yet.

"I asked Halfdan to come when he saw you and the boys head this way," Gudbjartur told Ingerd. "Yonder he comes." He raised his chin toward the figure striding across the barley field.

"What is it, father?" Ivar asked.

"Be patient. We will wait for Halfdan," Gudbjartur said.

Halfdan smiled as he walked up. "Ingerd. Boys." He acknowledged them with a nod. He looked at Ivar and Lothar with a twinkle in his eye. "I understand that today is your birthday. Let me be the first outside your family to wish you both a happy birthday."

"Thank you, Halfdan." Ivar spoke for both boys; Lothar seemed tongue-tied in Halfdan's presence.

"Turn toward the village and close your eyes, all three of you." Gudbjartur included Yola in the request.

The three complied, and Gudbjartur walked a short distance into the woods and retrieved the gifts. He handed the bows and quivers of arrows to Halfdan, by prior arrangement. He wanted his sons and Yola to receive their bows from the hand of their chieftain. Gudbjartur stepped to Ingerd's side and nodded to Halfdan.

"Turn around, boys, and open your eyes." Halfdan grinned from ear to ear. "I have these fine bows and arrows for each of you. Gudbjartur had Herjulf the Bowyer make them for this occasion. He wanted you to receive them from your chieftain, here, in the Sacred Grove of Odin." He handed each boy his bow and quiver. "Gudbjartur will teach you how to use these weapons. As your chieftain, I welcome three young warriors to the ranks of our people in the name of Odin, the god of war. May you use these weapons with honor all the days of your lives."

Even Ivar was speechless with the honor Halfdan had bestowed on mere boys. He looked from Gudbjartur to Ingerd and back to Halfdan. He smiled. It was all he could manage.

* * *

Gudbjartur leaned against the end wall of a longhouse. He watched Ivar, Lothar, and Yola as they practiced with their new bows. The boys were shooting their blunt arrows at the circle he had marked with a bit of charcoal in the center of a hide stretched between two of several trees left within the palisade walls. Ivar had complained to Gudbjartur about the necessity of practice. He thought they already knew enough about the art of the bow.

Out of character with his usual brusque personality, Gudbjartur allowed the boys to play unsuccessfully with their new bows for a time before he showed them the right way to shoot an arrow.

"Come here, all of you. Let me show you how to use your bows." He took Ivar's bow from the hand of the reluctant boy.

A look of utter frustration passed between the boys. Gudbjartur did not notice.

"We already know how to shoot, father." Ivar's voice was tinged with irritation.

"Not with these bows, Ivar. You have not hit the hide, much less the mark. I will show you what you are doing wrong whether you want me to or not." He spoke sternly to his stubborn son. "So listen and learn, Ivar." He shoved at the boy's shoulder to get his attention.

The boy, arms crossed, stared defiantly at his father. Then he scuffed angrily at a pebble in the dust with the toe of his shoe. Lothar and Yola stood silently beside him.

Gudbjartur tried his best not to smile while he sternly regarded his recalcitrant son. Finally the boy shrugged.

Gudbjartur continued. "I had Herjulf make you real bows. These are not toys, nor are they weak like the Haudeno bows you have been using. The reason you are having trouble hitting the mark or the hide," he said, glancing at Ivar, "is the way you are shooting. You are trying to push the bow toward the mark, instead of extending your bow arm and drawing the arrow back on the string as you line up, releasing the arrow as the mark and the arrow are aligned. Like this!" In one fluid motion he raised the bow, drew the arrow to its blunt tip, and loosed. The arrow sped to the center of the mark and bounced from the hide to the ground.

Irritation forgotten, Ivar yelled excitedly and ran to retrieve the arrow, with his brother and Yola in close pursuit.

Gudbjartur took the arrow from Ivar's outstretched hand and continued his object lesson. He believed a demonstration always had more worth than mere words. "When you can shoot like that you will not need to listen to me anymore." Gudbjartur looked at the upturned faces of the three boys. His eyes came to rest on Ivar. "Do we understand each other?"

"Yes," Ivar said, his eyes on his father's face. "Show us how to shoot like that."

For the remainder of the morning, Gudbjartur schooled the boys in the use of their new bows.

Gudbjartur pulled one of the hunting arrows from Ivar's quiver. "You each have two of these. Be careful with them, for they are dangerous. They are the same as the arrows we use to hunt game and fight our enemies.

A crowd of boys and girls gathered as the lessons progressed, turning the impromptu practice session for his sons into a school of archery. He used an assortment of Haudeno and Norse bows and arrows for the instruction.

Ingerd walked up unnoticed and stood to the side, leaning against the wall of a longhouse. She watched her husband with a slight smile on her face. Gudbjartur caught sight of her as he moved from one child to the next, correcting mistakes in stance or shooting style.

"All of you practice what I have shown you. Take turns shooting. Do not go get your arrows until the others are finished. I will be watching you from over there." He gestured toward Ingerd and walked over to join her.

Ingerd smiled at him. "I have never seen such patience from you, Gudbj. I like it."

"Ivar is so stubborn. It took patience to get his attention. He thought he already knew everything there was to know about archery. I showed him he had a lot to learn." He watched the practice.

Lips pursed, Ingerd regarded her husband. "Stubborn, you say. I wonder where he got that."

"From you, I think," he said, laughing as he gazed fondly at her.

"No, Gudbj. He is your son, and if you have ever wondered what you were like at his age, look at him, for you are alike."

"I guess we are." He watched Ivar as the boy confidently shot arrow after arrow at the mark. "I am proud of how he defied me. Few grown men will stand up to me, but that little boy will."

"Have you ever told him you were proud of him for anything?"

"Maybe not. I do not want to spoil him with praise. One day, perhaps I will."

"Do not wait too long, Gudbj. Time has a way of getting away from us. Before you know it that little boy will be a man and it will be too late to praise the accomplishments of the boy who is gone."

* * *

Daily life for the residents of Halfdansfjord gradually assumed a comfortable level as the hard work and anxiety of building and the stocking the larder for winter gave way to the more-settled pursuits of an established society.

With new fleeces available once again, every woman and girl spent the majority of her day spinning the long wool fibers into the yarn from which clothing and other wadmal products would be made over the long winter.

Ingerd, Frida, and Thora sat with their legs dangling over the edge of a high platform particularly suited to spinning. The platform was on the shady side of one of the longhouses, and the three women had joined a large group of other women and young girls. Spinning was the object, and the young girls learned the art in the process. Gossip, of course, was an added benefit.

Ingerd explained the spinning process to two young girls. All the other women were similarly engaged with other girls. "We separate the fleece and clean it of sticks and other trash. Then we card the wool with these flat, toothed brushes, to clean it further and separate the fibers. Hold a card brush in each hand and pull the wool fibers through the teeth, like this." She showed them how with a piece of fleece. "After you get the fleece carded, wind the fibers onto this staff until it is full. My staff is as long as my arm. Gudbj carved these designs in it when he made it for me." She passed it to the two girls for their examination. When you are ready to spin, hold the filled staff under your upper arm like this." She demonstrated. "Now we tie the end of the carded wool on the staff to the looped end of this twisted iron rod. Some of the rods will be made of hardwood, but I like iron best. The rod is two hands in length regardless of what it is made of. This weight on the end of the rod is called a spindle whorl. This one is made of soapstone. You see that the spindle whorl has a hole in the middle, and the rod fits through it. Like so." She showed them the different parts while she explained their use. "The rod and spindle whorl together is called a spindle. "Now, with the wool fibers tied to the spindle's looped end, I set the spindle to spinning by a twist of the wrist." She gave the spindle a spin. "See, I let the wool twist from the staff under my arm, through my fingers, to form a single strand of twisted yarn as the spindle spins to the ground." The spindle reached the ground and stopped spinning. "There, we have a length of hard-twisted yarn." She held it up for the girls to examine and then wound the yarn onto the spindle rod while she explained that step. "We wind the new length of yarn on the spindle rod between the looped end and the spindle whorl. The yarn accumulates in a continuous length until we come to the last step." She began to spin wool again while she explained the next step. "When the spindle rod is full of yarn, I will remove the spindle whorl from the end, take off the spun skein of yarn, and replace the spindle whorl so I can continue spinning. Here, you try it. Do not be shy. We all had to learn." Ingerd smiled at the youngsters and helped them through the process.

Skeins of hard-twisted wool yarn, from which all fabric products were made, accumulated rapidly by this simple yet tedious process until the annual wool production had been spun.

Just down the platform, Ingerd's friends gossiped while they taught other girls to spin.

"Tell us about you and Deskaheh, Thora. Something juicy," Frida said.

"I will, but only if you tell us something about Halfdan, Frida. We do not know anything about you two, and it is high time you told us."

"He is our chieftain, and I will not make gossip about him."
She saw their looks of disappointment. "But I will tell you he
is a very passionate, randy man."

Gales of laughter came from the group. They seemed satisfied by the brief revelation.

Thora came forward with news of her and Deskaheh. "He,
too, is randy, and I am pregnant. It happened during this moon,
so about the Sowing Time moon, our little one will arrive."

"That is a good thing, Thora!" Ingerd exclaimed. She and
her two youngsters moved down the platform and sat beside
Frida, her constant companion. "Deskaheh has really settled
in with us. Since he began to wear our clothing, the only way
we can tell him from anyone else is he is the only man without a beard."

"Yes, he has some facial hair but not enough for a decent
beard." Thora smiled at the thought.

"I, too, am pregnant," Genevra the Thrall announced from
her seat near the end of the platform. Her announcement
silenced the group. She continued in a nervous tone of voice.
"I have known for some time now but I still do not show. It
is Sigmund's baby, and I do not know what to do. I am frightened at what Brodir will do when he finds out, because I am
his thrall." Her eyes brimmed with tears. She hung her head
in misery.

The women listened sympathetically but none could offer
the young wretch any encouragement.

"The baby will be Brodir's chattel, as I am. Born a slave—I
cannot stand the thought of that."

Frida set her spinning aside and came to stand in front of
the girl. "I know that you and Sigmund have had a good time,
and so does everyone else, including Brodir. Sigmund is a freeman and it is forbidden for him to marry a thrall. Any children belong to your owner. It is the way of things. It is our
law and it is inviolate. It cannot be changed except by an
edict from the council during the *thing*. Or Brodir can set you
free at any time. As you say, you are his chattel to do with as
he wishes." Frida placed a hand on the wretched girl's shoulder. She continued in a firm but not unkind voice. "I will
speak of this to Halfdan. Not to intercede in your behalf,

because that I cannot do. It is not my place. But he is our chieftain, and he must know of this. What he does about it is entirely his business, not mine, and certainly not yours. After Brodir returns from his voyage, Halfdan may mention it to him. But if nothing happens after Brodir's return, you will know that either Halfdan did not mention the matter to him, or Brodir decided to do nothing about it, in which case you will be left as you are."

"Thank you, Frida. I feel a little better now."

"Well, regardless of what happens, you will have your baby, and that is all that is really important. You have never been treated poorly by Brodir or any one of us, so long as you performed your tasks without slacking. And you have. Your baby will receive the same treatment, I should think." She looked from face to face. Many of the women had gathered around as she talked.

Genevra looked at the silent women through her tears of anguish. "Thank you, Frida, for talking to me. And thank you all for listening. I knew what I was doing, but it does not make it any easier to bear."

"Does Sigmund know that you are pregnant?" Ingerd asked.

Genevra looked up at Ingerd, who stood before her. "Yes, he knew when I did, but he has said little about it."

"There is nothing to say, Genevra. He knows it and there is nothing he, or anyone but Brodir, can do about it," Thora said. "My situation is similar. Deskaheh is a freeman but he is a prisoner here. I am a freeman, too, but I do not know how this will work out as far as he is concerned. We have spoken of it, of course, but until he is publicly accepted as one of us, by Halfdan and the council, he is still a prisoner, I think."

"That is a good question, Thora, and I will mention it to Halfdan also. But I think you need not worry about Deskaheh. I believe he has already been accepted by everyone." Frida looked at each woman. The topic was dropped as they returned to their spinning and other matters of interest.

That night, sleep eluded Gudbjartur. His mind would not release his body to the rest it so desperately needed. A jumble of thoughts rose unbidden to the fore. He lay on the comfortable sleeping platform beside Ingerd, hands clasped at the back of his head, knees drawn up to take the strain off his sore lower back. It had been a long day. His two sons and little Yola had been apprenticed to Herjulf the Bowyer for a few days, or until Herjulf deemed them sufficiently exposed to his craft. After the first full day, they were fairly bubbling over with all the knowledge they had gained. Each had proudly showed him the arrows they had helped make. Ivar was impressed with the process of turning a square arrow blank into a round shaft ready for fletching. He chuckled quietly to himself at the thought of his son's interest in the things he had also been drawn to when he was a lad. They would learn many usual skills under Herjulf's tutelage. His mind wandered for a time, dwelling on nothing in particular, rather a kaleidoscope of events, until sleep overcame him.

The settlement awakened to a cloudless day the next morning. A steady, heavy feeling, chill wind from the north brought with it the promise of foul weather.

Gudbjartur, one of the first risers, walked from his longhouse, sniffed the air, and surveyed the northern sky. *No sign of anything yet. But I feel Njord stir in his lair. He will bring a storm to us,* he thought.

The wind sucked the smoke from Athils's newfangled chimneys and scattered it asunder as the morning meals were prepared in the longhouses. He rubbed his growling stomach in anticipation as his eyes traveled over the settlement. He returned the wave of one of the tower guards—a sign that all was well—and strode to open the nearest gate as others began to walk from their longhouses.

Halfdan emerged from his house about the same time Gudbjartur propped the two gate halves open. The two men walked to greet each other. "Gudbj, I want to meet with you and Gudrod. I want you both there to voice your opinions on a couple matters that have come up."

Accustomed to Halfdan's methods, Gudbjartur just nodded. "I will find Gudrod."

"I have already told him. He came to me with something to discuss and, I told him to hold it until the three of us were present. He waits for us in my house."

The two men walked back through the village center. They passed the livestock pens as herders began to drive the animals out to pasture.

"We were lucky with the newborns this season. I cannot ever remember another time when not a single animal was lost," Gudbjartur said, as they helped the herders drive the easily handled animals out the north palisade gate.

"Let us hope we can duplicate that luck next year," Halfdan said.

They stopped for a time in the common area, between the animal pens and the first two longhouses, and observed the commerce between the various trades and the general population as people began their day.

"It is good to see our people plying their trades and bartering with each other," Halfdan said.

"Northmen do love to trade," Gudbjartur agreed. "This row of open-fronted lean-tos around the commons will soon be filled with all manner of wares."

"Aye. The tradesmen already produce goods to order," Halfdan said. "This is the aura of permanency we have all craved."

"I hope we see the Naskapi and other tribes from the interior trading here with us."

"They will come in time, I think," Halfdan answered.

The forge fire belched smoke as the coals were stoked for the new day. Haakon, Asgrim, and their mates produced the steel to make cutting tools, utensils, and weapons. In another lean-to, Jorundr the Carver, his magic with wood much in demand, plied his trade amid piles of fragrant wood shavings. Weavers, Frida and Ingerd among them, worked at looms to produce the bolts of wadmal from which everything from clothing to sails would later be made. Tradesmen skilled in leather goods displayed shoes, belts, scabbards, quivers, vests, and the like. The smell of the rich leather drew onlookers even if they did not buy. Ring split antler for combs and brushes. He smoothed the thin, flat sections with a file and sharkskin sandpaper, then carefully cut the removable teeth with small saws made especially for his trade by the smithies. And so went the industry of a viable society.

Money, in the form of gold and silver coin, was virtually
unavailable to the common man. Unlike their brethren in
Vestfold, Svealand, and the other areas of the homeland,
these former Greenlanders traded tangible goods for every
conceivable necessity. A wooden bowl for a haunch of veni-
son; a dressed lamb for a new knife or spearhead; a brace of
geese or ducks for a new pair of shoes; or as in Gudbjartur's
case, an entire dressed bear carcass for the bows, arrows, and
the quivers to carry them in. Herjulf drove a hard bargain.
Gudbjartur snorted at the memory.

"What is it?" Halfdan asked.

"I was thinking about my trade with Herjulf. He got the
better of me, I think."

"Not really. It took him some time to fashion the bows and
arrows you ordered. I would say you came out about even. Of
course, I did not spend an entire day getting that big black
bear like you and your sons did."

"I enjoyed hunting with them, and I will take them out
again. Ivar and Lothar both got a killing arrow into the bear
after my arrow stopped his bid for freedom. Even little Yola
stuck an arrow into the side of the bear's head. It would not
have killed him, but at least he hit him." He chuckled. "All
three of them learned much on their first real hunting trip,
and they already clamor for more."

"Good. I will go with you when you take them out next
time."

Gudbjartur looked at him in surprise. "They would certainly
enjoy having you with us, Halfdan."

"We will do it then. Just tell me when."

"I will."

"Let us go meet with Gudrod. They will have something
for us to eat on the hearth; I am hungry all of a sudden."

"Aye, and so am I," Gudbjartur said.

Gudrod sat on a bench near one of the hearths while he
ate a bowl of stew and talked to Thora. He looked up when
Halfdan and Gudbjartur entered the longhouse.

"Is the stew still hot, Thora? We have not eaten yet,"
Halfdan said, as he bent over to peer into the kettle on the
warming ledge of the stone hearth.

"Oh yes, it is still hot. Help yourself." She smiled at the two men. "I lit the lamps in the council room for you."

"Good, thank you," Halfdan said.

They each ladled a wooden bowl full of stew, selected a chunk of flat bread from a basket beside the hearth to sop up the juice, and made their way into the council room.

The large, open room contained portable benches along the walls and several trestle tables around a square hearth in the center. A charcoal fire glowed on the hearth, and soapstone lamps hanging from the timbers overhead cast a soft glow over the room. A bright patch of morning sunlight came through the open doorway.

Halfdan took a seat on one of the benches on either side of a long trestle table. "Frida has brought up a potential problem that I want your opinions on. Brodir's thrall, Genevra, is pregnant by Sigmund."

Gudrod laughed aloud. "Well, what a surprise that is. Those two have been coupling daily since we were at Snorrisfjord. One more thrall for Brodir, I would say."

"I have already told her that. She offered no opinion herself; she just wanted me to know of the situation. She hopes I will mention it to Brodir. Sigmund and Genevra want to live openly together, and maybe get married one day."

"Married!" Gudrod snorted. "That cannot be. Sigmund is a freeman."

Noncommittal, Halfdan made eye contact with Gudbjartur. "What do you think?"

"You know that I am one of the few who does not own a thrall. I have never told anyone why, even you, Halfdan." Gudbjartur put his spoon in the bowl of stew and leaned forward, his elbows on the table. "My father, Einar, spent five years as a Celt slave. He was captured during a raid on their territory when he was a very young man, long before I was born. Einar was set free by Gotar Vikings when they attacked the Celt village where he was held. He returned with the victorious Gotar warriors to Gotland. He later took a ship to Iceland, where he met my mother, and where I was born. Einar never kept a thrall. He told me he would not enslave another after he himself had been enslaved for so long. I am

Einar's son. I have always honored his memory by not owning a thrall. Others may do as they wish. It is of no concern to me. I do not judge them. But I think all of our thralls should be set free, to make their own destiny, instead of being eaters at another man's board. Especially in this new land, where we will share every success, or we will all perish together, freeman and thrall alike. That is my opinion, Halfdan, since you asked."

Both of his listeners sat in silent regard of him for a time.

Gudrod chuckled low in his throat, glanced at Halfdan, and stood to stretch. "I have always known that Gudbj carefully considers before he speaks. It is one of the many reasons he is your second-in-command. He has brought up something I had never considered before: how a thrall must feel to be a slave. I, for one, will think on this. Whatever you decide, Halfdan, will be fine with me."

Halfdan considered his response a moment. "I, too, will think on this, Gudbj. Thank you for telling us of Einar. You are correct in saying our destinies are entwined with our thralls; they are more so now than at any time in the history of our people. I doubt the council will ever reach agreement on freeing our thralls, but I will put it to them when our ships return. Until then we will not speak of this with anyone."

Gudbjartur and Gudrod waited for him to bring up his other concerns. "Frida also told me people wonder what Deskaheh's status is among us. She said Thora especially wants to know. She has an interest in the man."

"More than an interest!" Gudrod exclaimed.

"Deskaheh is a prisoner, Halfdan, until you say otherwise. He is a freeman among his people," Gudbjartur added.

Halfdan pulled at his beard a moment. "From this day hence, Deskaheh is free to do as he wishes. He is no longer a prisoner. I will make the announcement to our people. He has earned the right to be free."

"Aye, he has. He is a good man. We have become neutral toward each other. Someday perhaps, we will be friends. We can learn much from him about this land," Gudbjartur said.

Halfdan picked his teeth with a splinter as he thought things over. "Two more topics need discussion before we each go about our tasks." He gestured with the splinter. "Gudbj, I want you to take a scouting party to the salt water inlet Deskaheh spoke of. He told us the journey takes about seven days. Thoroughly scout the land between here and there. Determine if the people are hostile toward us and find out their numbers, that sort of thing. Leave when you judge Halfdansfjord to be completed and ready for winter in all respects. I leave that decision to you."

"I will think on this."

"We know you will." Gudrod chuckled and slapped Gudbjartur on the shoulder good-naturedly. Seeing him wince slightly, Gudrod immediately apologized for his lapse. "I am sorry. I forgot about your shoulder."

"It is all right." Gudbjartur eyed the contrite man. "I am overly protective of it. It is healed, but still a little tender sometimes."

"Especially when some fool forgets and slaps it in jest," Gudrod answered.

"Forget about it."

"What did you want to discuss, Gudrod?" Halfdan asked.

"I had a question about Deskaheh. You answered it."

Halfdan nodded. "When are we going hunting with the boys, Gudbj?" Halfdan asked.

"How about tomorrow, after they finish morning chores? We can spend the night in the bush, if you are agreed."

"That sounds good to me. I will be ready."

"I, too, would like to go," Gudrod said.

"Not this one. You must be in command here while we are gone. Maybe Gudbj will let you take the boys out at some other time." Halfdan glanced at Gudbjartur.

"They would enjoy that. I will tell them that you will take them out next time." Gudbjartur looked at Gudrod.

"Good," Gudrod said.

The three men walked from the longhouse together. They talked briefly about the progress that had been made and the feeling of permanency the village of Halfdansfjord gave to everyone, before each went their separate way.

As the shadows lengthened after midday, the populace gathered earlier than usual for the final meal of the day and the planned festivities to follow. The second of the two daily meals was usually a leisurely affair, but not today.

A horse fight between a pair of the village's six stallions was organized by some of the men when a mare came in heat. The event could best be enjoyed in the full light of day and was one of the peoples' favorite opportunities to wager all manner of personal goods.

* * *

Two leagues inland, along the banks of the river that flowed by Halfdansfjord, four Northmen killed and butchered a pair of moose. They loaded the quarters into their boat and hiked to the top a nearby hillock to survey the countryside.

One of them detected movement in a small fen in the distance. "Get down!" He warned.

His three companions dropped as one to the ground and looked questioningly at him.

"I just saw four native women!" Thorkell exclaimed excitedly.

"Where?" Ketill asked, rising up to look over the top of the brush.

"Get down, they may see you," Eyvindr said.

"I do not care if they do see me. I want to see what they look like."

"They are specks in the distance," Thorkell said. "After you see them, what do you intend?"

"All we have talked about lately is women." Ketill eyed his companions. "There are women in that fen, one for each of us. I say we sneak down there and have at them."

"Halfdan or Gudbj would kill us." Grimr acted frightened.

"Only if they found out," Ketill said. "How would they ever find out?"

"I do not know," Grimr answered. "They find out everything sooner or later."

"I wonder why there are no men with them." Eyvindr rose up to watch the women from the well-concealed vantage point.

"I, too, wonder about that, but I see only the four women." Ketill observed.

As time passed, the thoughts of two of the men became more sexual. Ketill and Eyvindr stroked themselves while they watched the progress of the women. Their ardor reached a fever pitch that could no longer be denied.

Ketill leered at the others. "I am sneaking down there and coupling with one of those women." He began to crawl away.

"I am not going." Grimr spoke with conviction.

Ketill stopped. He hissed in a lowered voice that dripped with malice and scorn. "You will come, you coward, or I will kill you."

"I am not a coward, and well you know it, Ketill. This is not right. I will not violate those women or my leader's trust." Grimr was resolute.

"I, too, feel the same. I stand with Grimr. I will not go." Thorkell eyed his companions.

"Well, I will go, Ketill. Come on, we do not need them to handle those women." He started to crawl.

Ketill's eyes shifted from Grimr to Thorkell.

"Do what you must. We will wait at the boat," Thorkell said.

Without another word Ketill and Eyvindr crawled down the hill. Grimr and Thorkell watched for a moment.

"I do not want to watch them, and I do not want to know what they do." Grimr crawled off the top of the hillock, got to his feet, and wound his way through the brush and down the hill toward the river.

Thorkell paused while he watched the two men crawl down the hill. He thought over what Grimr had said. Then he, too, made his way down the hill toward the river and the boat.

* * *

Colorful butterflies flew about in the humid summer air of the fen. Birds trilled from the edge of the forest. A fish slapped the water as it rose to bait fluttering on the surface. Across a small pond a beaver swam, his mouth full of green shoots for his dam.

The girl's presence seemed not to disturb the business of life in the fen, for they belonged to and were a part of it. All were young, and they wore their long black hair tied back. They wore plain, light brown, full-length buckskin dresses that were loose at the waist. They sat on the fen bank and laughed and chattered like squirrels, unconcerned, while they removed their leather shoes to keep them dry before they walked barefoot into the boggy fen where the berries grew.

As they got to their feet, they tied the thong laces of their shoes together and looped them around the backs of their necks to hang down the front.

"We saw you look at that young warrior in the hunting party," one of the younger girls said to the oldest of them.

"I can look. There is no harm in looking at them. I cannot touch, for it is forbidden until we mate with a man."

Her younger companions tittered in response.

"You all know we cannot mate before our time. Our people forbid it. It has always been so," she scolded them, being the older sister.

"Well, it is very hard to wait. We have thoughts of such things," one girl said.

"I know. I can tell you that the waiting becomes more difficult with time."

The other three giggled again. Then they all waded into the waters of the fen and began to pick purple sarvis berries from the head-high bushes. They talked as they worked, exclaiming and laughing happily at what they saw in the fen.

They stripped the berry bushes into small bark boxes that hung on thongs around their necks. These boxes allowed the women to use both hands to strip the bushes of berries as they waded through the fen. When the boxes were full, they dumped them over a shoulder and into a much larger, open-topped bark box each carried as a backpack. The weight of the large box was relieved by a broad leather tumpline strap secured to the outside bottom corners that then passed over the forehead of the bearer.

The four women were so intent on picking berries and having a good time in the process that their innate animal instincts failed to warn them of the peril that approached. They broke a cardinal rule of survival; they relaxed in a hostile land.

* * *

Ketill and Eyvindr crawled until they had an unobstructed view of their prey. Then the two men took cover along the game trail the women would use when they left one pond to walk to the next as they moved slowly through the fen. The men fantasized about what might be under the leather dresses and played with themselves while they waited for their prey to walk into the trap. They became fascinated by the efficiency and speed with which the women picked as they drew near to their place of concealment. The women were close enough now that features were discernible. Whispered comments were exchanged between the men.

"They are just girls," Eyvindr whispered.

"I do not care how old they are. I will take the first one. The one with the pretty face and the big breasts," Ketill answered.

"I will take the second. She is pretty, too, but her chest looks kind of flat. What about the other two?" Eyvindr asked.

"They will run."

"Let them run, I do not care. They can do nothing."

As the four women approached the men, brush, trees, and the hummocks of the fen served to funnel them naturally onto the trail between ponds. The woman in the lead parted the brush ahead of her across the path they followed and turned her head to say something to her companions. She laughed at some return comment. When she turned her head back to the front, her field of vision was filled by a large bearded man with a huge grin on his face. He seemed to materialize at arm's length in front of her. The trap was so unexpected and cunningly laid, the attack so well-timed and savage, that scarcely a sound escaped into the comparative silence of the fen.

Before she could move from her tracks, the man grabbed her upper arms in a grip from which she could not escape, cast her berry boxes aside, and threw her to the wet ground. Fright stilled any outcry for a heartbeat as her brain struggled to register what her eyes saw but her conscious mind could not accept.

Her feet and legs thrashed against him. She pulled a knife from a scabbard in her dress and tried to stab him. He grabbed her wrist and twisted the knife from her hand.

A savage, backhanded blow struck the side of her head. A single scream pierced the solitude of the forest. A hard hand covered her mouth. He dropped his hand to her throat and throttled her. The warning cry strangled in her throat. He leered at her and held a finger to his lips. Tears squeezed from her eyes. Then the man jerked her dress up and levered her legs apart with his knee. He pulled his tunic aside to free his engorged member and lowered his bulk onto her thin frame. His weight crushed down on her and his fetid breath fanned her face. Ketill grunted like a rooting hog as he sheathed his manhood in her body. He thrust violently in and out. Finally he shuddered and his seed flooded into her.

A similar fate befell the second woman in line when Eyvindr leaped from his hiding place and bore her to the ground.

The third young woman stumbled unexpectedly on Eyvindr and his prey just as he threw her to the ground. In shock, the woman stood with a hand to her mouth as she watched the hairy devil throw himself atop her friend. A scream up ahead shattered her shocked immobility; she threw her baskets aside and wheeled back the way she had come.

The fourth woman stood rooted in fright at the screams coming from the forest.

Her friend suddenly burst from the bushes ahead and screamed a warning. "Run! The devils of the forest have attacked!"

Not even pausing to don their shoes, the two young women ran like deer into the hinterland.

* * *

"What is the matter with you, and where are the other two girls?" The tall warrior held the young woman lightly by her arm as his black eyes bored into hers. Twelve other warriors clustered around them.

"We were attacked by hairy men while we picked berries," the young girl said miserably, her eyes downcast.

A growl came from the warriors.

"What men? What did they do?" The gorge rose in the tall warrior's throat for he already knew the answer.

"They have white skin and hairy faces," the girl squeaked in fright. "They forcibly took the other two girls." She lowered her eyes in shame.

He patted her shoulder and turned his hard, black eyes on his men.

Rage swept through the close-knit Naskapi hunting party, a fiery rage that could only be quenched with the blood of those who had visited this dishonor upon them.

* * *

The four hunters returned to Halfdansfjord, almost unnoticed given the level of activity, with the butchered carcasses as evidence of the success of their hunt. Nobody seemed to notice the furtive glances two of them directed toward Halfdan and Gudbjartur. Neither did anyone observe that two of their number shunned the other two.

Grimr and Thorkell were consumed with guilt over their erstwhile companions' deed. They had played no active part, but the betrayal of their leader's trust preyed on them.

Ketill and Eyvindr tried to put the matter behind them. A foul deed often turned men into opposing factions and eroded the foundation of their common bond.

* * *

Gudbjartur's horn signaled for an assembly before the stallions were brought together for the horse fight. He and Halfdan stood atop one of the palisade parapets facing the village common, in full view of the assembling crowd.

"Gudbj, have Deskaheh brought up here with us."

"I knew you would want him here so I sent Tostig to find him," he said, with a slight smile. "And yonder he comes." He gestured toward the upper end of the village where Deskaheh could be seen winding his way through the fringes of the crowd as he made his way toward them.

Halfdan laughed at his own predictability and made to punch his friend on the shoulder. Gudbjartur's narrowed eyes and braced posture arrested him midway through the punch. "Ha! You thought I forgot about your shoulder, huh? No, I did not forget, my friend. I thought to test your ability to defend yourself."

Halfdan's statement got only a brief hrumph! from Gudbjartur.

Both men turned toward Deskaheh as he topped the parapet ladder and walked toward them.

The three men greeted each other.

"I have an announcement that concerns you, Deskaheh. We felt you should be here beside us when I tell the people," Halfdan said.

"As you wish, Halfdan." Deskaheh eyes shifted between the two men.

Gudbjartur, uncharacteristically, offered an explanation. "There is no reason to be nervous. I think you will approve of what Halfdan will say when the people have finished gathering." He swept a hand over the throng.

Halfdan stepped to the edge of the parapet and looked out over the people. Conversation gradually subsided. "Thora, where are you?" Halfdan called.

"Here, Halfdan," she called from the front of the crowd and just below the parapet.

"Oh!" His surprise brought a ripple of laughter. "Come up here. You are part of this, too."

Thora came to join them on the parapet. She grasped Deskaheh's hand with a radiant smile on her face. He did not seem to know what was taking place, but she had confidence that it was something good for them.

Halfdan addressed the people in a voice all could hear. "This man, Deskaheh, has freely submitted to our way of life. He has by all outward signs become a useful part of our community. I, and the other two council members present have decided to free him from his status of prisoner. From this moment he is officially free. By the laws of the Northmen, and as a freeman in his native society, he is to enjoy all the privileges of a freeman among us." Halfdan turned to the beaming couple.

"Thank you, both of you." Deskaheh shook hands with Halfdan and Gudbjartur.

Speechless for once, Thora hugged both men and clutched Deskaheh's arm happily. Her eyes filled as she looked out over the cheering crowd.

The four of them climbed from the parapet and joined the people as they flooded through the inland gates to the open field where the horse fight would take place.

By the time Halfdan, Gudbjartur, and Gudrod arrived, the squeals of the stallions could be heard above the noise of the crowd.

A pall of dust hung over the arena. The excitement and cries of the crowd, the high heat, and the sweat of the keyed-up horses all served to create an air of bedlam.

Two men brought the mare into the midst of the encircling crowd where four men tethered the two blindfolded stallions.

The stallions were positioned at either end of the arena created by the boisterous crowd. The stallions' excitement increased by the moment. Handlers were kept busy as the spirited animals pulled and pranced to the limit of the tethers that held them.

The mare, too, became excited. She squealed, wheeled, and kicked at each stallion as her handlers led her by them. Her squeals and the scent of a mare in estrus fanned the flames of sexual excitement. The stallions arched their necks, snorted, and neighed. They became almost unmanageable.

The handlers quickly trotted the mare from the circle. People scattered helter-skelter as she pranced through an opening. The moment she was out of sight, the crowd filled in the gap.

The handlers jerked off the blindfolds and released the stallions. Both horses squealed and lunged toward each other. The fight was on.

Shouts from the crowd goaded the stallions on as they reared and struck at each other.

"Two bearskins on the black!" Gudbjartur shouted, as he and his two companions jostled for position among the press of shouting spectators.

"Done!" Gudrod shouted back.

"I will take those bearskins and wager my new chain-mail vest and sword against your chain-mail vest and axe that the bay beats the black." Halfdan had a look of cunning on his face.

"Not the axe. I will not wager that." Gudbjartur said with resolve.

Halfdan laughed uproariously. Impulsively he threw a thick arm around his friend's neck and pulled him to his face. "I know that, Gudbj." He released his hold on Gudbjartur's neck. "I will see your two bearskins and wager you one more that the bay stallion beats the black. It will cost both of you one more bearskin to stay in this wager." Halfdan's face split in a huge grin as he glanced from man to man.

"I will take that wager." Gudrod watched Gudbjartur to see what he was going to do.

"I will owe each of you three bearskins if I lose." Gudbjartur thought it over.

"Do you have six bearskins? Freshly tanned ones, now. Gudrod and I do not want any of your old, smelly, motheaten skins." Halfdan could barely contain his exuberance.

"Of course I have six good bearskins. But it will not matter. The black will win."

"We shall see. We shall see," Halfdan repeated.

They turned their full attention back to the fight as it developed before the shouting crowd.

The two stallions appeared equally matched to begin with. After a furious exchange of bites, strikes with their front hooves, and wheeling kicks with hind feet, the fight began to turn in favor of the black.

Under a pall of choking dust kicked aloft by the struggling stallions, the edge of the circling crowd ebbed to and fro as individuals shouted and waved their arms to keep from being run down.

"The black is winning!" Gudbjartur shouted over the tumult.

"Not yet! The fight is not over until the loser tries to get away!" Gudrod shouted.

Halfdan did not appear to be that certain that his wager was safe when the black delivered a hard strike to the bay's head. Gudbjartur happened to see the slight shake of Halfdan's head as he saw the bay recoil in pain.

"You may as well pay me the wager, Halfdan!" Gudbjartur exclaimed loudly above the din.

At that moment the bay clamped his jaws down on the top of the black's neck just behind his head. The black squealed and tried to buck the bay loose. The bay held on doggedly. His front feet pelted the black's chest and front shoulders. The two lunged and surged over the field of battle.

"He has him now!" Halfdan shouted. He pounded Gudbjartur on the shoulder.

Gudbjartur shrugged away from the blow.

"I am sorry, Gudbj. I forgot in the excitement."

"I will stay at arm's length from now on."

Both Halfdan and Gudrod laughed.

The black broke loose from the bay and ran in a big circle with the bay in pursuit.

"The black is finished!" Gudrod shouted.

"No, wait! He gathers himself for another attack. He does not run away." Gudbjartur waved his arms.

Halfdan and Gudrod cheered their choice on.

Gudbjartur remained convinced the black would prevail.

The black suddenly stopped his sham flight. He came up on his front feet. His powerful hind feet coiled under his rump. The bay bored in. The black's first kick missed. The bay came on undeterred. The black suddenly rocked forward again on his forelegs, bunched his hind legs under his belly, and recoiled. The hard hooves thudded into the bays neck and chest. The impact knocked the bay to the ground. He did not rise.

Pandemonium swept through the crowd. Men rushed forward to prevent the squealing black from pounding his downed adversary to a bloody pulp. The fight was over.

The winners in the crowd laughed and jested with the losers. Most took their losses good-naturedly.

A group of men worked over the bay. They got his head up and his front legs forward. The gallant stallion gathered himself. He finally lurched to his feet. His head hung until he got his breath and wits about him once again.

Gudbjartur, hands on hips, confronted his two companions. "Well, I guess that settles it. As soon as I collect from you two, that is."

"Yes, I guess it does. No doubt about which horse won that fight." Halfdan glanced at Gudrod, who shrugged.

"You won fair and square. But I still think the bay would have won if the black had not landed that last kick." Gudrod admitted defeat.

"Perhaps," Gudbjartur said. "They are evenly matched and anything can happen in such a fight."

Frida and Ingerd walked up with arms linked. Both were laughing.

"Who won?" Ingerd asked, as they stopped in front of the three men. Nobody responded for a moment. The two women glanced from man to man expectantly.

Halfdan raised his chin toward Gudbjartur. "Gudbj won. He beat us out of three bearskins apiece."

"Both of you lost?" Ingerd threw her arms around Gudbjartur. "Good! We can use more bearskin robes for winter."

"Which one of you won?" Gudrod asked the women.

"I did." Frida beamed. Her mood was triumphant. "I won the new pair of scissors and six needles that Ingerd just traded from Haakon and Askhold."

Gudbjartur glanced at Ingerd.

"I could have won. And Frida would have lost her sable pelt she traded from Essipit's people," she explained.

"I guess you will be visiting Haakon again for another pair of scissors." Mirth danced in Gudbjartur's voice.

Ingerd laughed and hugged him.

Ivar, Lothar, and Yola joined the adults. The conversation turned to the boy's involvement in the spate of wagering.

"Look, Gudbj, I won all four hunting arrows from your sons!" Little Yola cried excitedly as he held his prizes out proudly for all to see.

The adults all laughed.

Ivar clenched his jaws in anger. "I will win them back! It was not a fair fight anyway. The black kicked the bay while he was not looking."

Gudbjartur grabbed Ivar by the arm and pulled him forward. He bent down so they were face to face. "Listen, Ivar, and listen well. A wager is a game. It is not life or death. You lost fair and square. The horses were evenly matched. The fight could have gone either way at any time. Next time the bay may win. But this time the black won. That is the way of things; accept it. It is over. Now," he turned Ivar to face the other two boys, "apologize to your brother and Yola for being a poor loser."

The still defiant Ivar made his apologies.

Gudbjartur watched his son closely. *By the gods,* he thought. *The boy will be a great leader some day. A fire burns in his gut.* Gudbjartur glanced at Ingerd. Her eyebrow was arched. The beginnings of a smile played about the corners of her mouth. They had talked of Ivar's strength many times in the past. He realized she had been correct in her assessment of the boy's strong personality. Just like his father, she had said. He sighed and turned his attention back to the boys. "All right then, the matter is finished. Let this be the end of it."

"Yes, father." Ivar's facial expression belied his words. He met his father's eyes steadfastly. Then he turned and strode away, his two companions trailing behind.

The adults watched the boy's departure with a certain amount of amusement.

"I predict that Ivar will someday be the chieftain of our people." Halfdan watched the boys walk toward the settlement gate. "He has very definite ideas about things. Not unlike his father." His eyes shifted to Gudbjartur. Only Gudbjartur saw the wink.

The five of them walked back toward the gate with the crowd. Several people around them made mention of the chill wind and the feel of the air.

"This wind from the northwest is heavy with the smell of moisture. Njord and Thor stir in their lair. They will come to us tonight, I think." Gudbjartur gestured to the west as the sun's face began to dip into the heavy bank of dirty gray clouds that extended across the horizon.

Ingerd cuddled into Gudbjartur's shoulder as they walked. His arm draped over the back of her shoulders. "I am so happy to have a warm, snug house again." She looked up at him.

"And so am I." He smiled at her. "We will need it tonight."

* * *

In the dimness of the cloaking forest, a tall, grim-faced Naskapi and twelve warriors watched the procession of people file through the gate of their town. They had watched the spectacle of the interlopers since midday. The leader carefully observed everything the strangers did. He noted the guard towers, the high palisade wall, and the gates that secured the town.

With a lift of his chin the leader signaled to his men. They all melted into the shadows of the forest. As the distance from the town increased and the chance of detection decreased, the scouting party broke into a trot. They wound their way through the forest for some distance before coming to the banks of the river that had borne them here.

The leader had a brief conversation with his warriors.

"At dawn we will go to the town of the pale skins. I want to know their hearts before we go home."

The warriors agreed, to a man.

The leader nodded and he and his men began to pick their way through the dense brush along the river. Finally they stepped into a small clearing beyond the riverbank. The three canoes that had brought them waited there in the overnight camp, as did the four young women who had accompanied them.

The four women got to their feet when their men appeared from the surrounding brush.

The leader stopped in front of them. "Tomorrow before dawn, we will paddle down this river to the town of the pale skinned, hairy men. I will talk to their leader and tell him what two of his men have done to you."

"No, please, we do not wish to see them," one young woman pleaded. Her three companions recoiled in fright at the thought of seeing the hairy men again.

The leader chopped his hand down in the cutting sign. "I have spoken. It will be as I say. I have looked on their chief. He must know of this deed."

The women acceded, their eyes downcast.

* * *

"Come on, Gudbj, those are new skins. The bears were killed this summer. You saw me kill two of them!" Halfdan exploded in frustration over the way his friend picked through the hair of each robe as he peered intently into the depths of the luxurious, long brown hair, as if expecting to find a defect or nest of vermin.

"I am certain you are right. Summer pelts are not prime fur. I want to inspect them for blemishes and loose hair. These skins are acceptable to me. I can find no fault with them," he said with a twinkle in his eye and the beginnings of a smile at the corners of his mouth.

Speechless, Halfdan looked at Gudrod.

Gudrod shrugged.

Halfdan snorted in disgust. He dropped the last of the three skins on the ground at Gudbjartur's feet and stood with his hands on his hips regarding his friend.

Gudrod added his three skins to the pile on the ground.

Gudbjartur made no move to inspect them.

Gudrod glanced quickly at Halfdan to gauge his reaction and then he began to laugh as he realized the joke was on the both of them.

Halfdan looked from the laughing Gudrod to Gudbjartur when he, too, began to laugh.

"I jest with both of you." Gudbjartur laughed. "You know me better than that. I do not care about the skins, although we will certainly put them to good use. I won, and I am being smug about my victory." He looked from man to man. "Why, next time I might lose. I doubt it though.

Halfdan shook his head and smiled at them. "You had me going."

"He got both of us this time. Next time will be our turn, I think." Gudrod smiled at his friends.

Gudbjartur told the tale to Ingerd later that evening. They lounged comfortably on the platforms built against the interior walls of their longhouse. He laughed aloud as he told her of the men's reaction to his minute inspection of Halfdan's hides for defects. "You should have seen the look on Halfdan's face. He could not believe I might reject his bearskins. Gudrod knew I jested with them when I did not even look at his bearskins. As soon as he figured it out he started laughing. By that time, Halfdan was angry."

"You did not part with him still angry." Ingerd looked at her husband with concern.

"Oh, no, he went along with it finally. But I got him good. He will be laying for me, of that I am certain." He shook his head and grinned at the memory. The looks on their faces when they surrendered their payment for the wager had definitely been worth the wait.

* * *

People were fast asleep in Halfdansfjord. The men in the guard towers were wide awake when the storm came with a vengeance.

Gudbjartur awoke to the moan of the northwest wind. Rain pelted against the daub walls of his longhouse. He glanced at his family, dimly visible in the gloom of a single lamp. They were not the least disturbed from their slumber by the sounds of the storm. His thoughts drifted to the long journey to Vinland. *For the first time since we sailed from Greenland, my people enjoy uninterrupted sleep within houses safe from weather,* he mused. The most disquieting event of the day was that a group of moose hunters had found fresh human tracks in the hinterland. It put a damper on the spirits of everyone who knew of the discovery. He heard others stir as the storm increased in intensity, but unlike living in the tents, all were secure within the snug longhouse. He listened to the rain for a time as the wind-driven droplets hammered the stout walls. Then he slid into a deep sleep once again.

In the morning, Gudbjartur awoke to the sound of water slowly dripping from the roof into a puddle. He rolled easily off the sleeping platform to the floor without awakening his family. The door was open so he knew that someone had already gone outside. From the sounds coming through the door, the storm had passed. He washed the sleep from his face and combed his hair. His thoughts dwelt on the hunting trip he and Halfdan planned this day with his sons. He saw no reason not to spend the night in the bush just because the countryside was wet from the storm. *Being wet and miserable will be good training for them,* he thought. He finished dressing and turned to walk from the longhouse.

As he walked out into the common area Gudbjartur saw Halfdan standing under the entryway of his house. The men met halfway, avoiding the puddles and mud courtesy of the wide log walkways—a recently completed project—that connected each longhouse and the huts surrounding the central common area.

"That was some storm," Gudbjartur said.

"I did not stir. The puddles and light drizzle I saw at dawn were a surprise to me when I walked from my house. I must be getting too content with all this comfort and security," Halfdan observed. He waved to one of the tower guards.

"I am the same. I awoke for a very short time and do not remember going back to sleep. I think I prefer this comfort and security to what we had before we built Halfdansfjord."

The thread of their conversation was shattered by the wail of a warning horn from the inland tower guard.

"People! A party of people is standing on the riverbank at the edge of the barley field," the guard shouted through cupped hands.

"What are they doing?" Halfdan shouted as he and Gudbjartur quickly climbed a ladder to the parapet.

"Nothing, they are just standing there." The guard pointed as Halfdan and Gudbjartur gained the parapet below the guard tower and looked out over the barley field.

"There are women with them," Gudbjartur said.

"I see them."

Gudrod, Thorgill, and Tostig joined them on the parapet.

Halfdan turned toward them; his eyes mirrored the intensity of his feelings. "Tostig, find Frida, Ingerd, Deskaheh, and Thora. Meet us at the north gate."

"The men are armed, Halfdan." Gudbjartur turned to look at him.

"Arm yourselves." Halfdan turned to follow Tostig down the ladder.

* * *

"A gate is being opened. Here they come," the Naskapi leader said.

"There are six armed men and three women," a warrior said.

"One of the men looks Haudeno," another warrior observed.

"No matter, we come to parley." The leader looked at the young women. "And we will right a wrong."

* * *

Halfdan spoke to his retinue as they slogged through the mud of the field. "A great deal depends on this first meeting. Be open and friendly, but remain alert. Deskaheh, you and Thora will interpret for us. Are they Naskapi?"

"Yes, they are Naskapi. The tall man in the middle is the leader, I think," Deskaheh said, his eyes fastened on the Naskapi leader.

Halfdan stopped in front of the tall man. Gudbjartur stood to his right, Deskaheh to his left, and the others fanned out slightly on either side. Nobody spoke for a heartbeat. Halfdan held out his right hand, palm open. "I welcome you, in the name of my people."

The Naskapi said nothing. His hard black eyes bored into Halfdan. He paid no mind to the other Northmen. "We do not come in peace. Two of your people have done these women a great wrong." He gestured to the nervous young women. "I have come to tell you of this and to see what is in your heart."

"This man is Halfdan, the chieftain of his people," Deskaheh said. "He welcomes you and your people."

The Naskapi's eyes flicked to Deskaheh. "What is a Haudeno doing with these pale skins?"

"I live with them. They are my friends. This is my woman." He took Thora's hand.

The Naskapi looked at her.

"My people come in peace to Nitassinan." When Thora spoke in the Haudeno tongue, a flicker of surprise registered on the Naskapi's face, but he remained silent.

Deskaheh spoke to Halfdan. "Someone of us has done a bad thing to these women."

"What? When?" Halfdan asked, but the answer flashed in his mind before the words left his mouth.

Deskaheh repeated Halfdan's question.

The Naskapi took two of the young girls by the arm and stepped toward Halfdan with them. He spoke at length. "Two of your men had their way with these girls. As one leader to another, those men must answer for it. My people demand it. I demand it, or the blood of your people will soak this land." He spoke in a voice filled with hate and anger.

"When?" Deskaheh asked the Naskapi.

The Naskapi leader made the sign for the passage of two days.

Halfdan looked at Deskaheh.

"Somebody raped those two girls two days ago," Deskaheh said.

Halfdan turned to Gudbjartur. Anger seethed in him. "Who found the tracks a couple days ago?"

"Grimr, but I do not believe he would do such a thing. I will ask him." He looked at Thorgill and Tostig. "Come with me." The three men walked back toward the village gate.

"Tell the Naskapi leader what we are doing and ask him to come into the village." Halfdan spoke to Deskaheh, but his eyes were on the Naskapi.

Deskaheh spoke to the Naskapi. The Naskapi shook his head. "He will not enter the village. He will wait here," Deskaheh said.

"Halfdan, let us try to talk to the girls," Frida said.

Halfdan waved them forward and impatiently looked toward the village.

Thora spoke to the Naskapi leader. "We want to speak to the girls," she said. Frida and Ingerd were at her side.

The Naskapi looked at the three women for a heartbeat and then said something over his shoulder to his young women.

Thora nodded to him and the three women walked toward the four girls.

"They are so young," Frida said, smiling at one of the Naskapi girls.

Thora, Frida, and Ingerd quickly broke down the barriers of language and took the girls aside to do what only one woman can do for another in such circumstance.

Halfdan waited uncomfortably. He and the Naskapi leader had eye contact when the man's eyes shifted toward the village and he said something to his men.

"Gudbj comes, Halfdan," Deskaheh said.

Halfdan turned around. Everyone's eyes followed the progress of the men trudging across the barley field. Gudbjartur led; Tostig and Thorgill followed, prodding two men forward with spears.

Gudbjartur halted them in front of Halfdan. He pushed them a step away from their chieftain with the head of his axe. Nobody spoke.

Neither man could meet the rage in Halfdan's eyes.

Halfdan turned to the Naskapi leader. "Are these the men?"

The Naskapi spoke over his shoulder. His eyes never left the two accused men. The young women hesitated in fright. "Speak," the leader said in a low voice. "Are these the men?"

The older girl, wringing her hands in distress, her eyes downcast, unable to look on her attacker, whispered a single word. "Yes."

"Which one?" the Naskapi leader asked.

The girl raised a trembling finger and pointed to Ketill.

"Now, Halfdan, we—" Ketill's excuse caught in his throat.

Halfdan's fist crashed into the side of his head and he fell like he had been poleaxed. Halfdan turned on Eyvindr. "Run! Do not look back!"

"I . . ." The piteous plea died in the man's throat.

"Run for your life!" Halfdan screamed at him. Spittle flew from his mouth. Rage consumed him. With a visible effort of will he turned to the Naskapi leader and gestured toward Eyvindr as the man ran through the muddy field toward the forest. "He is yours."

The Naskapi leader said something to his men. Four of them set off in pursuit. They caught Eyvindr as he gained the forest. His screams came to them. The screams ended abruptly.

Moments later the four warriors trotted back to their leader. One of them dropped Eyvindr's manhood on the ground between his leader and Halfdan.

Ketill had feigned unconsciousness long enough to bear witness to Eyvindr's screams and the bloody remains of his friend's manhood. He bolted from the ground and made a bid for freedom.

Gudbjartur ran to the side, stopped, and threw his axe from the side. It hit Ketill in the back of the legs as intended. Gudbjartur ran to the struggling man and stilled him with a blow to the head.

The two groups gathered around him. The Naskapi watched Halfdan to see what he intended. Ketill stirred.

"Stand him up," Halfdan said through gritted teeth.

Thorkell jerked Ketill to his feet and held him up. The man's head lolled to the side.

Halfdan stepped in front of him, his face inches away. "You have endangered our people. You raped a defenseless young girl. You will die by the blood eagle."

"No, for the love of the gods, no! Not that!" Ketill screamed and struggled. Thorkell threw him face down on the ground and pulled his arms forward. Gudbjartur pinned his legs. Halfdan whipped out his knife and cut between the man's ribs below the shoulder blades on either side of his backbone.

A long, drawn-out scream was ripped from Ketill's soul.

Halfdan reached through each cut and pulled out a lung. He wiped his knife on Ketill's tunic and got to his feet. "You are free to go, you scum."

The man thrashed on the ground. His pink, bloody lungs lay on his back like wings, expanding and contracting with each breath. He whimpered and moaned in agony. He got slowly to his feet and began to walk away. His shambling steps carried him toward the forest.

The pitiless witnesses to his demise watched in silence as he disappeared into the shadows of the forest.

Halfdan sheathed his knife and looked up at the Naskapi leader. The man held his eyes for a moment, nodded, and without a word, turned away and led his people toward the river and their canoes.

Justice was served. Halfdan noticed the parapets of the palisade were lined with silent people. He shook his head and walked away alone. Frida made to join him. Gudbjartur took her arm. She looked at him, a question furrowing her brow. The shake of his head gave her pause. She looked at Halfdan's back. Ingerd took her arm, gently pulled her away, and everyone trudged back to the village gate.

Gudbjartur watched his friend for a moment and then followed after him. The two men walked slowly, one behind the other, through the field in the general direction of Yggdrasil.

Halfdan stopped and sat down near the spring beneath the world-tree. Gudbjartur joined him. Neither spoke. After a time, Halfdan glanced at the silent Gudbjartur. His friend had a peculiar look on his face. "What is it, Gudbj, is something amiss?"

Gudbjartur shook his head and continued to stare out over the country, his eyes unfocused and unseeing.

"Gudbj, my friend, what is the matter?" Halfdan repeated the question, a hand on the man's shoulder.

Gudbjartur caught himself. A shudder shook his body, and his eyes focused on Halfdan's face. "I was thinking of what has happened over the past two days. Not what we did to those two men; they deserved what they got. But rather what their deed might have done to all of us. If that Naskapi leader had returned to his people to tell them of the rapes instead of confronting us, we might have awakened one morning to face hundreds of Naskapi warriors. All we have done all our lives is fight against our enemies, both real and perceived. We have fought for the food we eat, fought for the land we live on, all manner of things. I am weary of the fight. I thought this place might allow me, us, to live in peace. But it all depends on each of us and what we do here each day. And it depends on them." He gestured to the countryside. "I hope those Naskapi are satisfied with the justice meted out here today, for our survival as a people will always depend on them. They hold our fate in the palm of their hand, whoever they turn out to be." He paused in thought. "All it will take is a mistake by someone, anyone, on either side, and we will be in trouble. I fear we will be doomed once hostilities begin. It will take a miracle to save us."

Halfdan held his friend's eyes. He knew in his heart that Gudbjartur's words were prophetic.

GLOSSARY OF NORSE TERMS

Einvigi—Norse duel to the death. Challenger chooses the weapons. Usually swords and shields but can also be knives. Usually fought on hides staked to the ground, with both men clenching a length of leather strap in their teeth.

Freemen—The largest social order among the Norse. Men capable of owning land. Women could be free but could not own land.

Frey—God of fertility, crops, peace, and prosperity.

Freya—Goddess of love. Sister of Frey.

Furdustrandir—Wonder Beach or Marvel Strand. Thought to be the forty-mile stretch of white sandy beach located south of Cape Porcupine, Labrador, Canada.

Gotar—The people of Gotland. One of the two main Germanic tribes, the other being the Svear, which became modern Sweden.

Hel—Norse goddess of death and the ruler of the realm of the dead. Daughter of Loki, who rules the abode of the dead. Hel lives among the roots of the world-tree, Yggdrasil, and has the appearance of a rotting corpse.

Helluland—Flat Stone Land, Baffin Island, Canada.

Leifsbudir—Leif's Booths or Leif's Camp. Found in 1962 on the northeastern tip of Newfoundland, Canada, by Helge and Anne-Stine Ingstad, of Norway. It remains the only substantiated Norse settlement site ever discovered in North America.

Loki—God of discord and mischief. At Ragnarok, the twilight of the gods, he will lead forth the hosts of Hel.

Markland—Wood Land, Labrador, Canada.

Njord—Norse god of winds, navigation, and the sea. Father of Frey and Freya.

Nordsettir—The northern hunting grounds of Greenland. The region along the northwest coast as far as 80° north latitude in waters free of pack ice during the Medieval Warm Period.

Otherworld—The world after death.

Ragnarok—Twilight of the gods. The final battle between the gods and their enemies that leads to the destruction of mankind.

Skyr—A mildly fermented drink made from the whey left from the making of cheese. A nutritious drink favored by Norse people.

Steerboard—large oar secured on the right aft side of the ship; a combination rudder and keel. Possibly the origin of the term starboard, or right side of a boat or ship.

Svealand—Land of the Svear, one of the Germanic tribes that became modern day Sweden, the other main tribe being the Gotar.

Sweep—Large, long oar, used to propel a ship in calm wind or close quarters. Usually plied from a standing position, the long sweeps were thrust out through holes spaced equidistant along a plank below the ship's rail.

Thing—The h is silent, thus literally Ting. An annual assembly that served as the governing body of Norse society and at which any Freemen could bring their concerns before the chieftain, or lawspeaker, for the rule of law. Although women could be heard at a thing, they had no vote.

Thor—Norse god of the sky and thunder. Thor may have been the favorite of all Norse gods. His hammer was a much favored amulet worn by both men and women. As in any Germanic combination of th, the h is silent, thus literally Tor.

Tornit—Pronounced Dornit. Native people of Greenland and the Canadian Arctic islands. Encountered by the Northmen in the early years of both Greenland settlements before the arrival of the Inuit from the west sometime in the twelfth century.

Thrall—A slave or chattel of a chief or freeman.

Underworld—A realm below the surface of the earth in which the spirits of the dead reside.

Valhalla—Odin's Hall of the Slain in the Underworld where the Valkyries take the heroes killed in battle.

Valkyries—The handmaidens of Odin, who select the heroes from the field of battle and transport them to Valhalla.

Vinland—An area somewhere in southeastern Canada or the northeastern U.S. Disagreement and conjecture surrounds both the meaning of the name and the location of the place.

Wadmal—Tightly woven wool cloth used for clothing. Also sewn together into panels to make sails and tents. Virtually waterproof due to the tightness of the weave.

Yggdrasil—The horse of Yggr, that is, Odin. A giant ash tree, the world-tree of Norse mythology. Odin impaled himself on a spear and hung from the world-tree for nine days to discover the secret of the runes. Believed to be supported by three main roots: one each in Asgard, the realm of the gods, Niflheim, the realm of the dead, and Jotenheim, the realm of giants in the earth. It is an eternal tree that will survive Ragnarok.

Sources:

Webster's New International Dictionary, (G & C Merriman Co. Springfield, MA, 1948).

John Haygood, *Encyclopedia of the Vikings,* (Thames and Hudson, Inc. New York, NY, 2000).

Turn the page for a look at *Confrontation*, the next in the *Axe of Iron* series by J.A. Hunsinger.

Axe of Iron—Confrontation

Halfdansfjord, Vinland, late summer, AD 1008

Out of long habit, the Northman, Gudbjartur Einarsson, carefully examined his surroundings every morning. He climbed a ladder to the palisade parapet and circled the settlement looking out over the bay, the fen, and surrounding countryside. Alert for the slightest danger or anything that did not belong in his world, the daily ritual, and a wave from the two tower guards assured him that all was well. He turned back toward his longhouse, his immediate thoughts being the coming adventure for his sons, Ivar and Lothar, and their small friend Yola.

He entered the house to find his sons finishing their morning meal. "When you have finished your meal, go and get Yola. Yesterday, I spoke to his mother about the hunt. He will be ready to go," Gudbjartur said.

Watching his sons run excitedly from the house, Gudbjartur shook his head at such exuberance on a full stomach. He rubbed his stomach at the thought of food, and smiled a greeting to his wife as she moved the kettle from the hearth tripod to the stone warming ledge.

She ladled the steaming fish chowder into a bowl and handed it to him. "They are really looking forward to this, Gudbj," Ingerd said.

Gudbjartur sat down in his high seat and began to eat. "It is time. This is their right of passage to manhood." He noisily slurped the thick liquid from the bowl, leaving a few chunks of cod in the bottom, which he ate with gusto. Suddenly he stopped chewing, pulled a long rib bone from his mouth, and examined it ruefully. "I could have choked on this, Ingerd."

She chuckled at him. "That is why we should *chew* our food instead of bolting it down in chunks. Honestly, you are as bad as the boys."

Grinning at her, he got to his feet and placed his empty bowl and spoon with the other dirty utensils. "Thank you, the chowder is delicious."

"It should be we made it with butter and milk. You ate so fast I am surprised you could taste it."

"I tasted it all right. I am in a hurry, the boys are anxious to get going." He watched her for a moment. "They will be men soon, Ingerd, whether we want them to or not," he said gently, mindful of her feelings on the subject.

She leaned against the wide shoulders of this man she loved so much, warm and content as he put an arm around her, she gazed up into his pale blue eyes. "I know. I know. But they seem so young."

"They are young. But soon they will be men. You were only two years older than Ivar is now when you birthed him."

"And well I know it. The birthing was very hard for me and that is why we have had no more children. Something came loose in me."

"I know, Ingerd. I think that is why the gods sent us Lothar. He is our son, too, as if you birthed him."

The boys rushed in with Yola in tow, effectively shattering the moment, much to Gudbjartur's relief.

He gave Ingerd a final squeeze, released her, and gave his attention to the three boys. "I have told you what you can take with you, and I see you have your packs and weapons in order. The only food we will have is dried meat. We will use it if the hunt is unsuccessful." His glance played over the three boys. A slight smile pulled at the corners of his mouth. Their barely checked exuberance, as they listened intently to him, caused a flush of pleasure through his chest. "Say good-bye to your mother, and we will be off."

The best the boys could manage was a perfunctory peck on her cheek before they ran from the longhouse. Gudbjartur hugged and kissed Ingerd, examined her appreciatively at arms length, and then hugged and kissed her again. Then he picked up his gear and walked from the longhouse to begin the much anticipated hunting expedition.

Ingerd watched him go, a heat rose in her, she smiled, and hugged herself with pleasure. She began to clean up the mess from the morning meal, whistling softly as she worked.

* * *

As Gudbjartur walked into the settlement commons he saw his chieftain, Halfdan Ingolfsson, talking to the two men tending the charcoal kiln. He joined them, not interrupting the conversation beyond a nodded greeting.

"It takes all day for the charcoal in the kiln to cool enough to shovel it out when we open it up in the morning," Grimr said, glancing from Halfdan to Gudbjartur. "After we empty the kiln it takes a short time to fill it back up with wood and light the fire. We throw the wood in through the vent hole on top until the kiln is full then we light it at the bottom opening." He gestured as he spoke. "After it catches fire we place the flat rock over the vent and roll another rock in front of the bottom opening. By dawn the next day we have a kiln full of charcoal." The man grinned through the grim that covered his face.

"The woodcutters haul the dry wood in for us," Barthur, his companion, said. "We would rather do this than cut wood, but I know we will be swapping jobs soon. As you told us, Gudbj, it keeps us from getting bored."

Gudbjartur acknowledged with a nod, and spoke to Halfdan. "The boys are waiting for us."

They took their leave of the kiln tenders, shouldered their packs and weapons, and headed for the landing beach to meet the boys.

"They gave me a report on the winter charcoal supply," Halfdan said, as he and Gudbjartur strolled slowly along the log walkway toward the main gate. "The bins in each longhouse are almost full. Then they will pile the excess charcoal under the shed roof next to the kiln until they judge there is plenty for winter. I left that up to them, they know more about it than I do."

"I spoke to them several days ago. Since they started using the new kiln their job is much easier. The charcoal is all made of dry birch wood. Birch will give us better heat than the pine we normally use," Gudbjartur said as they walked through the gate and down the hill toward the landing beach.

* * *

Further conversation about the charcoal supply ended when the three boys saw the men and ran to meet them.

"Which boat are we taking?" a breathless Ivar asked.

"This one," Gudbjartur said. He swung his pack aboard. "Your mother has already put a pack of dried meat aboard in case you boys do not kill us fresh meat."

"We will not fail, father," Lothar said, a determined look on his thin face.

Gudbjartur could not remember the boy ever calling him, father, before. He was taken aback.

"I never thought you would, Lothar," the big man said, his hand on the boy's shoulder in a rare display of affection. Gudbjartur glanced at the smiling Halfdan, and turned away, unaccustomed to the feeling one word had brought to him. He carefully laid his bow, quiver of hunting arrows, and axe across the boats thwarts. "Load your gear boys. We will launch the boat and get underway," Gudbjartur said.

The boys gathered their scattered gear and loaded it aboard. The two men, eagerly assisted by the chattering boys, pushed the boat's bow off the beach and all clambered aboard.

* * *

They sailed up a wide river until the wind off the bay became too variable from the dampening effect of the forest to be of any further use. The three boys had taken turns at the steering oar as the hunting party progressed inland. At the moment, Ivar had the helm.

Gudbjartur pointed ahead to the mouth of a tributary stream that issued from a small lake partially hidden back in the forest. "Steer for that stream, Ivar. Beach the boat anywhere along the left hand bank. Lothar, you, and Yola lower the sail just before the boat reaches the shore."

The two boys craned forward to watch the shoreline, the tag end of the halyard clenched in their hands, ready to jerk it loose from the cleat and lower the sail. Lothar glanced anxiously at Halfdan, who watched them from his seat on the bow thwart. He smiled and nodded at him, but said nothing.

Ivar put the helm over and the boat headed into the shore.

"Now Yola," Lothar hollered, as he jerked the halyard loose. The small sail plummeted down the mast as the boys lost their grip on the halyard, covering them as they lost their footing and fell in a heap when the boat ground to a halt on the stones of the stream bank.

"See, there is nothing to it." Halfdan said, as he and Gudbjartur pulled the sail off the two struggling boys. "You dropped the sail at just the right time."

Ivar, hands on hips, stood at his place in the stern with a smile on his face as he watched his brother and Yola regain their feet.

"What are you grinning at?" Lothar asked.

"I saw the whole thing," Ivar said, his superior attitude coming to the fore. "That was a pretty funny way to lower the sail. You are supposed to lower it hand-over-hand, not just turn loose of the halyard."

"We know that. It was heavier than we thought and the halyard slipped through our hands."

The grinning Gudbjartur caught a wink from Halfdan as the two men, barely able to keep from laughing aloud, enjoyed the moment with their young charges.

"All right, boys. You all did well. Roll the sail up on the boom, like we showed you, and secure the boat to a tree. Then

we will go find a good place to hunt around yon lake,"
Gudbjartur ordered, gesturing inland.

* * *

They walked in single file, with Halfdan and Gudbjartur in
the lead, around the shoreline to the north shore of the closest of the several small lakes in the area. Moose tracks seemed
to be everywhere. Well-used game trails naturally funneled
animals to the shoreline of the lake the men had selected for
the hunt.

Gudbjartur briefed the boys on his plan. "There is no wind
so the moose will not smell you. You all saw the deep game
trails winding down here from the forest. The moose use these
trails every evening when they leave their bed grounds to
water and feed on bulrushes on the lake bottom. Halfdan and
I will find hiding places for you that will allow us to drive the
animals to you. If we spring the trap at the right moment the
moose will come right by your positions when they run away
from Halfdan and me."

"How will we know when to shoot?" Lothar asked.

Ivar snorted at the question.

"That is a good question, Lothar." Halfdan entered the
conversation to show Ivar that questions were a part of learning. "Each of you knows your range limit for accurate shots.
Your quarry is a big moose. Even the calves are big, as you all
know. The target you are shooting at is an area in the chest
that is as big around as your mother's stew pot. About like so."
He held both hands out in a circle to demonstrate a diameter
equal to the length of a man's forearm. "The arrow must hit
that target to kill him. If you hit him anywhere else, he may
die, but he will run away and be lost to us because we probably will never find his carcass."

"Try to wait until your target is quartering and head away
from where you are." Gudbjartur demonstrated the proper
angle with his hands. "If you get that angle, aim for the
paunch, just back of the short ribs. There is no heavy bone
there and all his vital organs are lying low in his chest cavity
when he is on his feet. Your arrow will slice forward into his

chest cavity, hitting a tub full of guts, the liver, at least one lung, and maybe the heart. It will be a killing shot."

"Aye that is the best shooting angle on any game we kill with an arrow. Another important thing to remember when you get an arrow into him and he runs away: let him go, wait for Gudbj and me." Halfdan looked at each of the boys. "Yola, why should you wait?"

Yola looked at his two friends and then back to Halfdan. "Because we should give him time to bleed to death."

"That is right!" Halfdan exclaimed enthusiastically. "If the animal has not seen you he will not know what happened. Maybe the wound will only burn. He will feel secure because you have not scared him. As he weakens he will lie down. Why do we want him to lie down Ivar?"

"So he will bleed to death quietly rather than run away in a panic until he finally drops dead. We would probably lose him then. And the meat would not be any good if he was all heated up when he died."

Halfdan smiled and nodded. He winked at Gudbjartur and stepped aside.

"Good, Ivar," Gudbjartur said, looking from boy to boy. "Remember, we will all be focused only on animals coming to the lake from this game trail. There may be others but ignore them unless they are about to step on you." The boys laughed. "You will see the moose before they get to the lake. They will be nervous. Their senses will be on full alert. Stay still and do not take a shot no matter how tempting it is. Wait until they relax and Halfdan and I decide the time is right to drive them to you. You may get only one shot so take your time. Make your shots count. All it takes is one well placed arrow and the moose is meat on the board." He grinned at them. "All right, I think you all know what to do. Now, check your arrows and knives. Make certain they are sharp. You will have need of them, I think. Are there any questions before we lay our trap?"

The boys shook their heads. They busied themselves giving each arrowhead a final swipe or two with their whetstones. All were understandably nervous.

* * *

A short time later the boys were well concealed and the trap was laid. The men separated and each walked to a position across the lake from each other and with the targeted game trail roughly centered. When they sprung the trap each man would cover half the shoreline as they converged on the quarry, thereby ensuring the flushed animals would have to make their bid to escape right by the three hidden boys.

While he waited in concealment Gudbjartur cut a short piece of green willow shoot, chewed the end until it frayed and softened, and used it to scrub his teeth. For him it was a daily ritual. He watched the scene unfold much as he and Halfdan had told the boys it would. All three were concealed in the underbrush well back from the game trail.

* * *

As the shadows lengthened toward day's end, a trio of moose stepped from the dense forest surrounding the lake. The lead animal, an old cow, paused and carefully surveyed the lake environs. Her sensitive nose tested the still air while the huge ears turned this way and that listening to the cries of birds and the buzz of insects. Her senses told her that all was well. She continued down into the willow scrub along the lake shoreline. She and her calves nibbled at the tender tips of willow before stepping into the shallow waters of the lake. Their kind did this same thing, just before sundown every day, when hunger and thirst drove them from their bedding grounds to begin another night of foraging.

* * *

Gudbjartur watched the cow moose and two large calves walk with caution from the cover of the forest. The quarry grazed slowly through the thick willows along the shoreline before wading into the lake. The animals began to relax as they grazed along the lake bottom on an abundance of bulrushes and other underwater forage plants, oblivious to the threat lurking nearby.

Gudbjartur waved to Halfdan and the two men began closing in from both sides of the boys' position. They walked along the shoreline making no attempt at stealth. Gudbjartur figured that he and Halfdan would be almost up to the animals before they became alarmed. If everything worked as planned the three moose should pass the boys' hiding place as they ran from the lake.

* * *

Five hundred sea leagues to the northeast of Halfdansfjord, the four ships of the settlement's trading flotilla to Greenland rolled and plunged in the heavy swells of the strait separating Helluland and Greenland. The flotilla had sailed from the strait between Markland and Helluland, through the southerly current flowing along the Helluland coast the preceding morning, and into the open ocean area of relatively slack currents between Helluland and Greenland.

Seabirds had recently joined the ships, diving and swooping in their constant quest for food, indicating land was not far off. Estimating there were some fifty leagues remaining in the voyage for the ships bound for Eiriksfjord, Greenland, Bjorn Kjetilsson, flotilla commander, signaled the ships to heave-to into the wind as they approached a bank of thin fog and sea mist.

Fog banks of varying thickness and the pervading sea mist had been their constant companion during the twelve days of the voyage. Although it had not been necessary to heave to, the Fog Giant and reduced visibility preyed on Bjorn's mind. Command of more than his own ship weighed heavily on him. He thought the cargoes of green timber would be most welcome in both Greenland settlements and should induce the local farmers to part with all manner of trade goods from both Iceland and Vestfoldland. The ships had managed to stay in contact while running in the thin fog by sailing in close company and frequently sounding their bullhorns. The sound of the horns reverberating from ship to ship lent a surreal quality to the damp blanket as the ships alternately appeared and disappeared within its shroud.

After turning into the wind to heave-to, the heavily laden ships remained close together as they paid-off slowly downwind, their unfettered sails flapped loosely, and the crews shouted back and forth.

"If the visibility was not so poor the masthead would have the clouds of Greenland in sight to leeward. We will part company when the coast is sighted. As agreed, Athils and Sweyn will steer for Lysufjord and Brodir and I will make for Eiriksfjord," Bjorn shouted across the narrow expanse of water separating the ships. "Good luck trading with the Tornit on your return voyages. I hope you kill many walrus with them. We will see you at Halfdansfjord before winter."

"Brodir," Sweyn shouted through cupped hands, "I hope you fill your ship with the trade goods we need in Halfdansfjord. Good luck trading with the Thalmiut on your return voyage, Bjorn. Trade them out of another pair of those big dogs." He waved and turned back to his waiting crew to get his ship underway.

Shouted farewells drifted across the water as crews bid their opposite numbers farewell and sails were sheeted home. A freshening wind out of the northwest began to blow the tatters of fog away and the flotilla rapidly gathered way as each ship answered her helm and steadied on course.

The ships would shortly come under the influence of the current sweeping into the north along the coast of western Greenland, speeding them toward their individual destinations. This fast-moving current would be especially useful to the two ships bound for Lysufjord, more than one hundred leagues north of Eiriksfjord.

* * *